INSCRIBED POWER

Amulets and Magic in Early Spanish Literature

RYAN D. GILES

Inscribed Power

Amulets and Magic in Early Spanish Literature

UNIVERSITY OF TORONTO PRESS
Toronto Buffalo London

ISBN 978-1-4426-4607-0

Library and Archives Canada Cataloguing in Publication

Giles, Ryan D. (Ryan Dennis), author
Inscribed power : amulets and magic in early Spanish
literature / Ryan D. Giles.

(Toronto Iberic ; 23)
Includes bibliographical references and index.
ISBN 978-1-4426-4607-0 (cloth)

1. Spanish literature – To 1500 – History and criticism.
2. Magic in literature. I. Title. II. Series: Toronto Iberic ; 23

PQ6060.G54 2017   860.9'001   C2016-907860-4

University of Toronto Press acknowledges the financial assistance to its
publishing program of the Canada Council for the Arts and the Ontario
Arts Council, an agency of the Government of Ontario.

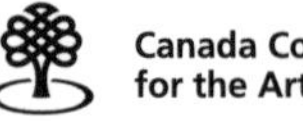

To Claudia

Contents

Illustrations

Acknowledgments

Completing a project like this would not have been possible without the support of family, and the encouragement of many mentors, colleagues, and friends – too many to acknowledge fully here. I am especially appreciative of the support of Suzanne Rancourt, my editor, and the University of Toronto Press, as well as the anonymous readers who reviewed my manuscript with care and expertise. Early versions of three chapters in this study appeared in *La corónica* 44.1, *Los jardines en la literatura medieval*; and the volumes *In and Of the Mediterranean: Medieval and Early Modern Iberian Studies* (Vanderbilt University Press) and *Objects of Culture in the Literature of Imperial Spain* (University of Toronto Press). I would like to thank the editors and evaluators of these publications for their feedback. Getting started on this book would not have been possible without support provided by a Franke Fellowship at the University of Chicago, and my participation in a 2009 NEH Summer Seminar led by Michael Gerli at the University of Virginia. My conversations with fellow participants were invaluable, as were my later discussions with colleagues and students at the University of Chicago and Indiana University. I greatly benefited from the encouragement of Frederick de Armas, Daisy Delogu, David Nirenberg and Steven Wagschal. I am also grateful for the continued support that I have received from the College of Arts and Sciences at Indiana University. During the process of revising my manuscript, I was fortunate to have the logistical support of two excellent research assistants, Victor Rodriguez-Pereira and Christina Cole.

INSCRIBED POWER

Literary Amulets

Near the end of the fourth century, a pilgrim from the Iberian Peninsula arrived in the Holy Land. Identified as Egeria, this traveller left a
written account of her voyage that was preserved in a medieval manuscript centuries later at the monastery of Monte Cassino. Most scholars
believe that the author of the *Itinerarium Egeriae* (Egeria's Itinerary) was
a wealthy religious woman from the Roman province of Galicia. The
pilgrim made stops in Egypt and Palestine, where she visited Mount
Sinai, the Jordan Valley, and other sites associated with the life of Christ,
before travelling to the city of Edessa in what is now Turkey (1960).
There she heard the story of a letter that Jesus purportedly wrote in
response to the Edessene King Abgar. According to the bishop, the precious document had protected Abgar and his subjects from invaders:
"Persians came against the city and surrounded it. And straightway
Abgar, bearing the letter of the Lord to the gate, with all his army,
prayed ... holding the open letter in his uplifted hands ... as often as
enemies determined to come and take the city, this letter was brought
out and read in the gate ... all enemies were driven back" (1919: 33–4).[1]
The *Itinerarium*, like later accounts of the king's defence of Edessa,
demonstrates how apotropaic power was believed to emanate from the
physical presence of the *epistola* in addition to the meaning and efficacious recitation of its inscription.[2]

Egeria describes how the bishop took her to a shrine, where he read
aloud the correspondence between Christ and Abgar before presenting
the pilgrim with a copy to take back to Hispania. The traveller notes
that this text was more complete than the versions found in her library
at home and probably hoped to benefit from its apotropaic promises by
carrying the *Epistolam Domini* (Letter from the Lord) on her person and

reading its promises during her subsequent travels (1960: 1.18.9). In his recent study of medieval textual amulets, Don Skemer has suggested that the bishop is "in effect giving her Christ's 'letter of protection' for the long and perilous journey home" (2006: 97).[3] The contents of the Edessene text can be gleaned from Eusebius of Caesarea's monumental *Historia ecclesiastica* (Church History), completed some sixty years prior to Egeria's pilgrimage and translated into Latin in the early fifth century. Having heard of Christ's powers to heal, exorcise, and resuscitate the dead with His words, Abgar first sent a missive inviting the Nazarene miracle worker to take refuge in Edessa. According to Eusebius, the king's letter recognized Jesus as the Son of God and petitions the Saviour for relief from a debilitating disease identified in later sources as leprosy. To reward Abgar for his belief, Jesus wrote back with a promise to heal the ailing ruler and bless the city.[4]

The Abgar tale persisted in the medieval imaginary, eventually making its way into chronicles of the First Crusade, such as the twelfth-century *Historia vie Hierosolimitane* (History of the Journey to Jerusalem) by Gilo of Paris (1997: 134–5) – this in spite of the Roman church having declared it, during the sixth century, to be apocryphal. According to some accounts, the messenger also brought Abgar a wondrous image of Christ's face known as the Mandylion (analogous to Veronica's veil), and the city was in later years Christianized by a disciple of the apostle Thomas.[5] The story was widely known through "bestselling" Latin literature like the *Legenda aurea* (Golden Legend, c. 1275) and the *Gesta Romanorum* (Deeds of the Romans, c. 1300). In medieval Iberia, it appears in a late thirteenth-century chronicle that combines historiography with more imaginative literary materials, the *Estoria de España* (History of Spain) compiled by the king of Castile-Leon, Alfonso X "El Sabio" (the Wise or Learned). In this rendition, as in the one told in the *Golden Legend*, a boy carries the letter and pronounces its words as defensive weapons against military aggression. Thus, the potency of the missive is implicitly likened to the sling young David used to confront the Philistines – since Jesus as the Incarnate Word of God was typologically linked to the projectile launched by Jesse's son (1 Sam. 17:48–50):[6]

> Cristo envió al rey Abgaro la carta escripta de su mano ... tomavan un niño bateado que sopiesse leer, et ponien lo en somo de la puerta de la cibdat et davan le aquella carta, et léyela; et aquel día mismo en que la leye, o fazien los bárbaros paz con ellos o fuyen con miedo. Et esto era por la vertud del escripto de Nuestro Señor.

(Christ sent to King Abgar the letter written by his hand ... they chose a baptized boy who knew how to read and put atop the gate of the city and gave him the letter and he read it; and that same day it was read, they either caused the barbarians to make peace with them or retreat in fear. And this was the virtue of the inscription of Our Lord.) (1906: 161)

Through such retellings an additional layer of figurative meaning was attached to the story of the amulet. By the end of the Middle Ages, narrative traditions had developed in which Charlemagne was said to have received the Edessene letter or other powerful texts, either from an angelic messenger or from Pope Leo III.[7] This physical document was attributed with protecting the Emperor from Saracen forces south of the Pyrenees. By bringing it into battle as a miraculous prophylactic, Charlemagne could expect to receive Davidic blessings and participate in the benediction given to Abgar, extended to those who possessed copies of the letter. Thus, the kind of divine text first reported by Eusebius and Egeria was adapted from the defence of Edessa against the Persians to storytelling about the advance of a perceived Muslim Goliath conquering Hispania and penetrating into the heart of Christendom. Like other examples that I will discuss in this book, the potency of the letter was recontextualized and transferred from the logic of one story to another. In other words, the written object came to function not only as what Skemer categorizes as a "textual amulet" but also as a literary one.[8] By the fourteenth century, the contents of the *Epistolam Domini* were being replaced by a growing number of formulas that Pope Leo purportedly gave to Charlemagne, amounting to a kind of standard compilation of elements that frequently appear on other amulets from the period.[9] During the reign of the Catholic Monarchs (1474–1516), a translation known as the "Oración de San León" was reproduced in Spanish as *Horas de Nuestra Señora* (Hours of Our Lady) or also copied on portable sheets of parchment and printed separately as a miniature pamphlet.[10]

In fact, the inventory of texts belonging to Isabel I indicates that the queen owned two copies of this prayer, both of which were meant to be hung around the neck. By this time, its promised efficacy has been expanded far beyond safeguarding the *miles Christi* ("Soldier of Christ"). Reciting and wearing a copy of the prayer is now additionally expected to shield travellers on land or sea from storms and sudden death, to offer protection from illness and difficulty in childbirth, liberate believers from captivity, release them from demonic possession, and assure a good death.[11] It provides an interesting example of what Karen

Jolly calls, in her study of amulets, "all purpose devices" that could "serve several functions" (2002: 43). Its promises not only correspond with the medieval literary *persona* of Charlemagne fighting the Saracens but also continue to include echoes of the legend of the Edessene king being miraculously healed and safeguarded from his enemies: "Cura a my que soy leproso, sana me que soy enfermo, resuscita me que soy muerto ... todos mis enemigos ... faze los tornar atrás ... defiende me" (Cure me, for I am leprous, heal me for I am sick, resuscitate me for I am dead ... make all of my enemies ... retreat ... defend me) (1502: 107v). The reader and wearer of the amulet in this manner enters into and identifies with Carolingian and christological subtexts intended to authenticate its power. During the sixteenth century, audiences were imagining the prayer being recited and worn by fictional characters in satirical theatrical works in Castilian and Portuguese. For example, it is one of the amuletic texts performed by an itinerant blind man in the 1554 *Farsa del molinero* (Miller's Farce) by Diego Sánchez de Badajoz (1970: v. 267). Another variation can be found in Gil Vicente's *Juiz da Beira* (Judge from Beira), written two decades earlier, when a fencer claims to have won a sword fight against three opponents, in spite of the fact that his opponents carried the shielding "Oraçam de Sam Liam" (Bouza 2001: 101).

It is clear from texts like the *Floresta española* (Collection of Spanish Fineries, 1574) that individual soldiers in Habsburg armies continued to wear textual amulets like this one, as did medieval knights before them: "traía consigo ... oraciones o nóminas" (he brought with him ... prayers and divine names) (Santa Cruz 1997: 876). In fact, the first of the Spanish Habsburgs, Carlos V (1519–56), was said to have carried a written amulet. A surviving printed copy of this text employs cruciform seals and christological invocations in Latin, similar to other popular examples. As we will see in this study, not only the apocryphal letter to Abgar but also several components of the later "Oración de San León" can be found on other Iberian amulets produced from the thirteenth to the sixteenth century. Among these are formulaic petitions for deliverance, exorcistic invocations, the first verses of the Gospel of John, set images from Revelation, evocations of the *Arma Christi* (Instruments of the Passion) and wounds of the Saviour, and amuletic names or *nomina divina* in Latin, Greek, and Hebrew.[12] Apart from general protection afforded later devotees such as Queen Isabel, the prayer was more specifically intended to ensure that its readers and wearers would prevail in violent conflict:

El santo padre León ... enbío la a Carlomagno rey ... mandó la escribir con letras de oro ... siempre consigo la tuvo ... qualquier día que esta oración leyeres y sobre ti la truxieres ... en batalla ... ninguno de tus enemigos avrá señorío en ti y vencedor permanecerás siempre ... En aquel día no morirá a fierro ... ni sus enemigos nin el dyablo avrá poderío sobre él ... ni será vencido en batalla.

(The holy father Leo ... sent it to king Charlemagne ... he had it written in golden letters ... he always had it with him ... whatever day this prayer is read and carried on your person ... in battle ... none of your enemies will prevail over you and you will remain victorious always ... That day he [the wearer] will not die by the sword ... neither his enemies nor the devil will have power over him ... nor will he be defeated in battle.) (1502: fol. 101)

The kind of potency ascribed to the Emperor's prayer was also enlisted in support of crusading propaganda, as represented in literary works chronicling efforts by Christians to conquer parts of the Iberian Peninsula that had been inhabited for centuries by Muslims. For example, in a Spanish reworking of earlier historical and epic literary sources that was also begun under Alfonso X, the *Gran conquista de ultramar* (Great Conquest Overseas, c. 1295), two famous participants in the First Crusade are reportedly saved from imminent death by a written amulet called a *nómina*. Baldwin, the count of Edessa and future king of Jerusalem, at one point takes refuge in a marsh not far from the Holy City after being severely wounded by Muslim warriors. There, he is first plagued by leeches that slither beneath his armour and attach themselves to his profusely bleeding flesh, and later nearly burned to death when enemy forces learn of his presence and set fire to the surrounding reeds. Thomas of Marle, however, manages to rescue and resuscitate him in time: "traía una nómina muy buena, e púsosela el cuello de Baldovin, e lavantóse luego en pie ... e ficieron curar de las llagas de Baldovin e de su caballo" (he carried a very good *nómina*, and put it around neck of Baldwin, who arose to his feet ... and they managed to cure the wounds of Baldwin and his horse) (1858: 345). In another scene, when Thomas manages to scale the gates of Jerusalem, an awaiting Bedouin woman crushes his helmet with a club, causing him to fall perilously from the wall and into enemy hands. Just when his situation seems hopeless, the same amulet that healed Baldwin enables the crusader to ward off and escape an onslaught of attackers: "hirieron en él cuanto pudieron, mas traía una nómina de tal virtud, que mientra la trujiese sobre si non le podrían herir de muerte e ... salió de entre ellos" (they wounded him as much as they could, but he carried a *nómina* of such power, that so long as he had it on him they could not deliver a fatal wound and ... he got away from them) (1858: 346).[13]

The Spanish term used for his amulet seems to be a translation of the "brief" (Latin *brevis*) carried by Thomas in the early twelfth-century *Chanson de Jérusalem* from the First Crusade Cycle (Thorp 1992: vv. 3833, 4287). The same word describes the amulet given to the Arthurian hero, Perceval, in preparation for his quest for the Holy Grail. In the first part of Gerbert de Montreuil's *Continuation*, he wears a small, round text ("petit, roont, tota compas") in a piece of silk to protect himself from being defeated in battle, since this "brief" contains a holy "letre" (1922: vv. 238–41). Whereas the Old French *brief* refers to a document that is small enough to be worn around the neck, the Latin *chartae* and *nomina* were adapted into Spanish as "cartas" and "nóminas" to describe the same sort of parchments as having sacred "names" inscribed on them. Skemer has found that these were most commonly placed in bags or other containers that could be hung from a cord or chain. It is interesting to consider what early Spanish audiences of works like the *Gran conquista de ultramar* might have assumed to be the contents of these texts. While the inscription on the *nómina* carried by crusaders in the Alfonsine work remains unspecified, readers might have imagined a conventional litany of holy men and women liberated from earthly and spiritual enemies. Certainly, this is consistent with appeals and invocations in the "Oración de San León" legendarily carried by Charlemagne, as recorded in the late medieval *Horas de Nuestra Señora*: "Líbrame ... de los enemigos míos ... enfaqueciendo y venciendo las batallas y fuerças suyas, desterrando el poder suyo ... Líbrame ... assí como libraste a David ... y a Daniel del lago de los leones, y a Susaña de falso testimento" (Deliver me ... from my enemies ... weakening and defeating their forces in battle, vanquishing their power ... Deliver me ... just as you delivered David ... and Daniel from the den of lions, and Susanna from false testimony) (1502: 104v, 110v, 111r–112v). As Michael Gerli (1980) has pointed out, this vernacular formula was related to the *Ordo commendationis animae* or ritual prayer for the dying in which the soul is commended in preparation for its journey into the afterlife. Its petitions appear in a number of medieval narrative poems: in particular, verses invoking the deliverance of David or Daniel, along with Susanna, who was falsely accused of the capital crime of adultery by two lustful men in the Old Testament.

Spanish poets employed similar prayers in the context of preparing for war against infidel armies in the twelfth-century *Poema de mío Cid* (The Song of My Cid) and later *Poema de Fernán González* (c. 1260). The list of sacred figures builds on the overall meaning of these literary works by introducing a series of allusions that parallel and complicate the characterization of the hero and his journey, while simultaneously providing an oral – and for manuscript readers, written, tangible – blessing. In the former epic, the Cid's wife chants the prayer as the storied warrior embarks on a journey into exile that ends with his conquest of the Muslim city of Valencia: "salvest a Daniel con los leones en la mala cárçel ... salvest a Santa Susaña del falso criminal" (you saved Daniel from the Lions in the evil cell ... you saved St Susanna from the false criminal) (1980: vv. 340, 342). Scholars have noticed that the prayer intertexually anticipates the Cid, reminiscent of Daniel, remaining unharmed by a lion that escapes from a net.[14] In the later, more clerical work, recounting the deeds of the first count of Castile, the hero intones the same sort of appeals before going to battle against the Moorish ruler of Andalusia, Al-Mansur (c. 938–1002): "Señor, tu que libreste a Davit ... librest' Susana de los falsos varones, / saqueste a Daniel de entre los leones" (Lord, you who delivered David ... delivered Susanna from false men, freed Daniel who was among the lions) (1983: 107a, 108ab). Here, the inserted prayer suggests that the invading Moors could be compared to the lustful enemies of Susanna, implicitly figuring Hispania as a virtuous woman under threat. At the same time, Christian defenders again appear to be likened to David facing the Philistine giant.

During the fourteenth century, verses almost identical to the *Poema de Fernán González* prayer were inscribed on a small piece of clay tile discovered near Burgos during the 1960s. The object, to which I will return in chapter 3, also includes *nomina divina* that are not present in the poem, but which are commonly found on other extant amulets from the period. This suggests that a fragment from the *Poema de Fernán González* was being reframed by early audiences as an apotropaic material text.[15] Such a reading appears even more likely considering that comparable clay objects were carried by Christians as pilgrim badges and also employed as amulets by Iberian Muslims during the Middle Ages.[16]

Although *briefs* and *nóminas* like the ones carried into battle by French and Spanish literary heroes were not uncommon, their use had been restricted on a number of occasions by Church authorities. These prohibitions shed considerable light on how written amulets were thought to work in medieval culture. For instance, in the case of Abgar's letter, the twelfth-century theologian Hugh of St Victor declared that the magical missive was not only an apocryphal fiction but also demonic in origin (1854: 4.15).[17] Like other clerical leaders, Hugh drew his conclusion in part from an understanding of linguistic signs developed by Augustine of Hippo. According to this view, any power seemingly derived from textual amulets, even if gospel elements are mixed with pre-Christian ones, could be brought about only through an idolatrous reliance on the intervention of demons. Just as the uncorrupted sacred language (*sacra verba*) of prayer intoned by the faithful communicates through a linguistic convention with God, the efficacy of such verbal magic would be possible only through "previously established assumptions about language shared in common with malevolent spirits and binding us to them ... superstitions, like other sign systems, are conventional arrangements (*pacta, conventa*) between symbols and audiences; they achieve meaning and influence behavior in accordance with a consensus (*consensio*)" (Stock 1996: 201–2).[18] Augustine's view remained largely unchanged during the Middle Ages, until Arabic works translated on the Iberian Peninsula (most notably at the Alfonsine court and the Toledan school) and Italy began to circulate more widely.

In the early part of the thirteenth century, a bishop of Paris named William of Auvergne argued against the idea that words inscribed on amulets could be invested with or exert the kind of natural potency theorized in newly available Arabic treatises like Al-Kindi's *De radiis*. This work described how celestial rays conferred power to the sublunary world and suggested that spoken and written language could be infused with *virtus* and project its influences. Equally problematic was the translation of Avicenna's *De Anima* made in twelfth-century Toledo, with its proposition that matter could be naturally obedient to expressions of the soul, enabling it possibly to affect the health of human bodies and other elements of nature.[19] Contesting such theories, William told the story of a magician who claimed that a single word might be capable of exerting such a deadly force that its letters had to be written in water so as to vanish instantly (Auvergne 1963: 90).[20] Either pronouncing this vocable or viewing its inscription could be fatal. William contended that sound could kill only on the basis of its extreme volume (as opposed to its composition or linguistic signification), and that only material infused with poison would potentially result in death (regardless of the sound or signs carried by these materials). In accordance with Augustine, he maintained that such *virtus verborum* would bring about changes in matter only by calling on demons who then acted on the basis of material stimuli. William similarly disapproved of investing the physical presence of textual objects with power, including those inscribed with Holy Writ. He saw these practices as a form of linguistic idolatry, tantamount to the ancient Israelites losing faith in God and worshipping graven images (Peters 1978: 165).

Other thirteenth-century thinkers were less apt to prohibit categorically the binding of sacred texts to the body in hopes of healing and protection. After all, early saints had relied on the written words of the gospel, in keeping with the promised efficacy of Christ's name.[21] Later holy men also possessed portable sacred texts, such as Francis of Assisi, who gave to a companion a folded parchment or "chartula" inscribed with a combination of scriptural quotations described by the saint as "meditatus sum in corde meo" (meditated on in my heart) (Skemer 2006: 174). Medieval scholastics permitted these practices so long as the objects were understood strictly as signs of devotion and omitted extra-biblical language, especially occult writing or *characteres*. They stressed that the safety and health of believers carrying inscriptions of orthodox prayers such as the Pater Noster or divine names like those of the Three Kings could be hoped for but never promised. Most important, any perceived efficacy should be attributed to divine grace rather than the objects themselves. This last criterion would seem to prohibit the use of the amulets legendarily carried by Charlemagne and other heroes portrayed in Arthurian romance and Alfonsine literature.

Yet, as will be demonstrated in this study, authoritative warnings against non-orthodox content and promises stemming from a text's material presence were consistently and richly violated in medieval and early modern life and art. Some thinkers who were more receptive to the Arabic sources of knowledge about nature that were being transmitted from Iberia and Italy allowed that a potency that could reside in sacred – and, to a lesser extent, other – types of words, and that a soul's will and devoted intention might convey and infuse this force into the materiality of an amuletic inscription and thereby affect changes in the world. Notably, Roger Bacon told of an innocent boy who once cured a man from epilepsy by binding him with the holy names of the Magi inscribed on parchment. The epileptic continued to safeguard himself by carrying this text around his neck. His wife, who was having affair with the local priest, one day removed the amulet under the pretext of bathing her husband. When the seizures immediately returned, the wayward woman was moved to return his protective parchment. Such stories, such as the literary examples cited earlier, were not uncommon in the Middle Ages and seemed to confirm the idea that textual objects could exert a curative apotropaic force by the grace of God working through the spiritual and material nature of the written word. Bacon's tale also shows how the outcomes of narratives were sometimes constructed around the supposed potency of words contained within them. Of course, this influence was extended from allegedly true stories to overtly fictional tales.

The miracle recounted by Bacon is also consistent with uses of textual amulets in medical literature from the latter part of the Middle Ages.[22] Bernard de Gordon's popular *Lilium medicina* (Flower of Medicine, c. 1303), which was translated into Castilian during the fifteenth century, recommends that incurable epileptics wear a parchment inscribed with the names of the Three Kings along with verses from the gospels in hopes of expelling demonic beings afflicting the patient. The Magi had long been closely associated with astrological magic due to their prowess as star gazers.[23] Throughout the Middle Ages, their names were viewed as especially efficacious whether written or pronounced, as in the litany from the earlier-quoted *Poema de mío Cid*: "tres reyes de Arabia te vinieron adorar, Melchor, Gaspar y Baltasar" (three kings of Arabia came to adore you, Melchior, Gaspar and Balthazar) (1980: 336–7). However, the famous doctor from Gordon suggests resorting to this kind of logotherapy only when other remedies derived from classical scientific sources fail.[24] Another physician from the famed medical school at Montpellier, the Catalan Arnau de Vilanova, is credited with providing instruction on how to treat disease with a Christian text combined with occult astrological knowledge transmitted from Muslim Andalusia. Skemer finds that the *De sigillis* (On Seals), which was written in the early fourteenth century, is dependent on the *Picatrix* (The Aim of the Sage), which was first translated from Arabic under the direction of Alfonso X in 1256 (2006: 132).[25] It provides evidence of how scriptural passages conventionally inscribed on amulets were sometimes made to convey additional, non-Christian meanings.

In keeping with the *Picatrix*, the work attributed to Arnau de Vilanova (1504: fols. 194v–196v) shows how to prepare talismans in harmony with corresponding signs of the zodiac. An extant example of the seal of Leo, or *sigillum leonis*, features an astrological image stamped on one side of a gold medallion, with an inscription from the Book of Revelation on the other: "vincit Leo de tribu Juda, radix David" (the lion of Judah's tribe has conquered, the root of David) (5:5). The golden seal was intended to draw power from the constellation Leo while the physician recited from Revelation and the Psalms, positioning the object over the stricken part of his patient's body. In this manner, Arnau seems to have used the *sigillum leonis* to cure Pope Boniface VIII of chronic illness, as the pontiff himself later reported in a letter.[26] Apart from linking astral and allegorical meanings, the potency ascribed to scriptural language is at the same time derived from its exorcistic attributes. On medieval crosses and church bells the same verse from Revelation traditionally appears after the words, "ecce crucem domini, fugite partes adversae" (behold the Cross of the Lord, flee you hostile forces) (Skemer 2006: 132). The formula was incorporated in surviving amuletic texts like the "Oración de San León," where the influence of Leo is additionally linked with the canonized pope, and an earlier prayer copied in the manuscript of *Razón de amor* (Love's Reason), a thirteenth-century Spanish poem that I will examine in first chapter of this book.[27]

Christian amulets that, in different ways, made their way into literary texts rarely served simultaneously as talismans like Arnau's seal did. As Skemer has pointed out, the preparation of talismanic texts required more specialized knowledge of the movement of "heavenly bodies" found in learned books like the *Picatrix*, and in many cases access to precious metal or stones (2006: 131).[28] However, in the context of late medieval and early modern Spain, amulets without such sophisticated elements were in no way free from potentially problematic resemblances to objects produced within other religious traditions. In recent decades, protective textual objects belonging to Muslims have been discovered in different parts of the peninsula and seriously researched by scholars. For example, a small lead tablet bearing an inscription in Arabic was unearthed during the 1990s in the province of Cadiz (Alberite). Its writing was identified as having been produced in North Africa or Andalusia during the second half of the twelfth century (Martínez Enamorado 2006). The text consists of praises to Allah from the well-known ninety-nine divine names listed in the Hadith or Koranic commentary.[29] In addition to metal artefacts, surviving pieces of parchment and paper produced in medieval Iberia include the same Islamic holy names. Like Christian *briefs* and *nóminas* portrayed in the sequel to *Perceval* and the *Gran conquista de ultramar*, these were evidently meant to be carried by believers, whether folded and hung around the neck in small sacks made of cloth or leather, or rolled and similarly worn in capsules of metal or wood. It is also clear that miniature copies of the Koran could be carried as a means of protection or healing, analogous to medieval Christians relying on the power of small portable gospels in imitation of saints depicted in hagiographic literature (Coffey 2010).

Further evidence of amuletic practice among Iberian Muslims can be gleaned from a discovery made during a construction project in the province of Toledo (Ocaña) during the late 1960s. Workers uncovered Romance texts written in Arabic characters (known as "aljamiado" script), as well as several late medieval Arabic manuscripts, including one that has been given the Spanish title *Misceláneo de Salomón* (Solomonic Miscellanea). This part of the cache includes instructions for the production and implementation of healing amulets, presented in the context of a Judeo-Hellenistic legend that first emerged in pseudoepigraphical work dating back to early centuries of the Common Era. It is one of several surviving *aljamiado* manuscripts relating to the powers of sacred written text, spells, and charms.[30] According to versions of this hermetic *Testament*, which circulated among Jews, Christians, and Muslims, the proverbial wisdom of Solomon, along with his magic seal or ring, enabled the king to subdue and control demons during the building of the first temple of Jerusalem.[31] In the *Misceláneo de Salomón*, he confronts a malevolent female spirit or Jinn who, in keeping with the mythical Jewish figure of Lilith, was popularly attributed with causing infant mortality, death in childbirth, or even inspiring acts of infanticide and the abandonment of newborns (see Hurwitz 1992). What follows is an amuletic sequence of sacred names and qualities of Allah that could serve as a shield when inscribed on virgin parchment and carried on the body. According to the manuscript, this text could offer protection against a demonic enemy of mothers and their offspring during and after childbirth. It could also heal fevers, indigestion, convulsions; remedy fits of terror and madness; and safeguard travellers, along with innocent victims of unjust accusations or persecution. Solomon's sealing pentacle and the use of birthing amulets were no less popular among Christians, as attested by codicological evidence compiled by Skemer, as well as literary representations considered in later sections of this book.

Other texts worn by Muslims on the peninsula invoked the Arabized names of Old Testament angels with whom Solomon legendarily communicated or received his wisdom. Not surprisingly, the same angelic invocations were also transliterated for the production of amuletic prayers in Latin and Romance, such as the one that accompanies the *Razón de amor* poem. One of these celestial names, Raziel, provided the title for a Hebrew treatise that Alfonso X ordered translated into Latin during the 1250s, not long after the *Picatrix*. In the decades following the reconquest of the Andalusian cities of Córdoba and Seville by his father, Fernando III, Alfonso had fostered collaborative, productive relationships with members of Jewish and Muslim communities serving his court – though his reign was also marked by policies that led to persecution or displacement of religious minorities.[32] The Hebrew work had already been circulating on the peninsula for centuries when Alfonso ordered its translation, as indicated by references found in the writings of an early eleventh-century Jewish convert to Christianity, Petrus Alfonsi.[33]

The surviving *Liber Razielis* claims to have been supernaturally recorded on a sapphire, known as a celestial stone, and presented to Adam by the archangel Raziel, following his exile from Eden and the introduction of sickness and death into the world. This angel, whose Hebrew name alludes to him keeping the "Secrets of God," was known in Jewish cabbalistic traditions for standing by the throne of God, listening to His words, and recording them in a heavenly book that could benefit humanity by providing a way to recapture an Edenic knowledge of their Creator. According to the prologue, the book enabled Adam and his postlapsarian heirs, from the time of Solomon to the reign of the learned Spanish king, to reacquire wisdom of the eternal and recuperate access to divine language that had been lost as a consequence of the Fall:

And this was done by the angel Raziel, as Raziel brought the Sepher, and this means that he brought the Secret Book. Adam who was in sorrow and pain, seeing that he was separated and distant from wisdom. And this book was written on a sapphire stone. And God sent the book to him in order that by the power and virtue of the words written in this holy and treasured book he might recover the highest good that he had lost for himself and others so that after it they might follow the commandments and traces of his presence in creation and preserve this book ... It pleased God that this book, being so holy, should be presented to king Solomon, son of king David; a ruler who was so noble and accomplished in science that he was called Wiseman in the Holy Scriptures ... the lord of justice in our time who is known as good and earnest and is pious and a gatherer and a lover of philosophy and all kinds of learning ... is lord Alfonso ... our king from whose hand this noble and treasured book is provided, that is the *Sepher Raziel*, which in Hebrew is to say the book of God's secrets.[34]

In addition to allowing the initiated to look into the future, sections of the *Liber Razielis* show how to invoke and inscribe sacred names onto parchment and other media that are called "Semiforas" (from the Greek word for bearing signs).[35] The book demonstrates how the spoken and written word can exert control over the forces of nature, including fire, ice, rain, and hail storms, which were believed to be ruled over by supernatural beings. As such, Raziel purports to impart a verbal significance that transcends the fallen nature of language functioning merely on the basis of convention. The source of this mystical power is the Tetragrammaton or four-letter ineffable name of God given to Moses (יהוה), transliterated as Yahweh (YHWH). Variations of the Tetragrammaton are common on premodern Christian and Jewish amulets and also appear in literary works from the period. In the *Libro de Alexandre*, a Spanish legend of Alexander the Great written during the reign of Alfonso's father, we will see how this divine name enables the heroic emperor to look into the future when it is presented to him on a "carta."

The *Liber Razielis* was widely translated and adapted over the centuries, in spite of repeated condemnations by church authorities. In Iberia, versions of text were censured by the Inquisition during the late Middle Ages and into the early modern period. Most famously, a copy was confiscated in the 1430s after being discovered in the library of the accused necromancer Enrique de Villena. The Dominican responsible for burning the book, Lope de Barrientos, observed that copies of such esoteric works were easier to find south of the Pyrenees than elsewhere.[36] Villena's own writings reveal that he was interested in learning how to employ medicinal amulets derived from learned Jewish sources.[37] The contents of objects employed by Jews living in medieval Iberia can be extrapolated from a relatively small number of surviving examples, such as the ones preserved at the Sephardic museum of Toledo. In addition to pieces of parchment, this collection includes a number of small metallic amulets dating from the fifteenth century, some of which were fashioned to be hung around the neck. The medallion-shaped objects are inscribed with divine and angelic names in Hebrew that also appear in cabbalistic writings, including the Tetragrammaton inscribed on an image of the ark, and sealing concentric circles similar to those found on Christian *nóminas* from the same period. For instance, one of the artefacts at the museum in Toledo also features the biblical word, Jabbok (López Álvarez 1986: inv. 0026/001). It thus alludes to a tributary of the Jordan and spiritual threshold where Jacob, having prayed for deliverance from his murderous brother Esau, famously wrestled with and received a blessing from the divine before taking the name Israel and arriving in the Promised Land (Gen. 32:22–32).

On Christian amulets produced in late medieval Iberia, a reference to the same scriptural episode was sometimes added to the earlier-cited petitions that coincide with the *Ordo commendationis animae*. This can be seen once again in the "Oración de San León": "libra me ... como libraste ... a Iacob de las manos de Esau su hermano" (Deliver me ... as you delivered ... Jacob from the hands of Esau his brother) (1502: 111r–112v). Regardless of the intention behind such practices that appear to be shared or somehow related to other faith traditions, anxieties over the possibility of contamination from Judaism and Islam fuelled the efforts of the Spanish Inquisition from the late fifteenth century onward.

Following the isolation of Granada as the last Muslim kingdom on the peninsula and the mass conversion of non-Christians, Inquisitors began investigating reports of "Judaizing" by converts and their descendants, who were known as *conversos*. The family of one author whose work I will examine in the pages that follow, Fernando de Rojas, was famously investigated by the Inquisition. Two other writers under consideration in this study, Francisco Delicado and Francisco de Quevedo, portray *conversos* engaging in amuletic practices and attempting to elude the Holy Office in Spanish novels written during the early sixteenth and seventeenth centuries. In Old and New Castile, as well as former Andalusian frontier towns, a growing number of suspects were accused of disseminating, carrying, and hiding, concealed on their person or stowed away in their house, "una nómina de ebrayco" (a Hebrew *nómina*) or "una nómina escripta en hebrayco" (a *nómina* written in Hebrew) (Gitlitz 2002: 194). Some of these descriptions could refer to the mezuzah, or placing of an enclosed parchment inscribed with Torah verses. According to the files of the Holy Office, these consisted of portable sheets of parchment and metal inscribed with spherical designs, citations from the Torah, and esoteric names like the ones given in the *Liber Razielis*. Presumably passed on from Jewish ancestors and copied by successive generations – who sometimes introduced Christian elements, such as patron saints – such material objects purported to heal any number of ailments, guard the wearer from visible and invisible enemies, and offer safety from sudden death during childbirth. *Moriscos*, or Muslim converts to Christianity, and their families were similarly accused by the Inquisition of carrying what officials described as "nóminas de moros" (Moorish *nóminas*) or "herçes," a Hispanicized Arabic term for phylacteries (Labarta 1983: 167). In some cases, investigators from the Holy Office found that these texts incorporated images of the cross, together with the *hamsa*, or apotropaic figure of the hand of Fatima believed to counteract evil and long associated by Muslims with the five pillars of Islam. On a number of occasions, *conversos* and *moriscos* who were detained and interviewed by Inquisitors claimed to be unaware of the meaning of Hebrew or Arabic words written on amulets found in their possession.

Prohibitions against heterodox Christian uses of *nóminas* were also vigorously investigated by Inquisitors and exposed by reformers following the expulsion of Jews and Muslims from the peninsula. Such efforts were no doubt frustrated by the tens of thousands of cheaply reproduced "pliegos de nóminas" or chapbook amulets sold by major printing houses, such as the one operated by the Crombergers in sixteenth-century Seville (Skemer 2006: 230–1). A number of amuletic prayers studied in the chapters that follow were explicitly banned by the Holy Office through the *Index of Prohibited Books*. In one particularly striking case, I will discuss a round paper *nómina* inscribed with the letter to Abgar, Tetragrammaton, and other features that was hidden in a wall in the Extremaduran countryside during the first half of the sixteenth century – together with other texts banned by the Index, including the classic picaresque novel, *Lazarillo de Tormes*.

Once again, an understanding of the characteristics and powers ascribed to amuletic texts can be gleaned from contemporary prohibitions. Notably, a professor of theology in the early sixteenth century, Pedro Ciruelo, wrote a condemnation of popular superstitions while serving in the court of Carlos V. He devotes a long chapter to the problem of *nóminas*, described as brief documents or "cédulas" consisting of holy names and prayers in Latin, Romance, or combined with words from foreign languages: "vocablos ... de otras lenguas peregrinas" (1978: 77). Ciruelo observed that amulets with difficult-to-decipher writing were in some cases supposed to lose their power if unsealed or read aloud: "palabras ignotas ... que solas aquellas palabras escritas .... en solamente traer la nomina cerrada y cosido ... será sanado y librado del peligro " (unknown words ... and only with those written words ... in only carrying the *nómina* sewn shut ... he will be healed and freed from danger) (1978: 82).[38] Here, he might be alluding to the inclusion of transliterated Hebrew components, since the threat of the Inquisition is directly evoked ("merece ser castigado por los ... inquisidores"), and the treatise also warns against amuletic words whose significance defies comprehension, as in the case of the ineffable four-letter name of God (1978: 75). At the same time, Arabic or aljamiado inscriptions could also be implicated in Ciruelo's prohibition, or what Inquisitors called "oraciones moriscas y otras cosas escritas en algarabía" (*morisco* prayers and other things written in their Arabic) (Labarta 1983: 171). He notes that heterodox amulets – that is, *nóminas* that combine orthodox elements with other (*hetero*) supersticiones – were typically hung from the neck and included promises of safety from drowning, fires, pestilence, "o la muger en el parto" (or a woman in labour) (1978: 74). In general terms, his approach to the problem hearkens back to St Isidore's definition of *superstitio* as baseless observances wrongly added to (*super*) institutionally prescribed forms of devotion (2008: 8.3.4).

Ciruelo disapproved of the requirements of using virgin parchment and specific kinds of silk thread, along with other superfluous rituals.[39] In this treatise, he seems to be describing the kind of *nómina* employed by the eponymous old bawd in Fernando de Rojas's *La Celestina* (1499–1502), as will be discussed later in this book. Ciruelo finds that preferences for certain words in lieu of others also stray from accepted worship. He was equally suspicious of amuletic functions attached to numbers or shapes, whether through folding patterns or contents. Following Augustine, Ciruelo stresses that words are signs, and the matter on which they are written can have no natural power, and so they only seem efficacious as a result of demonic intervention. He categorizes such abuses as idolatrous and calls the texts themselves records of "heregía o mentira o blasfemia" (heresy or lying or blasphemy) (1978: 77). The only licit *nóminas* are those that are recited out loud, never concealed, and restricted to brief readings from the gospels, "tan claras que todos las entiendan, o en latín, o en la lengua común de todos" (so clear that all can understand, either in Latin, or in the vernacular of everyone) (1978: 77).[40] Apart from Hebrew, Arabic, or other incomprehensible words, it seems that Ciruelo also censors the amuletic efficacy believed to reside in prayers and holy names that have been abbreviated as sequences of majuscule initials, not unlike INRI, the *titulus* of the cross (*Iesus Nazarenus Rex Iudaeorum*, Jesus of Nazareth King of the Jews). This element, as we will see, characterizes a majority of the amulets that I have investigated from the high Middle Ages to the Renaissance. A contemporary friar, Martín de Castañega, similarly wrote that *nóminas* must always be "muy claras en la escritura y sentencia, no habiendo alguna cosa ... que en sí traen sospecha" (very clear in their writing and meaning, not having any thing ... that in itself attracts suspicion), and must refrain from promising deliverance from sudden death in battle or any other danger (1997: 131). Drawing on the letters of St Paul, Ciruelo goes on to designate the potency attributed to *nóminas* on the basis of their inscribed materiality as an adherence to the closed "escritura muerta" (dead writing) of the old Jewish law, in contrast to the "palabras bivas" of Christ (living words) (1978: 82). His discussion also seems to be influenced by commentaries on a passage from the Gospel of Matthew, in which Jesus condemns the Pharisees for their "phylacteria," understood as tefillin inscriptions of the law being misused as amulets (23:5). In contrast, Ciruelo likens Christian prayer to a little open book: "un librito abierto que le pueda sacar del seno a cada hora que quisiera leerlo, o hazerlo" (a little book that can be brought out from the bosom at any hour one might wish to read it, or have it read) (1978: 83).[41]

The Spanish reformer in this way demonstrates how believers might still wear approved amulets against their bodies, but must refrain from concealing their contents. He cites from the legend of St Cecilia, who read from a gospel that she literally carried over her chest but was also portrayed as spiritually hearing its truth within her heart. At the same time, as Skemer observers, textual amulets were understood as *lorica* (armour) positioned to shield the heart as the central gateway to the soul and the body's vitality. This proximity can also be related to the heart's role in the faculty of memory and the capacity for reason and conscience thought to connect human beings to the divine. Within this inner dwelling place, God was believed to have inscribed His Word, to be read through a process of conversional, interior recollection of the kind evoked in Augustine's *Confessions* and explicated by other church fathers. Theologians like Ciruelo sought to contrast a renewing notion of the externally and internally worn divine text with what they viewed as the dead letter of Pharisaic phylacteries and adherence to Jewish law, physically bound to the body without spiritual fulfilment.[42] For this reason, implicit in Spanish efforts to reform the abuse of *nóminas* among Old and New Christians alike are increased concerns over what Inquisitors characterized as Judaizing tendencies. Of course, the preoccupation itself was nothing new: even during the comparatively more tolerant reign of Alfonso X, we will see how an anxiety with regard to Jewish amuletic influence feeds into the Galician-Portuguese *Cantigas de Santa Maria* (Songs of Holy Mary, c. 1250–80).[43]

Not long after Castañega and Ciruelo published their treatises, the Inquisitor Fernando de Valdés published an *Index of Prohibited Books* that banned the same *Oración de San León* (1559) that I have referred to in this discussion. It was included in a list of prayers that were derived from or contained fictional sources or legends and promised to bring about healing and protection on the basis of their textual, material presence. Thus, copies of the amuletic text that appeared decades earlier in the inventory of Isabel I "La Católica" (The Catholic) were now to be confiscated and destroyed. What is more, as Joseph Gwara has recently shown, "cultre," the term used in this and other royal inventories for prayers and seals inscribed on parchment, rolled or otherwise enclosed in ornate capsules to be worn around the neck, was almost certainly derived from a rabbinic Hebrew word for amulets, *glturi* ("A Possible Hebraism" 2012). The examples of this lexical borrowing that Gwara examines are once again suggestive of a potential *mudejarismo* or tradition of religio-cultural hybridizing of amuletic practices in medieval and early modern Spain. Objects designated as "cultres" were also owned by Isabel's daughter, Juana "La Loca" (The Mad), and again appear in the record of a gift exchanged between the queen's grandchildren, Carlos V and Catalina de Austria (Gwara "A Possible Hebraism" 2012: 13–16). The same word is later used by Juan de Pineda in his *Diálogos familiares de la agricultura cristiana* (Familiar Dialogues about Christian Agriculture, 1589), where superstitions surrounding *cultres* are exposed in the same way that Ciruelo condemns *nóminas* (1963: 3.340).

Even more interesting for the purposes of this investigation is a satirical reference from a literary work written during the reign of the Catholic Monarchs. Gwara observes that the Hispanicized Hebrew term – possibly introduced into Spanish by early fifteenth-century *conversos* – is employed in the novel by Juan Flores, *Grisel y Mirabella* ("A Possible Hebraism"). In a final scene, offended damsels take their revenge on a misogynist by tearing him to pieces and reducing his body to ashes that can be dispersed like relics: "algunas hovo que por cultre en el cuello la traían, por que, trayendo más a memoria su venganza, mayor plazer les diese" (there were some who had it [his remains] around their necks like a *cultre*, because, reminding them more of their revenge, it gave them more pleasure) (2003: 370). Significantly, the Hebrew *glturi* was itself adapted from *ligatura*, a common Latin word for amulets intended to tie and bind through the power and presence of words. Believers would be reminded of this binding potency by the attached cord or chain from which the object hung, touching and materially enveloping their body. Such contact is implicated in *Grisel y Mirabella*, as the ladies' *cultres* provide a tactile means of inwardly activating the memory. It is not surprising that a word most often linked with the practice of carrying enclosed written prayers has been applied in this way to reliquary amulets. In his reproval of *nóminas*, Ciruelo compares the dead-letter problem of textual amulets with that of capsules containing relics that were also superstitiously worn around the neck and encouraged an improper devotion to "cosas muertas" (dead things), as opposed to what he views as an orthodox Christian faith in the Pauline living spirit and the spoken word (1978: 80). In a subversion of mnemonic textual objects carried over the hearts of saints like Cecilia, reminding them of the sacrifice of Christ and His martyrs, the tactile function of *cultres* in Flores's novel would have perversely recalled the mock martyrdom of an enemy. This prompting of an internal recollection – etymologically conveying the idea of re-gathering (*re-colligere*) – parallels the material *pars pro toto* of relics as bodily fragments possessing the martyr's integral, efficacious presence. The corporal mementos carried by vengeful ladies in *Grisel y Mirabella* also satirize what Skemer calls the "bidirectional" power of amulets to bestow inner healing while at the same time projecting an outward apotropaic force – in this case, by providing a morbid inward pleasure and a physical shield to ward off further misogynist attacks (2006: 138).

Analogous to the potency of relics worn like *cultres*, some of the written amulets that concern me in this study draw power and meaning through uses of material and textual *pars pro toto* or synecdoche. Brief or partial inscriptions and majuscule abbreviations were made on these objects and bound to the body as a means of seeing, touching, and elliptically bringing to mind and making present the whole of an efficacious text. This process is noted by Skemer and aptly described by David Frankfurter as an infusion of performative meaning through materially manifest words, extracted from the gospels and other holy sources, as in the case of the opening phrase *in illo tempore* (at that time) from the Vulgate versions of Luke and John:

> The power inherent in sacred scripture could be tapped simply by writing gospel incipits ... often there was an analogical relationship between the contexts ... and the apotropaic or curative function for which the amulet was intended ... quotation, therefore, worked not only by its ... writing, but also as a *historiola*, invoking a specific power that was performed and guaranteed *in illo tempore* ... and ... might convey power to present human situations ... when one narrates or utters ... the words uttered draw power into the world and towards (or against) an object in the world ... an additional sense to narrating power: a power intrinsic to any narrative, any

story, uttered in a ritual context, and the idea that the mere recounting of certain stories situates or directs their narrative power into the world. (2001: 457)

We have seen how imaginative, storytelling elements were inherent in the elaboration of texts like Abgar's letter or the "Oración de San León." Frankfurter's notion of "narrating power" suggests how amulets can be retold and redeployed in ways that work intrinsically within new literary frames and extrinsically through whatever attributes are believed to reside in their visible, tangible writing.

In recent years, Caroline Walker Bynum has shed further light on the paradoxical role of materiality in premodern Christianity. She points out how medieval religiosity emphasized transcendence of the worldly realm and spiritual interiority beyond the material realm – to include what Ciruelo calls "escritura muerta" and "cosas muertas" – while at the same time upholding an incarnational understanding of sublunary, corruptible matter based on the central christological doctrine that God literally took on human flesh. On the one hand, bodily fragments and objects in contact with them, as well as texts and images recorded on parchment or other materials, were by definition subject to decay and destruction. On the other hand, these seemingly transient things could be infused with and serve as mediating witnesses to the power of the divine Word overcoming the perilous mortal corruptibility of the fallen world.[44] Bynum also finds that medieval ideas about material agency were less figurative than theories focused on contemporary culture: miraculous objects were believed to speak, act, and make things happen, not just in a discursive or performative sense but as if they were living things. They also harboured the potential literally to defy boundaries we perceive as separating matter that can actively make things happen from inanimate matter.

In keeping with Bynum, my study is primarily, though not exclusively concerned with what she calls "theories of those contemporary with the objects" and "evidence about the attitudes and assumptions of those who shaped and were shaped by the objects themselves" (2011: 280–1). In addition to modern critical approaches to examining issues related to influence and intertextuality in literature, this book has been informed by the work of scholars researching medieval and early modern materiality from the standpoint of manuscript culture and the history of the book. In recent decades John Dagenais and others have provided new models for studying these early materials, less encumbered by editorial or disciplinary impositions that sometimes misleadingly divided canonized literature from what is deemed non-literary, tended to isolate authorized texts from other accompanying written and visual components, and separated authorial attributions from audience interactions.[45] In keeping with this movement towards greater interdisciplinarity, each chapter in this book will concentrate on the ways in which literary history intersects with the tradition of written amulets used on the Iberian Peninsula to heal, protect, and otherwise provide a blessing or curse. In addition to Gwara's work, Skemer has touched on medieval stories about and fictional representations of amulets that provide evidence of how they were used in different contexts. What is suggested by but lies beyond the scope of their important studies is the relationship between the power assigned to such inscribed objects and the construction of the narratives in which they are evoked. My intention is to address this question by analysing the meaningful evocation of amulets in literature as a means of harnessing and redirecting their efficacy – in this sense, considering the notion of the textual objects themselves as a point of departure for interpretation.

By considering a variety of emblematic examples from medieval manuscripts, early printed books, and picaresque novels, I hope to shed light on how their power was drawn on and fictionalized at critical junctures in the development of imaginative literature on the Iberian Peninsula. While my primary focus is on works written in Spanish, this study also considers examples of amuletic and literary texts that were composed in Latin, Portuguese, and – to a much lesser extent – other languages. My investigation centres on the function of prayers, divine names, and incantatory formulas that were inscribed and printed on parchment, paper, or other media, and at the same time inserted into literary works dating from the High Middle Ages to the early modern period – from an era of conflict and exchange between Jews, Christians, and Muslims on the peninsula to one of Inquisitorial persecution, following the forced and voluntary exile of religious minorities and their converted descendants. While the amulets I have selected are primarily composed of Christian elements, in a number of instances they cannot be fully understood without also considering their uses and connotations in relation to Muslim and especially Jewish and *converso* traditions. If, as Bynum has found, the potency of such objects was viewed more literally in the premodern imaginary, I am interested in understanding how this perspective transitioned and changed in literary works that figuratively reinterpret and ironically redirect the amuletic attributes of the written word. To this end, I will begin by examining in chapter 1 the lyrical *Razón de amor* and Alfonso X's well-known *Cantigas de Santa Maria* (Songs of St Mary, c. 1250–80), followed in chapters 2 and 3 by texts written in the same narrative verse form: the thirteenth-century *Libro de Alexandre* (Book of Alexander) and *Libro de Apolonio* (Book of Apollonius of Tyre), as they relate to the archpriest of Hita's classic *Libro de buen amor* (Book of Good Love, 1343). My analysis then turns to interrelated classic works of Renaissance satire, *La Celestina* and *La Lozana andaluza* (The Lusty Andalusian Woman, 1528) in chapter 4, before considering final examples from two picaresque masterpieces, *Lazarillo de Tormes* and Quevedo's *El Buscón* (The Swindler, c.1604) in chapter 5. Over the course of this itinerary, I hope to demonstrate how written amulets were imbedded into, intervened in, and came to shape the creation of fictional lives in medieval and early modern Iberian culture.

Chapter One

Amuletic Manuscripts

One telling narrative account of the powers attributed to the spoken and written word during the Middle Ages can be found in a miracle from the earlier-mentioned *Cantigas de Santa Maria*, compiled by Alfonso X "El Sabio." The story is set in Auvergne, a mountainous, formerly Occitan-speaking region of France that is known for its Romanesque churches, convents, and abbeys. Miracle number 125 tells of a clerical devotee of the Virgin who fell so desperately in love with "ũa donzela fremosa a maravilla" (a wondrously beautiful maiden) that he resorted to summoning demonic assistance in his campaign to woo her (1986–9: v. 11). Meanwhile, the object of his affections has been instructed by the Virgin to protect herself from this malevolence by reciting the Ave Maria "e ten sempr' en mi a voontade" (while keeping your will directed towards me) (1986–9, vol. 2, vv. 15–16). The demons report that they have failed to penetrate her apotropaic barrier of prayer, but the priest sends them back to afflict the maiden with such a grave illness that her parents consider ending their daughter's life.[1] In this weakened state, she forgets the words of the Ave Maria ("a oraçón da Virgen, lle fezo que se ll' obridou") (1986–9: vol. 2, v. 35). Finally, when the priest comes to visit her, the vulnerable maiden is so stricken with mad love that she threatens to commit suicide unless the two are not immediately allowed to wed.

To undo this illicit betrothal, the Holy Mother visits the would-be groom as he chants the Hours of the Virgin. After first causing him to forget the mid-afternoon prayer of Nones ("sas oras, essa vez obridou-xe-lle a nõa"), she demands that the cleric renounce his allegiance to the devil and honour his priestly vows (1986–9: vol. 1, v. 66–7). Significantly, the prayer in question, during the season of Advent, evoked the Ave Maria and then Mary's spiritual beauty and redemptive power against the encroachment of evil, as well as her maternal victory over sickness and death: "Be mindful, author of our health, that you sometime did take on yourself of a pure virgin being born, the form of our humanity" (*Office of the Blessed Virgin Marie* 1599: Hymn, vv. 1–4).[2] As a result of the Virgin's intercession, the lovers are moved to call off their espousals and commit themselves to lives of Christian asceticism. Thus, efficacious prayer in the story is linked to the memory and the will recollecting and turning to its maker. The sins of the lovers temporarily obliviate this memory, and their wrongly directed volition becomes disunited from the sacred meaning of the Ave Maria and *Officium Beatae Mariae*. In accordance with Augustine and later theologians, postlapsarian language seems to be understood strictly as a system of signs, with no natural power beyond the capacity to express what is in the heart and willed by the speaker.[3]

At least, no further effects are made explicit in the verses of the song. The maiden's initial invocation corresponds with a rightly turned will ("en mi a voontade") that calls on Mary for protection. In the case of the lecherous priest, however, his incantation coincides with a misaligned heart and communicates with evil forces. In either case, it appears that language cannot, in and of itself, cause any benefit or harm. Words only makes things happen by furnishing audible signs that are consensually understood to be calling for Marian or demonic intervention in human events. Yet the deployment of language in this context is not restricted to the articulation of sound but is also associated with written materiality. Although denounced as idolatry by thirteenth-century writers like William of Auvergne, we have seen how it was permitted for believers to bind themselves with amulets inscribed with Holy Writ in hopes of attaining protection and healing. As discussed earlier, these objects were in theory viewed merely as signs of devotion, and the attainment of any benefit from them attributed solely to divine grace. In practice, such texts were often superstitiously thought to exert power through their material presence and physical contact with believers, and in some cases it was postulated that the natural potency of incantatory words could be projected and conferred to the matter of amuletic objects. Material representations of the efficacious language used by the priest and maiden can be seen in an illustration of the storied lovers from a thirteenth-century Alfonsine codex at the Escorial library (the "codice rico" or MS. T.j.I, Alfonso 2011).

The lascivious cleric is pictured with an outward-facing, open codex, gesturing from the centre of a pentagram and encircled by seals and keys that he utilizes to summon a devilish gathering (Figure 1).[4] This image draws on early grimoires in which Solomon was legendarily credited with employing and recording verbal formulae that combine astrological invocations with the names of fallen angels, along with other written signs. These were believed to bind supernatural beings to the conjurer's will and often employed on amulets from the period. Significantly, the illumination suggests that the priest has, as it were, entered into his book, and that its inscribed contents have then spilled out into the exterior space that surrounds him – and onto the parchment of the miracle collection itself. Thus, the bidirectional effect of his words appears to be emanating from a physical manifestation of writing, and not just from oral recitation. In a subsequent panel (Figure 2), the maiden is shown safeguarding herself by wielding a codex that apparently represents a prayer book containing the Ave Maria. The presence of this object, together with the Virgin's intercession, enables her to drive away the diabolical assembly. Her open book is held sideways and pointed at the retreating devils in a way that calls attention to its potentially amuletic, shielding function, while deemphasizing her oral pronouncement of an immaterial, memorized text. By extension, of course, this depiction of a Marian codex calls attention to the materiality of the *Cantigas* manuscript itself. The manuscript on which the illuminations appear is, after all, analogous to the prayer book insofar as it praises the Virgin by invoking the protective Ave Maria in numerous collected songs as means of counteracting and expelling evil.[5]

In this way, the Auvergne miracle seems to illustrate a clear distinction between sinful versus devotional uses of powerful books and the invocations they contain. This differentiation, however, becomes more vexing in two other thirteenth-century examples that will be considered in what remains of this chapter. I will first examine a previously mentioned manuscript that was preserved in France (BNP lat. 3576) and contains a number of Spanish works, including the poem known as the *Razón de amor*. These verses were copied together with a Latin text that combines the language of Christian prayer with words intended to summon and bind demonic forces. My discussion will show how, comparable to miracle 125, the conjuring of demons and efficacy of *sacra verba* affects the meaning and outcome of an illicit affair between a priest and maiden in this earlier love poem. I will then return to the *Cantigas de Santa Maria*, examining another illuminated manuscript

Figure 1. Cleric conjuring demons. *Cantigas de Santa Maria*, Escorial MS. T.j.I, pt. 1, panel 5, detail (photo: Album/Art Resource, NY).

Figure 2. Lady defended by the Virgin. *Cantigas de Santa Maria*, Escorial MS.T.j.I, pt. 1, panel 6, detail (photo: Album/Art Resource, NY).

that is housed in Florence ("F" or Biblioteca Nazionale Centrale B.R.20, Alfonso X 1991). My purpose is to demonstrate how the text and imagery of this particular codex further complicate and problematize delineations between prayers to the Virgin and a potentially superstitious reliance on the efficacy of a Marian text. We will see how the illustration of an amuletic book and the materiality of the Alfonsine codex itself are not just implicitly suggested, but literally conflated in *cantiga* 209.

The Exorcistic Prelude to the *Razón de amor*

During the 1880s, a French Hispanist who was working in the manuscript department at the Bibliothèque Nationale made an important discovery. While preparing a catalogue of Spanish language works in the collection, Alfred Morel-Fatio came across a codex containing an expansive compilation of Latin sermons copied sometime during the first part of the thirteenth century.[6] Between these materials, he found three texts in Castilian, copied in the same hand and dating from the same period as the homilies: a poem about two lovers meeting in a garden, a debate in verse between water and wine, and a penitential treatment of the Ten Commandments. Although Morel-Fatio (1987) published the two poems separately, the Spanish philologist Menéndez Pidal later combined them under the title "Siesta de abril" or "Razón de amor con los denuestos del agua y vino," taken from descriptions given by the poet who is identified at the end of the text as Lupus or Lope from the Aragonese town of Moros (1905).[7] Immediately before this text is an exorcistic prayer that, as I will show in the pages that follow, relates to and even affects the outcome of the love poem set in an idyllic garden. What I am interested in is how this prayer sheds light on notions of outer and inner spaces of fertility and desolation in the medieval imaginary, pointing to natural and supernatural settings that are threatened by sin and purified by the church. As I hope to show, the exorcistic text is efficacious as a physical, textual presence in the codex and also as a source of meaning prefiguring imagery from the poetic work that it precedes in the manuscript.

The poem, which has received a great deal of attention from critics, begins with a Latin invocation of the Holy Spirit: "Sancti Spiritus adsid nobis gratia amen" (Franchini 1993: v. 1). What follows is a springtime encounter between a priestly lover identified as an "escolar" and a beautiful lady who comes to meet him in her "huerto" (1993: vv. 6, 21). The *locus amoenus* is complete with an ever-flowing spring, blooming flowers, and ripened fruit trees – specifically an olive, apple, and pomegranate. The scholar enters into this allegorical space during the heat of the day, removes his clothing as if returning to Edenic innocence, and then takes rest under the "olivar" (1993: v. 12).[8] As we will see, this spatial "conventional language," as Laura Howes puts it in her study of later, Chaucerian gardens, sets the stage for expressions of ambivalence as opposed to providing a landscape of unequivocal moralization (1997: 36). In the branches of the apple tree, the scholar sees that the owner of the garden has left a covered silver chalice full of red wine for a male visitor. As James Burke and others have pointed out, this "surely evokes Eucharistic imagery whatever else it might imply" (1998: 144). On a higher bough is perched a glass filled with cold water that the scholar believes to be enchanted: "ovi miedo que era encantado" (1993: v. 33).[9] The clerical narrator approaches the spring to take a drink from what are described as its healing waters, plucks a flower from among the roses, lilies, and violets growing there, and begins singing of love.[10] A lady then appears, also picking flowers and singing praises to her lover. While this setting has been viewed as conventionally symbolic, it also opens up a discursive space for worldly, carnal representation – like other gardens in medieval literature it is the kind of textual *locus* that John Ganim has described as "dialectical, dynamic, and creative" (2007: xv). The lady immediately recognizes the scholar, removes her mantle, and the two kiss, exchange their feelings for one another, and, as Connie Scarborough (2011) has recently argued, probably make love in the garden: "una grant pieça ali estando, / de nuestro amor ementando" (tarrying there for a good while, speaking of our love) (1993: vv. 134–5). Fearing that she will be caught with him, the lady hastily departs and leaves him in a state of sorrow. As the scholar begins to doze off, a white dove enters the garden to drink from the spring, becomes frightened by his presence, and then flies up into the apple tree to refresh itself in the glass of water. The bird spills some of the water into the wine below, previously described as being covered. This veiling and unveiling of the chalice might recall the Eucharistic *pallium* or linen cloth, ornamented with the cross and designed to protect the vessel's contents from impurities during the mass until the taking for communion (Thurston 1908: 3.563–4).

The dove not only evokes the consoling grace or *paracletus* of the Holy Spirit from the opening of the poem but also brings about a mixture of liquids that recalls the Eucharistic drink. John the Baptist was understood as preparing the way for the sacrifice of Christ, when blood and water poured from the right side of Saviour's crucified body.[11] For a medieval audience, I would suggest that the bird may have also brought to mind dove tabernacles, known as the *peristerium* or *columba*, that held consecrated hosts in a pyx or behind the bird's neck to bring to the sick. Hung from chains over the altar, these vessels were positioned above the priest offering the sacrifice of Christ's body and blood, recalling the Paraclete that appeared in the form of a *columba* or dove above Jesus during his baptism.[12]

Critics like Enzo Franchini (1993) have considered how this scene introduces and relates to the debate poem that follows in the manuscript. In accordance with Latin versions of the dispute between *aquam et vinum*, water is accused of being easily contaminated with filth but also takes wine to task for impairing reason and encouraging sinfulness. The two disputants attempt to defend themselves by mentioning their role in the sacraments of baptism and communion. In this way, the mixing of imagery linked to worldly lust and spiritual *caritas* – that is, the fruit of the mutual love between the Father and Son expressed in the person of the Holy Spirit – is extended to the "denuestos" section. Franchini compares this to what Andreas Capellanus famously calls "mixed" as opposed to "pure" love, in the late twelfth-century *De amore* (1993: 398). Fittingly, the *Razón de amor* ends with a colophon that seems to refer ambivalently to Eucharistic and/or goliardic imbibing: the usual "qui me scripsit scribat, semper cum domino vivat" (may he who wrote me keep writing and live always with God) is written as "qui me scripsit scribat, semper cum domino bibat" (may he who wrote me keep writing and drink always with God) (1993: vv. 146–8).[13] Scholars have also connected the problem of *amor mixtus* versus *amor purus* to the Castilian manual on the Ten Commandments that appears after the poems. For example, Colbert Nepaulsingh observes how this section emphasizes the role of the senses in committing and penitentially reflecting on sins, and in particular the danger of lust and fornication being incited by the taste of wine, the sound of "cantares" (poetic singing), and touching women "en las tetas o en otro lugar de vergonça" (on the breasts or other shameful places) (1986: 60).

However, the significance of the Latin text that immediately precedes these three interrelated Castilian works, which are known collectively as the Spanish *cuaderno*, has been largely ignored. It features an exorcistic prayer against bad weather, together with liturgical elements, and a series of petitions, divine names, and scriptural citations or *nomina sacra* and *verba divina*. Critics following more traditional philological models have tended to either view these as unrelated to the vernacular, literary portion of the codex – in spite of the fact that it employs Hispanicized Latin from the period that Franchini has traced to peninsular dialects ("Abracalabra" 1991). In more recent years, John Dagenais has suggested that there could be meaningful links between it, the *Razón de amor con los denuestos*, and the *Diez mandamientos*.[14] Without fully exploring this possibility, Dagenais notes that the enchantment of water in a garden of love not only brings to mind a warning in the confessional treatise against "los que façen encantaciones o conjurios por mulleres" (those who make incantations and conjuries for women), but could also be tied to language employed against Satan in the exorcistic text: "uas signatum no designavis ... aqua piissima" (you will not unseal the sealed vessel ... most holy water) (1994: 50). As he puts it, just as the "the *Razón* seems to create the very state of sin that the prose text's confession and penance seek to correct ... a folio containing prayers and formulas of exorcism ... establishes at the beginning ... the atmosphere of veiled danger picked up in the *escolar*'s fear of the enchanted water" (1994: 50). My intention is to build on his suggestion by closely considering how efficacious sacred imagery from the prefatory folio containing the Latin prayer resonates in the love poetry and garden space that follows. Understanding this medieval "textual situation," to use the title from Andrew Taylor's book (2002), requires us to first examine what has been seen as a non-literary intrusion that happens to immediately precede the *Razón de amor*.

Franchini (1991) has noted that part of the exorcism against inclement weather was adapted from, or at least coincides with, the Mozarabic liturgy for baptism. The practice of abjuration as part of the baptismal ceremony was intended to counteract the power of evil, as a remedy for original sin. Accordingly, the Evil One was renounced by taking an oath prior to administering the sacrament: "Recordare Sathanas quod tibi mando a pena confideris ... [quem] Deus meus ad suam sanctam gratiam vocare dignatus es ... fugas ... uas signatum non designavis adjuratus es in nomine patris filii spiritus sancti amen" (Remember, Satan, what is in store for you ... [by what] my God and Lord has deigned to call to his grace ... retreat ... you will not unseal the sealed vessel, you are sworn against it in the name of the Father, Son, and Holy Spirit, amen) (Matt. 3:16, Franchini 1991: 82).[15] This exorcistic process was described as an *exsufflatio* or breathing out of demonic influences, followed by an *insufflatio*, or breathing in of the Holy Spirit believed to descend on the newly baptized (Toner 1909). It thus reenacts the coming down of the Paraclete from the heavens like a dove (*columba*) in the Gospel of Matthew, just as Christ emerged from the waters of the river Jordan. What is more, a similar abjuration could be used in blessing the baptismal font itself, as well as other vessels and sacred objects such as the Eucharist chalice and altar bells.[16] Rituals for purifying water can also be related to practices associated with the feast of St John on the summer solstice, when believers lit bonfires to drive away contaminating demonic storms and gathered pure, healing waters said to have been purified by the Baptizer.[17] Similarly, the folio preceding the *Razón de amor* conjures the heavens with words for expelling malevolent forces ("demones" and "diaboli") from the air in the context of taking in the Spirit, and evoking the opening up of the sky for the descent of the Paraclete (1993: 123v). Its prayer calls on the Holy Ghost to drive away a storm (*timphanis*) that torments the community and individual souls and instead to bring "sol in celum" (1993: 123v). In this way, the text anticipates the *locus amoenus* setting in the Spanish poem, threatened by the contamination of "agua encantada" (enchanted water) and sanctified by the "paloma" (dove).

Significantly, the Latin prayer provides a telling example of how such abjurations could be intoned in combination with litanies that were also common in vernacular literary works. It invokes the deliverance of Susanna and the young Shadrach, Meshach, and Abednego from the book of Daniel ("sancta susanna de falso crimine liberavi, tres pueros de camino ignis eripuit") (1993: fol. 123r). The same kind of petition also made its way into Spanish prayers that were inscribed on textual amulets, as well as previously mentioned narratives from the period such as the *Poema de mío Cid* and the *Poema de Fernán González*, as well as Gonzalo de Berceo's *Milagros de Nuestra Señora* (Miracles of Our Lady, c. 1260). These pleas for deliverance, related to the *Ordo commendatio animae*, are followed in the prayer by the amuletic Trisagion, or tripartite invocation in Greek of "agios, agios, agios" (holy, holy, holy) that was adapted from Revelation (4:8) and also employed in the Order of Mass as a Latin prayer recited prior to the Eucharistic consecration, "sanctus, sanctus, sanctus" (1993: fol. 123r).[18] The next section of the parchment moves from divine invocation to the naming of malevolent spirits. Richard Kieckhefer has documented analogous exorcisms in which thundering armies of demons are verbally bound by their names (sometimes derived from those of pagan gods), forced to desist from causing hail storms or to redirect their damaging storms to the sea. For example, he translates an eleventh-century German version:

"I abjure you O Devil and your angels ... I abjure you or Mermeut (a supernatural maker of bad weather in Norse mythology) with your companions, you have power over the tempests" (1989: 74). Not surprisingly, premodern abjurations were often copied and in some cases pronounced by priests such as the French lover depicted in Alfonso X's song 125.[19] Such formulas could be expected to call on demonic forces, either to exert or relinquish their power to torment mortals and punish enemies. They might be made to seize or surrender control over the skies, summoning or withdrawing storm clouds known to destroy crops, cause flooding, and contaminate the water supply. The appearance of darkening, threatening skies on the horizon was sometimes likened to the advance of an invading army. For instance, in the earlier-mentioned *Poema de Fernán González*, the "conjuramientos" of Moorish enemies are blamed for causing demonic tempests (1983: st. 477). In later centuries, witches were sometimes accused of diabolically conjuring storms, as can be seen, for example, in the *De lamiis et phitonicis mulieribus* (Of Female Witches and Sorcerers, 1498) by Ulrich Molitor (Luber 1999).

In keeping with the legend of Solomon, medieval conjurers sought to seal or capture tempestuous demons by naming them. It was believed that their "conjuros" were put in effect not just by reciting powerful words but also by the presence of the parchment onto which these were inscribed – in some cases placed by clerics in agricultural fields, attached to trees, or even livestock (Skemer 2006: 167). Such practices persisted throughout the Middle Ages to the extent that early sixteenth-century reformer Pedro Ciruelo singles out and condemns this particular superstition, urging believers to rely instead on rogative processions and the ringing of church bells to ward off storms:

> Conjuradores de los nublados en tiempo de la tempestad ... hazen creer a la simple gente que los diablos engendran el nublado, el granizo, y el pedrisco, y toda la tempestad de truenos, relampagos, y rayos: y que en quellas nuves vienen los diablos: y que con ellos harán huyr de allí a los diablos con sus nublados y les harán echar el granizo, y pedra a otro cabo donde ellos quisieren ... hazen otras cosas vanas ... ni ellas ni sus palabras tienen virtud alguna natural ni sobre natural para hazer lo que dizen ... Y si por ser clérigos tienen virtud divina sobrenatural contra los demonios: ellos no tienen más esta virtud que los otros clérigos ... en este caso de la tempestad ... que hagan tañer en torno y a soga las mayores campanas que ay en las tores de las yglesias... ansí la nube se disuelve o derrite en agua

limpia sin granizo o piedra ... con devotas oraciones [y] procesiones. (1978: 115, 118–19)

(Conjurers of cloud formations in stormy weather ... make simple people believe that devils create the clouds, all kinds of hail stones, thundering storms, and lightening: and that in those clouds devils are coming, and with them [the conjurers] the devils with their clouds will be made to flee from there, and make them drop their hail stones further away wherever they wish ... they do other vain things ... neither these claims nor their words have any natural or supernatural power to do what they say ... And if because they are priests they have divine, supernatural power against demons, they do not have more power that other priests ... in the case of tempests ... they should have the largest bells found in church towers swung from ropes and sounded at intervals ... this way the cloud dissolves or melts in clear water without hail or stone ... with devout prayers [and] processions.)

The Hispanicized Latin prayer that precedes the *Razón de amor* features all of the elements studied by Kieckhefer and warned against by Ciruelo, as it calls on the names "Mercorim," "Gubim" (a name for Jupiter), and "Yrcole" that correspond with medieval grimoires, in hopes that "grandine" or hail stones will turn to rain, fall "in medio mare" – or, in any case, not within the limits of "ista villa" (Franchini 1991: fol. 123v). What is more, the series of *nomina sacra* and *verba divina* added to the exorcistic text are also characteristically found on amulets whose written words were believed to confer more general protection and healing through their material presence. Another early sixteenth-century treatise against heterodox practices, written by the Franciscan Martín de Castañega, specifically denounces the practice of relying on textual objects to assuage demonic tempests:

Tienen unos conjuros supersticiosos compuestos ... por excelencia los tienen escriptos en pergamino virgen en que están muchas partes del Canon de la Misa, y las palabras sacramentales, porque piensan que como con aquellas palabras convierten el pan en cuerpo de Jesucristo, y vino en sangre, así con aquellas palabras consagran la nube, y la piedra converte en agua ... [como] *agios* ... y cuantos nombres hebráicos y griegos." (1997: 167)

(They have composed certain superstitious conjurations ... characteristically they have them written on virgin parchment on which are many parts of the Order of the Mass, and sacramental words, since they think that just as those words convert the bread into the body of Jesus Christ, and wine into blood, so with those words they consecrate the cloud, and convert the hail stone into water ... [such as] *agios* ... and many Hebrew and Greek names.)

In the case of the Latin conjurations in the manuscript that I have been discussing, inscriptions on the parchment could have also been understood as working in tandem with the power of spring water and Eucharistic imagery evoked in the *Razón de amor*: "en al mana quan comiesse ... nuncas mas enfermarya" (he who ingests from its flow ... will never again get sick) (1993: vv. 24–6). By verbally abjuring and converting hail stones into water, this amuletic text also anticipates the transformation of wine into Christ's blood that is represented in the subsequent poem and debate. Accordingly, the *verba divina* of the exorcistic prayer include the repeated elliptical phrase from the Gospel of Matthew, "in illo tempore" (at that time), and the first words of John, "In principio [erat Verbum]" (In the beginning [was the Word]) to conjure what Frankfurter (2001: 457) calls the "narrative power" of a *historiola* (Matt. 12:1, 14:1, 22:34). The latter gospel was believed to be effective particularly when deployed as an amulet, with its emphasis on the power of the Word becoming flesh. Other common elements in the Latin prayer that are also found in amulets studied by Skemer include a triad of binding pentacles, comparable to the ones pictured in the Escorial *Cantigas* manuscript; the triune naming of God from Exodus and Acts, "Deus Habraham, Deus Ysaac, Deus Iacob" (God of Abraham, God of Isaac, God of Jacob); and "Abracalabra," an esoteric seal that dates back to second-century talismans that Latinized the Aramaic *ibra* (אברא) and *k'dibra* (כדברא) to mean roughly, "I have made it so through my words" (Franchini 1991: 83; Ex. 3:6, Acts 3:14).[20] In consideration of this close connection with extant medieval amulets, it seems likely that the prayer in the manuscript was meant not only to be intoned, but also could have been recopied on parchment and employed as an efficacious textual object.

Several other demonic and divine names in the text, as well as numbers (such as the repeated reference to thousands) and other esoteric allusions, either explicitly or indirectly allude to the Apocalypse.[21] For example, the prayer evokes the serpent and lamb, the dragon with seven heads and ten horns, the darkening of the sun, moon and falling stars, angels from the east and west, and a demon from the bottomless pit called "Abaddon" and "Apollyon" also invoked in grimoires (fol. 123v) (Rev. 9:11; Franchini 1991: 87).[22] Not just the sound but also the visual material inscription of these names could have been understood as granting protection against damaging weather, along with other forms of evil encroachment. The prayer in this manner evokes the storm from Revelation, described by John the Divine: "upon the rivers and the fountains of waters ... there was made blood ... There were bolts of lightning and voices and thundering ... The cup of the wine of the indignation of his wrath ... Great hail ... came down from heaven upon men: and men blasphemed God, for the plague of the hail because it was exceedingly great" (16:4–21).[23] In keeping with apocalyptic *nomina sacra* found on other amulets, the text also invokes Christ as the "Alfa" and "Omega" (First and Last), as well as the earlier-mentioned "agios, agios, agios" (holy, holy, holy).[24] These words, together with performative commands like "liga illos, ligati sunt ... fugiatis" (bind them, they are bound ... may you flee) are no doubt intended to capture and drive away malevolent powers through the promised efficacy of the Saviour's name (1991: 82).

Images of binding work in combination with exorcistic elements, as believers hoping to be saved from the damning tempest prophesized in Revelation are reminded of the clearing skies and baptismal winged descent of the Holy Spirit. The apotropaic language is thus dependent on the promised return of sinners from the *locus eremus* or stormy wasteland of their exile as a result of original sin to a celestial garden paradise eternally free from the menacing clouds of this world. At stake are long-standing notions in medieval culture of an inner "garden of the soul," where virtues are cultivated by a prelapsarian Adam, vitalized by the tree of life and the fountain of the soul (Jeffrey 1992: 224). Outside of this sanctuary, however, is a sensual garden, where humankind is tempted by flights of the imagination – a seemingly idyllic space that is in fact always subject to diabolical storms. Christian redemption could thus be understood as a return from an outer torment to an inner garden of peace, figured as calm, clear skies. Gonzalo de Berceo, in his *Signos que aparesçerán ante del juiçio* (Signs That Will Appear before the Judgment, c. 1250) envisions such a homecoming at the end of time: "Abrán entri todos caridat y amor ... por la paz ... nin clamor, / Nin catarán las nubes si tienen mal color ... Do tantos bienes iaçen e tanta alegria ... Que es fuente de graçia e mana cada dia" (Love and charity will open up for all ... in peace ... neither noise, nor clouds will be perceived if they are of a malefic colour ... where so many good things abide and such joy ... which is the fountain of grace and manna that flows each day) (2003,

59bc, 60bd). The same kind of end-time din and ominous skies that Berceo imagines being quieted and pacified are evoked in one of the final songs in Alfonso X's *Cantigas*. In expectation of the day of judgment, the Galician-Portuguese poem describes a time when "será a ayre de fog' e de suffr' / u verrá do çeo sõo miu fort' e rogido" (the air will be aflame with fire and sulphur … when there will come from the heavens a loud and roaring sound) (1986–9: vol. 3, no. 422, vv. 10–11).

The amuletic text that prefaces the *Razón de amor* also represents the last punishments and reconciliation of humankind as the planting of a vine root, "una radice plantata est in terra" (1993: 123v). This scriptural metaphor, used to signify the flourishing or withering of Israel in the Hebrew Bible, was reinterpreted as the Eucharistic body of Christ by New Testament commentators.[25] A similar meaning can be attached to the phrase "dic nomina in montem Saron" (speak the names in the mountain of Sharon) (1991: 82). The same place-name appears in the book of Isaiah, telling how a desolate wilderness will be made to flourish and bloom (33.9, 35.2). As Franchini (1991) observes, it is also a traditional setting for the Song of Songs when the bride describes herself as a flower blooming in the plain, situated between mountains, and goes on to praise her lover's name, comparing him to a ripened apple tree and a sweet wine (Cant. 1–2). She is additionally likened to a lily, an enclosed garden, a sealed fountain or spring, and pomegranates, and both lovers are described as doves.[26] Critics like Nepaulsingh (1986) have analysed clear parallels between the Song of Songs and the amorous encounter in the *Razón de amor*, focusing in particular on the ever-flowing spring, fruit trees, and flowers that grow in a garden where the lover finds "claro vino … vermejo y fino" (pure wine … red and fine) kissing and embracing his beloved before the arrival of the dove (1993: vv. 15–16). Scholars have thus come to view the poem as a kind of allegorical *epithalamia* or nuptial song.

What has not been considered is how such connections might shed light on the exorcistic amuletic text that precedes the poem. We have seen how it pleads for christological redemption from a tempest of damnation. Significantly, its blending of imagery corresponds with influential readings of the Song of Songs as a typological prefiguration of the Apocalypse. Eleventh and twelfth-century commentaries by Robert of Tombelaine and Honorius of Autun were widely disseminated through the *Glossa ordinaria* or standard biblical gloss of the church fathers consulted during much of the Middle Ages.[27] These interpreters connected the eschatological image of the bride and the lamb with the moral failings of the clergy and the implementation of Gregorian and later reforms (Rev. 21:9). Increasingly, the Song of Songs was viewed as a typological expression of the ultimate triumph of the church over the tribulations, heresies, and corruptions prophesized in the Apocalypse, so that the hidden purity of *Ecclesia* would be in the end symbolically embraced by her bridegroom Christ. This embrace is sometimes depicted in manuscript illuminations of the word *osculetur*, from the first verse of the Song: "let him kiss me with the kiss of his mouth, for thy breasts are better than wine" (1.2).[28] As Ann Matter has shown, the sixth-century Spanish bishop Gregory of Elvira was the most important precedent for interpreting the Song of Songs and the Apocalypse as interlinked allegories of the church (1990: 87–9). His commentary established the tradition of linking the dove from the Old Testament Song to the Second Advent of Christ as the Alpha and Omega in Revelation:

> He calls the Church a dove ... in that she is not steeped in the bile of malice; but also because among the Greeks a dove is called "peristera," and that letters of this name, reckoning according to the Greek method of counting, add up to total of eight hundred and one; but one and eight hundred are denoted in Greek by Alpha Omega. Hence the Lord himself, whose flesh is the Church says, "I am the Alpha and the Omega" (Rel. 1:8) by which number the name dove is signified. Hence to the Spirit descending as a dove upon Christ in the Jordan manifests the Trinity ... and the Holy Spirit is the dove. (Norris 2003: 85–6)[29]

Matter finds that this interpretation was a commonplace during the Middle Ages, making its way into numerous glosses of the Song of Songs and Apocalypse (1990: 89). Significantly, the numerical Greek alphabet was not only applied by Christian interpreters but also had become even more conventional in the production of amulets, grimoires, and other esoteric texts. This tradition sheds further light on how the baptismal healing power of the *Spiritus Sancti* and *Alfa Omega* in the apocalyptic prayer might resonate in the *Razón de amor* that follows in the manuscript, with its invocation of the Holy Spirit and symbolic dove flight. The poem represents the problem of ecclesiastical impurity through its characterization of a scholar falsely imitating the christological role of the bridegroom in the Song of Songs. He sinfully embraces and kisses his lover in a way that, as we have seen, is subsequently condemned in the *Diez mandamientos* section of the Spanish *cuaderno*. At the time the poem was being composed, the Spanish clergy was especially notorious for worldliness and the practice of keeping concubines. The text was written during a period of attempted clerical reform on the peninsula, coinciding with eschatological interpretations of the Christian defeat by the Moors at Alarcos in 1195 and the crusaders' even more troubling surrender of Jerusalem in 1199. Both losses could be attributed to the iniquity of the church, and followers of Joachim of Fiore – whose works I will examine in the next chapter – were even predicting the arrival of the End Times of the Holy Spirit by 1260.

In this context, the dove implicated in the amuletic prayer can be seen as, in effect, resurfacing in the subsequent love poem as a means of exorcizing the violated garden of *Ecclesia*, as if to purify and consecrate its enchanted space and thereby protect against the threat of a punishing storm. Its flight would have also brought to mind the function of *columba* vessels during the period, used to bring Eucharistic healing to the sick and, by extension, the hope of reconciling the fallen condition of humankind. The *Razón de amor* alludes to a dove whose purpose was to bear the transformative Word made flesh, just as the divine conjuration that prefaces the poem was apparently meant to convert a diabolical, apocalyptic downpour into clear, life-giving waters. Instead of embracing the *caritas* or divine charity symbolized by the Spirit's descent, the scholar and his lady exemplify a corruption of the church. They engage in the *cupiditas* or lust of worldly doves as described in a thirteenth-century Castilian translation of Brunetto Latini's *Tesoro*: "las palomas ... muevensse a luxuria besando ... en la Santa Escriptura ... fabla de ... otra que aparesçó al bautismo de Ihesu Christo" (doves ... are moved to lust by their kissing ... the Holy Scriptures ... speak of ... another [kind of dove] that appeared at the baptism of Christ) (1982: 27).[30] The love of this spiritual *columba* would be extended to sinners who purified themselves by the Spirit. Similarly, the winged Paraclete of the *Razón de amor* offers protection and healing to the faithful who are sick in body and soul and show themselves to be remorseful lovers of Christ, unlike the couple in the poem. Read in conjunction with the Hispanicized Latin prayer that introduces the Spanish portion of the codex, the poem's representation of an impure embrace can be read *in bono* as revealing the sealed, uncontaminated truth of love. The purified and profaned garden of the *Razón de amor* is a discursive space of dynamic ambivalence, in keeping with the earlier-mentioned studies of Ganim and Howes – but one that derives power and significance from the materiality of the manuscript itself. The representation of a dove in the amuletic text, followed by the *Razón de amor*, signifies both the veiled inner *Ecclesia* in the garden and the Alpha Omega appearing in the heavens at the beginning and the torrential End Times of the church.[31] These meanings, as we have seen, emerge from the relationship in the medieval imaginary between the dove that takes flight in the garden setting of the Song of Songs and the creative destruction and tormentous renewal that takes place in Revelation. The church's *columba* symbolized the Holy Spirit at the baptism of Jesus, in contrast to the lustful cooing of worldly doves, and also inspired the production of dove vessels carrying eucharistic sustenance to the sick and dying. Its flight has been invested with powers to assuage and purify tempests and pollutions that threaten the garden of the soul, storms that are at once fictional and perceived to be real.

Alfonso X's Open Book

We have seen how similar powers of prayer and the occult are represented in the *Cantigas de Santa Maria*, compiled during the second half of the thirteenth century by Alfonso X. Apart from the earlier-discussed miracle 125, further evidence of the king's approach to amulets can be found in a more well-known biographic song to Mary that celebrates his recovery from illness in the town of Vitoria in Basque Country. In what remains of this chapter, I will demonstrate how his *cantiga* 209 sheds further light on the dangers of contamination and the healing, conversional powers that could be ascribed to amuletic manuscripts. By returning to commentaries from the *Glossa ordinaria*, we will see how these anxieties and efficacies once again relate to images of the Incarnation and the Last Judgment during the period.

By the fall of 1276, Alfonso X had travelled to Vitoria in hopes of staying abreast of his army's movements to defend Navarra from French invaders.[32] Here, the aged Alfonso was confined to his bed, gravely ill, suffering from severe pain and reportedly near death. One of his best known songs to Mary (*cantiga* no. 209), with the refrain "Muito faz grand' erro e en torto jaz, a Deus quen lle nega o ben que lle faz" (He who denies God and His blessings commits a great error and is grievously wrong), recounts in the first person how the king was wondrously cured of sickness:

> Vos direi o que passou per mi, / jazend' en Bitoira enfermo assi / que todos cuidavan que morress' ali / e non atendian de mi bon solaz … … ũa door me fillou atal / que eu ben cuidava que era mortal, / e braadava: "Santa Maria, val, / e por ta vertud' aqueste mal desfaz" … os fisicos mandavan me põer / panos caentes, mas non o quix fazer / mas mandei o livro dela

aduzer / e poseron mio, e logo jouv' en paz ... que non braadei nen senti nulla ren / da door, mas senti me logo mui ben / e dei ende graças a ela por en, ca tenno ben que de meu mal lle despraz ... Quand' esto foi, muitos eran no logar / que mostravan que avian gran pesar / de mia door e filla- van s' a chorar, / estand' ante mi todos come en az. / E pois viron a mercee que me fez / esta Virgen santa, sennor de gran prez / loaron a muito todos dessa vez / cada ũu põend' en terra sa faz. (1986–9: sts. 3–8)

(I will tell you what happened when I lay in Vitoria so sick that everyone be- lieved that I was going to die there, and had no hope for my wellness ... I felt such pain that I myself thought that it was fatal and cried out: "Holy Mary, help me, and with your power take away this sickness!" ... The physicians or- dered hot cloths to be placed on me, but I refused them and, instead, had them bring her book; they put it on me and soon I was calmed ... I stopped screaming and felt less pain and soon found myself well, and so I gave her thanks for this blessing of mine, that my maladies should displease her ... When this happened there were many who showed great pity for my pain, shedding tears with all who gathered around me ... Then they saw the mercy that was bestowed upon me by the holy Virgin, lady of great fame, and on that occa- sion they all praised her highly, bowing their faces down to the floor.) [33]

Scholars have been primarily concerned with the biographical and historical context of this *cantiga*.[34] They have considered how it relates to other miraculous cures in the collection, and speculated on what sort of illness might have led to Alfonso's near-death experience in Vitoria. One exception is a recent groundbreaking study by the art historian Francisco Prado-Vilar, who reexamines the relationship between these lyrics and accompanying illustrations in an unfinished thirteenth-century manuscript preserved in Florence (Manuscript F, Alfonso X 1991). Spe- cifically, he observes that the head physician in the first panel is wearing the same characteristic hood as other Jews in the collection. In keep- ing with a contemporary prohibition against Christians receiving direct medical attention from Jews, Prado-Vilar notes how this hooded figure is absent in two subsequent scenes that show the king refusing the hot compress and instead accepting a *Cantigas* manuscript that is brought by a priest (Figure 3).[35] The Jewish character then appears once more in the next panel as a witness to the miraculous cure that has been brought about by Alfonso's open codex, held face up beneath his chest (Figure 4). In final images, only worshipful Christians are shown as the king first kisses the book and then raises his hands in prayer.

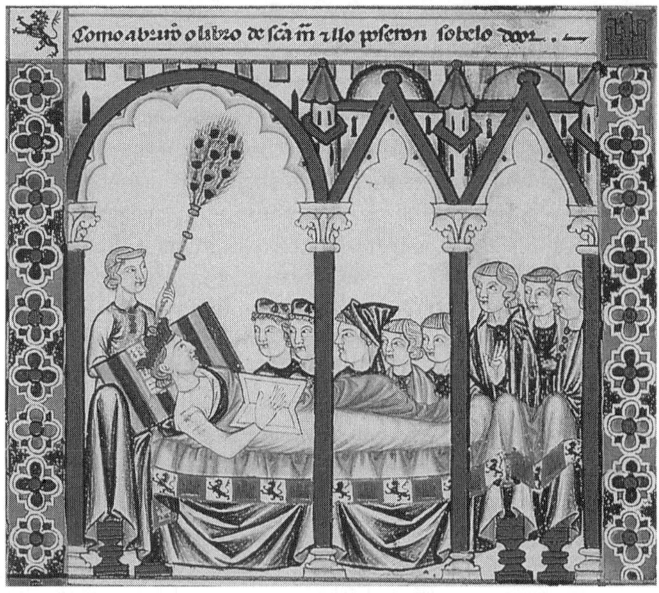

Figures 3 and 4. A codex is brought to heal Alfonso X. *Cantigas de Santa Maria* no. 209, Biblioteca Nazionale Centrale, Florencia ("F"), MS. B.R.20, fol. 119v, details (photo: Album/Art Resource, NY).

Some scholars believe that this healing codex was meant to represent an early manuscript of the *Cantigas* that had been similarly bound with a red leather cover and brass clasps before being preserved at the Cathedral of Toledo.[36] Prado-Vilar finds that the miracle works as a "subtle proselytizing *exemplum*" in which the visual presence, absence, and reappearance of a Jew positions him as both "friend and foe, kin and stranger, the other within the self" (2011: 123). Thus, the amuletic text – in conjunction with Mary's purported intervention – is not just efficacious in relieving physical pain, but more importantly also reaffirms the faith while at the same time potentially converting non-Christian witnesses, consistent with Alfonso's aim of promoting religious unity in his kingdom. In this sense, the inclusion of a Jewish doctor (possibly based on one of his actual physicians) relates to the song's refrain against denying the redemptive significance attributed to the Son of Mary, and by extension the blessings of "her book." Yet the physician's role is much more complex than might be suggested by the typical vilification of Jews found in non-biographical songs in the collection that were adapted from earlier sources.[37]

Prado-Vilar also examines links between *cantiga* 209 and other miracles that also revolve around the central theme of conversion. Of particular interest are songs that feature Jews being figuratively reborn through baptism, in spite of their coreligionists' persistent denial of the Virgin Birth and the theology of the Incarnation. For example, a Jewish woman is denounced by her community after Mary saves her from a life-threatening delivery of twins (a boy and girl), restores her health, and convinces the new mother to "wait no longer for the Messiah" ("que non atendeu Messias") (Alfonso X 1986–9: vol. 1, no. 89, v. 66).[38] In another case, a wise Jewish physician engages in a debate with the Arthurian wizard, Merlin over the Christian teaching that God chose Mary as a pure vessel for the Incarnation (1986–9: vol. 2, no. 108). A richly illustrated manuscript at the Escorial library (E2 or the *Codice rico*) depicts him pointing to a container that might be used for preparing medicines, along with a book that could represent the Scriptures or Talmud. In this way, he exemplifies Jewish resistance to the healing Christology promoted by Alfonso's *Cantigas*, asserting that "God could never enter into such a place ... How could He who contains so many things be contained?" ("non podo Deus nunca entrar en tal logar ... ca o que foi ensserrar en ssi quantas cousas son, como ss' enserraria?") (1986–9: vol. 2, vv. 31–6). After praying to Mary, Merlin causes the Jew's son to be born with his head turned backward in a monstrous display of the old law understood as unfulfilled by the new and resistant to conversion. In later panels, Merlin can be seen preaching to the defiant father, along with a more receptive gathering, while the boy – now pictured as a young man – undergoes a bodily and spiritual rebirth in the waters of conversion, surrounded by women.[39] His forward-facing head is now indicative of typological readings of the Old Testament believed to prefigure the Incarnation, such as the linking of the Song of Songs with the Nativity and Apocalypse. In this way, his malformed and then rectified body appears to symbolize the Christian topic of perversion (*perversio*) and conversion (*conversio*), or wrong and right "turning."

In another tale, a Jewish student is befriended by his Christian schoolmates and attends Easter mass, where he accepts a consecrated host from a wondrous image of the Virgin. When his father, a local glassmaker, learns of this communion miracle, he flies into a fit of rage and throws the boy into his oven. Whereas the Bread of Life is prepared in an oven to become the sacrificial Body of Christ, the young victim is shoved into the fire where his father causes sand to become glass.[40] Yet, the glassmaker's son is found to be unscathed by the flames in what Prado-Vilar calls a "metaphorical equivalent of the scene of baptism ... being pulled out of the oven, emerging from the womb of the Virgin" (2011: 130). In this way, the book that Alfonso seems to be employing as a curative amulet evokes the Incarnation in order "to imagine and promote conversion of ... the Jew excluded from his community and reborn to a new life out of the womb of the Virgin ... into the Christian community" (2011: 131–3). Prado-Vilar perceptively describes a kind of liminal space or threshold between religious identities as simultaneously conferring a status of exclusion and inclusion.[41]

What has yet to be explained is how Alfonso's seeming reliance on the *Cantigas* as a written amulet might relate to the conversional agenda in *cantiga* 209 and the collection as a whole. The practice of textual binding that he appears to be engaging in can be further contextualized by turning to commentaries found in the *Glossa ordinaria*. Notably, Jerome discusses this problem in his explication of verses from Matthew that I mentioned earlier, in which Christ condemns what is described as the false prayerfulness of the Pharisees (Matt. 23:5).[42] His commentary shows how early Christian superstitions were sometimes associated with the Jewish practice of wearing tefillin during prayer. Jerome erroneously assumes that these objects always contained the Ten Commandments and identifies them solely as amuletic texts rather than considering their function as signs and mnemonic devices:[43]

> The Lord, when he gave the commandments of the Law through Moses, added at the end: "you will bind these … they will be unmoved before your eyes" … The Pharisees interpreting this perversely, wrote on small parchments the Decalogue of Moses, that is, the ten words of the Law. Folding them up they even bound them to their forehead … Thus just as circumcision gives the sign of the Jewish nation in the bodies, so their clothing has some differentiation … They called those brief texts (*pictaciolum*) of the Decalogue "phylacteries" (from a Greek word meaning to "safeguard" or "ward off") because whoever had them had his own protection and fortification … Now the Pharisees did not understand that these things need to be carried in the heart, not on the body … Among us there are superstitious ones … who keep doing this up to the present day with little Gospels (*parvula evangelia*). (2008: 259–60)[44]

John Chrysostom was mistakenly attributed with writing another well-known commentary that compares amuletic exploitation of the gospel with the Saviour's condemnation of phylacteries worn by the Pharisees. During the Middle Ages, this saint was famed for his eloquence and devotion to the Virgin, to the extent that his martyrdom is retold in the *Cantigas* (no. 138). The *Opus imperfectum in Evangelium Mattheum* (Incomplete Work on the Gospel of Matthew) of Pseudo-Chrysostom makes further connections between perceptions of the tefillin and Christian superstition. Like Jerome, the writer of this work is clearly influenced by the epistles of Paul in denouncing the use of textual amulets among followers of Christ as a kind of neo-Pharisaic reversion, in keeping with later prohibitions of Spanish reformers like Ciruelo. In his letters to the Romans and Corinthians, the apostle – himself a former Pharisee – advocated an incorporeal circumcision of gentile Christians, not "outwardly" by the "letter" of the law, but "inwardly" by the "spirit" that is "written on the heart" and believed to be revealed newly through the Incarnate Word (Rom. 2:28–9, 2 Cor. 3:2–7).[45] As Peter Brown has pointed out, Paul employs the word "heart" (*kardia* translated into Latin as *cor*) to convey what might be called the "hidden core of the self" (1967: 35). In addition to these influences, Pseudo-Chrysostom links the production of amulets bearing angelic names, comparable to the kind Alfonso recorded in his

Liber Razielis, with the Pharisaic misinterpretation of God's command to bind His words:

> Many people now discover some Hebrew names of angels and write them down and bind them to themselves ... they are [doing this] in vain just as the Scribes and the Pharisees [did] ... so when we explain about people of our own time, we seem to be explaining about the Scribes and Pharisees. Therefore, because some priests want to seem righteous to people, they bind on phylacteries ... some with a written portion of the gospel ... Then where is the power of the gospel – in the shape of the letters or in the understanding of its meaning? If it is in the shapes then you do well to have it around your neck, but if it is in the understanding, then it helps you more to place it in your heart. (Pseudo-Chrysostom 2010: vol. 2, 346)[46]

As Skemer has observed, Jerome and other patristic writers evidently (and incorrectly) viewed the wearing of the Jewish tefillin as a direct "antecedent" to the circulation of written amulets among Christians, insofar as both seemed to draw on a "physical propinquity to Holy Writ" instead of an internalized spiritual understanding of divine law (2006: 35). Interestingly, the *Cantigas* manuscript that a priest brings to Alfonso in song 209 appears to draw on both the material and the immaterial power of the Word, insofar as it purportedly heals the king through its physical presence and contact with the body, while at the same time representing the christological significance of its contents being opened up to a Jewish viewer. Its meaning and potency in this way extend beyond that of the open books used to summon and drive away demons in song 125 to portray notions of what Prado-Vilar calls "the other within." The conversional threshold between religious identities in *cantiga* 209 implicates a Pauline relationship between the mortal body and the divine text – that is, between visible, tangible expressions of the "letter" (through clothing, phylacteries, circumcision) and the spirit taken into the "heart" and potentially transforming the old man through rebirth and the sacrifice of the Word made flesh.

By singling out what were seen as idolatrous or pharisaical misuses of Scripture, these writers most likely refer to the widespread tradition of carrying protective or healing copies of the Gospel of John. Early evidence of John's words being redeployed on amulets can be found on pieces of papyrus and small codices in Greek and Latin dating from the fourth to the sixth century. Later examples from the Middle Ages, like the previously discussed "Oración de San León" and exorcistic prayer, are also inscribed with verses from the prologue to this evangel: "In the beginning was the Word: and the Word was with God: and the Word was God ... And the Word was made flesh and dwelt among us ... full of grace and truth" (1:1–14).[47] John's opening encapsulates the "core" belief that a Jewish father denies in his debate with Merlin and that the stricken Spanish king reaffirms throughout his amuletic book – from his first song addressed "pola Sennor onrrada, / en que Deus quis carne fillar / bêeyta e sagrada" (to the Honoured Lady in whom God chose to take on blessed and sacred flesh) to a concluding feast-day hymn to the Virgin: "con sa deïdade / en ela pres carne que el non avía" (His divinity took on flesh in her which He did not have before) (1986–9: vol. 1, *cantiga* 1, vv. 4–6; *cantiga* 413, vol. 3, vv. 5–6). In the illumination to *cantiga* 209, Alfonso's Jewish doctor appears willing to consider healing incarnational texts and imagery that are being projected bidirectionally from the book held against the king's body.

During the twelfth and thirteenth centuries, the hagiographic legends of Hugh of Avalon and Caesarius of Heisterbach tell of the Gospel of John being carried and its first words recited as a weapon against evil spirits that could afflict the bodies of individuals and groups of believers (Skemer 2006: 88). Numerous extant amulets from this period include the Latin prologue to John, and portable copies of the gospel were frequently invested with an apotropaic potency. As a result, it is sometimes difficult to maintain a clear distinction between the accepted efficacy of John's words being recited and interiorized by Christians and superstitious powers commonly attributed to the material presence of the evangel or what Pseudo-Chrysostom calls the "shape" of its "letters" bound to exterior bodies. To cite one example, the Venerable Bede wrote a *Vita* (c. 730) that tells how St Cuthbert sought to replace written incantations against plague with the John's *sacra verba* (Skemer 2006: 50–1). By the mid twelfth century, however, a small Johannine manuscript supposedly owned by the saint was said to exert curative powers, and sometimes hung like an amulet around the necks of pilgrims at the cathedral of Durham.[48] Alfonso's role in *cantiga* 209 draws attention to this kind of amuletic, potentially heterodox practice and might even seem to be suggestive of a persistent Pharisaism among "people of our own time" that biblical glossators repeatedly condemned. Yet the ultimate purpose of the author appearing to rely on a textual amulet is apparently to represent himself as a devotee favoured by Mary and an exemplary witness to "the power of the Gospel" being "placed in your heart."

This perceived tension between the redemptive significance of a holy book taking root within and its potency as a medicinal object that is physically applied to the body can be further clarified by turning to another commentary found in the *Glossa ordinaria*. In his *In Evangelium Joannis tractatus* (Tractates on the Gospel of John), Augustine goes further than Jerome and Pseudo-Chrysostom in denouncing those who would attempt to cure themselves with written amulets and extolls the spiritually medicinal properties of the gospel as an immaterial text that instead abides in the heart:

> What a remedy the Lord has provided for the sicknesses of the soul! … Instead of having recourse to an amulet (*ligaturam*) … So lamentable is the estate of those who have recourse to amulets (*ligaturas*), that we rejoice when we see a man who is upon his bed, and tossed about with fevers and pains, placing his hope on nothing else than the gospel … not because it is done for this purpose, but because the gospel is preferred to amulets … to allay the pain is it not placed at the heart to heal it from sin? … Let it be placed at the heart, let the heart be healed. It is well – well that you should have no further care regarding the safety of the body, than to ask it from God … The Apostle Paul besought Him that He would take away the thorn in his flesh … For this he found in the voice of the [divine] Physician (*Medici*), "My grace is sufficient for you, for my strength is made perfect in weakness." (1888: *Tractatus* 7.12; 2 Cor. 2:9)[49]

In keeping with this debilitating "thorn in the flesh," Augustine's image of the heart inscribed and healed with the gospel once again hearkens back to the letters of Paul – specifically, the image of God's law being interiorized on what are called "tablets of human hearts," written with the "Spirit of the living God" as opposed to being carved as "tablets of stone" (2 Cor. 3:2–3). The apostle sees the heart's tablet as a record of the conscience and a witness to redemptive grace, while he imagines the stone tablet of Mosaic Law unremittingly exposing and convicting humanity of wickedness (Rom. 7:7). As Eric Jager has shown in his study of this imagery (2000), the biblical figure of the open book in Daniel and Revelation was first identified as a scroll but later re-envisioned as a codex being opened to reveal what is written in the hearts of believers (7:10, 20:12).[50] In my view, a similar hope of salvation could be conveyed by the intimate relationship between the Spanish king and the visible folios of the codex he holds beneath his heart.

Figure 5. Last Resurrection and Judgment (Rev. 20:11–15). The British Library
Board, Add. Ms. 35166, fol. 28r., detail.

Augustine's theological mentor, Ambrose of Milan, warned those who
refused to recognize the sacred text within and instead, as it were, rein-
scribed their books with iniquity: "What are these opened books, if not
our consciences which, like books, contain the long story of our sins …
the book of your heart (*liber cordis tui*) shall be opened … read aloud …
if you have lived righteously, God's writing shall remain. See that you
do not remove the grace of the Holy Spirit … erase it and write with the
ink of your evil deeds" (qtd. in Jager 2000: 25).[51] The same idea made its
way into medieval (and Renaissance) visual depictions of the risen dead
being judged on the basis of a text displayed on the open codices of their
hearts (Figure 5).

In his illuminated *cantiga* 209, Alfonso is comparably holding open
the bifolios of his book so that its pious autobiographical text can be
read by witnesses in this world and presumably the next. Unlike the
apotropaic prayer book of the maiden turned sideways in song 125, his
manuscript is positioned to be read. In fact, the king's will specifies that
manuscripts containing the *Cantigas* should be kept in the same church
where his body is entombed and that its miracles should be sung on

Marian feast days. In this way, they would provide a testimony of his devotion not only to those who survived him but also to the heavenly final audience envisioned by artists depicting the Last Judgment.[52] As Joseph O'Callaghan has pointed out in his biography of Alfonso X, the *Cantigas* as a whole exhibit the king's "deep-seated fear" of this final "dread-day" (1998: 206).

In his *Confessions*, Augustine again draws on the figure of the *liber cordis* in a way that is reminiscent of Ambrose. The bishop of Hippo tells a story of his guilt and shame, along with a deeply reflective account of his *conversio* or "turning" back to the truth through what is portrayed as an inward reading of the heart. This change taking place in his inner being reaches its fruition in a garden setting when Augustine famously hears a voice telling him to open the folios of a codex containing the letters of Paul. Scholars have connected this conversional moment to a celestial vision, described near the end of the narrative, of angels reading the heavenly book: "Their book is never closed ... because thou thyself are this to them" (1955: 427).[53] Throughout his autobiography, he at the same time metaphorically describes the experience of redemption as the healing of his soul through the medicinal Word or Logos. This context would seem to suggest that Alfonso, by holding open the *Cantigas* manuscript in view of his Jewish doctor, is ultimately evoking the idea of a spiritual cure brought about by what Augustine calls the divine "Physician." Thus the king's seeming utilization of a textual amulet not only contributes to his overarching agenda of conversion but also seems to be responding to and seeking to transcend what commentators describe as the Pharisaic "character" of certain "present-day" Christians. The superstitious were said to be reverting back to the mere physical presence of "letters" bound to the body as opposed to the Pauline meaning that is carried "in the heart." For this reason, the king's healing book ultimately serves as a kind of anti-amulet, insofar as its correct interpretation has the effect of spiritualizing the power attributed to material texts. The text that he uses *as if* it were a healing amulet contains expressions of biblical truth but was composed under his own direction, unlike the Word of God that brings about Augustine's conversion.[54]

By the same token, his ailment might be understood to convey a fear of spiritual sickness and contamination, not unlike allusions to healing and the threatened purity of a symbolic vessel in the earlier *Razón de amor*. In contrast to the kind of relief offered by his earthly physician, drawn from Galenic tradition and observation, Alfonso cries out to the Virgin and deploys her book in a way that recalls Augustine's discussion of the divine Physician in his *Tractates*: "When it happens that we are scourged in the body, let us pray to Him for relief ... Is he cruel who does not listen to the man crying out, or is he not rather merciful in following the wound, that he may heal the sick man? These things have I said, my brethren, in order that no one seek any other aid than that of God" (1888: 52).

We have seen how Augustine's *Tractates*, like his earlier *Confessions*, recommends a scriptural, readerly curing of the *cor* as the alternative to relying solely on physical contact with textual amulets. As Jager points out, Augustine's "heart-centered reading ... from letter to spirit, from the external law and Scripture to the word inscribed within" is anticipated by earlier converts in the narrative opening up and reading biblical or hagiographic codices in a way (known as *sortes sacrae* or a holy, textual drawing of lots) that would not be possible through the unrolling of scrolls containing Torah or the works of ancient pagans (2000: 33).[55] The meaning of the opened bifolio in his *Confessions* thus comes to represent a binding of the Hebrew Bible to the gospels, and a Pauline movement from the old to the new man – from a status of convicted sinner to the hope of salvific rebirth through Christ. In the words of Jager, this imagery would deeply impact "the medieval symbolism of the codex, whose diptychal form was used to contrast the Jewish Law with its 'fulfillment' in the Gospel" (2000: 37). The presentation of Alfonso's open folios could have held a similar kind of christological symbolism, implicitly extending the book's healing efficacy to the potentiality of a conversional "turning" in the heart of a Jewish onlooker.

Further connotations can be gleaned from the twelfth-century sermons of Petrus Comestor, whose *Historia scholastica* provided a major source for Alfonso's historiographic work.[56] For this influential theologian, the open pages of humanity's *liber cordis* can be understood first as a Christian reading of the Decalogue, and second as the *perversio* or "wrong-turning" of the past versus the salvific repentance and conversion of the reconciled sinner:

> In this first folio are written those commands that pertain to the love of God himself, and in which the Trinity is expounded ... in the second folio you are to write those commands that pertain to the love of your neighbor ... man speaks to his own heart reading attentively about his own deeds in the book of his heart. This book has two folia. Sinners read one, and penitents the other ... let us read in the leaf of penitence lest ... we be exiled from the new land. (Jager 2000: 56–7)[57]

In this sense, the representation of the bifolial layout of the *Cantigas* book itself could be understood as conveying what Prado-Vilar deems as the "potentiality" of the Jew (figured through a Pauline understanding of Mosaic law) to "become" internally, ontologically Christian. Gazing at the opposing folios from the other side of a column, he is at once connected and separated or "excluded" from Alfonso and his sacred codex. The Marian text has been implicitly invested with a power to turn liminal viewers away from what is perceived as humanity's intrinsic state of sin and exile, and towards repentance and rebirth – consonant with what Paul described as a condemnatory law etched in stone being converted into a new covenant through the Word incarnate. Yet the material presence of the object coming into contact with the body, and not just its visual display and interiorized meaning, remains central to the Christianizing "process of becoming" that is implicated in the *Cantiga*. In other words, it exhibits what Caroline Walker Bynum has described as the seeming "paradox" inherent in medieval Christianity, with its emphasis on inward spirituality and immaterial holiness, coupled with its Incarnational belief in the sacred "manifested and conveyed in matter" – extending from the central ritual of the Eucharist, belief in the corporal resurrection of the dead, to a growing cult of bodily and contact relics and superstitious reliance on the amuletic physicality of the word written on parchment and other corruptible media (2011: 269). Alfonso's literal pain and suffering is alleviated by efficacious prayer combined with the tangible materiality of the *Cantigas* in a scene of redemptive healing that figures and anticipates transcendence of the material world. At the same time, the music of Marian praise recorded in the manuscript could further contribute to this efficacy, in accordance with Augustine's experience of the new song of Christianity infusing the heart with truth (*"Confessions"* 1955: 9.14).[58]

This relationship between textual matter and the immaterial word is explored once more in *cantiga* 384, near the end of the collection (E or *Códice de los músicos*, without narrative illuminations), when a monk inscribes the name "Maria" in gold, blue, and rose-coloured ink in order to celebrate her precious nobility, celestial splendour, and virginal purity. He is said to kiss frequently the name and carry it on his person as a defence against evil. Like the Spanish king, the monk relies on the mediation of the Holy Mother after falling ill from what appears to be a fatal malady. It is revealed that his own name will be recorded in the Book of Life, and the Virgin herself promises to welcome him into heaven. It seems clear that he physically venerates and binds himself with the written image, suggesting that "aqueste nome santo o monge tragia sigo" (this sacred name the monk carried with him) should be understood as a logotherapeutic material object and not wholly as a symbolic, intangible text written in the heart (1986–9, vol. 3, v. 19). An even more telling, final example can be found in the thirteenth-century *Legenda aurea* (Golden Legend) of Jacobus Voragine: before being martyred in the arena, St Ignatius famously claims that the Saviour's name has been inscribed in his *cor* – a term for heart that, as we have seen, could be expected to signify the incorporeal "inner core" of his mind and soul. In what appears to be a grotesque misunderstanding of this final pronouncement, infidel witnesses physically open up the martyr's chest, only to find that "Jesus Christus" is in fact written on his heart in letters of gold. Because they are moved to convert by this literalized "heart-centred reading," it would seem that the same name has been figuratively, spiritually copied into their own interior selves. However, the conversional scribal process need not stop there, since subsequent copies of the inscription could be seen as continuing to bear witness for medieval readers of the *legenda*. Similarly, Alfonso X's amuletic codex is attributed with a power to open up the potentiality for an incorporeal, inward change in the hearts of present and future audiences as they witness and come into contact with *Cantigas* manuscripts.

It has been shown in this chapter how what John Dagenais calls the "bothersome residue" of manuscript culture, along with its visual representation, could provide an amuletic presence that contributed to the logic of poetic works like the *Cantigas de Santa Maria* and *Razón de amor*. The efficacy of this presence, however, was problematized and denied on the basis of the Christian "spirit" of an intangible text inscribed within versus the physicality of the unrevealed "letter" adhering itself to corruptible flesh and other writing surfaces. Spoken words of prayer and conjuration, nevertheless, were visualized as devotional and imaginative literary texts being held in the hands of Christians, who wielded them like shields and bound them against their bodies as a means of communicating with or protecting themselves from supernatural forces of good and evil, and thereby affecting change in the sublunary world. We have observed how this power sheds light on the intertextual relationship between an amuletic prayer and the verses of the *Razón de amor* that begin on the next folio of a codex preserved at the Bibliothèque Nationale de France. Written at a time of eschatological expectation and church reform, the language and material presence of the former text is invested with the power to assuage an apocalyptic tempest and restore the pristine garden evoked by the Song of Songs. Its exorcistic call to exhale or blow away demonic influences (*exsufflatio*) and inhale or take in the Holy Spirit (*insufflatio*) sets the scene for and contributes to the meaning of the carnal sin and the flight of the dove in the *Razón de amor*. Operating in conjunction with imagery put to use in this amuletic text, the poem evokes a dangerous enchantment and pollution of the clergy, followed by a healing renewal of the Edenic spring, typologically associated with the divine love of Mary and the *Ecclesia* bearing the saving waters of baptism and the redemptive body and blood of Christ. Similarly, I hope to have demonstrated how physical contact is central to the cure brought about by Alfonso X's book, and how this relates to the longstanding tradition of the gospel codices restoring the health of believers. In keeping with the earlier Latin prayer and love poem, the opposing folia of the king's codex ultimately reflect inner penitence and conversion, while at the same time warning of the judgment of worldly sinners. In both cases, the purpose of amuletic manuscripts extends beyond attributes believed to be present in their residual matter and points to a salvific Word that transcends – while at the same time manifesting itself through – the material realm.

Chapter Two

Naming God

A 2008 ruling by the Vatican prohibited the pronouncement of a sacred name that occurs frequently in scripture and which God revealed to Moses following the wondrous vision of the burning bush, unconsumed by flame (Exodus 3:15). These four letters (הוהי) were known in Greek as the Tetragrammaton, as noted in the introduction to this study. They were transliterated into Latin script as IHVH or YHWH and are conventionally vocalized by modern biblical scholars as "Yahweh." Although the word's original pronunciation cannot be determined, it is believed that the name must have conveyed God's creative, eternal self-existence, in keeping with the preceding verse in Exodus: "God said to Moses: I am who I am. He said: Thus shalt thou say to the children of Israel: He who is hath sent me to you" (Ex. 3:14). In ancient Israel, temple priests are thought to have spoken the name aloud and signalled it with a hand gesture on the Day of Atonement, a tradition that was lost after the Roman destruction of Jerusalem. In Torah manuscripts, the four consonants appeared with diacritical vowel points reminding readers to say instead the word for Lord, "Adonai" (יָנֹדֲא). This practice led some humanists during the Reformation to mistranslate the Tetragrammaton into English as "Jehovah."[1] According to the Curia, by forbidding this "expression of the infinite greatness of God" from being read, sung, or uttered in prayer, the church remains faithful to its "tradition, from the beginning, that the sacred Tetragrammaton [four-lettered word] was never pronounced in the Christian context nor translated" (Arinze 2008: 3).

It is, of course, true that YHWH has never formed part of the Latin rite, and the Vulgate gives the title *Dominus* for *Adonai*. Early translations into the vernacular follow St Jerome, as in the case of Castilian renderings of the biblical text from the thirteenth to the fifteenth century that use "Adonay" or "Señor," or omit the word altogether and instead express the idea of God's name solely on the basis of variant formulations of the previous verse, "I am who I am" (*ego sum qui sum*). Examples of the latter approach demonstrate how premodern translators struggled with the task of expressing a sense of eternal being: "'Él que fue y él que será' ... 'so él que seré' ... 'so él que siempre fue & seré' ... 'él que es de sienpre' .. 'él que es será' ...' so lo que so'" ("He that was and he that will be" ... "I am he that I will be" ... "I am he that always was and I will be" ... "he that is forever" ... "he that is will be" ... "I am what I am").[2] In spite of the official omission of the Tetragrammaton in scripture and liturgies, it was at the same time expropriated by early Christians in a number of other ways. In the discussion that follows, we will see how the holiest name was not only considered at length by medieval theologians, polemicists, and mystics but also copied onto amulets and employed in imaginative literary works.

A legendary origin for such expropriations was dramatized in the sixth-century *Toledoth Yeshu* (Biography of Jesus), a counter-gospel that circulated among Hebrew readers on the Iberian Peninsula and elsewhere in medieval Europe. The earliest Christian reference to this work appears in the writings of Agobard, the ninth-century archbishop of Lyons. On the Iberian Peninsula, the *Toledoth Yeshu* was later paraphrased by the Dominican polemicist Raimundo Martín in his *Pugio fidei adversus Mauros et Judaeos* (Dagger of Faith against Moors and Jews c. 1275) and cited again in the treatises of two Jewish converts to Christianity, Alfonso de Valladolid's *Mostrador de justiçia* (Teacher of Justice c. 1330) and the fifteenth century *Fortalitium fidei* (Fortress of the Faith) by Alonso de Espina.[3] In the version of *Toledoth Yeshu* transmitted by these Spanish writers, the miracles of Jesus are made possible only by his theft and sorcerous misuse of the Tetragrammaton, referred to as the "Semhameforás" or *Shem ha-Meforash* (preeminent name of God): "In the Temple ... [were] engraven the letters of God's ineffable Name. Whoever learned the secret of the Name and its use would be able to do whatever he wished ... Yeshu came and learned the Name; he wrote them [the letters] upon the parchment" (Sainz de la Maza 1992: 804; Goldstein 1950: 147–50). Drawing on canonical and apocryphal gospels alike, the legend tells how these inscribed letters enabled Jesus to cure a lame man and a leper, bring a corpse back to life, magically set to flight a flock of clay birds, float on a millstone, and ascend into the sky. Hebrew inscriptions of the Tetragrammaton have been found on amuletic scrolls dating back to the sixth and seventh centuries BCE, and the *Toledoth Yeshu* appears to identify the ministry of Jesus with a corruption of this longstanding practice in the production of textual amulets in Greek, Syriac, and Latin.[4] In this context, the anti-evangel not only seeks to expose a false messiah and his superstitious followers for abusing the power of the four letters but also implicates what it perceives as the misapplication of God's name to Christian revelation.

By the tenth century, this Christianizing appropriation extended to imaginative literary works like the debate poem, *Ecloga Theoduli* (Eclogue of Theodulus, c. 900). One of the most frequently copied poetic dialogues of the Middle Ages, the *Ecloga Theoduli* formed part of the textbook of *Auctores octo morales* (Eight Moral Authors) and survives in hundreds of manuscripts. Testimony of the poem's influence on the peninsula can be found in a passage from Alfonso X's *General estoria* describing representations of Falsehood (Pseustis) and Truth (Alethia) exchanging a series of pagan and scriptural exempla in an allegorical debate that ends when Wisdom (Phronesis) decides in favour of Truth. As I observed earlier, the same king ordered a translation of the esoteric wisdom of the angel Raziel, which was tied to the power of the Tetragrammaton. The Alfonsine chronicle interprets the title "Theodolo" as an etymological combination of Greek and Latin words signifying both divinity and deception: "El uno *theos* ... los latinos dezimos Dios. Ell otro nonbre es *dolus* ... quiere dezir como libro de Dios e de enganno" (the first *theos* ... we Latins say God. The other name is *dolus* ... meaning the book of God and of deceit) (1957: 65). This combination can be most clearly seen near the end of the poem, when Truth responds to the mythology of Falsehood with a typological invocation of YHWH:

[Falsehood] When Proserpina went down to gloomy hell, a law / was given Ceres for her daughter's safe return. / Now tell me who, first in treachery, revealed her meal, /. and you'll be praised for knowing Troy's great mystery. [Truth] When the sea's beneath the world and world beneath the sky / And hanging air is always in-between, now say / when earth will rise above sky's light air. Guess this / and I will grant you'll say God's Tetragrammaton! (Rigg 2008; Osternacher 1902: vv. 317–24)

According to Falsehood's myth, the goddess Ceres cursed and devastated the face of the earth after Pluto abducted her daughter, Proserpina. It was then that the treacherous Ascalaphus – the answer to the first part of the riddle – condemned her to return forever to the underworld by revealing that she had eaten pomegranate seeds, the food of the dead. This is likened to the "secret of Troy," the *fatale Palladium* or the protective effigy of the goddess Athena that had fallen from heaven in answer to the prayers of the city's founder, Ilus, and was famously stolen by Odysseus and Diomedes in anticipation of the Greek invasion. Thus, Falsehood evokes the underworld, the devastation of earth, and the talismanic power of the heavenly Palladium as a prelude to Truth's enigma of the Tetragrammaton, when "earth will rise above heaven's vault" (*levem caeli supereminet axem*).

Significantly, her riddle seems to draw on the hermeneutic resonance of this Latin verse for learned medieval audiences. In particular, scholars have noticed that the celestial ascent of earth recalls a well-known poem by the early Christian writer, Avitus (c. 500). Prior to assuming the form of a serpent, Satan laments his fall from heaven and the subsequent raising up of humankind in the Garden of Eden: "this clay succeeds to my angelic honors, earth now possesses heaven, the very soil exalted!" (1997: 2.92–4).[5] Such an allusion would have encouraged readers to apply a Christian interpretation to Falsehood's preceding riddles, mythologically linking Proserpine's *raptus* and the fall of Troy with the problem of sin. At the same time, as Henry Fairclough observed, the particular phrase "heaven's vault" (*caeli ... axem*) can be traced back to a prophesy in the *Aeneid*, when the offspring of the Trojan refugee is "destined to ascend beneath the mighty vault of heaven" (*progenies magnum caeli ventura sub axem*) (1916: 109).[6] In an influential fourth-century commentary, Servius interprets this verse as a reference to the apotheosis of Aeneus's imperial heirs ascending to "divinos honores" (Fairclough 1916: 109). This may explain why the fourteenth-century *Enigmata* of Claret gives the solution to Truth's riddle in *Ecloga Theoduli* as the ascension of Christ and the resurrection of the body of Christians, "altior est caelo tellus? cum corpore sumpto" (when is the earth higher than heaven? when the body ascends) (Peachy 1957: 43).[7] To arrive at its full significance, however, the reader must harmonize the answer Claret gives with Avitus's description of the Garden of Eden, "earth now possesses heaven." This is because the "when" of Truth's riddle in the conclusion of the *Ecloga* alludes to sacred history as a whole, and the divine temporality associated with the Tetragrammaton as "I am who I am" and "he who is": Christ first served as the New Adam, vanquishing Satan and offering redemption from Original Sin, and will come again in the Second Advent that church fathers typologically linked to his ascension. Following the example of Christ, believers will rise at the

End of Days "above heaven's vault," as part of the fulfilment of prophecy in Revelation, "the stars from heaven fell upon the earth ... And the heaven departed as a book folded up" (*stellae caeli ceciderunt super terram ... caelum recessit sicut liber involutus*) (1957: 6.13–14).[8]

In this way, the appearance of the Tetragrammaton in the final stanzas of the *Ecloga Theoduli* symbolically brings together the form and content of the entire poem. Immediately after invoking YHWH, Truth victoriously calls on the "four evangelists and their great books, which tell how God took on our human body" (*quatuor imprimis evangelicae rationis / nitar codicibus, nostrum de virgine corpus / ut Deus accepit*), and in doing so recalls the numeric structure of quatrains established by Knowledge at the beginning of the *Ecloga*: "you will speak in fours, Pythagoras decreed this number's role" (*sit tetras in ordine vestro, Pitagorae numerus*) (Rigg 2008; Osternacher 1902: vv. 330–2, 35–6). The Pythagorean reference introduces this number as an intrinsic symbol that will be mythologized over the course of the poem. Medieval scholars not only attributed the writing of a book on the *quadrivium* to Pythagoras but also the discovery of a cosmic power of the tetrad manifesting itself in the elements.[9] In keeping with Christian exegetes like the Venerable Bede, the *Ecloga* poet concludes by connecting this number to the Tetragrammaton and the quadripartite numerology of Revelation: "I saw four angels standing on the four corners of the earth, holding the four winds" (7.1). YHWH is intended to function both as a unifying poetic device and a sacred apotropaic that protects Truth from Falsehood, in contrast to the defeated talismanic idol of the Palladium. Allegorized as a Christian descendent of David, Truth reinterprets Yahweh from Exodus, "one God ... what was, is and shall be" (*idemque Deus ... quod fuit, est et erit*) through a Trinitarian faith in "three names, three persons" (*tres personae, tria nomina*) that prevails over Falsehood's invocation of the "names of many thousands of gods" (*Nomina mille deum*) (1906: vv. 9, 181–8).

In the end, Truth triumphs by confronting Falsehood with what is the irresolvable enigma. Unlike the secret Palladium of Troy, the real presence of God in the pronouncement of His name transcends all predicates and verbal signifiers. The only way to solve this metaphysical riddle is to know the unknowable *when* of eternity and speak the name of the ineffable *who* – "answer this and I will grant that you can pronounce God's Tetragrammaton." In other words, it entails no longer seeing "through a glass darkly" but encountering the Divine, as it were, "face to face" (Cor. 1:13). As Eleanor Cook has recently shown, this figure from Paul's epistle served as a master trope for the use of enigmas in imaginative literature throughout the Middle Ages (2006). In the case of the Tetragrammaton, the secret's infinite meaning can be neither kept nor told. Its essence is, in the words of Northrop Frye, "hid divinity, hidden because all language about such a being dissolves in paradox or ambiguity ... descriptive inadequacy" (2008: 111).[10] This kind of apophasis at the same time coincides with the premodern belief that the letters YHWH inscribed on textual amulets were never to be spoken for fear of unleashing God's wrath, or that attempting to pronounce other *nomina sacra* might cause them to lose their power (Skemer 2006: 144). The veil of secrecy surrounding God's ineffable name was, however, spoken *about* – through what Frye calls a "mythical and metaphorical language" that is "spiritually descriptive" and "spiritually conceptual" (2008: 122) – as in the case of the *Ecloga*, and through the *via negativa* of early theologians like Tertullian: "that which is immeasurable is known only to itself. This is what determines what God is, but it is a determination that cannot be grasped. Thus, the power of his greatness is made present and held before (*obicit*) humanity as both known and unknown" (1917: 57; *Apologeticus* 17.2–3). In keeping with Truth's tetradic, sacred defence against Falsehood in the *Ecloga*, Tertullian's choice of the verb *obicio* implicitly likens his apophatic idea of God to a shield "held before" the believer and an obstacle placed before an advancing enemy. As we will see in the remainder of this chapter, Spanish writers during the thirteenth and fourteenth centuries continued to speak figuratively about and around the Tetragrammaton by inserting the unvoiced name into their works as a revelatory shielding apotropaic. In each case, YHWH exerts a kind of hidden amuletic power in the shaping of a poetic structure of divine truth (*theo*) besieged by internal and external deceptions (*dulus*).

Jadus's Forehead: Interpreting the Tetragrammaton in the *Libro de Alexandre*

Arguably the most significant invocation of "YHWH" in medieval Spanish literature can be found in the previously mentioned *Libro de Alexandre*. This anonymous early thirteenth-century poem depicts Alexander the Great's rise to power, his early conquests, victory over Darius of Persia, and expedition into the exotic lands of India.[11] Infused with Christian symbolism and composed in monorhymed quatrains, the work is presented as the product of a "mester ... de clerezía ... rimado por la quaderna vía ... ca es grant maestría" (clerical poetic craft ... rhymed the fourfold way ... that is great in learning) (1988: st. 2). The Tetragrammaton appears in a crucial scene when Alexander encounters Jadus, the high priest of Jerusalem, who has already visited the hero in a dream: "Tenié quatro caróctoras en la fruente debujadas, / de obscura materia e obscurament dictadas; / non las sope leer que eran muy çerradas ... semejavan sagradas" (He had four characters traced onto his forehead, obscurely written of a similar, obscure material. He could not read them as their meaning was very much closed ... they seemed to be sacred) (1988: st. 1155). Alexander scandalizes his troops by prayerfully kneeling before Jadus: "fizo ant' el obispo su gynojo flecçión, / postrado sobre tierra fizo grant oraçion ... en la fruent' una carta que era bien ditada, / que de nombres de Dios era toda cargada" (he genuflected before the bishop, and prostrate on the ground said a great prayer ... on the forehead was a finely inscribed parchment, completely covered with the names of God) (1988: st. 1139).[12] In the dream-vision, Jadus promised victory over the Persians, as foretold in a prophecy from Daniel that is now read to Alexander in the temple: "leyó en Daniel ... que tornarié un griego Asia en monarchía; / plazió' a Alexandre ... dizo: 'Yo seré esse'" (he [Alexander] read in Daniel ... that a Greek would turn Asia into his kingdom; this pleased him ... he said "I will be this man") (1988: st. 1145; 11.2–3).

Critics have observed that this section of the poem elaborates on Walter of Châtillon's *Alexandreis* (c. 1180), where the four-letter name displayed by the high priest is identified with the Greek word "tetragrammata" (1978: 1.525). The *Libro de Alexandre* also seems to draw on a twelfth-century version of the *Historia de preliis Alexandri* (History of Alexander's Deeds) in its description of Jadus's mitre, "*laminam auream in qua erat scriptum Dei nomen*" (a plate of gold on which was etched the name of God) (emphasis mine, Steffens 1975: 66).[13] María Rosa Lida de Malkiel has pointed out that by reimagining this metal as a "carta," the Spanish poet evokes an object that would have been more familiar to his audience: an amulet or *nómina* produced on parchment and inscribed with divine names (1957: 191n7). Its appearance in the context of Alexander's promised military victory can be compared with legends of other heroic figures. For example, we have observed how a celestial messenger was said to have delivered a letter to Charlemagne containing a prayer written by Christ that was intended to provide the knight with supernatural protection during his campaign against the Saracens. In Jean Le Névelon's late twelfth-century *Venjance Alixandre*, it is the son of Alexander the Great, Alior, who relies on the power of mysteriously inscribed vellum to avenge his father (1931: vv. 627–8).[14] The *Libro de Alexandre* responds to and transcends the literary convention of using textual amulets to access divine assistance in battle. The pages that follow will demonstrate how the Jerusalem episode implicates modes of interpreting the Tetragrammaton in thirteenth-century clerical culture and consider how this relates to the poem as a whole.

An early commentary on the subject can be found in the *epistolae* of Jerome, where God's names from the Old Testament are enumerated: El, Elohim, Eloe, Sabaoth, Elion, Eie, Adonai, Ia, Tetragrammaton, and Shaddai. Jerome explains how the sixth and ninth of these were directly given to Moses by God: one expressing His essence with the affirmation "I am" (*Qui est*), and the other ineffable word transliterated as "YHWH" (1845: nos. 25, 15). Isidore, following his predecessor's list, adds that this ineffability (*ineffabile*) does not only refer to Jewish prohibitions against pronouncing the holy letters outside of the Temple – where they could be desecrated by heathens – but more importantly indicates that the meaning they convey can "in no way can be bounded by human sense and intellect ... nothing can be said worthy of it" (2007: 7.1–14). Unlike other words, the original meaning of the name cannot be etymologically reconstructed. It is likely that this explanation of the Tetragrammaton's incomprehensibility influenced the *Libro de Alexandre*, especially as the *Etymologiae* is cited elsewhere, and also informs commentaries on YHWH written not long before the poem.[15]

Armand A. Maurer (1979) has studied discussions of the Tetragrammaton in scholastic works from the latter part of the twelfth-century. Petrus "Comestor" (the "devourer" of books), whose earlier-cited *Historia Scholastica* has been identified by scholars as another one of the Spanish poet's sources, notes that the four letters are not meant to signify in the same way as any other word (1855: 1408A).[16] A later treatise, known as the *Dialogus Ratii et Everardi* (Dialogue of Ratius and Everardus), develops this idea even further: "saying 'Tetragrammaton' is not the sign of any mental concept ... or anything else ... it is ineffable, not naming but named" (Haring 1953: 266).[17] Referring to Aristotle's *De interpretatione*, the anonymous writer concludes that names can be properly applied only to those forms that are knowable to the human mind. Medieval scholars studied Boethius's translation and commentary of this book, in addition to the *Etymologiae*, as part of their training in the Trivium – the first phase of Alexander's tutelage under Aristotle in the Spanish poem: "entiendo bien gramática ... bien sé los argumentos de lógica formar" (I have a firm understanding of grammar ... and know well how to formulate the arguments of logic) (1988: sts. 40–2).

Because human language is predicated on and semantically tied to the realm of created things, it is impossible to convey the Creator's essence by what Boethius describes as "imponens nomina rebus ... secundum positionem hominum" (imposing names on to things ... according to the imposition of man) (Reynolds 1996: 46–8). For this reason, the pagan hero and, by extension, medieval readers of the *Libro de Alexandre* cannot hope to interpret the Tetragrammaton through grammar and logic, whether or not they understand Hebrew. The most sacred name functions as a sign of the "inner word" that Augustine identified with the unmediated, unspoken voice of God being received by Adam's soul prior to the Fall and the Confusion of Tongues, biblical events that are described in the Spanish poem's digressions.[18] As a result of these semiotic displacements, the Tetragrammaton not only remains indecipherable for Alexander but also goes unexplained by the author – being derived from "strange material" and "obscurely written." Its opacity is described at length in a widely circulated sixth-century Greek treatise, erroneously attributed to St Dionysius, and known as *De divinis nominibus* (On Divine Names): "we cannot know God in his nature, since this is unknowable and beyond the reach of mind or of reason ... He cannot be understood, words cannot contain him, and no name can lay hold of him" (Pseudo-Dionysius 1987: 108; 7.3).[19] The characters of the Tetragrammaton are not, as Joseph Dan puts it in his study of Pseudo-Dionysius, "derived from their position in communicative language, but in their intimate, meta-linguistic relationship to the mystical divine being ... the mystical power of a name is increased, when its linguistic meaning is diminished" (1996: 232).

As the meaning of the underived name could not be understood through etymology and onomastics, the Tetragrammaton was interpreted through a kind of cabbalistic Christian typology. This approach can be traced back to the influential work of a Sephardic convert, Petrus Alfonsi, whose *Dialogus contra Iudaeos* (Dialogue against the Jews, c. 1120) survives in dozens of manuscripts, three of which were produced in Iberia during the twelfth and thirteenth centuries. In one of his most elaborate explanations, Alfonsi argues that "the very subtle name of God ... a name of three letters (although it is written with four characters [*figurae*], for one of them is written twice, doubled) ... If you examine it you will see that this same name is both one and three. But that one refers to the unity of the substance, whereas the three refer to the Trinity

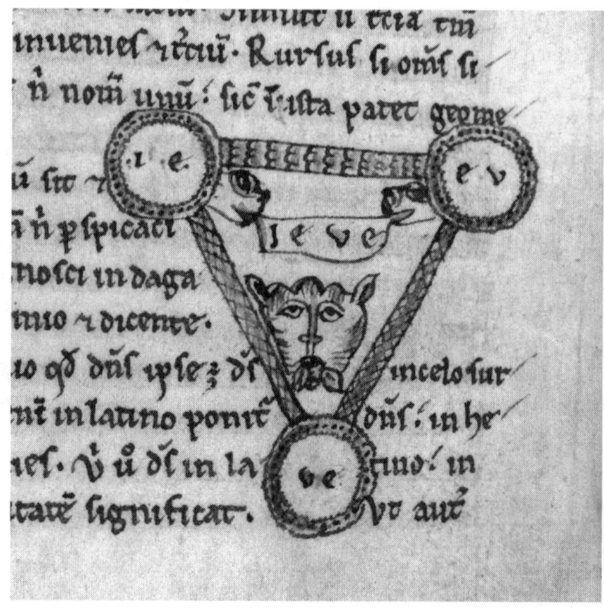

Figure 6. Trinitarian diagram of the Latinized Tetragrammaton. *Dialogus adversus Judaeos* of Petrus Alfonsi, MS. E.4, fol. 153v, detail by permission of the Master and Fellows of St John's College, Cambridge.

of persons" (2006: 172).[20] He goes on to describe how the four letters can be geometrically conjoined and delineated in three combinations. An early diagram (Figure 6) arranges intersecting spheres to form an equilateral triangle inscribed with the transliteration "I-E-V-E."

The polemic's author thus employs a cabbalistic procedure to persuade his imagined Jewish interlocutor of Trinitarian doctrine: "consider then, O Moses, how hidden and subtle and ineffable that name is, and that it can only be known by the insight of a perspicacious mind and by a profound investigation" (2006: 172). Late twelfth- and early thirteenth-century theologians and preachers like Garnerius of Rochefort replicated and developed variations on Petrus Alfonsi's Trinitarian reading.[21] The prevalence of such interpretations during this period suggests that the Tetragrammaton in the *Libro de Alexandre* could have similarly functioned as a figure of Christian revelation.

Petrus Alfonsi's typological approach can be compared to the earlier work of the Venerable Bede, who saw the name as a prefiguration of

God's servants being sealed with "His name on their foreheads" in the Book of Revelation (7.3, 22.4):

> The Lord incarnate ... bearing the ensign of the cross, with which to seal His own in their foreheads ... For, again, the figure of the cross itself represents the kingdom of the Lord extending everywhere, as the old saying proves: 'Behold the world four-square, in parts distinct, to shew the realm of faith possessing all.' And not in vain was the sacred Name of the Lord, of four letters, written on the forehead of the High Priest, inasmuch as this is the sign on the forehead of the faithful. (1878: 7.2–3)[22]

The Bede's *Explanatio Apocalypsis* thus links the quatriliteral word appearing over the high priest's brow with redemption by the cross and the apocalyptic image of "four angels standing on the four corners of the earth" (1878: 7.1).[23] As Maurer has pointed out, it was the "Bede who passed on to the later Middle Ages" the idea of the Tetragrammaton "inscribed on the forehead of the priests" (1990: 66). His gloss of "the world four-square, in parts distinct" can also be related to quadripartite visualizations of the *mappa mundi* found in numerous illuminations of the eighth-century *Commentarius In Apocalypsin* of Beatus of Liébana. (Sáenz-López Pérez 2014) In such schemes, a *terra incognita* is added to the symbolically cruciform design of the tripartite "T" map: the landmass of the known Earth falls into three divisions, with Asia positioned ("oriented") above Mediterranean Europe and Africa, stretching from north to south, and separated by the ocean from a far or reversed side of "opposing feet" or Antipodes. In the words of Isidore, "Besides these three parts of the world there is a fourth, across the ocean and in the south. This is unknown to us ... Legends place the inhabited Antipodes there" (2007: 9.2.13). The same type of geographic configuration is implicated in the *Libro de Alexandre*, as the conquering hero, in his quadripartite tent and on other occasions, views his progress on a "mapamundi" with "tres partes" forming the figure of the "cruz," and sails to the end of the Earth in search of a fourth area occupied by the monstrous race of "antípodes" (1988: sts. 2576, 2578, 280, 2293b, 2440ab).[24] For an audience familiar with connections between the Tetragrammaton and religious cartography, Alexander's contemplation of "quatro caróctoras" not only signals his coming triumph over the Persians, but could also allude to the End of Days and the Kingdom of God "extending everywhere."

Undoubtedly, the most important example of the Tetragrammaton being used as a eschatological symbol can be found in the earlier-mentioned mystical work of Joachim of Fiore, whose prophesies have been linked to the divine vision of "tre giri" (three circles) in Dante's *Paradiso* (1996: *Canto* 33, vv. 115–20). By the early thirteenth century, Joachim's ideas had found their way into the writings of Robert of Auxerre, along with tracts and sermons.[25] In his mystical *Liber figurarum*, which has been linked to the *Dialogus* of Petrus Alfonsi, three interlocking spheres are traced around the four letters to signify the Trinity (Figure 7).

Joachim designates segments as the "Vetus Testamentum" and "Novum Testamentum," identifies three ages with the Father, Son, and Holy Spirit, and includes a quadripartite chronology: "before the law," "under the law," "the time of the Gospel," and finally the "understanding of types" prior to the "Finis mundi" (*Tavola* XI 1940). His figure also links the Trinitarian name to the first and last letters of the Greek alphabet, Alpha (A) and Omega (Ω), used as a divine name in Revelation – and inscribed on amulets, as we have seen (1.8, 21.6, 22.13).[26] The impact of Joachimism in thirteenth-century Iberia can be seen in a treatise by Arnau de Vilanova (c.1238–c.1310), in which a representation of YHWH similarly "prefigures the shape of history, which is nearing its climax" (Lee 1974: 52–3). In his *Allocutio super Tetragrammaton* (Discourse concerning the Tetragrammaton), Arnau likens this interpretation of "sealed and closed" letters to "opening" a "closed book" (2005: 357). He specifically cites a verse from Daniel (7.10), "the books were opened" (*libri aperti sunt*), referring to the vision of Babylonia, Persia, and Alexander's empire as beasts that give rise to a "little horn" symbolizing Antiochus Epiphanes (2005: 35–7, 65). A strikingly similar image appears in the *Libro de Alexandre*, when the tomb Apelles sculpts for Darius's wife is compared to "un libro abierto" (an open book) depicting the Babylonian tower, the time of Old Testament prophets, and Persian ascendancy (1988: 1244d).

This representation of Alexander's place in sacred history forms part of a larger revelatory process in which time and space are "opened up" in the poem to reveal typological meanings implicit in the "closed" characters of the Tetragrammaton. In keeping with the ekphrastic tent and his "open book" sculpture, Apelles at another point in the poem selects a biblical epitaph for Darius's tomb that echoes the initial prophecy given to Alexander in the temple, following his viewing of the ineffable name on a *nómina*: "un cabrón mal domado, / quebrantarié los cuernos al carnero doblado. Este fue Alexandre ... Dario fue el carnero de los regnos doblados" (an untamed he-goat will break the dual horns of the ram. The first was Alexander ... Darius the ram of the dual kingdoms)

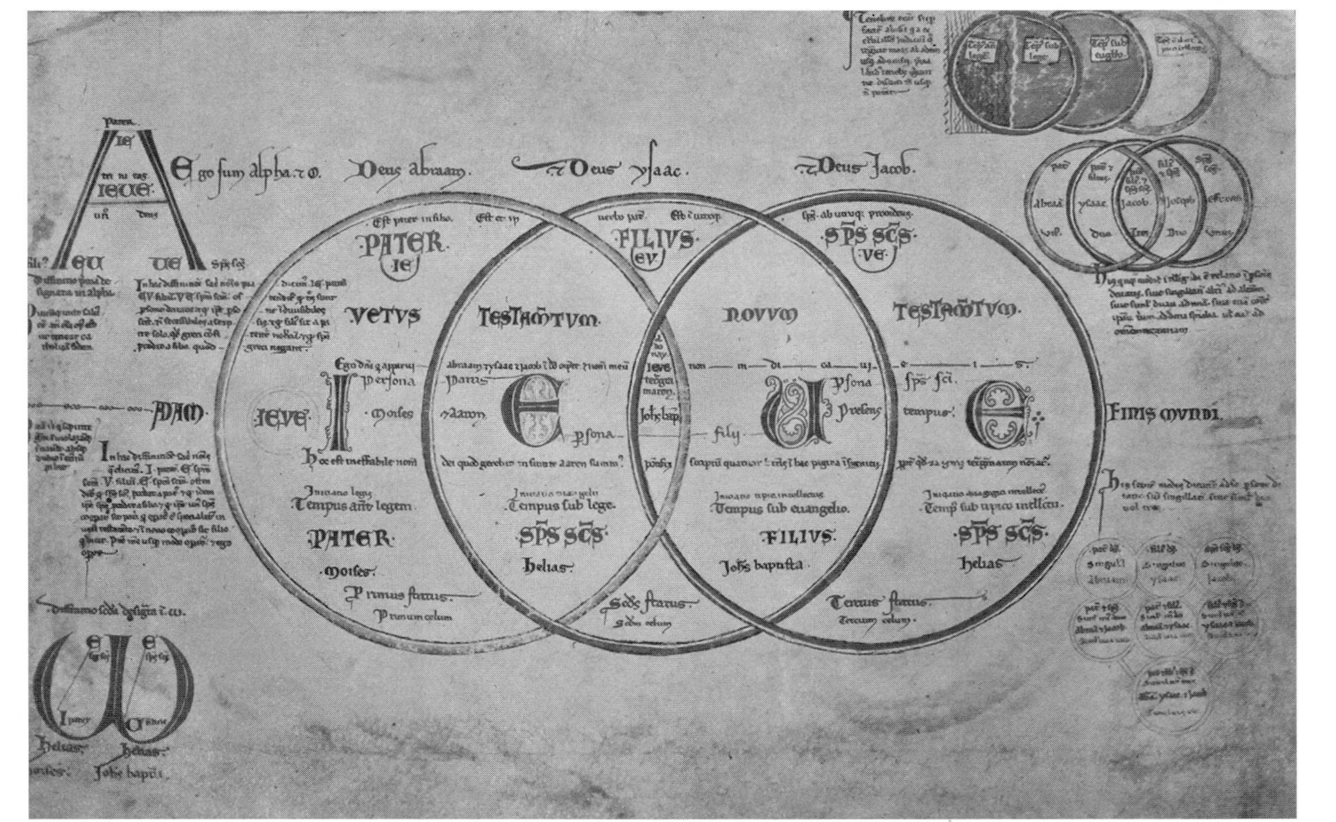

Figure 7. Sacred History as the Tetragrammaton. *Liber figurarum* of Joachim of Fiore, public domain, detail.

(1988: st. 1339).[27] In this apocalyptic vision, Daniel imagines the Persian "pushing with his horns against the west, and against the north, and against the south," only to be crushed by Alexander, whose empire will extend over the "face of the whole earth" and lead to the iniquitous reign of Antiochus, laying "all things to waste" (Dan. 8.1–26). The Spanish poet makes yet another reference to the Seleucid ruler when Persians fighting to the death against Alexander's forces are compared to Judas Maccabeus, the Jewish leader of a martyrs' revolt (1988: st. 1756).[28] Because Antiochus violated and desecrated the sanctuary, glossators from the time of Jerome consistently identified him as a type of Antichrist, the figure expected to "erect his throne in the Holy Temple" and "pretend that he is the son of Almighty God" (Adso 1979: 91). In the *City of God.* (1984), Augustine also explains how Alexander's earlier arrival in Jerusalem prefigured that of his infamous successor: "Alexander, indeed, offered up sacrifices in the temple of God ... but thinking, with impious folly, that He was to be worshipped along with false gods ... Then Antiochus ... filled the temple itself with sacrilegious superstitions" (1841: 18.45).[29] Seen in this light, the pattern of scriptural allusion in the *Libro de Alexandre* points to the hero's apocalyptic role as the predecessor of Antiochus and suggests that God's occluded name can be understood through what Joachim calls the "understanding of types" leading up to the "End of the World."

In a crucial later episode, Alexander's connection to the End Times is explicitly revealed when the hero encloses the forces of evil behind the Caspian Mountains (1988: sts. 2098–116). The poet adapts this from the *Historia de preliis* and *Historia scholastica* – sources that, as we have seen, also appear to have impacted his earlier depiction of the Tetragrammaton. Both texts conflate the story of Alexander erecting a gate to hold back the Scythians with interpretations of the apocalyptic vision of John the Divine: "Satan shall be loosed out of his prison ... over the four quarters of the earth, Gog and Magog ... together to battle, the number of whom is as the sand of the sea" (Rev. 20.7–10).[30] Medieval legend identifies the captives as the ten lost tribes of Israel who would be released by the Antichrist to wage war against the Kingdom of the Lord. In the poem's treatment of this material, Alexander walls up these multitudes and prays for their enclosure to hold until the events of the Apocalypse unfold:

"Rrey," dixo un sabio ... "Judíos son, que yazen en captividade, / gentes a que
   Dios fizo mucha de piadade, / e porque non sopioron guardarle lealtade, /

por ende son caydos en esta mesquindade ... de los prophetas assy pro-
phetizado" ... "Otorgo," diz el rrey ... "fasta la fin del mundo deve yazer
encerrado ... y las pascuas por siempre çelebrar" ... rogó al Criador ... Pero diz
la escriptura ... avrán çerca la fin ende a estorçer, / avrán el mundo todo en
quyxa a meter." (1988: sts. 2104–15)

("King," said a wiseman ... "These are Jews that remain in captivity, peoples that were very pious before God, but have fallen in this misery because they could not remain loyal to Him ... as revealed by the prophets" ...
"I order," said the king ... "that they should remain enclosed until the end
of the world ... and forever celebrate Passover" ... he prayed to the Creator ...
But the scripture says that ... near the End they will finally be freed, and
bring all of the world to despair.")[31]

On the one hand, the scene can be read as a fulfilment of the prophetic
trope of opening up the closed-off text of divine providence introduced
in Alexander's vision of the amuletic "carta" and prayer in Jerusalem,
followed by his temple reading from Daniel. On the other, the interpretive metaphor of occlusion and aperture in the *Libro de Alexandre* has
been transferred from the underived sacred name of the Old Testament
to enclosed adversaries cryptically mentioned in Revelation – but subjected to a lengthy anti-Judaic catalogue in the Spanish poem: "de flaca
conplexión ... astrosos, de flacos coraçones, / non valen pora armas ...
de suzia mantenençia ... cobdician dineruelos ... malastrugos ... mesqui-
nos e lazrados" (weak of complexion ... filthy, faint of heart, no good in
war .. unclean in appearance ... greedy for money ... ill-fated ... miser-
able and wretched) (1998: sts. 2102, 2105, 2109). The poet imagines these
fallen Jews celebrating an apocalyptic "Passover" and foresees the Antichrist, instead of Moses, releasing them from captivity.

In recent years, Julian Weiss (2006) has related this section of the poem
to the interpolated sculptures of Apelles. He finds that the Hebrew sym-
bolizes "Jewish writing and history" as the "indispensable ground of
Christianity" but also represents an "undercurrent of treachery" that
comes to the surface in the scene of the lost tribes – and later when
Alexander is tricked into drinking poison and tries to induce vomit-
ing with a feather that has also been laced with venom (2006: 132–42).
Weiss associates Apelles's status as a Jewish "clérigo letrado" with the
poet's scholarly quill, observing that both must negotiate the histori-
cally tense relationship between political compromise and religious
ideals, the here-and-now and the hereafter. Both artists are complicit

in the promotion of Alexander's sinful self-aggrandizement but at the same time function as moralizing practitioners of allegoresis. My findings suggest that eschatological readings of YHWH not only relate to the narrator's prophetic interventions over the course of the poem but also to the ultimate significance of Apelles's work as an ekphrastic witness to Christian truth. This can be clearly seen when the poet – speaking through a "wiseman" – reinterprets images of the Passover from the tomb of Darius's wife, placing them in the context of the End Times: "las plagas de Egipto, el ángel crüel, / el taü en las puertas de sangne de añel … las plagas de Egipto, la muerte de Faraón, como fue por la ley Moïses el barón" (the plagues of Egypt, the cruel angel, the mark on the doors in lamb's blood … the plagues of Egypt, the death of Pharaoh, how Moses, the man was entrusted with the law) (1988: sts. 1242cd, 2106bc).

It has been shown how Petrus Alfonsi's dialogue with "Moses" partially inspired Joachim's well-known Tetragrammaton figure. The millenarian writer eagerly anticipated a final conversion and even claimed in his *Expositio in Apocalypsim* that diagrams of the wondrous name could persuade Jews of the Trinitarian nature of God, in keeping with Alfonsi and contemporary polemicists like Peter of Blois.[32] This perspective sheds light on the *Libro de Alexandre*'s overall preoccupation with Last Things and Christianizing *interpretatio* of the high priest of Jerusalem as a "bishop" wearing a "miter," and crowds waving "palms" on the "via" where Alexander visits the "stations" (1988: sts. 1139–43). The priest's *lamina*, displaying the Hebrew ineffable name is likened to an amuletic text of the sort Sephardic Jews inscribed on metal but also a Christianized parchment bearing a plurality of sacred *nomina*. The power of this material object is then subjected to an allegorizing reinterpretation that can be compared to what we have seen in the *Razón de amor* and the *Cantigas* manuscripts.

In an era of apocalyptic expectancy, intensified by the earlier-mentioned capture of Jerusalem, the Muslim victory at Alarcos, and Joachimist predictions of Doomsday arriving in the year 1260, readers of the poem would have been especially inclined to view the Macedonian's entry into the Holy City as part of an end-time sequence, leading from the desecrations of Antiochus to the paschal arrival of Christ, the coming of the Antichrist, and the Second Advent.[33] As I hope to have shown, the Tetragrammaton "carta" in Spanish narrative provides a focal point for this kind of reading. Its symbolism during the twelfth and thirteenth centuries not only maps Alexander's spatial and temporal advance as a prefigurement of the End of Days – set into motion by the release of

Gog and Magog in the form of treacherous Hebrew tribes – but also projects beyond these tribulations to a messianic age in which believers expected discordant Jewish and Christian understandings of scripture and the ineffable name to be reconciled. As such, what is described as the textual amulet attached to Jadus's forehead is analogous to the prophetic vision of Apelles's sculpture and exemplifies the typological design of the poem through its inscribed "narrative power." In this way, the poet subjects this Hebrew inscription to a process of Christianizing reinterpretation that is central to his literary composition as a whole and its resonance for learned medieval audiences. In what remains of this chapter, I will show how a later poet recreates and re-inscribes the divine *nómina* found in the *Libro de Alexandre*.

The Trinitarian Shield and the Name of God in
the *Libro de buen amor*

The archpriest of Hita concludes his fourteenth-century allegory concerning "quales armas se deve armar todo cristiano" (the weapons with which all Christians should arm themselves) by evoking the "shield of faith" from the epistles of Paul, "scutum fidei in quo possitis omnia tela nequissimi ignea extinguere" (wherewith you may be able to extinguish all the fiery darts of the most wicked one) (Ruiz 1988: sts. 1579–1605; Eph. 6.16). This is followed by an enigmatic description of the shield that has yet to be explained fully by scholars: "contra esta enemiga que nos fiere con saetas / tenemos escudo fuerte, pintado con tabletas; / spíritu de buen consejo, encordado destas letras" (against this enemy who wounds us with darts, we have a strong shield, painted in tablets; the Spirit of Good Counsel, corded with these letters) (1988: st. 1598ab). In his edition of the work, Joan Corominas suggested that the letters could refer to initials appearing as a device on the shield, possibly "*SC*" for *spiritus consilii* or "spíritu de buen consejo" as the last of the seven gifts of the Holy Spirit named by the archpriest: "Spíritu Santo de buena sabidoría ... temer a Dios ... de piedat ... fortaleza ... entendimiento ... çiencia" (Holy Spirit of good wisdom ... fear of God ... piety ... strength ... understanding ... wisdom) (Ruiz 1967: sts. 1588–96). Subsequent editors have approached Corominas's hypothesis with a degree of scepticism, noting that the meaning of the emblazoned letters remains unclear.[34] It is my intention to demonstrate how the image specifically evokes the *Scutum fidei* or Trinitarian Shield of Faith and does so in a way that sheds light on the overall function of sacred names in the *Libro* in relation to the *Libro de Alexandre*.

It has long been observed that the archpriest's treatment of the seven deadly sins draws on the *Summa de vitiis et virtutibus* (Summa of Vices and Virtues), written by William Perault (1519) in the 1230s.[35] The *Libro*, in keeping with the Dominican's widely read treatise, represents each mortal sin as a consequence of worldly love or "amor loco" and catalogues virtues used to defend against vice (1988: sts. 181–473, 1579–1605). For this reason, it is not surprising that the archpriest's "escudo fuerte" bears an intriguing resemblance to an illumination of the Christian knight in a thirteenth-century manuscript of the *Summa de vitiis* (Figure 8). Here, the knight appears on horseback, facing a list of the seven gifts of the Holy Spirit, and holding a couche-shaped shield with orle lines that connect nodes at each of its three corners.

The nodes are inscribed with the *nomen sacra* or abbreviated names of the persons of the Trinity, "PR" (Pater), "Fili" (Filius), "Spc" (Spiritus Sancti), and linked by pall lines to a fourth, inner circle around the name "DE" (Deus).[36] What this illustration of Perault's work suggests is that the archpriest's "letras" refer to abbreviated names for the persons of the Trinity.

Analogous medieval illuminations of the Trinitarian shield studied by Michael Evans also include Paul's image of wounding projectiles, in keeping with the "saetas" in the *Libro* (1988: 653d, 1598b). For example, in the De Quincy *Apocalypse*, a female personification of repentance holds a shield identified in French as "l'escu la fei" and used to deflect arrows shot by a devil. Similarly, in an English *Collectanea* compiled at the Benedictine monastery of St Alban, two demonic archers identified as "demones vel heretici" (demons or heretics) assault the "scutum fidei" beneath an inscription of the same verse from Ephesians that the archpriest paraphrases (Evans 1982: 73).[37] As Evans has pointed out, such visual and textual representations of spiritual warfare against "the fiery darts of the most wicked one" were believed to offer amuletic protection against evil (1982: 26). The image in the *Collectanea*, like other Shields of Faith from the period, is invested with further apotropaic power by the inclusion of a crucifix extending from the centre roundel (*Deus*) to the bottom (*Filius*). Significantly, as Skemer has shown, textual amulets from the period frequently featured Latin names and majuscule invocations of the three persons, as well as cruciform shield configurations. The orle and pall of this figure are also decorated with a pattern of interweaving lines, similar to the corded cross blazon, "cum

Figure 8. Shield of Faith. *Summa de Vitiis* of William Perault. The British
Library Board, Harley MS. 3244, fol. 28r, detail.

cruce plana cordata," illustrated in a fifteenth-century version of the *Liber armorum* (Book of Arms) (Dallaway 1793: 20). It seems likely that this sort of heraldic design would have been evoked by the archpriest's use of the term "cordado."[38] It could also allude to the use of cord (*ligatura*) in binding sacred names as a textual shield against malevolent forces.

At the same time, a deeper underlying significance for the shield's cording is suggested by a model for Trinitarian diagrams found in the previously discussed *Dialogus contra Iudaeos*. We know that Petrus Alfonsi's twelfth-century explanation of the Trinity was illustrated by positioning a version of the Tetragrammaton, "IEVE," inside a triangle of lines braided like rope to connect three pairings of the name's letters "ie," "ev," and "ve" (Figure 6). We have also seen how Joachim of Fiore, in his *Liber Figurarum*, uses a triad of interlocking golden spheres to combine visually Alfonsi's letters with the names *Pater, Filius*, and *Spiritu Sanctum* in way that may have influenced Dante's "tre giri." This configuration can in fact be traced back to St Augustine's *De Trinitate*, where the Trinity is likened to three connected "rings from one and the same gold" (2002: 9.5.7). A particularly striking version of the image was found in a thirteenth-century manuscript at the Chartres Municipal Library and reproduced in iconographic manuals before being destroyed in a wartime fire in 1944. It built on Joachim's scheme by inscribing the separated syllables "Tri-ni-tate" and "Tri-ni-tas" inside three symmetrically interlaced rings (forming what is known as a Borromean knot), at the centre of which appear the unseparated words "unitas" and "unitate" (Julien 1994: 178). This was apparently intended to demonstrate the doctrine that God is both "Three in One" (*Trinitas Unitate*) and "One in Three" (*Unitas Trinitate*). The same folio featured two other Borromean figures, comparable to an extant fifteenth-century *Scutum fidei* appearing in a set of three shields, with orle lines labelled "erat," "est," and "erit," (was, is, shall be), representing the omnipresent *Esse* of God's ineffable name, "I am that I am," in conjunction with the tripartite unity of the Trinity (Evans 1982: 24, 73).[39] Such variations show how diagrams in the tradition of the Shield of Faith continued to elaborate on Petrus Alfonsi's cabbalistic interpretation of the Tetragrammaton's letters.

Similar to the Chartres image, captions in numerous thirteenth-century examples of the *Scutum fidei* discussed by Evans reflect propositions from the *Quicumque vult* or Athanasian Creed: "Alia est enim persona Patris alia Filii, alia Spiritus Sancti … Deus Pater, Deus Filius,

Deus Spiritus Sanctus" (there is one person of the Father, another of the Son, another of the Holy Spirit ... the Father is God, the Son is God, and the Holy Spirit is God) (Schaff 1919: 2.66). In the *Collectanea*, the corded lines of the pall leading from *Deus* to the Three Persons are labelled "est" (is), while segments of the orle linking *Pater, Filius*, and *Spiritu Sanctum* all read "non est" (is not). The De Quincy *Apocalypse* gives the same statements in French ("est" and "ne est"), and the illumination of Perault's *Summa de vitiis* adds the Latin "e converso" (and vice versa). Because nearly every extant version of the *Scutum fidei* reproduces these affirmations and negations, it seems certain that they are implicated in the Trinitarian naming of the *Libro*'s "letras encordados."[40]

Athanasian logic could also be applied to the three faculties of the soul from St Augustine's *On the Trinity*: "these three are one ... But they are three ... I remember that I have memory and understanding, and will; and I understand that I understand, and will, and remember; and I will that I will, and remember, and understand" (2002: 10.11.18). In Matthew of Paris's *Chronica majora*, the *Scutum fidei* appears next to a "scutum animae" inscribed with the statements "est" and "non est" to demonstrate the trinal oneness of "memoria," "voluntas," and "ratio" (memory, will, and understanding) (Lewis 1987: 194–6). This example, probably more than any other, illustrates how the meaning of the shield of faith in medieval culture relates to the central concerns of the *Libro*. In the celebrated prologue to his poem, the archpriest describes how the soul's three faculties lead to *bonus amor* or the good love of God. However, in contrast to Augustine's theological censure of *cupiditas*, or Perault's moralizing rejection of *amor inordinatus* (disorderly love) as the root of all mortal sin, the narrator warns that his poem can also instruct readers in the ways of carnal desire:

> El alma, con el buen entendimiento e buena voluntad, con buena rremembrança, escoge e ama el buen amor ... empero ... so algunos, lo que non los conssejo, quisieren usar del loco amor, aquí fallarán algunas maneras para ello ... conssejo e quien lo viere e lo oyere que guarde bien las tres cosas del alma ... Dios sabe que mi intención ... por que sean todos aperçebidos e se puedan mejor guardar de ... loco amor ... dize Sant Gregorio que menos firién al onbre los dardos que ante son vistos, e mejor non podemos guardar de lo que ante hemos visto. (1988: st. 110)

> (The soul, with good reason, good will and good memory, chooses and embraces good love ... on the other hand, as it is human nature to sin, if

anyone would like to enjoy mad love, and I do not so counsel him, he will
find here means to that end ... I counsel anyone who reads or hears this
book to hold fast to the three parts of the soul ... God knows my intention ...
that everyone might be more aware and better guarded against ... mad
love ... St. Gregory says that the darts a man sees do him less harm, for we
can protect ourselves better against that we have seen.)

Here, the archpriest cites a homily from the Divine Office in which
Gregory evokes the Pauline metaphor of spiritual armour: "we are
harnessed against them with the shield (*clypeum*) of foreknowledge"
(Crichton-Stuart 1879: 2.35).[41] The prologue in prose then concludes
with an invocation of the Anthanasian Creed that is followed by an
opening prayer to "Dios padre, Dios fijo, Dios Spíritu Santo": "començé
mi libro en el nonbre de Dios ... la Santa Trinidat e de la fe cathólica,
que es 'Quicunque vult,' el vesso que dize: 'Ita Deus pater, Deus filius,
e çetera'" (I began my book in the name of God ... the Holy Trinity and
the catholic faith, that is "Whosoever shall," the verse that says, "So
the Father is God, the Son is God, etc." [the creed continues: "and the
Holy Ghost is God, and yet they are not three Gods, but one God"])
(1988: p. 111, st. 11a). We have seen how these same propositions were
consistently represented on the *Scutum fidei* that the archpriest later
describes as "corded with these letters" and identifies with the spiritual gift of "good counsel" to guard against the "wounding darts" of
worldly sin. The prologue shows how this shield can be understood as
a symbol of the *Libro*'s contradictory functions, protecting the faithful
with wisdom centred on the divine love of the Three Persons, while
at the same time providing sinful counsel and exposing readers to the
weaponry of mad love – in other words, serving at once as an apotropaic and a malediction.

These functions pose an interpretive problem that is subsequently
illustrated by the first story told in the *Libro*, the celebrated "disputa-
çión" between the Greeks and Romans (1988: sts. 44–70). The archpriest
begins by warning his audience, "entiende bien mis dichos et piensa
la sentencia; / non me contesca contigo commo al doctor de Greçia /
con el rribaldo rromano" (understand well my words and ponder their
meaning; lest it happen to me with you as it happened to the Greek doctor and the Roman rogue) (1988: st. 46abc). In this tale, the worthiness
of the Latins to receive divine law from the Greeks is to be determined
by a disputation conducted in sign language. The simpleton chosen
to represent the Romans, having misconstrued the Greek's one raised

finger, first menacingly holds up his thumb, index, and middle digit. He next responds to the Greek's open palm by making a fist. Whereas the Roman believes that his opponent threatened to poke and slap him, and for this reason responds with retaliatory gestures of gouging and punching, the Greek understands one and three raised fingers to signify the Athanasian truth of *Unitas Trinitate*: "Yo dixe que es un Dios: el rromano dixo que era / uno e tres personas, e tal señal feziera ... Desque vi que entendién e creyén la Trinidad, / entendí que meresçién de leyes çertenidad" (I declared there is one God; the Roman replied by making the sign that He is one in three persons ... When I saw they understood and believed in the Trinity, I knew they deserved to be confirmed in our laws) (1988: 59cd, 60cd). The archpriest applies this tale of Trinitarian miscommunication to conflicted interpretations of his *Libro*. Those who correctly understand its meaning are on the one hand promised success in finding a lover, and on the other urged to search for signs of good love in the book's deceptive gesturing:

> Entiende bien mi dicho e avrás dueña garrida. / La burla que oyeres, non la tengas en vil; / la manera del libro, entiende la sotil ... los cuerdos con buen sesso entendrá la cordura; / los mançebos livianos guarden se de locura ... Las del buen amor son rrazones encubiertas: trabaja do falleres las sus señales ciertas. (1988: 64d–65a, 67bc, 68ab)

> (Understand my words well and you will have a choice maiden. Do not despise the jest that you hear, understand the manner of this book as subtle ...the wise with good sense will understand wisdom; foolish youths beware of folly ... the teachings of Good Love are hidden, work to find its manifest signs.)

Critics have pointed out that this warning to the "reader trying to make sense of the *Libro*" contrasts with earlier thirteenth-century applications of the story (De Looze 1998: 144).[42] As Michael Gerli (2002) has shown, the *Libro* version can be related to St Augustine's treatment in *De doctrina Christiana* of the contingent and potentially ambiguous meaning of letters and words that are written and/or pronounced the same way in Greek and Latin.[43] I have found that the archpriest's tale also recalls a strikingly similar case of theological hand gesturing in *De Trinitate*. Here, the bishop of Hippo observes that "we know what a trinity is, because ... we can easily have this whenever we will, to pass over things, by *just holding up three fingers*. Or do we indeed love not every trinity, but the Trinity that is God? We love then in the Trinity… because God is One" (emphasis mine, 2002: 8.5.8). Early audiences of the *Libro* familiar with *De Trinitate* and aware of its influence on the prologue could have readily linked Augustine's image of *digitis tribus* with the Roman's misconstrued "trinity" of upheld fingers.

In contrast to this sign of worldly ambiguity and disorder, the meaning of One in Three in the archpriest's poem ultimately hinges on the Augustinian notion of the Holy Spirit as the love shared between the Father and Son – the *dilectio* reflected in the soul's will to embrace the straight path of *bonus amor* and reject the perverse ways of *malus amor* (*City of God* 1984: bk. 14, chap. 7). By the time the *Libro* was being written, *De Trinitate* had been expanded on by theologians like Anselm of Canterbury, who portrays the memory and understanding of the Father and Son coming together in the love of the Holy Ghost (Ngien 2005: 35). Richard of Saint-Victor identifies the Spirit as the co-beloved (*condilectus*), or the love that is freely bestowed by the Father and reciprocated by the Son (*caritas*). He compares this to the intimacy of two persons who "embrace each other with supreme longing and take supreme delight in each other's love … it is necessary for them to have someone who shares in love" (1855: bk. 3.15; Ngien 2005: 67). Thomas Aquinas later asserts that love is the Spirit's proper name, in both the intra-trinitarian and human sense, "for he makes us lovers (*amatores*) of God" (1957: bk. 4:21.2).[44] Bonaventure arrives at a similar conclusion after elaborating on Augustine's chapter from *De Trinitate* concerning the Tetragrammaton (1841: 5.2.3). He imagines two angels in the Holy of Holies, the first gazing at the ineffable name from the Old Testament, while the second contemplates the gospels' identification of God as the Good (Luke 18:19; Matt. 19:17). Bonaventure interprets this vision of being and goodness as the triune *caritas* of "one who gives" (the Father), another who "receives" (the Son), and "one mediating … in whom love is mingled [*amor permixtus*] from both" (the Holy Spirit), analogous to the conjugal fruit of a bride and groom (1864–71: 1.2.4).

Sophisticated medieval readers could have readily applied these kinds of theological interpretations to Trinitarian imagery in the *Libro*. Following the example of the Greek, they are encouraged to see in the disputants' upheld fingers a vision of the oneness of the Tetragrammaton as well as the love of the Holy Spirit; a triune sign that corresponds to Petrus Alfonsi's earlier-mentioned polemic description of the Jewish priestly blessing following his diagram of "IEVE" in the *Dialogus*

> When he said "Lord" [the Tetragrammaton] which we said above, he
> expressed in Hebrew by that name as threefold and one, and he raised
> up the three primary fingers, namely, the thumb, the index finger, and the
> middle finger … tell me, O Moses, how can the excellence of the Trinity
> be expressed allegorically better than by the elevation of three fingers?
> (2006: 175)

This same gesture was used as a benediction in Christian iconography
and liturgical practices. Similarly, the three fingers of the medieval
scribe holding his pen was interpreted as a sign of the Trinity (Wellbery
et al. 2004: 32). It is likely that Alfonsi drew on this context, as his image
of the temple priest's blessing – not surprisingly – differs from Jewish
accounts like that of the thirteenth-century Andalusian cabbalist, Abraham Abulafia.[45] In any case, early readers of the *Libro* are faced with a
choice between employing the three faculties of the soul to find in the
Trinitarian gesture a representation of the good and loving essence of
God's being, or electing to, in the words of Augustine, "pass things
over" by "just holding up three fingers" like the loutish Roman. The
sign can, in other words, be used to convey the apotropaic defence of
the *Scutum fidei* or represent a demonic assault – to communicate the
transcendent ineffable name or expose the pitfalls of human language,
to confer the blessing of *bonus amor* or the curse of *malus amor*.

Subsequent invocations of "good love" in the *Libro* have the effect
of confusing this opposition. Over the course of the poem, the narrator continues to employ the phrase "buen amor," initially used in an
Augustinian sense, to his ongoing pursuit of carnal lust or "amor loco."
Prior to the disputation between the Greeks and Romans, for example,
the archpriest calls on God to help him write a "libro de buen amor"
that will both delight the flesh and profit the soul, "que los cuerpos
alegre e a las almas preste" (1988: st. 13). Later, he reminds the audience that the redeeming wisdom of his book's "buen amor" lies hidden
beneath "fea letra" (uncomely letters) and again blurs the distinction
between good and mad love on the comic epitaph for his go-between:
"El que aquí llegare … dé Dios buen amor e plazer de amiga" (he who
comes here … may God grant him good love and the pleasure of a
lover) (1988: 1578ab). Such an inscription is particularly fitting for an
old bawd who identified herself by the same name that provides a title
for the archpriest's book.[46] She is to be called *Buen Amor*, as opposed
to Trotaconventos, Urraca (Convent-Trotter, Magpie), or a long list of
other epithets that, as John K. Walsh (1983) has shown, bring to mind

the enumeration of divine titles in works like Ramon Llull's *Cent noms de Déu* (The Hundred Names) (1988: sts. 924–7; 2006). Such an association anticipates her final ironic depiction on the epitaph as seated in celestial glory, "en paraíso … assentada" (1988: 1570c). The apophatic treatment of the procuress – cataloguing attributes that should *not* be used to name her – can also be interpreted as a subversion of the medieval theology of negative predication or the *via negativa* in which God is described through the insufficiency of finite names applied to what is infinite and ineffable. In the context of the *Libro*'s Trinitarian preliminaries, the positive, equivocal naming of the bawd and book as *Buen amor* can be understood as a parodic simulation of the Holy Spirit and, by extension, the *Fructus Spiritus Sancti* reflected in Christian *caritas*. The narrator thus applies the kind of sexualized *amor mixtus* described by Andreas Capellanus (1982) to the properly named *Amor* of the Trinity. In other words, he associates erotic mixing with the third member of the godhead designated as *condilectio* and *amor permixtus* in the works of Bonaventure and other theologians and figuratively identified with the mediation between and reciprocity of lovers, their amorous procession and spiration.

In this way, the three faculties leading the soul to the good love of God in Augustinian Trinitarianism and the archpriest's prologue are linked with the three temptations: "las almas quieren matar …. la carne, el diablo, el mundo, destos nasçen los mortales; destos tres vienen aquellos, tomemos armas" (they want to kill our souls … the flesh, the devil, and the world, from these three the deadly sins are born; from these three proceed all the rest, so let us take arms) (1988: 1584abc). As Donald Howard (1966) has shown, this notion of an unholy trinity was associated with the tripartite evil of suggestion, delectation, and consent in the Garden of Eden, an inheritance of Original Sin that can undermine the divinely ordained guidance of the soul through memory, understanding, and will. To arm themselves, readers of the *Libro* are challenged to decipher the sacred meaning of the letters on the Shield of Faith, in spite of the slippage of Love's name being alternatively used in reference to the fruit of the Holy Spirit, the sinful mediation of the go-between, and the ambivalence of the archpriest's poetics. This indeterminacy threatens to re-inscribe the protective *Scutum* with anti-trinitarian "uncomely letters," leaving the audience defenseless against the Enemy's arrows. It contributes to the risk of reading the archpriest's book as a kind of heretical performance of doctrinely wrong choices, as Gerli (2012) has recently demonstrated.

Such a process of re-inscription is on display in a celebrated section of the poem concerning "la pelea quel arçipreste ovo con don Amor" (the quarrel that the archpriest had with Sir Love) (1988: sts. 372–87). This episode subverts the propositions of the Athanasian Creed that we have seen in the captioning of medieval *Scutum fidei*, the invocation at the close of the *Libro*'s prologue ("in the name of God … the Holy Trinity and the Catholic faith, that is 'Whosoever shall,' the verse that says, 'So the Father is God, the Son is God, etc.'"), and also implicated in the misunderstanding of Greek and Roman hand signals ("the sign that He is one in three persons … I saw they understood and believed in the Trinity"). After appearing in a dream vision, Don Amor is identified with the Devil fathering each of the seven deadly sins, as Gerli (1982) has also shown. He inspires accidia by impassively neglecting love of the spirit and instead energetically misapplying the elevated language of the Canonical Hours to lower, bodily pleasures. At one point, while reciting fragments from the Divine Office that culminate in the first words of the Trinitarian creed, he even calls on a procuress as if she were God and arranges to deflower his mistress:

Comiienças luego prima: / "Deus in nomine tuo [salvum me]" rruegas a tu xaquima … e si es tal que non usa andar por las callejas, / que la lieve a las uertas por las rrosas bermejas; / si cree la bavieca sus dichos e conssejas, / "quod Eva tristis [abstulit]" trae, de "Quincunque vult [salvus esse]" rredruejas. (1988: st. 377b, 378)[47]

Then you begin prime: "God, in your name, [save me]" you plead for your go-between … and if she is reluctant to come through the alleys, she can be taken to the gardens for red roses; If the silly woman believes her sayings and counsel, / she will have "what hapless Eve [lost]" from "whosoever shall" [be saved] withered blossoms.

Gerli (1982) links Don Amor's spawning of the mortal sins to the central problem of *amor inordinatus* in the *Summa de vitiis* and later penitential literature. He rightly traces this back to the Augustinian notion of the will perverted ("voluntas perversa") when disorderly love is misdirected to fleeting, undeserving things of this world in place of the eternal, inestimable goodness of God (*Confessiones* 1841).[48] My further investigation reveals how, as a result of the overarching problem of *voluntas perversa*, the true relationship between the members of the Trinity and the voluntaristic function of the three faculties is perverted and misdirected so that the flesh, the devil, and the world lead the soul to sin through a triadic process of suggestion, delectation, and consent. As Augustine puts it, "the soul plays the unfaithful lover" by mounting a "grotesque and twisted" imitation of God's love ("*Confessions*" 1955: 2.14). Immediately following the text of the Athanasian Creed cited by Don Amor is a doctrinal statement that echoes the invocation from the *Libro*'s prologue and the subsequent disputation: "one God in Trinity, and Trinity in Unity" (*Deum in Trinitate, et Trinitatem in unitate*). The *Libro*, in its parody of the Canonical Hours, thus misapplies triune doctrine to a go-between bringing together an arch-seducer and his fallen lover, as opposed to the Holy Spirit uniting the divine love of the Father and the Son. Amor's imposturous godliness is further clarified by additional phrases inserted from the Hours that either explicitly or elliptically invoke the name *Dominus*: in the erotic serenade of a Moorish woman, "domine labia mea [aperies]" (O Lord, thou wilt [open my lips]), and the pleas of other female devotees, "en legem pone [mihi Domine]" (Set before me for a law … [O Lord]) and "[Domine, vigilantes] custodi nos" ([O Lord, keep us waking,] guard us) (1988: sts. 376–86). Through his perverse simulation of God's love, Amor effectively defaces and rewrites the triadic inscriptions on Shields of Faith like the one found in the illuminated *Summa de vitiis* manuscript.

The same kind of defacement of Trinitarian meaning is at work in a later celebration of the triumph of Don Amor on Easter Sunday. In keeping with other passages in the *Libro de buen amor* that parody material from the *Libro de Alexandre*, this climactic scene ironically resituates images from Alexander's triumphal entry into Jerusalem.[49] What the earlier poet describes as a "noble procession" of "all the clergy" in the temple city honouring the victorious emperor with "flowers" and "palm branches" is echoed in the archpriest's springtime scene: "todos van a rresçebir … con rramos e con flores … grandes proçesiones: muchos omnes ordenados … los clérigos … vienen con el grand emperante" (all come in greeting … with branches with flowers … great processions: many ordained men … the clergy … comes with the great emperor) (1988: sts. 1142a, 1140a, 1141; 1227a, 1235, 1245a). Instead of the sacerdotal gathering to greet Alexander and reveal the holiest name of the Tetragrammaton in the form of a textual amulet, the priests attached to the cathedral of Toledo herald the "emperante" Amor with fragmented, elliptical lines from the paschal liturgy that misname him as God the Father, the Son, and the Holy Ghost. This echoes earlier invocations in the *Libro* that have been similarly shown to misidentify Love as the *Dominus* of the Divine Office and *Deus* of the Athanasian Creed:

Venite exultemus [Domino]... Te Amore [Deum] laudemus [...Sanctus, Sanctus, Sanctus ... Patrem immensae maiestatis: Venerandum tuum verum et unicum Filium; Sanctum quoque Paraclitum Spiritum ... laudamus Nomen tuum] ... [Haec est dies quam fecit Dominus] exultemus laetemur ... Benedictus qui venit [in nomine Domini] ... Mane nobiscum domine. (1988: sts. 1236d, 1237d, 1238d, 1239d, 1241d)[50]

(Come let us exalt [the Lord] ... We worship you [God] Love [...Holy, Holy, Holy ... Father of an infinite Majesty ... true and only Son, also the Holy Ghost, the Comforter... we worship thy Name] ... [This is the day the Lord as made,] let us be glad and rejoice ... Blessed is He who comes [in the name of Lord] ... stay with us, Lord.)

The poet then builds on the intertextual association between Alexander in Jerusalem and Don Amor in Toledo in the episode of Love's "tienda." In place of the *mappa mundi* that will be depicted in the Macedonian's pavilion with its segments reflecting the four letters of the ineffable name and alluding to sacred history, Amor's tent is decorated with the seasons of the solar year, broken down into four tripartide personifications of the months: "tres caballeros ... tres fijos dalgo ... tres rricos onbres ... tres labradores ... son quatro tenporadas" (three knights .. three noblemen ... three rich men ... three farmers ... these are the four seasons) (1988: sts. 1271a, 1278a, 1287a, 1294a, 1300b). Instead of mapping a course in space and time to the ends of the world, the ekphrastic pavilion in the *Libro de buen amor* represents a worldly landscape that satisfies material needs and bodily appetites. The end of the liturgical year and the onset of spring is marked not by paschal mystery and revelation but by an erotic rendering of "omnes, aves y bestias .... en amores ... tres diablos ... ellos e ellas andan en modorría" (men, birds and beasts ... in love ... three devils ... men and women going about madly) (1988: sts. 1281d, 1282a, 1284b). The archpriest's parodic re-inscription of the amuletic allegorized Tetragrammaton in the procession scene, followed by this remapping of the God's name as Amor in the pavilion, is emblematic of the anti-Trinitarian predication of Love throughout the poem.

In this way, the fourteenth-century work can be read as a subversion of the typological interpretation of YHWH that characterizes the *Libro de Alexandre*. We have shown how, in the Castilian legend, the temple priest shows Alexander a "carta" or *nómina* with four obscurely written "characters" and other inscribed divine names whose "closed" significance is opened up by the hero's prophetic conquests and the spread of his power across the cruciform map as a prelude to the coming of Christ, the revelation of God's triune nature, and the eschatological fulfilment of time. The poetics of the archpriest, however, make it possible for the unwary reader to participate in corrupting Athanasian truths, misleading the faculties of the soul through the three temptations, and re-inscribing "corded letters" on the apotropaic diagram of the Shield of Faith with its Trinitarian interpretation of the ineffable name. We have seen how the materiality and Pharisaism that was associated with Jewish amulets during the Middle Ages is spiritualized and, as it were, opened up through Christian reinterpretation in the *Libro de Alexandre*. This process is systematically, ironically subverted in episodes of the *Libro de buen amor* that show how an amuletic text can be made to work against itself, both in terms of its apotropaic, externalized power and transcendent Christian notions of an interiorized, immaterial potency of the word inscribed within the heart and soul. Using "uncomely letters" to name *Amor* as bawd, book, and false god, the darts of mad love warned about in the prologue take the form of a misdirected reflection and perversion of the Holy Spirit's amorous mediation – the *Amor permixtus* that proceeds from the Father and the Son, uniting Christians through the triadic unity of God's love. Just as the reader of the *Libro de Alexandre* must open up the truth occluded in "quatro caróctoras," the archpriest's audience must determine whether the signs of the Roman and Greek disputants, and the three fingers of the poet holding his pen, will be used as a weapon against the faith or as a means of protecting the faithful from themselves.

Chapter Three

Amuletic Voices

Some fifty years ago, in a remote region of Spain, a centuries-old tile (Figure 9) was found near an abandoned hermitage dedicated to St Marina. Possibly the red clay object had been discarded at some point in the process of constructing an *arábiga* ceramic roof. A native of the nearby village of Villamartín de Sotoscueva, just north of the province of Burgos, first noticed that the shingle was inscribed with medieval poetry.[1] He brought the object – roughly the size of an automobile license plate – to the attention of a scholar from the University of Valladolid, who found that the verses in gothic script on this ostracon-like artefact very closely coincided with a prayer recited by the count of Castile in the late thirteenth-century *Poema de Fernán González*, as I noted in the introduction to this book.

Near the beginning of the poem, preserved in a single manuscript at the Escorial library, Christian territories are invaded by the tenth-century chieftain Al-Mansur. The Castilians are urged to fight and resist the temptation of succumbing to a Moorish invader whom the poem identifies with the forces of evil. The Christians pray for deliverance by invoking a series of prophets and saints who were liberated from their enemies in Scripture and hagiographic lore:

Señor, que con los sabios valiste a Catalina ... e del dragon libreste a la virgen Marina ... tu que libreste a Davit del leon ... a los jodios del rey de Babilon, /saca nos e libra nos de tal cruel presion ... saqueste a Daniel de entre los leones, / libreste a San Matheo de los fieros dragones, / libra nos tu, Señor, d'aquestas tentaciones. (1983: sts. 106–8)

(Lord who with the wise men saved Catherine ... and from the dragon freed the virgin Marina ... You freed David from the lion ... and the Jews

Figure 9. Photograph of clay tile, found in Villamartín (36 × 23 cm.),
Burgos (photo: Isabel Velázquez).

from the kingdom of Babylon / take and liberate us from such a cruel prison ... You took Daniel away from two Lions / freed St. Matthew from the fierce dragons / Lord free us from these temptations.)

It has been shown that the vernacular formula of this litany as it appears in the Escorial manuscript and on the early fourteenth-century Villamartín tile was adapted from the rite known as the *Ordo commendationis animae* or Recommendation of the Soul Departing. In addition, it shares important features with a blessing known as the *Itinerarium*, bestowed on clerics and monks as they set off on long journeys.[2]

We have seen how similar prayers can be found in the epic *Poema de mío Cid*, when the hero's wife blesses him at the monastery of San Pedro de Cardeña, and in works by Gonzalo de Berceo composed in the same clerical metre of *cuaderna vía* or mono-rhyming quatrains as the *Poema de Fernán González*.[3] Critics have pointed out that in Latin hagiography and French epics (including the *Chanson de Roland*), these kinds of prayers are often associated with the heroic journeys of saints and knights. The purpose of this formulaic petition for deliverance parallels the Recommendation of the Soul Departing, insofar as the passage from death to eternal life was often envisioned as a voyage during the Middle Ages, and the post-lapsarian exile of humankind was similarly seen as an itinerary back from the expulsion and exile brought about by Original Sin to redemption through Christ. It can be hypothesized that a fourteenth-century scribe prepared the tile for a pilgrim to the local hermitage of Marina, since this saint is invoked its prayer.

What has yet to be fully explained is the relationship of this inscription to another literary text from the period. The poetry recorded on the tile not only includes verses matching with lines from a prayer in the *Poema de Fernán González*, but these are preceded by part of another *cuaderna vía* verse that coincides with a riddle found in the mid-thirteenth-century *Libro de Apolonio* (Book of Apolonius): "... de fuera so rraýda" (... I am rough on the outside) (Gwara 2005: 117).[4] Thus, it would appear that the scribe has selected and pieced together texts from, or at least shared by, two separate works composed in the same poetic metre. Gwara has hypothesized that the riddle fragment seemingly taken from the *Libro de Apolonio* could have been meant as an allusion to the blank and inscribed surfaces of the clay tile itself: "De dentro soó vellosa e de fuera raýda" (I am smooth on the inside and rough on the outside) (1987: 518a; 2005: 132–3). The exiled hero from the poem, Apollonius, responds to this clue by identifying the exterior and interior of a leather ball stuffed with horsehair, just before recognizing his long-lost daughter, Tarsiana, and thereby completing a spiritual journey in which he is restored to and reconciled with his family.

I am in agreement with Gwara's suggestion that the partial verse from the riddle of the ball is used to make the clay tile vocalize its own "rough" inscription. It has been shown in this study how features of the *Ordo commendationis animae* were commonly found on medieval amuletic texts produced in Spain and elsewhere, including the *Oración de San León,* the prayer found in the *Razón de amor* manuscript, as well as examples studied by Skemer (2006: 257). In the case of Villamartín shingle, this litany, combined with the riddle inscription, suggests that it was intended to conjure divine protection or healing through its material presence – a presence that can be accessed visually and verbally, as well as through touch. Viewed in this light, the tile should be understood not only as a possible early witness to works that formed part of the thirteenth-century *mester de clerecía* or poetic "craft of the clergy." It also provides evidence of how a narrative prayer of deliverance, common in epic and priestly writing, was used to produce an amuletic object.

A problem that confronts scholars as they unearth such remnants from centuries past and consider their relationship with imaginative literary works is a tendency to overlook the *potentia* believed to reside in the physical inscription of sacred language – not as just performative "speech acts" in the modern sense, but as "speaking" texts whose efficacy was, in the words of Bynum, "manifested and conveyed in matter" according to "theories of those contemporary with the objects ... who shaped and were shaped by the objects themselves" (2011: 269, 280–1). As I intend to demonstrate in this chapter, the power of amulets in the medieval imaginary to be efficaciously vocalized and, in this way, assume a voice sheds considerable light on the relationship between the Villamartín tile, its prayer for deliverance, and its citation from the *Libro de Apolonio.* Finally, I will consider how the fourteenth-century *Libro de buen amor* parodically repurposes earlier traditions surrounding prayer and voices invoked in *mester de clerecía* works and on amulets like the Castilian ostracon.

To understand the potential meaning and relationship between the verses inscribed on this tile, it is helpful to first consider David Frankfurter's earlier-mentioned theory of "narrating power" as an account of amulet production that developed in early Christianity. According to Frankfurter, *historiola* are fragments extracted from narratives to be used in a spell or on an amulet as an efficacious analogy that could be brought into a present circumstance. The application of the analogy often, though not always, remained unspecified and implicit. Citations from one or more stories were traditionally inscribed on objects such as papyrus, stone, or parchment in order to bring supernatural healing or protection in this way. Their potency was derived from extractions from these stories being recited as speech acts, in addition to the physical presence of the inscribed words themselves. Frankfurter notes how fragments taken from narratives often replicated and made present the voices of powerful, holy, and heroic figures pronouncing "dramatic monologues" from a "mythic" past – be it pagan, Christian, or syncretic in origin – so that the power of these words could be brought into the present (2001: 461). In the case of the tile that I have been discussing, the powerful voices are spoken by long-ago Christians whose mythic fight against evil forces was led by the hero Fernán González; and by the pagan heroine, Tarsiana, whose story was Christianized in medieval culture. Frankfurter describes the *historiola* as an evocation of particular characters involved in an event or situation within the logic of the story that "is often a crisis" that can be applied "to the present condition" of the user of the spell or amulet (2001: 462). Often without explaining this crisis, they extract "focal words of power," referencing a "past accomplishment" or citing from a "direct speech" that

> effectively collapses the story with the reality of the performance ... In one form of application the *historiola* concludes with an invocation or prayer that is framed as the culminating speech of a character ... The specific declaration to apply the *historiola* may be only implicit ... uttering the same vital invocation as the character ... taps into the power of the entire story. (2001: 462)

The Villamartín tile evokes parts of "dramatic monologues" spoken by the Castilians and Tarsiana at critical junctures in the *Poema de Fernán González* and *Libro de Apolonio*. While the story of Apolonio and his daughter was well known throughout Western Europe and thus would have provided a widely accessible *historiola*, the specifically peninsular legend of Fernán González corresponds with another typical convention, offering what Frankfurter calls an "articulation within a local Christian discourse" (Frankfurter 2001: 475). It is not surprising that the tile combined elements associated with two separate though thematically and generically related narrative traditions. Frankfurter cites examples of magical and amuletic *historiolae* that individually and collectively can be described as a "bricolage," as "compilations and syntheses of diverse lore," and "deliberate acts of blending" that "tap into several authoritative symbol systems" (2001: 472–3). It is my contention that fragments from the vernacular *Poema de Fernán González* and *Libro de Apolonio* work as interlinked systems and sources of narrative power on the Villamartín amulet. While variations of the kind of prayer for deliverance found on the tile most likely circulated independently, this version follows the *Poema de Fernán González* text too closely to be dismissed as a mere coincidence. The same can be said for the direct match of the Castilian riddle fragment on the tile with the *Libro de Apolonio*.

This is not to say that using the Villamartín amulet would necessarily entail a deep familiarity – oral or literate – with the contexts of the poetic fragments inscribed on it – or, for that matter, sufficient literacy to recite them. As Frankfurter observes, power imparted by *historiolae* was also attributed to the presence of the physical object itself. In this way, the text might be expected to "lock in the power of the uttered words for ongoing effect" even in a "semi- or non-literate society," expressing "mythic episodes as continually powerful" (2001: 463, 464). Nevertheless, the most efficacious production and most powerful utilization of such amulets would require some knowledge of the stories they implicated. Skemer explains that "there were obvious benefits to verbalizing amuletic texts. The rhyme, repetition, and alliteration of charms produced a sonorous effect," and by hearing it one would be "better able to deter evil spirits" (2006: 153). Recitations could even require "a more dramatic presentation … late medieval amulets and charms often required performative responses" (2006: 154). Of course, the exact ways in which the Villamartín object was employed during the Middle Ages cannot be determined. Its power could benefit a traveller carrying it on their person, as I have suggested, but it might also have functioned as an apotropaic inscription in the construction of the Marina shrine, as Heather Bamford has recently pointed out (2012). Whatever the specifics of its provenance, the shingle can be best understood as at once an amuletic object and a literary text. We can therefore explain aspects of its referencing of *historiolae* and horizon of expectations, or what Frankfurter describes as an "active analogizing … a guarantee or rationale, an explicit precedent, for the directive utterance" (2001: 466). Combinations of texts used in spells and amulets were characterized by "structural resemblances, links and overall relationships among *historiolae*" with "liturgical recitations, texts, and other forms of mythical expression" (2001: 474). The potency of *Poema de Fernán González* and *Libro de Apolonio* on the tile similarly rely on the way rearticulated fragments from these narratives can be associated with Latin prayers and hagiographic legends of saints like Marina and Catherine. Among the most traditional stories implicated in amulet production, Frankfurter includes hagiography, along with what he calls "iconographic vignettes" extracted from the bible – pointing out how some examples drew on *historiola* for "generalized, apotropaic value," while others "were designed for specific ailments and problems" (2001: 464).

As I briefly discussed in the opening to this book, Don Skemer has shown how Frankfurter's work sheds light on medieval amulets that continue to draw on the potency of *historiolae* from saints' lives, magical legends, and scriptural narratives. In case of objects inscribed during the early centuries of Christianity, "it is the performative aspect of the *historiola* – its very utterance or inscription – that holds power … the force of that utterance explicitly comes from that 'I' who says the words" (2001: 463, 467). Skemer edits and comments on examples from the Middle Ages that follow this pattern by identifying "ego" with the divine speaker quoted on the textual amulet or the efficacious voice of the object itself (2006: 247, 287, 291, 299). In keeping with this tradition, it is the *persona* of the "yo" implicated on the Villamartín text that concerns me. By unpacking the storied identity of this speaker, my intention is to shed light on the amuletic power believed to resonate from her voice.

The Efficacious Voice of Tarsiana

It is a verse from Tarsiana's final speech in the *Libro de Apolonio* that has been recorded on the tile of Villamartín. It potentially "taps into the entire story," in keeping with Frankfurter's theory, and is emblematic of how the heroine's voice makes things happen in the poem. To fully perceive the potential resonance of her voice on the amulet, we must consider who it was that came to speak the words "de fuera so rayda." The verse comes after the hero's daughter is nearly martyred ("martiriada") by treacherous guardians in Tarsus, kidnapped by pirates, and sold at a slave market in Mytilene (1987: 382b). The ruler of the city, Antinágora, lusts after Tarsiana and tries to purchase her, but is outbid by a pimp who forces the beautiful maiden to work at his brothel. This turn of events enables the anonymous Spanish poet to introduce a series of Christian allusions that are absent from Latin models that were based on the *Historia Apollonii regis Tyri*.[5] When Antinágora comes to visit Tarsiana at the brothel, the "cordera" or lamb prays for her protection and liberation from the corruption that surrounds her: "rogó al Criador ... 'Senyor, la tu uertud me deue anparar / que non me puedan el alma garçones enconar'" (she petitioned the Creator ... '"Lord, your virtue must protect me / so that my soul cannot be defiled by these lusty young men") (1987: 403cd). The poet specifies that her prayer is heard and immediately answered by God: "en esta oración, / rencurando su cuyta e su tribulaçión, / ouo Dios de la huérfana duelo e compasión, / enviól' su acorro e oyó su petiçión" (in this prayer, bemoaning her suffering and tribulation, God felt pity and compassion for the orphan. He sent aid and heard her petition) (1987: 403, 382d, 384).

She continues to worry that visitors to the brothel will "contaminate" her: "que non me puedan el alma garçones enconar" (1987: st. 403b). Tarsiana greets the ruler with a tearful account of her misfortunes, accompanied by the kind of sermonic warnings that characterize the work as a whole, "cayerás por mal cuerpo, tú, en mortal pecado" (for evils of the flesh, you will fall in mortal sin) (1987: 408b, 409b). Antinágora has a sudden change of heart and offers a "donation" for her release along with his blessing, in lieu of the money he brought to "sin with her" (1987: 416, 417c).[6] Other clients undergo what is described as a spiritual awakening and conversion in the girl's presence: "non fue violada ... quantos ahí vinieron y a ella entraron, / todos *se convertieron*, todos por tal pasaron" (she was not violated ... all of those who went to see her, all of them *were converted*, all that passed through there) (emphasis mine, 1987: 419ab). My objective is to show how Tarsiana's characterization as a prayerful agent of conversion draws on a long tradition of holy virgins forced into prostitution. This martyrological tradition is used to characterize Tarsiana as a purifying presence, in spite of the corruption that surrounds her. In this manner, it functions as a *historiola* that channels power into the Villamartín tile, and like the *Poema de Fernán González* verses, could be a source of power for those seeking to protect themselves from evil and resist threats of violence and sinful temptations.

Patricia Grieve has observed that for a thirteenth-century audience, Apolonio's daughter could have represented the idea of a "virgin-martyr" (1998: 162).[7] Her study builds on the work of Marina Brownlee, who pointed out that the Spanish author evokes a Christian *peregrinatio vitae* (pilgrimage of life) in his portrayal of the journeys and travails of Tarsiana and the status of Apolonio as a "palmero, por tierras de Egipto anda como romero" (pilgrim, through the land of Egypt he travels as if he were a pilgrim) (1983: 171–4; st. 360cd). While these studies do not mention the Villamartín amulet, its inscription appears to testify to the poem's early reception in a way that could support such a thesis. As we have seen, the ostracon combines words spoken by Tarsiana with a prayer of deliverance for spiritual travellers – one that is comparable to the efficacious petition of Apolonio's daughter during her "suffering and tribulation."[8] What is more, the *Poema de Fernán González* inscription petitions two female martyrs, Catherine and Marina, calling on their power to overcome evil torturers and Satanic beasts. One issue that has yet to be explored is how Tarsiana's voice can be linked to particular virgin saints and their efficacious presence and prayers.

A hagiographic text that has close parallels with the *Libro de Apolonio*'s characterization of Tarsiana can be found in the thirteenth-century *Golden Legend*. In this collection, Jacobus de Voragine closely follows a sixth-century work that was falsely attributed to St Ambrose, the *Gesta Sanctae Agnes* (1863). Purportedly named after the *agnus* or lamb, Agnes was said to have been forced into prostitution at age thirteen, after refusing to sacrifice to the goddess Vesta. With the help of an angel, the virgin transformed the brothel into a luminous "place of prayer" (*locus orationis*) and later brought about the Christian rebirth of a Roman prefect's son: "in a fury he rushed in to force himself upon Agnes, but the same light engulfed him ... Agnes prayed, and the youth came to life and began to preach Christ" (1993: 2.9; 102–3).[9] Condemned as a "witch" and "sorceress who turns people's heads and befuddles their wits," the saint received her martyrdom from a Roman soldier's blade (1993: 103). The *Libro de Apolonio* poet seems to have drawn on the passion of this saint for key details that are not present in the *Historia Apollonii*: in particular, Tarsiana's identity as a "cordera," her age specified as "XIII años," and the conversional efficacy of her presence and prayer (1987: st. 348). The first-person voice on the amulet from Villamartín can, for this reason, be interpreted as reconveying the words of a saintly lamb of thirteen years, implicitly evoking the power and authority of a hagiographic *historiola*.

The way in which the story told in the *Gesta Sanctae Agnes* informs the *Libro de Apolonio* shows how the latter text, like the foundational *Libro de Alexandre* and other thirteenth-century works, reinterprets pagan material through a process of allegoresis. Such vernacular translations and adaptations arose from the practice of medieval commentators engaging in a Christianizing cultural "resignification" of "particular verbal usage" and "conceptual coherences" (Copeland 1991: 80, 156). Applying this method of *interpretatio* to the *Historia Apollonii* would have seemed particularly fitting, as early versions of the Latin text already contained images that also occur in hagiographic works – most notably, when Tarsiana describes her preservation from corruption: "virginitatem meam inter naufragium castitatis inviolabiliter" (I kept my virginity intact in the midst of a shipwreck of chastity) (1991: 160–1). This phrase corresponds with language used in a well-known sermon for the feast of St Agnes that was, like the *Gesta*, attributed to Ambrose of Milan: "ubi semper naufragaverat castitas, illic est coronata virginitas" (where chastity is always shipwrecked, there is the crown of virginity) (1879: 727).[10] These sources demonstrate a clear and longstanding connection between Tarsiana's characterization and the legend of Agnes in medieval literature. Accordingly, Tarsiana's voice on the Villamartín tile can be interpreted as recalling a fictional heroine as a type of St Agnes, rearticulated in the vernacular.

The plight of a closely related virgin saint, whose martyrdom is also recorded in the *Golden Legend*, offers more details concerning the hagiographic significance of Tarsiana in the *Libro de Apolonio* and, in particular, the girl's meeting with her father following her release from the brothel. In his treatise *De virginibus* (On Virgins), Ambrose recounts the passion of this unnamed martyr in the context of commemorating the feast of St Agnes and advocating a Christian alternative to the pagan office of "Vestal Virgins and the priestesses of the Palladium" (1997: 4.15).[11] The "Virgin of Antioch," like her counterpart from Rome, was ordered to renounce Christianity or face being sent to a bordello. The theologian maintains that such a virgin can be forced into prostitution but "cannot be made to commit fornication" (1997: 4.26). When visitors flock to the brothel, a scenario plays out that closely correlates with image of a *locus orationis* in the *Gesta Sanctae Agnes*. The maiden intones a prayer for liberation in which saints are petitioned in a manner that is similar to the litany inscribed on the Villamartín amulet. It provides a medieval example of what Frankfurter identifies as "structural resemblances, links, and overall relationships among *historiolae*":

> She raised her hands to heaven, as if she had come to a house of prayer and not a den of wantonness ... "O Christ, you tamed savage lions for the virgin Daniel's sake .... Susanna knelt down for punishment and triumphed over the adulterers ... now your temple itself is being threatened. Do not allow this *sacrilegious incest* (*incestum sacrilegii*) ... so that I who have

come to a place of defilement may depart a virgin." (1997: 2.4.27, emphasis mine)

The Virgin of Antioch's prayer is answered when a menacing soldier comes to copulate with the girl. Approaching her, he suddenly identifies the girl as his spiritual *soror* (or sister), and miraculously converts, becoming spiritually healed by the girl's words and presence: "I have come here as your brother to save my soul, not to destroy it ... Having come in as an adulterer, I shall, if you wish, go out as a martyr" (1997: 2.4.29). At the same time, a figurative relationship between father and daughter is also implied by Ambrose's use of the term *incestum*, as it forms part of his ongoing contrast between the ideals of Christian chastity and what he views as the unholy vows of the Vestals. Having left their fathers to become daughters of the Roman state, any sexual act committed with these priestesses was considered to be both incestuous and treasonous. Of course, the concept of a father-daughter relationship also marked the status of religious women in early Christian culture, insofar as paternal authority was transferred to bishops and other ecclesiastical officials and violations of vows continued to be viewed as acts of *incestum*.[12]

Apolonio's coming encounter with and recognition of his daughter implicates the Virgin of Antioch as a kind of hagiographic double of St Agnes. Both are prostituted virgins whose prayers of deliverance bring about a conversion in the writings of Ambrose and whose passion figures into the characterization and voice of Tarsiana in the *Libro de Apolonio*. Whereas the prefect's lecherous son in the *Gesta Sanctae Agnes* becomes a preacher after being brought back to life through the virgin's intercession, the soldier in *De Virginibus* is redeemed when he perceives his Christian kinship with the maiden from Antioch, following a petition that God save her from "sacrilegious incest." Similarly, Tarsiana's prayers are answered when the lustful Antinágora acknowledges that he has a daughter the same age, subsequent visitors to her brothel are "converted," and finally in the scene when Apolonio is brought to Mytilene by a storm and eventually identifies her as his offspring. The physical presence of these saintly virgins and their prayers for liberation from evil exert an apotropaic and exorcistic power, in each case, to resist and overcome malevolent adversaries who threaten their purity. Their legends could therefore be "tapped into" as effective *historiolae* in the production of amulets like the Villamartín ostracon. In accordance with Frankfurter's theory, invoking them can make things happen through the implication of a "mythic time," analogizing a "crisis" or "focal action," deriving power from part of a "culminating speech" that has been inscribed on the amulet (2001: 459, 462).

The Spanish poet begins his story by recounting how the first king of the biblical city, Antíoco, was possessed by the Devil, violated his maiden daughter, and then attempted to hide his crime in the obscure language of a riddle: "'la verdura del ramo escome la raýz, / de carne de mi madre engruesso mi seruiz'" ("the leafy branch consumes the root, from mother's flesh bred in my womb") (*Libro de Apolonio* 1987: 17ab).[13] The king of Antioch then offered his daughter's hand in marriage as a reward for solving this enigma and promised to punish incorrect solutions with death. Apolonio studies the riddle and arrives at the truth, but is forced into exile when he refuses to offer the incestuous king a more acceptable solution. This experience will feed into the hero's sense of growing uneasiness when Tarsiana comes to his bedside in Mytilene and entertains him with riddles that identify her as his child. Whereas the pagan daughter of Antíoco is represented by the shameful riddle of the branch that foreshadows the danger of incest inherent in this reunion, it has been demonstrated how Apolonio's daughter is closely associated with sacred language and a potent spiritual affinity with St Agnes and the Virgin of Antioch:

> "Otro mester sabía qu' es más sin pecado, / que es más ganançioso e es más ondrado ... meta yo estudio en essa maestría" ... El sermón de la duenya fue tan bien adonado / que el coraçon del garçon amansando .... ricamientre adobada ... priso huna viola buena e bien tenprada / e sallió al mercado violar por soldada / Començó hunos viesos e hunos sones tales / que trayén grant dulçor e eran naturales. / Finchiénse de omnes apriesa los portales, / non les cabién las plaças ... Quando con su viola houo bien solazado, / a sabor de los pueblos houo asaz cantado, / tornóles a rezar hun romançe bien rimado ... Cogieron con la duenya todos muy grant amor. (1987: 422c–430a)

> ("Knowing another office that is without sin, and more beneficial and honorable ... may I enter into the mastery of this profession" ... The lady's speaking was so artful / that the pimp's heart softened ... richly dressed up ... She took a fine and well tuned vihuela / and went to the market to play for money. She began with lyrics and notes that were full of sweetness and harmony. The market could not hold all the men, they filled up the plazas ... when she had sung and played for the joy and pleasure of all, she began to recite in well rhymed vernacular ... everyone had great love for the lady.)

This scene can be understood as a poetic restaging of Tarsiana's earlier power to bless and transform those who came to her with lust in their hearts. It may additionally emphasize that God has safeguarded her holiness, in accordance with a folkloric belief that stringed instruments would play out of tune in the presence of a deflowered virgin (Kelly 2000: 66).

Critics like J.C. Musgrave (1976) have observed that the girl's abilities as a minstrel relate to the composition of the *Libro de Apolonio* as a "romançe de nueua maestría" (new style of vernacular poetry) and its place in the context of the thirteenth-century poetic movement known as the *mester de clerecía* (1987: st. 1c).[14] Tarsiana becomes a kind of prosopopoeia for the poem itself, just as she is made to speak the voice of the Villamartín amulet. The earlier *Libro de Alexandre* was also identified as the product of a learned "mester ... sin pecado," but set apart from the kind of irregular metre and more corruptible "juglaría" heard in markets and plazas (1988: st. 2a). In the *Libro de Apolonio*, the topic of preserving virginity in the midst of a moral "shipwreck" comes to represent the purifying potency of the text's form and interpretation. The versification recorded on the Villamartín amulet can, in this sense, counteract evil through its sonorous recitation and performance, in keeping with Skemer's findings.

The redeeming power of poetry can be seen most clearly when Tarsiana comes to work in the court of Mytilene, and Antinágora sends her aboard Apolonio's newly arrived ship. The dejected, bedridden pilgrim has been told in Tarsus that his long-lost daughter succumbed to disease. Tarsiana's efficacious purity is here associated with the unadulterated artistry of the *Libro de Apolonio* itself:

Leuáronla al lecho ... Dijo ella: "Dios te salve, romero o merchante" ... Sue estrumente en mano parósele delante. / "Por mi solaz non tengas que eres aontado, / sy bien me conoscieses, tenerte yes por pagado, / qua non só juglaresa de las de buen mercado, / non lo é por natura, mas fágolo sin grado. Duenya só de linatge, de parientes honrrados, / mas dezir non lo oso por míos graues pecados;" ... mouyó en su viola hun canto natural, / coplas bien assentadas, rimadas a senyal; bien entendié el rey que no lo fazié mal. (1987: 489a–498b)

(They brought her to his bed ... She said: "God save you, pilgrim or merchant" ... She stood before him with her instrument in hand. / "Don't take my consolation as a dishonour; if you knew me well, you would be satisfied /

that I am not a cheap minstrel from the market. I do this not by nature, but unwillingly. I am a lady of lineage, of honourable family; / I dare not speak more for my grave sins" ... She began to play a harmonious song on her vihuela, with well-made lyrics, perfectly rhymed; the king surely understood that she had not performed badly.)

Most of the enigmas that Tarsiana poses to her father relate to the family's separation at sea, as in the case of "ships," "anchor," "fish," and "reeds."[15] Just as one part of the *historiola* narrative can elicit power from the whole, the one riddle inscribed on the tile can evoke the others. Tarsiana's mother, Luciana, was thought to have died giving birth to the girl at sea, was set adrift in a coffin, and washed up on a shore, where a physician restored her body with heated ointments. Clues to the riddle of the "sponge" conjure images of pregnancy ("prenyada") and immersion in water (1987: st. 514). In order to solve the enigma of Tarsiana's identity, Apolonio must hear and understand the allusion to her birth among the waves and the fish as a call for spiritual rebirth ("nací entre las ondas on naçen los pescados") (1987: 491c). Implicitly at stake is the recognition of her Christian identity, since "juglaresas" also could be of Jewish and Islamic background – and were in some cases exchanged between princes of differing faiths (Judith Cohen 2001). A convent is then built for the resurrected mother of Tarsiana, as opposed to the Pagan temple in the *Historia Apollonii*: "Por amor que toviese su castidat mejor, / fiziéronle vn monesterio ... sierua su eglesia e reze su salterio" (That she might cultivate her love of chastity, they made her a convent ... may she serve her church and sing her Psalter) (1987: 324ab, 325b).[16] Luciana's chaste devotion in this nunnery serves as a reflection of her daughter's holy presence in a brothel, reminiscent of St Agnes and the Virgin of Antioch transforming the spaces of their shipwrecked chastity. The voice on the Villamartín tile can be associated with virgin saints but also Tarsiana's connection to her mother's holiness. The fullness of the ostracon's potency could have implicated characters linked to Tarsiana within the story. This is another example of the power of mythic narratives referenced on amulets to imply "structural resemblances, links, and overall relationships" (Frankfurter 2001: 474). A subsequent enigma alludes to the fate of Apolonio when his ship capsized off the coast of North Africa, the same riddle that is partially inscribed on the Villamartín object, "de dentro ssó vellosa e de fuera raýda" (I am smooth on the inside and rough on the outside) (1987: 518a). Tarsiana's voice evokes the "ball" that Apolonio was playing with when Luciana's father first invited the shipwrecked exile to his palace in Pentapolis: "entré desbaratado / si non fuesse por essa ... non me oviera ayuntar conbidado" (I came dispossessed by the sea / were it not for this ball ... I wouldn't have been invited to the feast) (1987: 519bd). It was here that the hero first sang and played the vihuela with Luciana, and where she fell in love and chose him for her husband. The ball sets in motion a series of events that leads to Tarsiana's birth, and for this reason it provides what Frankfurter calls the "focal words of power" on the amuletic tile (2001: 462). We have seen how, according to Gwara (2005: 117–18), the same clue on the Villamartín object is used as a tactile reference to its inscription while also evoking the auditory presence of Tarsiana.

The climactic scene in the narrative comes when Apolonio recognizes the singing, riddling girl as his long-lost daughter:

Fuele amos los braços al cuello a echar / Ouosse ya con esto el rey a enssanyar, ouo con fellonía el braço a tornar ... començó de llorar, començo sus rencuras todas ha ementar ... Reuisco Apolonyo, plógol' de coraçón, / entendió las palabras ... Vio bien Apolonyo que andaua carrera ... diziendo: "¡Valme, Dios, que eres vertut uera!" / Prísola en sus braços con muy grant alegría diciendo: "Ay, mi fija, que yo por vos muría, agora he perdido la cuita ... ahora he plaçer; / siempre auré por ello a Dios que gradeçer." (1987: 527d–45d)

(She threw her arms around his neck / the king was enraged with this / and grievously twisted her arm.. she began to cry, recounting all of her sorrows ... Apolonio came back to life his heart was moved, / he understood her words ... Apolonio clearly perceived that he was on the path ... saying: "O God, you are true virtue!" he took her in his arms with great happiness, "O daughter, I was dying because you were lost, now my suffering is gone ... for this joy that I now have / I will always be grateful to God.")

Apolonio is in this manner redeemed by a saintly virgin whose characterized draws on the legends of St Agnes and the Virgin of Antioch. In the "blending" context of the Villamartín text, the hero might also be likened to Christians saving themselves in the *Poema de Fernán González* and even provide a model for how to hear and recognize the potent words of the amulet.

In Christian liturgy and drama, the Resurrection provided the subject of anagnorisis, as in the Easter trope, *Quem quaeritis*? (Whom do you seek) (Hardison 1965: 178).[17] Thomas Heffernan has even found that the ancient poetic device could have impacted the depiction of martyrdom in *Acts*, as Luke creates a likeness between the Passion of Christ and the death of St Stephen that extends beyond typology. What Heffernan has called the "associative faculty," allows for a "deeper recognition" that Stephen has "mysteriously become one with Christ" (1988: 115, 117). Scenes of reintegration in later hagiographic texts are also based on a discovery of inner oneness. As evidenced by the joy of Apolonio, this Christian discovery is meant to produce a reaffirmation of eternal truth (*gaudium*) and what has been aptly described as the "new departure" of conversion (Boulhol 1996: 158).[18]

In its use of hagiographic anagnorisis, the *Libro de Apolonio* is not only concerned with the anticipation of a final moment of saving recognition. In keeping with the example of virgin martyrs, the danger faced by Tarsiana enables her to exert power over Apolonio and other characters in the poem, causing them to be transformed by the "vertut uera." Tarsiana's performance reverses and exorcizes the evil logic of Antíoco's riddle: instead of hiding shameful acts in cryptic verses, the holy seduction of her song and enigmatic language of her riddle ultimately has the effect of unveiling truth and purifying and redeeming listeners.

On the tile of Villamartín, this kind of hagiographic deliverance and recognition is represented by a vernacular prayer in *cuaderna vía* and the inscribed clue "de fuera raýda ..." The textual amulet thus relates plight of Christians from the *Poema de Fernán González* and Apolonio's voyage to Mytilene as an ailing "romero" to the tradition of blessing travellers in life and death (the *Ordo commendationis animae* and *Itinerarium*). By assuming the poetic, revelatory voice of Tarsiana, the amulet might have drawn on her power to deliver suffering pilgrims like Apolonio – calling them back to their true selves and healing and reviving them, body and soul. In what remains of this discussion, I will briefly consider how the fourteenth-century *Libro de buen amor* redeploys the kind of amuletic prayer that was inscribed on amulets like the one from Villamartín, and also draws on the tradition of texts that can efficaciously speak.

Ironic Efficacy in the *Libro de buen amor*

Early critics imagined the *Libro de buen amor* as the poetic work of someone who had been imprisoned. This idea emerged as a result of the claim made by an early fifteenth-century scribe attached to the University of Salamanca, Alfonso de Paradinas, that the archpriest of Hita composed his work "seyendo preso por mandado del cardenal Don Gil, Arçobispo de Toledo" (while imprisoned by order of the Cardinal Lord Gil, Archbishop of Toledo) (1988: 467). Paradinas seems to have extrapolated this notion from a final episode in which the first-person narrator comically recounts how this reforming bishop forced the clergy of Talavera to renounce their concubines (1988: sts. 1690–1709). Such a reading appears to be corroborated by the archpriest's opening prayer for liberation from imprisonment. Whether or not the author was ever confined, scholars have shown that the first stanzas of his poem reproduce a version of the same vernacular prayer that we have seen in earlier *cuaderna vía* works and that was being used as an amuletic text during the first half of the fourteenth century:

> Señor Dios ... a Daniel sacaste ... saca a mí coitado desta mala presión ... a Santa Marina libreste ... a Santa Susaña ... da me tu misericordia, tira de mí tu saña. A Jonas el profeta del vientre de la ballena ... sacaste lo tú sano, así ... Mexías, tú me salva, sin culpa e sin pena. (1988: sts. 1–5)

> (Lord God ... who saved Daniel ...free me from this harsh prison ... you delivered St. Marina ... St. Susan ... grant me your mercy, save me from your wrath. From the belly of the whale ... you led Jonah safe and sound ... now save me, Messiah, without guilt and free of punishment.)

The archpriest's litany not only closely follows the *Commendatio animae* formula used on the Villamartín tile but also other textual amulets from the period, such as the incantatory repetition of holy names on an early fifteenth-century French roll studied by Skemer: "liberasti ... Danielem ... Jonam de ventri ceti ... Susannam de falso criminie ... de carcere libera me ... miserere mei ... absoluare me" (you delivered ... Daniel ... Jonah from the belly of the whale ... Susanna from false accusations ... liberate me from prison ... have mercy on me ... absolve me) (2006: 306). Skemer notes that this kind of textual "repackaging" for a *nomina* meant to be carried or worn on the body could offer hope from above to believers threatened by the dangers and temptations of the world (2006: 257). The *Libro de buen amor* engages in another kind of repackaging. Its narrator invokes the amuletic holy names at the start of a poem that, from start to finish, combines apotropaic language with ribald songs and the tales of a minstrel revelling in carnal attractions. What is more, as Veronica Menaldi has found, the poem makes numerous references to objects, charms, and potions that were used in magic among Christian as well as Muslim and Jewish communities in medieval Iberia (2015). Like the Villamartín tile, the poem offers a fourteenth-century reception of the *mester de clerecía* tradition – but one that creates burlesque reinterpretations of the power of sacred language.

This process begins with the narrator's ironic plea for liberation and its relationship not only to prayers inscribed on amulets but also found in thirteenth-century poems like the *Poema de Fernán González* and the work of Berceo, as we have seen. In his ground-breaking study, John K. Walsh (1979) was the first to suggest that the *Libro de buen amor* engages in a parodic restaging of the form and context of an existing *corpus* of *cuaderna vía* texts, including poems that have since been lost. His thesis has been accepted by scholars such as Julian Weiss, who more recently suggested that the archpriest's "protean and elusive persona itself develops a potential contradiction inherent in the narratorial presence of earlier didactic texts" (2006: 8). While Weiss does not fully develop this idea as his study deals exclusively with thirteenth-century productions, my findings suggest that such a contradictory quality can be seen in the archpriest's reworking of scenes from the *Libro de Apolonio*.

Not long after his parodic opening prayer, the narrator of the *Libro de buen amor* echoes a claim of earlier *mester de clerecía* poets: "trobas e cuento rimado: / es un desir fermoso e saber *sin pecado*" (songs and rhymed narrative: an eloquent composition and wisdom *without sin*) (emphasis mine, 1988: st. 15bc). Yet, in contrast to the sanctified presence of Tarsiana in the *Libro de Apolonio,* and on the Villamartín amulet, the archpriest's poem continues to bring together expressions of holiness and concupiscence. His initial plea for deliverance and later prayers are combined with obscene transpositions of sacred language, as when a chorus of clergy sing Psalmic verses from liturgy and divine office in praise of Eros, accompanied by minstrels playing vihuelas and a cacophony of other instruments.[19] The sinful effects of this performance can be contrasted with the efficacy of the purified performance of Tarsiana, as well as the healing effects believed to be produced by sonorous recitations of the amuletic texts during the Middle Ages, including those that cited verses from the Psalms (Skemer 2006: 153, 84–6).

While the *Libro de Apolonio* is compared to a saintly performer whose pure presence and voice blesses listeners – in the poem's narrative, and through the *historiola* power of the Villamartín amulet – the *Libro de buen amor* identifies itself as akin to "all instruments" – a composition performed by readers in ways that can bring a blessing or impart evil:

> De todos instrumentos yo libro só pariente, / bien o mal qual puntares, tal te dirá çiertamente, / qual tú desir quisieres, y fas punto y tente, / si me puntar sopieres, siempre me avrás en miente. (1988: st. 68–70)

> (I, the book, am akin to all instruments, / I will speak good or evil depending on how you play me, / in whatever way you wish me to speak, make your period and stop there; if you know how to interpret my notes, you will always have me in mind.)

As a speaking, self-identifying object, the book is presented as a riddle as well as a kind of all-encompassing instrument that plays the songs of pious and devious readers alike. Accordingly, its imagery combines the healing sounds of angelic harmony and Gregorian chanting with the *cantiones impudicas* of sin, the liberating song of David's harp with cursed noisemaking and the "bonds of inequity" (Acts 8:23). Whether or not the archpriest was directly influenced by the *Libro de Apolonio*, at stake in his masterpiece are the sanctifying claims of the earlier poetic school to which this anonymous work belonged, claims personified by Tarsiana. While the author of the *Libro de buen amor* seems to parody these claims and strip the language of earlier poets of its purifying effects, other readers continued to view *mester de clerecía* versification as a source of powerful authority. The *mester* was, in other words, not quite as antiquated as Walsh has suggested. In the case of the Villamartín ostracon, hundred-year-old poetry was still potent enough to provide an apotropaic voice in the production of an amuletic object.

We have observed how, on the tile, Tarsiana's first-person, self-referential riddle was applied to a tactile surface, being smooth on one side and roughly inscribed on the other side – so that the object is made to speak and self-identify. Interestingly, the *Libro de buen amor* also adopts the image of a ball to identify itself. It is even possible that the archpriest has deliberately reworked verses from the earlier poem. The crucial riddle of the ball in the *Libro de Apolonio*, as noted earlier, evokes the origins of Tarsiana – when the hero met her mother, after playing with a ball: "salliénse los donzelles fuera a deportar; / comenzaron luego la pellota jugar ... '*ando de mano en mano*, / tráenme escarnida; / quando van a yantar nengún non me conbida'" (The young men went outside to make sport; / and then began to play ball ... "*I am passed from hand to hand*, stripped leather, when it is time to eat no one invites me") (emphasis mine, 1987: sts. 144bc, 518cd).[20] In keeping with Tarsiana's status as a personification of the *Libro de Apolonio*'s poetry, and her identification through the riddle of the ball, the archpriest uses similar language to compare his text to a ball being passed around: "mi librete ... qual quier omne que lo oya, si bien trobar sopiere, / puede más ý añadir e enmendar, si quisiere; / *ande de mano en mano*, a quien quier quel pidiere; / como pella a las dueñas, tome lo quien podiere" (my little book ... whoever hears it, if he is a skilled poet, / let him add and revise if he wishes; / *may it be passed from hand to hand*, to whomever should ask for it; / like a ball thrown to the ladies; let it go to the one who can handle it) (emphasis mine, 1988: st. 1629). It has been shown how the ball from the *Libro de Apolonio* provides an amuletic voice on the surface of the Villamartín tile and does so through the *historiola* of Tarsiana's identification with St Agnes and Virgin of Antioch, martyrs who pled for deliverance from evil like the Castilians in the *Poema de Fernán González*. The voice identified with the ball is, as Frankfurter puts it, meant to "lock in" saintly power (2001: 463). In the *Libro de buen amor*, however, the text compares itself to a ball whose significance is designed to remain unfixed.

Tarsiana's first-person voice of the ball in the *Libro de Apolonio*, and the *Libro de buen amor*'s "instrumento" and "pella" comparisons, recall the many ways in which objects could be made to "speak" in the first person during the Middle Ages – apart from riddling.[21] In his study of the Villamartín amulet, Gwara has pointed out that wooden instruments were often carved with statements in the first-person that enabled them to "speak" of having been crafted from particular trees or attesting to the identity of their creators (2005: 133).[22] Over the course of the Middle Ages, words inscribed on church bells attained more of an amuletic power to bring about hoped-for effects in the sublunary world through *virtutes* believed to emanate from the heavenly sound of their ringing, as mentioned earlier: "Dissipo ventos, pello nociva, fleo mortua, consolo viva" (I drive away winds, I strike the injurious, I weep for the dead, I console the living) (Price, P. 1983: 128). Such inscriptions could also be taken from texts that modern readers identify as literary in nature, not unlike the case of the *mester de clerecía* poetry found on the Villamartín votive tile.[23] The examples that Skemer catalogues of a self-identifying "ego" voice include amuletic texts from England, France, and Spain (2006: 247, 287, 291, 299). These voices were inscribed to promote healing and protecting through the binding apotropaic *potentia* of their vocalization. The *Libro de buen amor* is the first text that I have found to be parodically evoking these powers, just as it subverts the power of God's ineffable name. It does so primarily by irreverently recontextualizing a prayer of deliverance from evil and the dangers of sin and playfully instrumentalizing its text to speak like an amuletic object.

At the same time, the power of hagiographic *historiola* could also be implicated.[24] Notably, the archpriest at one point falls in love with a saintly nun at prayer, and in her presence seems to be on the verge of receiving the same sort of redemptive blessing that softened the hearts of persecutors and transformed brothels into figurative convents in the lives of St Agnes, the Virgin of Antioch, and Apolonio's daughter. The narrator, plagued by lust, confesses his inability to escape from evil temptations: "¡Ay Dios! e yo lo fuese aqueste pecador, / que feçiese pentiençia desto" (Oh God! if only I could be that sinner, and do penance for that crime) (1988: 1501). Despite this admission, it appears as though the archpriest has resisted demonic urges and will undergone a true conversion – that is, until his hagiographic praise of the nun is quite suddenly reversed, and the poem once again turns away from the language of prayer:

> Mucho de bien me fiso con Dios en limpio amor ... Dios fue mi guiador. / Con mucha oraçión a Dios por mí rogava, / con la su abstinençia mucho me ayudaba / la su vida muy limpia en Dios se deleytava, / en locura del mundo nunca se trabajava. / Para tales amores son las religiosas, para rogar a Dios con obras piadosas, / que para amor del mundo mucho son peligrosas, / et son las escuseras, peresosas, mentirosas. (1988: sts. 1503c–1505)

> (She did me much good with God's pure love ... God was my guide. / With much prayer to God she pleaded for me, / with her chastity she helped me greatly; she lived innocently to take delight in God, and never strove for the madness of this world. For such loves religious women are well-suited, to petition God with pious deeds; / as worldly lovers they are dangerous, excuse-makers and lazy liars.)

In short, the "narrative powers" that the narrator seems to be drawing on for protection from sinful temptation are designed to fail. The archpriest cannot safeguard himself by extracting sacred, hagiographic, and potentially amuletic voices from earlier *mester de clerecía* poetry, as did the creator of the Villamartín amulet. Unlike characters in the *Libro de Apolonio* or users of this Castilian ostracon, the narrator of the *Libro de buen amor* fails to heal himself and instead turns the apotropaic textuality associated with earlier poets on its head. The *Libro de buen amor* is ironically efficacious only insofar as it provides a source of resistance to the prophylactic purity of clerical poetry. Its "yo" voice reinscribes the kind of amuletic language of prayer recorded on the Villamartín tile, imbuing it with the irrepressible lure of sin.

Chapter Four

The Bawd's Amulet

In the foothills of Gascony, not far from France's border with Spain, generations of matrons and midwives passed down a folded sheet of parchment torn from a fifteenth-century book of hours. The sheet contains a series of apotropaic prayers, along with a marginal illumination depicting the wound made in Christ's side during the crucifixion. As Skemer has observed, this kind of amulet or *nómina* was traditionally placed on the abdomen of women giving birth, in order to protect them and their newborns during delivery – but could also offer more general protection from harm and accidental death. In the case of the parchment found in Gascony, the life-sized side wound (known as the *apertione lateris Christi* and *mensura vulneris*) is ascribed the power to safeguard those who carry it from the piercing blades of their enemies – analogous to the point of the lance that pierced the Saviour's body – along with the dangers of childbirth and other common causes of an untimely demise:[1]

> Cy apres est la mesure de la benoiste playe du cousté Nostre Seigneur ... Et dit que celui ou celle qui a ladite mesure le jour verra ou sur soy la portera ne mourra de mort soudaine, ne en feu, ne en eaue, ne tempeste, ne trait, ne lance, ne cousteau, ne espee, ne aucuns ennemis ne lui pourront nuyre. Et si femme la porte sur elle quant enfantera legierement se delivrera.

> (This is the measure of the holy side wound of Our Lord ... It is said that he or she that is born under the protection of this measure or that wears it on his or her body, that person will not die of sudden death, whether by fire, water, tempest, arrow, spear, knife, sword nor by any enemy. If a woman wears this measure during labor, she will give birth easily.)

The inscription goes on to claim that this measure, originally taken from Christ's body, was – like the Heavenly Letter – brought from Constantinople by Charlemagne, "affin que aucun ne lui peust nuyre en bataille" (so that he might never be harmed in battle) (fol. 2).

Also kept in a silk bag together with the parchment was a printed ribbon reading, "La medida de nuestra señora de Montserrat" (The Measure of Our Lady of Montserrat). Similar measures objects continued to be sold at the Catalan shrine well into the nineteenth century, and many examples survive in museums and private collections. In earlier centuries, Marian statues and other saints associated with maternity or labour pains – such as Margaret, who was believed to have miraculously emerged from the body of a dragon – were also measured by visitors who brought with them "hilos y cordones" (threads and cords) that could be used as birthing girdles (Herradón Figueroa 2001, 41). It was believed that such *medidas*, similar to tapes employed by seamstresses and tailors, acquired a supernatural potency by capturing the dimensions of a miraculous icon or other sacred object. Medieval pilgrims and devotees were known to create second-hand contact relics by, for instance, wrapping a thread or cord around a pillar in Jerusalem where Christ was purportedly scourged. Some *medidas* were believed to have appeared miraculously. For example, a girdle now preserved in the cathedral of Tortosa was legendarily presented to a medieval priest, and for centuries after employed as an amulet in childbirth (Christian 1981a: 53–4).[2] A similar medieval cult of the Virgin's *cinta* arose in Huelva. In addition to measurements taken on site and then recorded on parchment amulets, broadside paper *medidas* promising to ease childbirth had been circulating in Spain since the 1480s (Skemer 2006: 247). During the Counter-Reformation, these practices were repeatedly condemned by local authorities, such as the 1565 Council of Valencia: "Que nadie mida las imágenes de los santos con hilos o cualquiera otra cosa para llevar las medidas ... pues todo esto respira superstición" (no one shall measure images of saints with threads or anything else to take measurements ... for all of this has an air of superstition) (Christian 1981b: 246).[3] In spite of repeated prohibitions, it is clear that generations of midwives continued to employ *medidas* from Montserrat and other peninsular shrines together with images of the side wound accompanied by amuletic inscriptions. The objects in Gascony provide evidence of how an apotropaic, curative power was attributed to measurements of the Holy Mother's body, together with life-sized representations of the opening in her son's side. The vulnerary image on the Gasconese parchment is also suggestive of a mouth with full lips (Figure 10).[4] When positioned vertically instead of horizontally, the image instead seems to resemble the vulva.

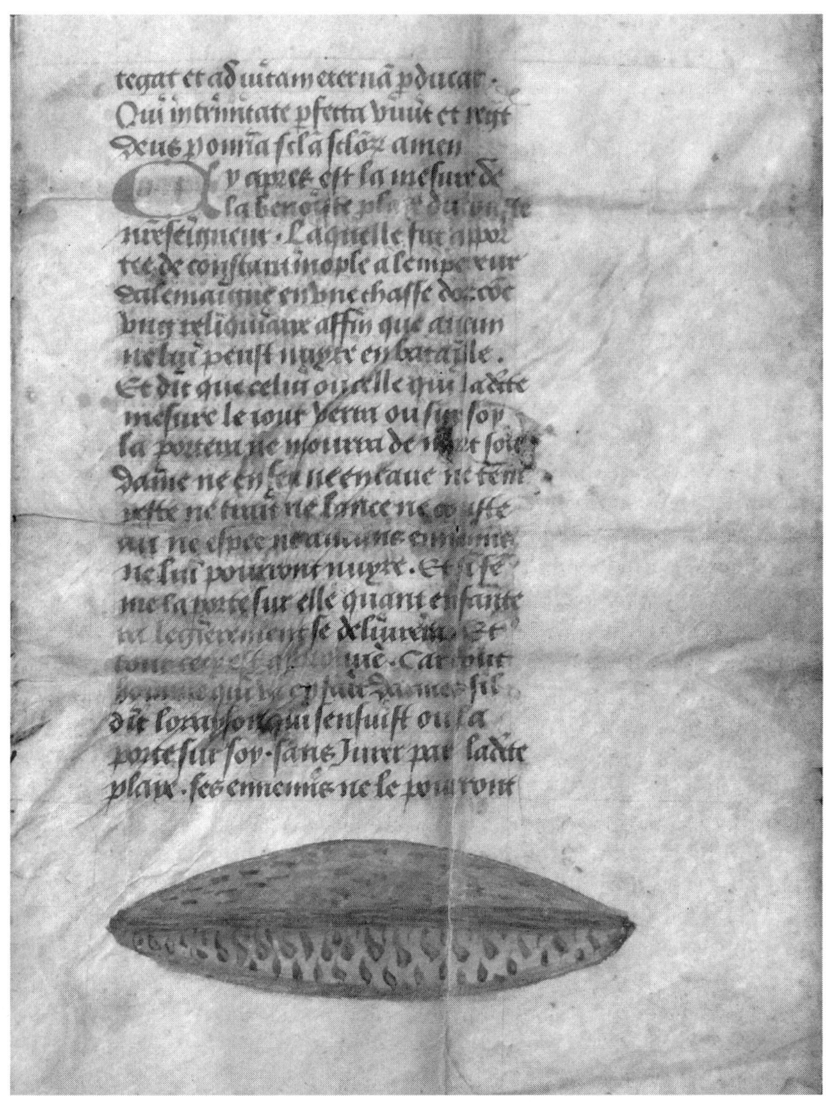

Figure 10. Birthing amulet. Parchment folio removed from a fourteenth-century French prayer book. Princeton University Library, Ms. 138.44.

Bynum has found that this visual parallel reflects its parturient function: "identification of the side wound with the vagina is most obvious in objects ... that use it as an amulet against difficult childbirth...
Depictions of the side wound were bound onto the laboring mother
in the hope that one gaping slit would aid another in opening" (2011:
197–200). The amuletic potency of Christ's wound to encourage vulvar
dilation not only deploys the homeopathic axiom *similia similibus curentur* (like cures like) but also relates to medieval interpretations of the
Saviour's side being "opened up" (*aperuit*) to release Eucharistic blood
and water (Bynum 2011: 200; John 19:34).[5]

Historians have also begun to consider the potentially erotic and even
queer valence of depictions of Christ's labial, vulvar wound during the
late Middle Ages. For example, the work of Wolfgang Riehle and Karma
Lochrie (1997) calls attention to the likely punning of the Latin *vulnus*
and *vulva* in James of Milan's thirteenth-century *Stimulus Amoris*. This
influential Franciscan portrays union with Christ as entering into the
vulnerary opening and as "vulnus vulneri copulatur" (wound coupled
with wound) (Riehle 1981: 46). Sarah Alison Miller has studied similar
imagery in the mystical *Showing of Love* of Julian of Norwich. In the
writings of this fourteenth-century female mystic, the way to salvation
"resides in the openness of Christ's birthing wound ... for children to
come up into him," leading to an "affective encounter with the wound"
that "includes her desire to penetrate ... at the site where bodies exit in
childbirth ... a boundary zone between fertility and eroticism" (2010:
122–4). More recently, Bynum has provided evidence that this cult was
not immune from bawdy reinterpretations. In particular, she considers
a kind of late-medieval pilgrim badge that features erect penises holding aloft a crowned and seemingly aroused vulva, similar to the depictions of the *mensura vulneris* I have been discussing (Figure 11).[6] Bynum
compares these to devotional imagery from a book of hours that depicts
angels lifting the side wound heavenward from an empty tomb.

In this chapter we will see how the old bawd of Fernando de Rojas's
La Celestina exerts an incantatory power through her erotic evocations of the lover's wound. The efficacy of her verbal appeals will be
shown to subvert the meaning of verses devoted to the wounding of
Christ in the original and revised preliminaries and epilogues of the
late fifteenth-century masterpiece. At the same time, in her capacity
as a midwife and purported witch, Celestina draws on the supposed
material potency of a textual amulet, along with a fetishized cord and

Figure 11. Phalluses carry a mandorla vulva in procession. Lead pilgrim
badge, c. 1400 (photo: Jean-Gilles Berizzi/RMN-Grand Palais/
Art Resource, NY).

thread – suggestive of objects used to measure devotional statues and
contact relics at shrines, and apotropaically wrapped around the bodies of women as they gave birth. In the second part of this chapter, I
will discuss the amuletic connotations of woodcuts printed in Francisco
Delicado's early sixteenth-century *La Lozana andaluza,* a dialogue whose
title character is explicitly based on Rojas's bawd. Whereas Celestina
utilizes language and material objects in a way that subversively evokes
the life-giving dilation of the *apertione lateris,* the power of incantation
and fictional representation of amulets in the story of Lozana will come
to signify an opening up of the mouth of Hell as demonic forces are
summoned and unleashed at the end of the narrative.

Wounds, Fetishes, and Incantatory Threads in the *Celestina*

Rojas first published his work as a *Comedia* in 1499 and three years later
released an expanded and revised *Tragicomedia*. The earlier version
included a preliminary poem appearing immediately before the text
that contemplates the *Arma Christi* (instruments of the Passion) along
with the wounding and crucifixion of Christ:

> Temamos Aquél que espinas y lança,
> açotes y clavos su sangre vertieron.
> La su santa faz herida escupieron …
> a cada santo lado consitió un ladrón.
> Nos lleve, le ruego, con los que creyeron. (1994: 75)

> (May we fear the One whose blood was spilled with thorns and lance,
> lash and nails. They spit in his holy wounded face … On each holy side he
> countenanced a thief. May he take us, we pray, with those who believed.)

In the tragicomedy, the same verses are moved to the end of the narrative, where they precede an epilogue that was written by the editor.
This version of the poem also includes alterations urging readers not to
"fear," but rather to love ("amemos") their wounded Saviour and identify the Good Thief positioned on His right side ("buen ladrón, de dos
que a sus santos lados pusieron") (1994: 343).[7] In the same place where
the original preliminary poem appeared in the comedy – with its evocation of soldiers piercing, flogging, and lancing Jesus – the 1502 edition also inserts new verses that caution unchaste lovers: "a otros que
amores dad vuestros cuidados. / limpiad ya los ojos, los ciegos errados …
no os lance Cúpido sus tiros dorados" (give your care to something
other than love affairs. Wipe your eyes, you who are lost and blind …
let not Cupid fling his gilded arrows at you) (1994: 75–6).
  Critics have tended either to emphasize the potential didacticism
of this poetry or dismissed it as an unconvincing gesture of religious
conformity. Setting aside these questions, my purpose is to unpack the
cultural resonance of these verses to show how their sacred meaning
is corrupted and demystified by the action of the tragicomedy. Scholars
have noticed that the two poems in the *Celestina* contrast the wounding cupidity of worldly paramours with the *caritas* or redemptive love
of Christ suffering on the cross, similar to earlier Spanish texts such
as the *Libro de buen amor*.[8] Imagery of a lover experiencing would-be

christological wounding can also be found in a bestselling text that influenced Rojas, Diego de San Pedro's 1492 *Cárcel de amor* (Prisoner of Love). What has not been considered is the deeper significance in Rojas's tragicomedy of implicating a relationship between the injuries made by the lance ("lança") and the arrows of Cupid ("os lance ... con tiros"). We have seen how the introductory verses warn against the characteristic blindness of the pagan god and his followers ("ciegos errados"). This anticipates the concluding poem, since the lateral flow from the body of Christ ("su sangre vertieron") legendarily restored sight to the unnamed soldier who wielded the lance, as well as other, figuratively blinded sinners ("limpiad ya los ojos"). The converted soldier came to be known as Longinus, derived from the Greek word "λόγχη" (longche) for lance.[9] In medieval visual art, the penitent thief on the right side of the cross faces the salvific aperture made by Longinus, in some cases opening his mouth to receive Eucharistic blood flowing from the *Corpus Christi*. On the left side, the unbelieving "sinister" thief turns away from the saving blood, his eyes forever closed in death.[10]

Devotional imagery from the late Middle Ages further clarifies the potential meaning of the wounded and crucified Christ making an appearance at the end of the tragicomedy, "por que nos lleve con el buen ladrón / de dos que a sus santos lados pusieron" (so that we might be brought with the good thief, of the two placed on either holy side of Him) (1994: 236–7). Bynum has found that the final injury caused by Longinus's lance was understood as a kind of a sacred *"pars pro toto"* that stood for all wounding and bloodshed during the Passion (2010: 97). Manuscript illuminations and woodcuts from the period characteristically separate and foreground the *apertio lateris*, situating previously inflicted wounds and the *Arma Christi* as a framing background. By the time Rojas wrote his verses, it was also common to depict the synecdochic, mandorla-shaped *vulnus* as an opening in the sacred heart of Jesus.[11] The pain of the weapon entering His body was not felt by Jesus, who had just died on the cross, but instead experienced by His mother. In the Gospel of Luke, Simeon prophesized that Mary's soul would be pierced, and in John the Saviour's Passion is compared to birth pangs (2:34–5, 16:21–2). For example, in one of Berceo's *Milagros de Nuestra Señora*, the maternal suffering of the Holy Mother during the Passion is said to be renewed when Toledan Jews purportedly crucified a wax effigy of her Son, reopening His side wound (2003: no. 18). Specifically, the Virgin was thought to have suffered Longinus's stab to the heart as if undergoing the labour pains that she had miraculously been spared during the nativity.[12] This widely held belief no doubt contributed to the supposed efficacy of the side wound on birthing amulets like the Gascony parchment. Marian miracle collections from the Middle Ages like those of Berceo and Alfonso X describe how parturient mothers and sinful daughters of Eve were spared from labour pains, not to mention the often fatal complications of delivery, through the Virgin's intercession – including, in one case, a seemingly amuletic allusion to the Holy Mother's sleeve physically covering and protecting a woman's body during a dangerous childbirth (2003: nos. 19, 21; 1986–9: vol. 1, cantigas 7, 89, vol. 2, 184).

Popular contemplative works, such as Ambrosio de Montesino's Spanish translation of the *Vita Christi* (published the same year as the revised *Celestina*), urge Christian readers to imagine themselves – like Mary and her son – being pierced in the heart by a lance of *caritas*.[13] At the end of tragicomedy, a kind of imitative participation in the Passion seems to be implicated by the call to love "Aquél" whose blood was spilled by the "lança." Analogous examples of affective piety consistently ask the audience to reflect on the wound in Christ's side and heart as an aperture made from the inside out and a pathway forged for their salvation. Not unlike earlier-mentioned mystics like Julian of Norwich, Montesino portrays this as a quasi-vulvic orifice opening up for the rebirth of sinners while simultaneously providing entry and a loving refuge within. He describes how Christ, as the true God of love, pierces the hearts of his spiritual lovers:

> Una grande llaga … de nuestra renovación y de nuestro nuevo nascimiento … fue abierta … [para que] podamos entrar … por la puerta del costado a sus sacratissimas entrañas … por la puerta de amor … te suplico que llagues mi coraçón con la lança de tu caridad … [que] en la abertura de tu divino coraçón abriste … la puerta de la vida … aunque esta llaga … no la ya sentido nuestro Salvador … la sintió la benaventurada virgen su madre … esta madre sancta fue … amortecida … deste abrimiento … se llaga y lastima … nuestro coraçón para compadecer y amar. (1608: fols. 133–5)

> (A large wound … of our renewal and our new birth … was opened … [so that] we may enter … through the side portal to His most sacred inside … by the doorway of love … I plead that you wound my heart with the lance of your charity … [that] in the aperture of your divine heart you opened … the doorway of life … although this wound … was not felt by the Saviour … the blessed virgin felt it … this holy mother was … in a

swoon ... from this opening ... wounded and injured ... is our heart with compassion and love.)

A number of writers connected the wounded heart of Christ with the myth of Cupid in ways that can shed further light on the tragicomedy's combination of poems. Mythographers, theologians, and poets reinterpreted this Greco-Roman god through a process of Christianizing allegoresis. In doing so, they brought together imagery from the amatory works of Ovid along with readings of Song of Songs and the gospel: "vulnerasti cor meum soror mea sponsa ... Deus caritas est" (you wounded my heart, my sister and bride ... God is Love) (Cant. 4.9, John 4.16). Like Cupid, medievals pictured Christ not just as receiving, but also inflicting amorous wounds with weapons variously described as arrows, a lance, or a sword. An early example can be found in Hugo of St Victor's twelfth-century *De laude caritatis* (In Praise of Charity). First Christ, then His followers are pierced with arrows of Love, as if assaulted by the son of Venus: "many now bear your arrows fixed in their innermost hearts and desire to have them pierce yet more deeply. For they neither grieve nor blush to have received your wounds" (qtd. in Newman 2003: 38). Similarly, St Bonaventure composed a thirteenth-century prayer in which language associated with Cupid and his victims is applied to Jesus, Mary, and individual Christians: "wound, o most sweet Lord Jesus, the inner depths of my soul with the most sweet and salutary wound of thy love ... thy passion pierced the soul of Mary ... hasten, hasten, Lord Jesus, and wound me" (qtd. in Auerbach 1993: 76).[14]

Boccaccio's influential *De genealogia Deorum Gentilium* (On the Genealogy of Pagan Gods, c. 1374) draws on these traditions, distinguishing the pagan lust and pathologized lovesickness incited by Eros or *Cupido* (Greek and Latin words for desire) from the god's Christianized reinterpretation as a lover inflicting a redemptive wound of *Caritas* (1951: vol. 2, 453–4).[15] In sacred history, the former had long been associated with the cupidity of Eve and her iniquitous progeny, punished with labour pains, mortality, and what Augustine characterized in his *Confessions* as a *vulnus* of Original Sin that could only be healed by Christ (1841: Bk. 9, 2.3). Accordingly, the latter was identified with Mary, the new, sinless Eve who only felt the birth pangs of redemption when a lance was driven into the heart of Jesus, bringing to fulfilment her painless delivery of a Saviour sent to conquer death.[16] Early readers of the *Celestina* who were familiar with such traditions could have readily applied these connotations to the versified warning, "nos os lance Cúpido sus tiros dorados," as it relates to the sanctioned god of love being wounded by the "lança."

As we will see, the religio-cultural context that I have been discussing is not just applicable to Rojas's verses but also relevant for understanding the development of eroticized vulnerary imagery in the *Celestina* as a whole. In the first act, Calisto claims to have been wounded by love after following his hawk into a private garden where he has a brief encounter with a maiden named Melibea: "aquella ardiente llaga que la cruel frecha de Cupido me ha causado" (that burning wound that the cruel arrow of Cupid has caused me) (1994: 136). In hopes of materially benefiting from the situation, his servant Sempronio promises to send for the aged procuress, Celestina. Calisto's other servant Pármeno, having been raised in her house, tries to persuade the lovesick falconer of her treachery. While ostensibly working as a seamstress, she "restores" deflowered virgins in order to prostitute them: "los virgos ... curaba de punto ... tenía ... unas agujas delgadas de pellejeros e hilos de seda" (the virgins ... she cured by stitching ... she had ... some thin needles for leatherworking and silk threads) (1994: 112). When Celestina is nevertheless summoned, it is revealed that she – in keeping with accusations against surgeons – plans to increase her profit by allowing the lover's figurative wound to fester. She seems to delay infinitely the healing process before providing a remedy: "dañan en los principios las llagas y encarecen el prometimiento de la salud ... y nunca la llaga viene a cicatrizar" (at first they aggravate the wounds and so make the promise of health more dear ... and never does the wound come to be cured) (1994: 107, 121).[17] The infamous healer later brags about her ability to stitch cracked maidenheads. Before applying metaphorical sutures, Celestina looks forward to a prolonged diagnosis of Melibea's matching love wound. The old bawd specifically brags about her gynecological needlework: "pocas virgenes ... en esta ciudad que hayan abierto tienda a vender, de quien yo no haya sido corredora de su primer hilado ... no hay cirujano que a la primera cura juzque la herida" (few virgins ... in this city have set up shop to sell their wares, for whom I was not the broker of their first stitching ... no surgeon can judge a wound from the first dressing) (1994: 141, 143). The significance of amorous wounding extends beyond the tragicomedy's characteristic parody of courtly love or humanistic Ovidian and Petrarchan imitations.[18] Through this pattern of imagery, the first part of the tragicomedy creates a cupiditous link between *vulnus* and *vulva* that will reach its climax in later acts, perverting the significance of christological wounding in the epilogue.

Prior to visiting Melibea, Celestina performs a hex with a textual amulet and thread. The purpose of the ritual is ostensibly to cast a *philocaptio* spell that can bewitch Melibea's will, causing her to fall in love with Calisto. Invoking Pluto and the Furies, she appears to draw power from the inscription on the paper *nómina* and calls on a poisonous serpent to enter into the skein of thread.[19] This image recalls a description in the prologue of a maternal viper from the bestiary tradition who takes pleasure in consuming and fatally constricting the body of her mate, but then dies while giving birth after her vengeful newborn rips through the belly of its mother (1994: 78–9). The old bawd's conjury of material objects then evokes the ensnaring and opening of a love wound in Melibea's heart: "por la virtud y fuerza de estas bermejas letras ... por la gravedad de aquestos nombres y signos que en este papel se contienen ... este hilado ... te envuelvas en ello ... quede enredada ... su corazón ... y se le abras y lastimes" (by the power and force of these crimson letters ... for the gravity of those names and signs written on this paper ... this thread ... wrap yourself in it ... may it ensnare ... her heart ... and may you tear open and injure it) (1994: 147–8). As Jean Dangler has pointed out, these and other objects and substances in Celestina's house had long been employed by traditional healers but increasingly raised suspicions of witchcraft during the fifteenth century (2001: 90–1).[20] We have seen how the combination of a textual amulet and length of thread were commonly used in the birthing kits. The description of "bermejas letras" and "nombres y signos" on Celestina's *nómina* – said to be written in bat's blood – corresponds with *nomina sacra* and symbols written in red ink, as well as real blood stains found on medieval birthing amulets that also feature representations of the side wound.[21]

Such parallels come as no surprise, since Celestina is known as a midwife, among her other trades. She apparently learned these skills – as well as practices associated with witchcraft – from her mentor and Pármeno's mother, Claudina: "fue su principal oficio partera" (her principle trade was that of a midwife) (1994: 197). For this reason, when the go-between returns from her first interview with Melibea, Sempronio asks her, "dime si tenemos hijo o hija" (tell me if we have a son or daughter) (1994: 172). In another scene, Celestina shows off her famous skills in the art of gynecological healing. By therapeutically manipulating the genitals of Pármeno's beloved prostitute, Areusa, she provides

(homoerotic) relief from what was known as the "mal de madre" or
wandering womb, an ailment that – according to medical authorities –
could be definitively cured only by having sex and giving birth.[22] In
the medieval imaginary, this perceived problem of the restless uterus
was seen as a "monstrous synecdoche for woman and her dangerous
appetites … for childbearing" (McAvoy 2003: 57). Apart from wrapping
sacred apotropaic thread around parturient mothers, Celestina's *hilado*
might be used to tie off umbilical cords. And, of course, her skill with
slender needles designed for sewing animal skins could be employed
in closing incisions, in addition to reconstructing hymens.[23] Sealing and
unsealing the power of inscribed amulets also commonly involved sewing and opening stitches, whether made from paper or parchment skin.
Such practices are condemned in the *Directorium Inquisitorum*, written
a century before *Celestina*. They would also be denounced in Ciruelo's
earlier-cited treatise on superstition, which was completed not long
after the tragicomedy: "las nóminas … las ponen a las mugeres que
están de parto … algunos dizen que la nómina … ha de estar cosida
con sigro, o con hilo de tal o tal suerte" (*nóminas* … they put them on
women who are giving birth … some say the amulet has to be sewn with
silk, or with certain kinds of thread) (1978: 85–6). Typical uses of thread
together with *nóminas* suggest that Celestina's spell can be understood
as in some way linking tools of midwifery and female healing with the
power to treat Melibea's amorous wounding.

This seems even more likely, considering the old bawd's use of Melibea's *cordón*. Her girdle is said to have come into contact with and presumably enveloped holy objects and icons in Rome and Jerusalem ("es
fama que ha tocado todas las reliquias que ay en Roma y Jerusalem"),
similar to the *medidas* and *cordones* employed by healers like the midwives who preserved the Gascony birthing kit (1994: 164). Claiming
that Calisto suffers from a debilitating toothache – a euphemism for
erotic lovesickness – Celestina convinces Melibea to let her borrow the
cordón and also requests an amuletic *ensalmo* or written curative prayer
to St Apollonia.[24] In addition to attributes of the side wound, uses of the
objects that I have been discussing once again correspond with evidence
for the production and circulation of particular kinds of amulets during
the late fifteenth century. For example, Skemer cites legal testimony from
the 1470s in which a French book illuminator was said to have in his
possession a "toothache amulet dedicated to St Apollonia, purchased at
a tavern … and worn around the neck … a love amulet written on a small
piece of virgin parchment with cabalistic signs … and a paper sheet with

the painted image of the Measure of Christ" (2006: 163). In subsequent scenes from the tragicomedy, the efficacious presence believed to have been captured by the *cordón*, as Gerli has suggested, is fetishized when Calisto materially and "linguistically collapses Melibea and her girdle in his imagination" (2011: 93). When the object is first brought to him, the suitor begins his perverse veneration: "¡Oh bienaventurado cordón, que tanto poder y merecimiento tuviste de ceñir aquel cuerpo ... ceñidero de aquella angélica cintura!" (Oh blessed girdle that took such power and worthiness from being wrapped around that body ... encircler of that angelic waist) (1994: 186–7). Substituting the binding of Melibea's body for the capturing of a relic's presence and power, both the girdle and Calisto's words are shown to be empty signs.[25] They are corruptible objects of desire as opposed to material linguistic modes of access to divine transcendence. As Gerli puts it, Calisto is "seduced by the very pleasure and delight he takes in words, substitutions, and exchanges; a torrent of signs and signals that simultaneously produce delectation and frustration" (2011: 94).

Undoubtedly, the contact relic can also be understood as a fetish in the original, etymological sense of the word – that is, in accordance with the meaning attached to the late medieval Portuguese *feitiço* as a created thing or utterance believed (in this case, falsely) to exert a supernatural, binding force over another. This kind of belief is mimicked when Calisto personifies the object: "conjúrote ... por la virtud del gran poder que aquella señora sobre mí tiene" (I conjure you ... for the virtue and great power that lady has over me) (1994: 187).[26] Apart from a parody of the cult of relics, as Santiago López-Ríos (2012) has recently shown, Calisto's fetish brings to mind the kind of "plastic love" that the nineteenth-century psychologist Alfred Binet famously identified as a tendency to deify the beloved and to treat body parts or items of clothing as if they constitute the whole (1887). For this reason, the lovesick worshipper calls on the girdle's "poder ... de rodear y ceñir con debida reverencia aquellos miembros ... tienes abrazados. ¡Oh qué secretos habrás visto de aquella excelente imagen!" (power ... from having enclosed and bound with befitting reverence those members ... you embrace. Oh what secrets you must have seen of that worthy image!) (1994: 187). The potency assigned to girdles like the one that wrapped around Melibea's waist and abdomen is thus subverted in the tragicomedy to make present a sexual as opposed to a sacred materiality. In this way, Calisto's veneration and conjuring of the *cordón* eroticizes and demystifies the force that girdles such as the ribbon found at Gascony were believed to exert over the womb – that is, through the virtue of Christ's side wound as a measured amuletic figure of *pars pro toto* and vulvic *similia similibus curentur*.

Its efficacy is again implicated in the seamstress Celestina's final interview with Melibea, who at long last agrees to surrender herself to Calisto with the words, "en mi cordón le llevaste envuelta la posesión de mi libertad" (in my girdle you took possession of my freedom) (1994: 245). This dialogue begins with wordplay associating the dangerous openness and uncontainability of female speech with the dilatory sexuality of women in fifteenth-century culture. The female characters are made to speak in a way that brings to mind Patricia Parker's description of the gendered rhetoric of *dilatio*: "its verbal form meant not only to expand ... or spread ... but also to put off, postpone, prolong, or protract" (1987: 182). This context, in my view, sheds light on Melibea's growing impatience with Celestina during their most pivotal scene together. Repeatedly, she complains of the go-between's dilatory rhetoric: "sin más dilatar ... cuanto más dilatas la cura, tanto más me acrecientas y multiplicas la pena y pasión ... me muero con tu dilatar" (the more you delay the cure, the more you increase and multiple my shame and passion ... I am dying from your delaying) (1994: 161, 241–2). Fittingly, Melibea echoes God's command in the Garden of Eden to procreate, "crescite et multiplicamini," followed by the punishment of Eve for eating the forbidden fruit: "I will multiply thy sorrows" (*multiplicabo aerumnas tuas*), and thy conceptions: in sorrow shalt thou bring forth children" (Gen. 1:28).

Her blasphemous allusion contributes to the ongoing subtext of parturition with its connection to the linguistic and corporal openness of the daughters of Eve in medieval culture, and in relation to belaboured discursive delay and prolonged amorous suffering. As a subversion of Mary's role in miraculously easing and safeguarding childbirth, Celestina thus urges Melibea to speak "openly," so that her logotherapeutic "medicine" can take effect: "habla ... abiertamente ... el silencio tregua entre tu llaga y mi melecina" (silence gets between your wound and my medicine) (1994: 240–1).[27] Melibea has come to see her malady and its remedy as a wounding "birth" that can only be cured by opening up verbally to her healer: "mucho has abierto el camino por donde mi mal te pueda especificar ... nuevemente nacido en mi cuerpo ... lo que tú tan abiertamente conoces, en vano trabajo por te lo encubrir" (you have greatly opened up the path through which I can specify my ailment ... newly born in my body ... that which you so openly know, in vain I work to conceal from you) (1994: 241, 245). The dialogue continues to figure the cure for Melibea's lovesickness as a kind of delivery. Celestina plays the metaphorical role of a midwife leading her patient through the dilation of labour, complete with torn flesh and a risk of death that is simulated by Melibea's swooning:[28]

> [Mel.] lastime mi cuerpo; aunque sea romper mis carnes para sacar mi dolorido corazón ...
>
> [Cel.] Tu llaga es grande, tiene necesidad de áspera cura ...
>
> [Mel.] más agradable me sería que rasgases mis carnes y sacases mi corazón ...
>
> [Cel.] no rasgaré yo tus carnes para le curar... es ... una agradable llaga ... dulce y fiera herida, una blanda muerte ... Dios da la llaga, tras ella envía el remedio ... al mundo nacida una flor que de todo esto te delibre ... Calisto ... [aside] qué descaecimiento ... si muere, matarme han ... ya no podrá sufrirse de no publicar su mal y mi cura... [a Lucrecia] ¡verás amortecida a tu señora entre mis manos! baja presto por un jarro de agua. (1994: 242–5)

> ([Mel.] lacerate my body, even if you must tear open my flesh to remove my suffering heart ...
>
> [Cel.] your wound is large, it will need a rough cure ...
>
> [Mel.] it would be easier for me if you were to rip open my flesh and remove my heart ...
>
> [Cel.] I will not tear your flesh to cure you ... it is ... a pleasant wound ... sweet and fierce your injury, a gentle death ... God gives the wound, and then sends its remedy ... born to the world is a flower that will deliver you from all of this: ... Calisto ... [aside] what a fainting heart ... if she dies, they will surely kill me ... no longer will it be tolerable to not make public her malady and my remedy ... [to Lucrecia] ¡you will see your lady dying in my hands! quickly go down and get a pot of water.)

Even the call for water coincides with a common description of midwives practicing their trade during the late Middle Ages (Macdonald 2009: 33). Ironically, Melibea's agonizing experience is reminiscent of the earlier-mentioned image of Mary undergoing what are perceived as labour pains and the wounding of her heart, causing her to faint as the vulnerary-vulvic opening is made in Christ's side. Medieval sermons on the *apertione lateris*, commonly link this moment to God's creation of Eve by removing a rib from Adam's side, enabling humankind to "increase and multiply."[29]

We have seen how the meaning of the lover's wounded heart was reinterpreted and allegorized during the Middle Ages by likening the arrow of Cupid to the lance of Longinus, and how this tradition sheds light on verses found in the preliminaries and epilogue of Rojas's masterpiece. As previously discussed, writers from the period imagined *cupiditas* being replaced by divine *caritas* through the release of saving Eucharistic blood and water, forming a vulnerary mouth to speak the Word and an apotropaic womb to issue new life and provide a refuge for sinners. This mythographic tradition and its close connection to girdles and other textual birthing amulets sheds light on why Celestina portrays Melibea's *vulnus* and its remedy as if the result of a mystical wounding, "sin te romper las vestiduras se lanzó en tu pecho el amor" (without penetrating your clothes love was flung into your heart) (1994: 244). Her promotion of Calisto as Melibea's final cure at the same time recalls the old bawd's notoriety as a heterodox midwife and a gynecological healer who specializes in the surgical repair of deflowered maidens. Celestina's rhetoric of *dilatio*, evocation of the "llaga grande," and recurrent natal allusions combine to suggest that the power of Melibea's *cordón* as a potential birthing girdle is redeployed in the bawd's patter. This material object not only comes to signify the capturing of her will – and the fetishizing extremes of Calisto's desire – but suggests an erotic as well as a maternal dilation. Such a link between vulnerary and vulvic opening and closing seems even more likely, considering the way in which Celestina rhetorically conjures and inflames carnal passion by referring to her logotherapy as stitches – stitches that are perceived by Melibea as the suturing of one wound and the bursting open of another in anticipation of coital healing in a subsequent act of the tragicomedy. In these passages, the lover's piercing and lancing is at once aggravated and treated by the midwife's figurative needle, equated to the instrument of a surgeon or physician. A verbal penetration of wounded flesh is accomplished through her evocation of the name Calisto. At the same time, her linguistic prowess is linked with the earlier-mentioned binding power of lengths of thread brought to births and used in the sealing and unsealing or potent opening of stitches made in textual amulets:

[Cel.] Los ásperos puntos que lastiman lo llagado, doblan la pasión. Pues si tú quieres ser sana y que te descubra la punta de mi sotil aguja sin temor, haz para tus manos y pies una ligadura de sosiego, para tus ojos una cobertura de piedad ... verás obrar a la antigua maestra de estas

llagas ... no hay cosa mas contraria en las grandes curas delante los ani-
mosos cirujanos que los flacos corazones ... ponen temor al enfermo, hacen
que desconfie de la salud y al médico enojan y turban y la turbación altera
la mano, rigue sin orden la aguja ... sufre, señora, con paciencia, que es el
primer punto y principal. No se quiebre; si no, todo nuestro trabajo es perdido ... la cura del lastimero médico deja mayor señal ... No concibes odio
ni desamor ni consientas a tu lengua decir mal de persona tan virtuosa
como Calisto ... es otro y segundo punto ... primero te avisé de mi cura y
de esta invisible aguja ... sientes en solo mentarla en mi boca ... creo que se
van quebrando mis puntos.

[Mel.] quebróse mi honestidad, quebróse mi empacho, aflojó mi mucha
vergüenza ... cerrado han tus puntos mi llaga, venida soy en tu querer.
(1994: 242–5)

([Cel.] Rough stitches inflicted on the wounded double their suffering.
So if you want to be healed, and for me to uncover the point of my slender
needle without fear, make for your hands and feet a binding of calm, and
for your eyes a blindfold of piety ... you will see how an old master works
these wounds ... nothing is more of an obstacle for motivated surgeons carrying out great cures than feeble hearts ... they put fear in the patient, cause
them to distrust their own health, frustrating and upsetting the physician.
This disturbance unsteadies the hand, so that the needle is applied without
order ... suffer, my lady, with patience, that is the primary point and the
first stitch. May it not break, for then all of our work would be lost ... The
healing of an unhappy physician will leave a greater mark ... so do not
conceive hate or without love, nor consent that your tongue should speak
evil of a person as virtuous as Calisto ... this is another, second stitch ... first
I warned you of my remedy and now you feel this invisible needle ... only
as it is spoken from my mouth ... I think that my stitches are breaking ...

[Mel.] My honesty is ruptured, my modesty broken, and my shame
loosened ... your stitches have closed my wound, and I have now come to
do as you desire.)

In a reversal of the salvific *amoris vulnus* of Christ, patterns of vulnerary imagery in the *Celestina* have the effect of conceiving and giving
birth to a fictional, doomed love that can only end in death. Celestina will soon be fatally stabbed by Calisto's conspiratorial servants
when she refuses to share the profits she has gained from their master. Cupid's penetrating blades end in a homicide that is not motivated by erotic or spiritual love but rather a bottomless pit of soulless

materialism. Not long after consummating their illicit affair, Calisto suddenly dies after falling from the ladder used to enter his lover's garden, and Melibea commits suicide by jumping from the tower of her house. This turn of events constitutes a complete and devastating negation and reversal of the efficacy attributed to birthing amulets, such as the one found in Gascony, to safeguard new life and shield against "sudden death, whether ... arrow, spear, knife, sword nor by any enemy." It is as if the power of the side wound to bless and protect has been turned against characters inhabiting the desacralized material world of the *Celestina*.

The fuller meaning of this fatal curse is revealed in a final act of the tragicomedy, when Melibea announces that she has lost her virginity just before taking her own life: "perdí mi virginidad ... Cortaron las hadas sus hilos, cortáronle sin confessión su vida, cortaron mi esperança, cortaron mi gloria, cortaron mi compañía" (I lost by virginity ... the Fates cut their threads, they cut his life short without confession, they cut by hope, they cut glory, the cut me off from my companion) (1994: 334). Her father Pleberio's subsequent lament recalls Celestina's earlier warning against disturbing her needle, causing it to move "sin orden" or without order, "turbóse la orden del morir" (disturbed is the order of death) (1994: 292, 337). With these last words, the disaster of Celestina's gynecological stitching, procuring, and wounding midwifery over the course of the tragicomedy comes to be associated with medieval representations of the threading of the Parcae or three Fates (*Fatae*), and in particular the figure of Atropos. The Greek name of the third sister was etymologically interpreted as signifying the accident of death "sine ordine" (without order).[30] Known in Latin as Morta, she was understood during the Middle Ages as a personification of death who cut the thread of life and served as kind of morbid counterpart to Cupid. For instance, in a fourteenth-century Pisan fresco, she appears as winged figure wielding a scythe. Swooping into a garden setting, Morta harvests the souls of unsuspecting lovers, which resemble hovering cupids being intercepted by flying demons.[31] A variation on the same tradition can be seen in a fifteenth-century illumination of Christine de Pizan's *Epistre Othéa* (Letter of Othea, c. 1399) (Figure 12), in which an aged, emaciated antithesis of fertile motherhood rains down spears down on her cowering victims, illustrating the warning "keep watch at all times for Atropos and her spear, which strikes and spares no one" (1970, 34.2–5).

Figure 12. Atropos with spear, *Epistre Othéa* of Christine de Pizan, The British Library Board, Harley MS. 4431, fol. 111r.

A better known literary example can be found in the thirteenth-century *Roman de la rose*, when lovers are advised to "concentrate upon multiplying; in that way you will trick cruel, cantankerous Atropos, who hinders everything" (qtd. in Desmond and Sheingorn 2003: 66–70).[32] As noted earlier, by speaking this same line from Genesis, Melibea associates Eve's labour pains and mortality outside the

Figure 13. Atropos feeding Cerberus, *Roman de la rose*, Universidat de València, Biblioteca Histórica, Ms. 387, fol. 135r.

garden with an amorous suffering that Celestina prolongs and further inflames with dilatory speech acts. At another point in the *Rose* poem, the lover acknowledges that procreation will not enable him to elude Morta ("Atropos ce est la mort") and instead pleads for a sexualized *memento mori:* "may Atropos deign not to take my life except when I am engaged in your work; instead may she take me in the very act that Venus performs most willingly ... As for those who should mourn me ... may they be able to say ... 'your death was appropriate to the life you led'" (de Lorris and de Meun 1971: 10341–54).[33] In a fourteenth-century manuscript of the *Rose*, the old woman Morta is visualized in another illumination (Figure 13), her belly pregnant with death and her pendulous breasts providing fatal nourishment as she feeds the three-headed guardian Cerberus by casting the bodies of lovers towards the gates of Hell.

Whether or not Rojas was familiar with the *Rose*, he had probably read Petrarch's *Triumphus Mortis*, since a 1512 translation was later listed in the Spanish author's will. This text similarly cautions mortals that all must return to the same fatal "madre," Morta, who will cut down Chastity: "corta, hiere y siega" ([she] cuts, wounds and blinds) (Petrarca 1512: fols. 65r, 66v).[34] Whereas her sisters were mythologized as seamstresses drawing out and spinning thread as a symbol of birth and life, Morta was viewed as the aged mother and midwife of death, forever cutting the *filum vitae*. The opening eyes of the newly born will in the end be blinded by Morta.

In the tragicomedy, this link between Atropos's morbid delivery and the old bawd's role as a deadly "madre" and "partera" sheds further light on the eroticized, subverted revision of *vulnus-vulva* imagery and the aborted love of Calisto and the virginal Melibea that has concerned me in this chapter. Over the course of Rojas's work, the blindly flung arrow of Cupid will not be allegorized as the spear of Longinus, restoring vision and forging a pathway to immortality. Rather, Love's weaponry is revealed as the blade of Morta – a blade that eventually falls on Celestina herself. This once again contributes to the tragicomedy's reversal and undoing of amuletic power drawn from the wounding *mensura* of Christ to prevent accidental death in childbirth and by "arrow, spear, knife" and "sword."

Notably, the significance of the Fates and their connection to the use of threads by midwives extends beyond the mythographic cutting and blinding of Morta. Early churchmen, such as Eligius, cautioned against any woman heard chanting verbal formulas during her needlework, apparently out of a concern that curses and heterodox petitions could be woven or sewn into fabric (Flint 1994: 226). In his eleventh-century *Decretum*, Burchard of Worms urges penance for any sinner who has witnessed or taken part in "the vanities which women practice in their woolen work, in their weaving ... [so] that with incantations ... the threads of the warp and of the woof become so intertwined that ... he will perish totally" (1853: 961; 185).[35] Such warnings against the interrelated power of language and thread refer to the practice of textual or textile objects being worn on the body – objects classified as *ligaturas*, a term also used in the healing of Melibea ("ligatura") – and to sewing parchment in the production of amulets.[36] These binding texts often included invocations to provide the wearer apotropaic protection from evil forces by controlling malevolent spirits with words and signs meant to capture and bind, in keeping with the pretext of Celestina's hexing performance. *Ligaturas* could also be employed in combination with loosing spells, which were traditionally believed to liberate the body and spirit from harm. It is in this context that the tragicomedy connects the mending-piercing, binding-loosing discourse of Celestina and Melibea with mythic images of the Fates spinning from their distaff, measuring, and cutting the thread of Chastity.

The popular folkloric connotations of these figures and their spinning in medieval and early modern culture would seem to support such a connection, as the Fates had long been associated with damning transgressions. In a section of his penitential condemning the survival of pagan beliefs, for example, Burchard associates the Parcae with fairies (*silvaticae*) who were said to visit occasionally mortals or even copulate with them.[37] In Dante's *Inferno*, the Fates seem to have been similarly recast as witches: "le triste che lasciaron l'ago, / la spuola e 'l fuso, e fecersi 'ndivine; facer malie con erbe e con imago" (the wretched women who left their needles, their spindles and their distaffs, and became soothsayers; they cast spells with herbs and images) (1996: 20.121).[38] The belief in three fairy sisters was widespread enough that it also appears in the thirteenth-century *Golden Legend*, when the hosts of St Germanus await a trio of nocturnal female visitors whom the holy man identifies as demons and commands to leave (Voragine 1993: 2.28). Often in such tales, the Fates are recast as old, deformed sisters making a night visit to help their hostess spin flax or wool, as in the tale of the "The Three Spinners" that was eventually recorded by the Brothers Grimm (1892: no. 14).[39] Scholars have found that the grotesque aspect of these female figures, closely related to the "weird sisters" in Shakespeare's *Macbeth* (1975), hearkens back to medieval traditions of the Parcae as demonic female enchantresses. Their attributes of a needle and spindle were viewed as symbols of women's unruly speech, while distaffs were sometimes portrayed as verbal (and physical) weapons – in keeping with the earlier-mentioned fear of curses being imbedded in textile work, as well as the topic of Eve's spinning and its association with Original Sin, the fallen word, and the confusion of tongues.[40] Celestina can be identified with folkloric portrayals of the Parcae insofar as she similarly visits Melibea under the pretext of bringing thread to assist with a tapestry, although her real interest is verbal entanglement and seduction. As has been shown, the fateful visit of the procuress is not primarily used to warn against diabolical superstitions and the wiles of women, but instead evokes amuletic, material objects linked to midwifery, together with the "invisible thread" of incantation, as a means of transforming sexual desire into profit.

Significantly, the spinning sisters of mythology and popular lore implicated in Melibea's pronouncement, "cortaron las hadas sus hilos," also made their way into *ensalmos* or verbal chants that were common enough to be alluded to in other Spanish texts from the period.[41] José Manuel Pedrosa and other scholars have linked the healing of "tres hilanderas" to folkloric representations of the Parcae, and documented variations in Castilian, Catalan, and Portuguese.[42] In most cases, the holy woman invoked is St Lucy, whose eyes were legendarily gouged out by her tormentors, and whose name signified the *lux* of grace radiating without "being soiled; no matter how unclean may be the places where its beams penetrate," it "goes in straight lines," without deviation (Voragine 1993: 1.27–8). Three daughters are then assigned to this persona and, like the Fates, identified with the making and unmaking of needlework, but as a means of curing problems with vision.[43] The sisters' tasks can vary from embroidery to sewing, spinning, and weaving; and in a number of versions they are attributed with needles and balls of wool: "tres hijas" (three daughters) or "tres hermanas tenía ... una bordaba, otra cosía, y otra quitaba la rija ... una urdía, la otra tejía, la otra todo lo deshacía ... tres agujas tenía, con una cosía, con otra bordaba, con otra corría la belida" (she had three sisters ... one embroidered, one sewed, and the other cleared away the fistula ... one warped, one weaved, and the other undid everything ... she had three needles; sewed with one, embroidered with another, and another drove away the cataract) (Pedrosa 2000: 173–8). In some of these formulas, the textile undoing or unclouding of the eye is implicitly linked to a kind of textual erasure and reinscription: "tres libros tenía, en uno leía, en otro escribía, y en otro belidas deshacía" (she had three books; read from one, wrote in another, and in another undid cataracts) (Pedrosa 2000: 175). In this way, the third sister turns the mythological cutting and blinding of Atropos into a popular form of optical logotherapy in which a healing inscription is restored.

In effect, these *ensalmos* invoke a curse that is intended to cure the sufferer by calling on a folkloric incarnation of Morta to terminate or "undo" the malady itself, comparable to the rhetorical performative application and breaking of sutures in the *Celestina*. This can be seen most clearly in variations that evoke two sisters involved in sewing, followed by a third who "cures the evil traitor" ("y la otra cura el mal traidor") (Pedrosa 2000: 180). As we have seen in Rojas's tragicomedy, the old bawd's verbal needle piercings and stitching cure Melibea by undoing her chastity and further blinding her.[44] In fact, connections between the Three Spinners and ocular remedies in Spanish healing chants can also be related to patterns of visual imagery that a number of critics such as James Burke have noticed in the Celestina (2000: 49–62). Celestina not only makes ironic references to the dangers of the evil eye and the optical pathways of *amor eros* but also makes repeated allusions to the obscured vision of lovers. In keeping with the old bawd, Pármeno and Melibea also refer to the worsening problem of amorous blindness: "[Cel.] Pármeno, que hayas limpiado las turbias telas de tus ojos ... [Par.] Señor ... quitarse ha el velo de la ceguedad ... [Mel.] túrbome la cara" (1994: 128, 136, 241). Whereas the side wound of Christ legendarily restores the sight of Longinus, textual textile healing in the *Celestina* causes metaphorical vision loss, as if turning the curse of the Three Spinners *ensalmo* back on the sufferer. Similarly, in the *Libro de buen amor* – long recognized as a crucial precedent for and influence on the *Celestina* – we have seen how the worldly love mediated by a go-between subverts the apotropaic power of Trinitarian prayer inscribed into the pages of the literary text, turning the poem's shielding words into a malediction.[45]

In the tragicomedy, this kind of subversion can be correlated with eroticized binding-loosing language that cuts off, undoes, and blots out the protective efficacy of written and oral incantation. Words instead provide cover for willful sinning, as when Celestina conjures an inscribed *nómina* or "ligatura" and additionally evokes a "cobertura" or blindfold for Melibea that disguises Cupid's intentions as false piety. As has been demonstrated, the cut thread of the tragicomedy's outcome also redirects the apotropaic linguistic and material power invested in amuletic girdles and threads to safeguard parturient mothers and their newborns – and, by extension, the *potentia* of amulets depicting the *mensura vulneris* and superstitiously believed to offer protection against an unexpected demise. The deadly cupidity of Celestina, Calisto, and Melibea, as well as other characters, has the effect of aborting and shutting them off from the rebirth and redemption of the life-giving aperture in Christ's right side as a synecdoche for all of his wounds. In the tragicomedy, the metaphysical power of material objects in premodern religiosity gives way to what Gerli describes as a noticeable "lack of transcendence" and "brutal materialism" that will be more characteristic of modern culture (2011: 215). Within the disenchanted confines of Rojas's masterpiece, still-born lovers are enclosed and trapped by their own dilated language and fetishization of corrupt materiality. Like the impenitent, blinded thief on the sinister side, they are forever turned and twisted away from the eternal Word, closed off and denied entry into the bodily presence of Christ and the *apertione lateris* through which wounded sinners could hope to transcend the experience of death and perdition.

Wounds, Seals, and a Sense of Ending in
the *Lozana Andaluza*

An early literary reinterpretation of the *Tres hilanderas* spell can be found in a book published by Francisco Delicado, a Spanish writer living in Renaissance Italy. His 1528 *Retrato de la Lozana andaluza* makes numerous direct and indirect references to Rojas's tragicomedy.[46] This begins on the title page, where Delicado claims to have included "muchas más cosas que la *Celestina*" (many more things than in the *Celestina*) (1985: 165). It is believed that the author journeyed to Rome to escape persecution resulting from his status as a *converso* or Christian descendent of Jews. He might also have hoped to further his career as a priest and medical practitioner.[47] The Spanish exile not only wrote the *Lozana andaluza*, but also a manual for treating syphilis, *El modo de adoperare el legno de India* (On the Use of the West Indies' Wood, 1529). It is clear from these two extant works that Delicado suffered for decades from this disease, known among Spanish speakers as the *mal francorum* (French malady). He also exhibits an intimate familiarity with the criminal underworld of pimps and whores working in early sixteenth-century Rome. In fact, he apparently wrote most of the *Lozana andaluza* while recovering in a Roman hospital and finished it in Venice after escaping from Charles V's invading, mutinous army in 1527.[48] Three years later, while still living in the Republic, he completed an edition of the *Celestina* (Brakhage 1986: 11). Delicado's version of the Three Spinners *ensalmo* is recited early in the dialogue by a character named Rampín, Lozana's lover and partner in crime. The title character is an Andalusian *conversa* who has made her way to the Eternal City and gained notoriety as a prostitute, procuress, and healer, whose skills are said to rival those of Celestina.

Rampín, after falling and breaking open his head, claims that Lozana knows a spell for curing all manner of wounds, including those caused by the "mal francorum":

"Eran tres cortesanas y tenían tres amigos pajes de Franquilino, la una lo tiene público, la otra muy callado; a la otra le vuelta el lunario." Quien esta oración dijere tres veces a rimano, cuando nace sea sano, amén. (1985: 256)

("Once there were three courtesans who had three lovers, all of them pages of the One from France. The first keeps hers public, the second keeps it very secret, and the third's returns with the moon." Whoever recites this prayer three times in succession, at its birth be healthy, amen.)

Critics have yet to consider how this spell draws on the folkloric *Tres hilanderas* and possibly their connection to the Fates invoked in Rojas's tragicomedy. We have seen how the Spinners were called on to restore sight and in this way reverse the blinding effects of the third Fate, *Morta*, cutting and undoing spun or woven threads. Reminiscent of euphemistic links between textile work and sexual healing in the *Celestina*, the three sisters are identified as courtesans in the *Lozana*. While this connection seems to have gone unnoticed, Manual da Costa Fontes (2005: 213) rightly points out that the "pajes" refer to bodily symptoms of the *mal francorum* or French disease, personified by "Franquilino." Thus the first courtesan is said to have sores that are visible ("público"); the second hides her illness while it is in remission ("muy callado"); and the third discovers that lesions return with her menstrual cycle, thought to be influenced by the new moon ("lunario").[49] The cure for blindness attributed to the *Tres hilanderas* is especially fitting, since a gradual loss of sight was also common in syphilitic patients. Like other healing spells, this *ensalmo* in the *Lozana andaluza* conjures and performatively reverses the course of illness – or the opening and closing of its symptomatic wounds – but does so parodically. Costa Fontes has also noted that the promise, "cuando nace sea sano" (at its birth, be healthy) alludes to an "initial manifestation in an infected person" (1993: 198).

I would add that the appearance or "birth" of a lover's open sore recalls the hidden wound in the *Celestina*, recasting it as a visible sign of venereal disease. Like the earlier bawd, Lozana is paid to arrange sex acts and perform the duties of a midwife, including treatment for the wandering womb or *mal de la madre* (1985: 108). Delicado's female healer, however, is also known for alleviating the symptoms of the *mal francorum* through coitus. As discussed earlier, Celestina's erotically charged, queer gynecology and midwifery cause the metaphor of the wounded heart to take on vulvic connotations, as it figuratively opens, reopens, and festers, before being fatally cured. Delicado associates this kind of amorous *vulnus* with the syphilitic sores that afflict promiscuous lovers like Lozana.

Reminiscent of Melibea, the Andalusian bawd first claims that she was pierced by Eros in the "teta izquierda" or left breast (1985: 182). Her amorous wounding is later represented in a woodcut (Figure 14) that accompanies a satirical poem at the end of book. In these verses, Cupid condemns an unnamed lady to suffer "tan gran maldición / de Sodoma y Gomorra" (such a great curse as Sodom and Gomorra) and then consigns each of her bodily charms to ruin, including "la resplandeciente

Figure 14. Cupid's arrow, woodcut, *Retrato de la Lozana andaluza* (Venice, 1528) fol. 53v, detail. Tipografía Moderna Facsimile (Valencia, 1950). Courtesy Artes Gráficas Soler-Albatros.

frente" (the resplendent forehead) (1985: 493, 499–500).[50] Carla Perugini has pointed out that the image from the woodcut was also used in a 1521 Italian translation of the earlier-referenced *Cárcel de amor* ("Las fuentes" 2000). Delicado associates the *Celestina* with this sentimental novel when Lozana's house in Rome is called "la cárcel de amor, aquí idolatró Calisto" (here Calisto committed idolatry) (1985: 349).[51]

Lozana's initial wound or "herida" anticipates the syphilitic lesion that will leave a scar on her forehead, referred to by other characters in the text as her "estrella" (star) and "estrellica" (little star) (1985: 186, 193). This sign of the French disease or *"greñimón,"* together with her deformed nose, is used to identify the Celestinesque character on the streets of Rome (1985: 192). We will see in the pages that follow how it also relates to the apocalyptic outcome of the narrative, when Rome is destroyed by invaders.

A number of critics have linked this scar to Lozana's Sephardic background. For example, both Costa Fontes (2005) and Carolyn Wolfenzon

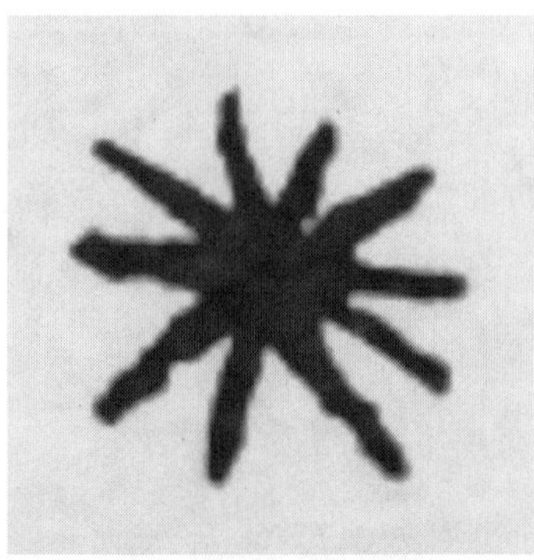

Figure 15. "Una estrellica." Woodcut from *Retrato de la Lozana andaluza* (Venice, 1528), fol. 53v, detail. Tipografía Moderna Facsimile (Valencia, 1950). Courtesy Artes Gráficas Soler-Albatros.

(2007) have suggested that the "estrella" or "estrellica" could allude to the Star of David, and in this way signal her Jewish ancestry and/ or possible adherence to crypto-Judaism (secret observance of Mosaic law among converts to Christianity).[52] Meghan McInnis-Domínguez has more recently related the mark on Lozana's face to the emerging idea of impure Jewish blood and the "alterity" of *conversos* introducing a "social disease" within the imperial state (2011: 311–13). One potential problem with such theories is that a woodcut in the book (Figure 15) depicts the "star" or "little star" as an asterisk detached from Lozana's body and not a Davidic hexagram.

In fact, it resembles the kind of *astriscus* used by printers to indicate omissions but also to mark places in the text containing essential truths or *sententia* (Parks 1992: 57). Similarly, Lozana's facial scar can be expected to reveal something about her that is not explicitly stated but is of the utmost importance – whether or not the mark was in some way meant to draw attention to her Jewish background.

Further light can be shed on this question by turning to another woodcut in which the scar appears on Lozana's forehead as an inverted "T" or Tau (Figure 16). The image is particularly significant, as it is the most detailed visual portrait of the title character in the *Retrato*.

There are a number of reasons to believe that its rendering of Lozana's scar is intentional. Since the book ends with the sacking of the

Figure 16. Lozana in her house in Rome, woodcut, *Retrato de la Lozana andaluza* (Venice, 1528), fol. 1v (and 32v), detail. Tipografía Moderna Facsimile (Valencia, 1950). Courtesy Artes Gráficas Soler-Albatros.

Eternal City and surrender of the Pope, it could be argued that this upside-down Tau refers to the inverted cross of St Peter as a symbol of the Roman Church in crisis. Lozana has come to embody a sexualized decadence that was seen as leading to the destruction of the city. Her literary depiction epitomizes the sinful decadence of "Roma," personified as a whore whose name written backward spells "amor" (1985: 505). The church taught that a treasure of divine grace, won by Christ's loving sacrifice on the cross, had been entrusted to the Roman Curia until the end of time. Delicado, however, portrays a worldly love of the flesh being bought and sold in the same Holy City where the freely given *caritas* or charity of the Holy Spirit was supposed to reign supreme.

Thus, the cruciform venereal scar on Lozana's forehead feeds into a sense of Rome's doomed meretricious faithlessness. Early sixteenth-century Spanish and Italian audiences would have been familiar with the idea that bodily signs could be interpreted as a means of predicting disaster. During this period, there was a growing interest across Europe in reading these *signa* as political and religious portents. A number of surviving woodcuts and texts claim that prior to catastrophic events, mystical letters and cross shapes appeared on the bodies of monstrous men and women living in Renaissance Italy.[53] In late medieval Iberia, Jews were sometimes said to have converted to Christianity after seeing cruciform signs, as in the case of Abner of Burgos (Williams 1935: 259).

In consideration of Lozana's identity as a new Christian, the mark might have taken on further connotations beyond its connection with St Peter's Roman cross. Shortly after baptism, the confirmation ceremony for new Christians and their children involved anointing the forehead with the sign of the cross.[54] Through what was called *signaculum, sigillum* or the "Sacrament of the Seal," the body and soul of the believer were sealed by God to receive the divine love of the Spirit, "unto the day of redemption" (Scannell 1908; Eph. 4:30). As explained in the medieval Spanish legal code known as the *Siete partidas* (Seven Divisions), this practice signified an open and unhindered disclosure of belief, in accordance with the gospel promise, "Every one therefore that shall confess me before men, I will also confess him before my Father who is in heaven" (Alfonso X 2004: 1.23; Matt. 10:42). Apparently, Inquisitorial officials suspected false converts would not heed the warning given in the subsequent biblical verse: "But he that shall deny me before men, I will also deny him before my Father who is in heaven." David Gitlitz has demonstrated that sixteenth-century *conversos* were sometimes accused of trying to remove chrism oil following the conferral of this sealing sacrament (2002: 147–8).[55] Such accusations bring to mind Lozana's attempt to conceal her scar by wearing a hood, as well as an earlier scene in which she claims to have struck herself on the forehead, ironically causing the mark to become more pronounced (1985: 186, 192–3).

The ritual of anointing that *conversos* allegedly sought to undo reflects an interpretation of the Book of Ezekiel that was central to the Christian understanding of sacred history. When the prophet foresees the siege of Jerusalem and pillaging of the Temple by the Babylonians, God tells him to mark the sorrowful witnesses so that they might be spared. St Jerome translated the Hebrew letter made on their foreheads as a Greek

Tau (9:4). The mark in Ezekiel ("signa thau super frontes") was interpreted as a prefigurement of the same sign – now identified with the *sigillum* of the cross – sealing the foreheads of the children of Jerusalem and faithful servants of God in Revelation. In John the Divine's vision, the Tau on their foreheads protects against punishments that include plagues and an outbreak of grievous wounds and sores ("factum est vulnus saevum ac pessimum") (7.1–8, 16.2). This might explain why the *signum thau* was often used as an apotropaic on medieval textual amulets and was specifically believed to confer protection against pestilence on fifteenth- and early sixteenth-century parchment and broadside charms. For example, a Tau-shaped cross appears on the earlier-mentioned Barcarrota *nómina* that was produced in sixteenth-century Italy before being brought to Iberia and which has been connected to a *converso* physician like Delicado. This amulet also features other characteristic written elements thought to protect against leprosy and the plague, including the Trisagion or thrice holy prayer from Revelation. The Tau's power "contra pestilentiam" or "contra peste" is explicitly invoked on other Italian examples from the period that have been studied by Skemer (2006: 180). In the text of the Apocalypse, sores are said to afflict those who instead bear the mark of the Beast, a sign ("character") that also appears on the forehead ("in frontibus suis") (13.16–17). Lozana's inverted Tau scar is thus suggestive both of the pestilent mark of the condemned, and ironically the divine sealing of those who will be spared. In other words, the mark on her forehead could be viewed as a damning curse or a kind of amuletic inscription, consistent with the character's role as a carrier and healer of syphilis.[56] It is both synecdochic and proleptic in relation to the book's ongoing characterization of Lozana.

Consonant with the apocalyptic expectations of Christians, Jews living in Italy during the Middle Ages were sometimes obliged to wear Tau-shaped badges (Damiani 1971: 59).[57] The cruciform letter was made to function as a mark of shame recalling the crucifixion of Christ and alleged perfidy of the Jews, as well as a sign of their protected status in expectation of a final conversion at the end of time.[58] This context sheds light on the way in which Lozana's bodily inscription anticipates the Last Judgment, as depicted, for example, in Alfonso X's apocalyptic song to Mary: "terrán escrito nas frentes quanto fezeron" (all have written on their foreheads what they have done) (1986–9: vol. 3, 422, v. 37). Over the course of the narrative, Lozana is marked as an outrageously sinful New Christian. Her "estrella" at the same time recalls the fallen star prophesized to open the smoldering, bottomless pit in

Revelation, leading to the destruction of those deemed unworthy to receive the divine seal first envisioned by Ezekiel ("non habent signum Dei in frontibus") (9:4). Parallels between the devastation of wicked cities in the Hebrew Bible, New Testament doomsday prophesies, and the 1527 sacking of Rome did not go unnoticed by witnesses like Delicado. In keeping with the significance of Lozana's upside-down Tau, characters in the dialogue make comparisons between the coming invasion of city of St Peter and the End of Days. Notably, Lozana and another syphilitic *conversa* named Divicia invoke the sixth angel of Revelation, who was prophesized to unleash a demonic army, after a plague of festering sores has afflicted those who bear the mark of the Beast (Delicado 1985: *mamotreto* 54; 16:2–14).[59]

Delicado's treatise on the *mal francorum* further clarifies his eschatological understanding of the disease that marks Lozana's forehead and the devastation of Rome at the end of her portrait. The author paraphrases and cites from the Old and New Testaments, translating the Latin *vulnus* (wound), *plaga* (blow, wound, or resulting scar) and *ulcus* (sore) as the Spanish "plaga":[60]

En Roma hizieron el año de mill y quinientos y veynte y siete los armigeros los quales no solamente pusieron sus sacrilegas manos en los pobres y en nos, los sacerdotes, y en las yglesias, hasta en la *Santa santorum*, temerariamente, por cierto, no guardando que Dios dize en el Salmo 7: "Como tomará el tiempo, las justicias juzgará." El Apocalipsis asimismo dize en el capítulo sesto décimo: "Porque blasphemaron el nombre del Altíssimo … y derramaron la sangre de los prophetas … es hecha la plaga [*vulnus*], seva e péssima." Esaías dize, primo capítulo: "Guay a la gente *peccatrice … blasphemauerunt sanctum* … enferma … [con] plaga [*vulnus … et plaga*] hinchada … no es ligada ni medicada con medicina ni ungida con olio" … En el Deuteronomij, capítulo vigésimo octavo, dize … "*[Percutiat te Dominus] ulcere pessimo … sanarique non possis a planta pedis usque ad verticen tuum*" … que quiere dezir claro de una plaga incurabile como ésta de que aquí tratamos. (Damiani 1971: 265)

(Armies entered Rome in the year one thousand five hundred and twenty seven, that not only placed their sacrilegious hands on the poor, on we the priests, on the churches, and even the *Sancta sanctorum*; fearfully, to be sure, not obeying what God says in Psalm 7: "As He will overtake time, judging right and wrong." The Apocalypse likewise says in chapter sixteen: 'Because they have blasphemed the name of the Highest … and spilled the blood of the prophets ... there fell upon them a wounding plague, fierce and grievous." Isaiah says, chapter one: "Woe to the sinful people ... they blasphemed the Holy One ... sickened ... [with] swelling plague wound that can neither be bound with ligatures, treated with medicine, nor anointed with balm" ... In Deuteronomy, chapter twenty-eight, it says: "[May the Lord strike thee with] a very sore ulcer ... and be thou incurable from the sole of the foot to the top of the head" ... which clearly is to say with an incurable plague wound like this one we are treating here.) [61]

Delicado's epilogues to the *Lozana andaluza*, the "Epístola" and "Digresión," create similar links between the wounding venereal disease, the destruction of Rome, and the fulfilment of scriptural punishments and judgments described in Scripture:

Oh Roma, oh Babilón ... ¿pensólo nadie jamás tan alto secreto y juicio? ... después del saco y de la ruina, pestilencia ... el fin de los munchos juicios que había visto y escrito ... mira este retrato de Roma ... "*¡Ve tibi civitas meretrix!*" ... ¡Oh gran juicio de Dios!, venir un tanto ejército "*sub nube*" ... para castigar los habitatores romanes ... corrigiendo nuestro malo y vicioso vivir. (1985: 489–91, 507)

(Oh, Rome, oh Babylon ... did anyone ever consider so lofty a secret and judgment? ... after the pillage and destruction, pestilence ... the end of the numerous judgments that I had foreseen and written about ... Look at this portrait of Rome ... "Woe to you, city of strumpets" ... Oh, great judgment of God! To permit such an army to come "beneath a cloud" ... to punish the Roman inhabitants ... for our evil and corrupt lives.)

By identifying "Roma putana" (Whorish Rome) with Babylon, the author not only evokes the city destroyed by God in Genesis, but more importantly its refiguration in Revelation as "the great whore ... on her forehead a name was written, a mystery: Babylon the great, Mother of the fornications and abominations" (1985: 43; 17:1–5).[62] This would suggest that the meaning of the symbol on Lozana's forehead extends beyond both her status as a *conversa* and the tradition of seals protecting and condemning the saved and the iniquitous in Ezekiel and Revelation. The sign is crucial to the ongoing personification of the Eternal City's corruption in the *Lozana andaluza*, through an apocalyptic mode of thinking and fictionalizing that Frank Kermode has called the "sense of an ending." Thus, a "shadow of the end" is cast by the inverted cross of St Peter when it appears portentously on the forehead of an unrepentant whore and hypersexual convert who is neither faithful to the new nor the old religion (Kermode 2000: 5).

Drawing parallels between the doomed whoredom of Rome and the divinely ordained fall of biblical cities, Delicado's epilogues to the *Lozana andaluza* also correspond with other testimonies of the 1527 sacking. For example, his image of troops advancing as if "sub nube" or under a cloud appropriates language from Isaiah's so-called apocalypse to describe the thick fog that purportedly enveloped Rome on the morning of the assault (25:5).[63] The Old Testament prophet foresaw the annihilation of a corrupt city and the coming of a Messiah who would restore justice and resurrect the dead. The church had long interpreted the inauguration of this millennial age as the Second Coming: "thou hast reduced the city to a heap, the strong city to ruin, the house of strangers ... Thou shalt bring down the tumult of strangers ... as with heat under a burning cloud ['calore sub nube'] ... He shall cast death down headlong forever: and the Lord God shall wipe away tears ... and the reproach of his people he shall take away ... And they shall say in that day: Lo, this is our God, we have waited for him, and he will save us" (25:1–9).[64] Comparable imagery can be found in an anonymous Spanish letter that likens Rome to Sodom awaiting God's wrath, or a prediction made by the papal adviser Pietro Corsi that Christ would soon return to drive out the invaders, together with other sinners, and purify the desecrated city or *Civitas diaboli*. Scholars like Pamela Brakhage and John Edwards have found that following the exile of 1492, messianic expectations of this kind circulated and proliferated among Jewish as well as Christian communities in Rome and elsewhere on the Italian and Iberian peninsulas.[65]

The author makes another telling reference to the *topos* of the fallen *Civitas diaboli*, deserving of God's punishment, when he cites the first part of St Jerome's condemnation of Alexandria. This description could be found in the ever-popular *Vitae patrum* or *Lives of the Church Fathers*: "Vae tibi, ciuitas meretrix, in qua totius orbis daemonia confluxere" (Woe to you, harlot city, into which have flowed together the demons of the whole world!) (1570: 213).[66] Such an allusion to converging demonic forces comes as no surprise, considering that witnesses like Corsi and historian Marino Sanuto described how the 1527 sacking transformed the Eternal City into Hell on Earth and the entrance to Hades. In addition to the assault itself, the mouth of Hell is pictured in a woodcut near the end of the text, receiving sinners who are characteristically dressed as fools (Figures 17 and 18).[67]

Figure 17. Invasion of Rome, woodcut, *Retrato de la Lozana andaluza* (Venice, 1528), fol. 53r, detail. Tipografía Moderna Facsimile (Valencia, 1950). Courtesy Artes Gráficas Soler-Albatros.

Figure 18. Dream of "Plutón," woodcut, *Retrato de la Lozana andaluza* (Venice, 1528), fol. 51r, detail. Tipografía Moderna Facsimile (Valencia, 1950). Courtesy Artes Gráficas Soler-Albatros.

This infernal entryway is presided over by the demonic figure of Pluto from Celestina's hex and also evoked in Lozana's dream about the coming destruction. In her prophetic nightmare, the ruler of the underworld is accompanied by Mars and Mercury. These gods were associated with war and the treatment of syphilis, respectively: "veía a Plutón caballero ... veía venir a Marte debajo una niebla, y era tanto el estrépito que sus ministros hacían ... sin otro ningún dentenimiento cabalgaba en Mercurio ... Finalmente desperté ... consideraba cómo las coasas que han de estar en el profundo, cómo Plutón que está sobre la Sierra" (I saw Pluto as a rider ... I saw Mars coming beneath the mist, and his ministers making such deafening noises ... without delay, I rode Mercury ... Finally, I awoke ... considering how things must be in the infernal depths, and how Pluto is atop the Mountains) (1985: 478–9).[68]

Like other eyewitnesses, Delicado emphasizes that this armed advance of Mars and hellish defilement of the city extended to "even the *Sancta sanctorum*" in the Lateran chapel – this in contrast to Pompey's famous refusal to violate the Holy of Holies in the tabernacle of the Jerusalem temple.[69] In fact, the same precedent can be found in contemporary disputes over whether the sacking should be blamed primarily on worldly excesses of the Church or the insatiable evil of her enemies. For instance, the papal defender Baldassare Castiglione observed that while pagans had left the inner sanctum of Solomon's temple intact, Christian mercenaries now violated the sanctuaries of their own Church.[70] According to Delicado, this sacrilege was worse than might be expected of the "great Turk" (1985: 504). In his *Diálogo de las cosas ocurridas en Roma* (Dialogue on Things that Have Happened in Rome, 1527), however, the imperial apologist Alfonso de Valdés provides an explanation for why God would allow Roman altars to be profaned: "could not God create in an instant a hundred thousand temples more sumptuous and rich than the temple of Solomon if that were what he wanted?" (1952: 69). Valdés urges believers to create a new Rome, filled with "living temples" of Christ. His vision is suggestive of the timeless city of peace once again prophesized by John the Divine: "I, John, saw ... the new Jerusalem ... prepared as a bride ... the wife of the Lamb... I saw no temple therein. For the Lord God Almighty is the temple thereof, and the Lamb ... the Alpha and the Omega" (21:2–22, 22:13).[71]

Just as the Tau seal from the beginning of Revelation is implicated in an earlier woodcut depicting Lozana, this eschatological combination of the first and last Greek letters is reproduced at the close of Delicado's book (1985: 51v). Following her own prophetic vision, the title character

Figure 19. "Este ñudo de Salamón," woodcut, *Retrato de la Lozana andaluza* (Venice, 1528), fol. 51v, detail. Tipografía Moderna Facsimile (Valencia, 1950). Courtesy Artes Gráficas Soler-Albatros.

decides to retire to the island of Lipari with her "peers," then promises to send her lover, Rampín, a mysterious gift: "Yo quiero ir a paraíso, y entraré por la puerta que abierta hallare ... si veo la Paz, que allá está continua, la enviaré atada con este ñudo de Salomón, desátela quien la quisiere. Y esta es mi última voluntad" (I want to go to paradise, and will enter through the door that I find open to me ... if I see that peace is continuous there, I will send it tied with this knot of Solomon, let whoever wants to untie it. And this is my last wish) (1985: 480).[72] The woodcut (Figure 19) showing this cross-shaped knot includes the mystical Alpha Omega in Latin script, symbolizing the eternal conjunction of the beginning and the end, together with the letters "P" and "Z" to spell out the Spanish word for peace ("PAZ").

Several critics have offered explanations for the inclusion of this esoteric image. For Costa Fontes (2005: 225–6), the cross-shaped Solomonic knot subverts the supersessionist relationship between Christianity and Judaism in a way that supports his theory that Delicado was a crypto-Jew. Comparing uses of Solomon's seal as a hexagram or six-pointed star in Jewish Kabbalah, Carla Perugini (1999) reaches a similar conclusion. On the other hand, Claude Allaigre and Ian Macpherson have related Lozana's "ñudo" to variations of the seal in which a pentagram or five-pointed star – consisting of lines interwoven without beginning or end – represents the timeless wisdom and power entrusted to the first temple builder. As Macpherson points out, medieval and early modern Christians also understood this star as a representation of the five wounds of Christ that could be employed as a healing charm.[73] He goes on to demonstrate how the *Lozana andaluza* knot relates to Christograms that combine the Alpha Omega with the first two letters of the Saviour's name in Greek, X and P – letters that Delicado seemingly changed to Z and P, so as to read "PAZ." Macpherson notes that the quadripartite form of the woodcut, with sacred letters configured around its four corners, mirrors "four points ... as the compass ... the fourfold design of Solomon's temple ... constructed on the model of the Tabernacle" (1998: 214). He finds that configurations of this seal were sometimes associated with the "indissoluble ties" of love knots during the late Middle Ages, visualized as endless loops not unlike the tying of Lozana's "ñudo" (1998: 219).[74] Finally, Macpherson agrees with other critics that the word "PAZ" on the woodcut anticipates Lozana's journey to a paradisiacal Lipari.

What has yet to be considered is the significance of powers attributed to Solomonic seals and knots in the late medieval imaginary, and how these might relate to the "sense of ending" conveyed by the earlier inverted Tau woodcut. Solomon's attributes can be traced to the *Historia* of Josephus and biblical passages, to the pseudepigraphic *Testament of Solomon*, Latin dialogues, and hagiographic legends.[75] As discussed earlier in this study, the king was famous for his attainment of divine knowledge and ability to command demonic spirits during the construction of the first temple. As a consequence of what was portrayed as his insatiable lust for foreign women, however, Solomon fell under malevolent influences and allowed himself to be seduced into idolatry, risking the future of his kingdom and his own salvation. We have seen how a similarly perilous seduction is represented by Delicado's Spanish prostitute. Solomon's legend was further developed in popular books of magic attributed to this wise yet dangerously flawed king, such as the *Liber iuratus or Sacer* (The Sworn Book of Honorius), the *Ars notoria* (Notary Art), and especially the *Clavicula Salomonis* (Key of Solomon). These texts emerged from ancient Jewish and Christian sources, and were also influenced by the related Islamic tradition of "Sulaiman" commanding an army of evil spirits known as "jinn." Variations claimed to offer secret knowledge that was recorded by Solomon, kept hidden under his throne, and later buried with him. The most widely disseminated among these was the late medieval *Clavicula*, which provided instructions for drawing on the power of invocations, pentacles, and other sealing formulas to call forth and bind demons.

Julio Caro Baroja (1967) has documented early references to this work circulating on the Iberian Peninsula. Already in the fourteenth century, the General Inquisitor of Aragón ordered the destruction of a text called the *Liber Salomonis*.[76] Subsequent burnings took place in Cuenca in 1434, again in Barcelona in 1440, and decades later in Salamanca. Not long after Delicado finished the *Lozana andaluza*, the reformer Pedro Ciruelo again condemned Solomonic books for invoking demonic forces, and they were placed on the *Index of Prohibited Books* during the 1550s (1978: 61). During the second half of the sixteenth century, the theologian Martín del Río explains how the *Clavicula* was first copied by Iberian Jews and Muslims, and later widely disseminated by Christians, in spite of failed attempts by the church to confiscate and destroy all existing copies (1991).[77] Warnings issued by Renaissance censors attest to the continued popularity of the *Clavicula* among Spanish speakers, strongly suggesting that a learned bibliophile like Delicado would have been aware of this text when he created Lozana's Solomonic "ñudo."

It is also clear that elements from the *Clavicula* were reproduced on textual amulets intended to be carried as a means of conjuring and protecting believers from demonic influences. This tradition would suggest that, like the Tau's supposed efficacy against the plague, Lozana's knot could be interpreted as an amuletic shield. Specifically, the image might be understood as offering protection against the violent incursion into Rome that the bawd foresees in her dream – and that Delicado and his contemporaries compared to an opening of the mouth of Hell and a demonic convergence on the city. Such an interpretation is supported by the prevalence of Solomonic features on amulets that were either produced in or brought to Spain from the High Middle Ages to the mid-sixteenth century. Earlier in this book, for example, I discussed a thirteenth-century Aragonese manuscript folio that was inscribed with hexagrams, the Alpha Omega, and other *nomina sacra* in order to control and exorcize tempestuous demons. We have also seen how a century later, amuletic seal markings like those found in grimoires were etched onto a clay tile in medieval Castile. In the next chapter, I will analyse related elements on a paper *nómina* dating from the mid-sixteenth-century: produced in Italy and evidently carried by an Iberian traveller, this object includes both a pentagram and sealing concentric circles of the kind found in the *Clavicula*.

As Skemer has shown, the efficacy commonly attributed to these kinds of seals is specified on a medieval amuletic parchment that has been preserved in the Canterbury Cathedral: "hoc este signum regis Salomonis quo demones ... signalauit, qui super se portauerit ... saluus erit, et si demon ei apparuerit iubeat ei quicumque uoluerit et obediet ei ... Salomon ut demones compelleret" (this is the sign of the king Solomon that ... summons demons; he who wears it ... is safeguarded, and if any demon whatsoever appears to him, he commands it and it obeys him ... as Solomon summoned demons) (2006: 302).[78] Similarly, the knot in Delicado's book might be construed as summoning or safeguarding against the demonic. Versions of the king's *signum* had long been copied together with the Tau and Alpha Omega to indicate divine and eternal protection, as in the case of the previously studied amuletic text that precedes the *Razón de amor*. For instance, Skemer has brought to light a particularly striking example on a textual amulet that was produced in Italy during the early sixteenth century. It features a knotted cross with the divine acronym "AGLA," flanked by the five-pointed star along with other Solomonic keys and *caracteres* (2006: 214–17).[79] Another characteristic element found on such objects is the Latin "pax," recalling the Vulgate pronouncements of Christ: "peace I leave with you, my peace I give unto you"; and "peace be in this house," a blessing that is parodically repeated by Lozana and Celestina before her (John 4:27; Luke 10:5). This might suggest how the efficacy of the word "PAZ" on the knot should also be taken ironically, calling into question the assumption that Lozana will peacefully escape to the island of Lipari.

The most relevant analogue for the Lozana's "ñudo," however, can be found in a 1527 Spanish translation of the *Clavicula*. This manuscript was surrendered to authorities on the Canary Islands weeks before the sack of Rome and preserved in the archives of the Spanish Inquisition. It begins with a series of promises and conjurations: "con esta atan todos los demonios que son el el mundo y son los que contratan los abysmos ... 'conjuro vos prynçepes de los demonios que morays en quatro partes del mundo'" (with this all demons are bound that occupy the world and those that are sworn to the abyss ... "I conjure you rulers of the demons that occupy the four parts of the world") (Lamb 1963: fol. 34r). In accordance with the "ñudo," this vernacular text invokes "alpha" and "O," and shows how to unbind "en paz con la vendyçión" (in peace with your blessing) (Lamb 1963: 135–6). Reminiscent of Celestina's diabolical hex, it also demonstrates how the obedience of demons could be ensured with threats: "de las maldyçiones que dyó sobre Sodoma y Gomorra

... y sobre la gran çibdad de Babylonia ... venga sobre vos las doze mal-dyçiones que son y an de ser en el dya del juiçio" (of curses that befell Sodom and Gomorra ... and the great city of Babylon ... may the twelve curses fall on you that are and will be on the Day of Judgment) (Lamb 1963: 136).[80] Because the Spanish grimoire and Delicado's work both cor-relate Solomonic binding with the topic of punishing the *Civitate diaboli*, we might expect the tying and untying of Lozana's "ñudo" to implicate an apocalyptic threat, together with the power to summon and control demonic spirits. Like the mark that anoints and curses the lover's fore-head, the image represented by the woodcut could potentially shield against war and plague or invite punishment and destruction.

The sign of Solomon in the *Clavicula* manuscript, comparable to Lozana's endless knot, is created by tracing the lines of a pentagram without start or finish and inserting a cross in the centre, surrounded by mystical letters: "este syno de Salamón y en medyo vna cruz ... y estas letras que tiene escrypto derredor" (Lamb 1963: 136–7). What follows are directions for casting spells and producing amulets, overwhelm-ingly intended to bind or unbind lovers, but also effective in conjur-ing armed avengers and healing various ailments.[81] The inclusion of this material once more attests to Solomon's reputation for compelling demons to submit to his will, yet proving himself powerless to resist the temptation of illicit lovers – and, in particular, exotic women from other nations, like Lozana. Fittingly, at one point in Delicado's work, his title character calls a doctor "Salomón" in a speech about the natural plea-sures of vaginal penetration (1985: 461). Near the end of the *Clavicula* manuscript, instructions are provided for binding lovers, just as the magician king controlled evil spirits who, according to end-time proph-ecy, will torment humankind before being vanquished by the Lord. This section explains the potency of Solomon's "nudos" in a way that further clarifies the meaning of the "ñudo de Salomon" in the *Lozana andaluza*:

Para ligar cualquyer persona, toma filo de alanbre ... y faz ... nudos y quando los dyeres dyrás ansy ... "enlego a fulana o fulano ... en nel nombre de ... quantos demonios nel mundo son ... ansy como lygó Salamón a los demonios ... ansy sea ligado fulano o fulana que no pueda ser deslygado de onbre ny de muger del mundo fasta que yo mismo los deslygue ... a cada nudo ... Conjuro vos dyablos todos los nombrados y por quantos soys por todas las quatro partes del mundo y por el juyçio que ha de ser sobre vosotros el dya temeroso del juyçio ... ansy como están ligados los nudos deste fylo" ... Para desfazer este ligamiento ... desfáz los nudos.

Dyrás estas palabras ... "Christus vicat, Christus rreyna, Christus enpera."
(Lamb 1963: 142–3)

(To bind anyone, take a wire thread ... and make ... knots and when they
are made you will say this ... "I bind such a person ... in the name of ...
all of the demons of the world ... just as Solomon bound the demons ...
thus will the person be bound so that they cannot be unbound by any
man or woman in the world until I myself undo ... each knot ... I conjure
you, all of the devils so named, as many of you as exist in the four parts
of the world, and by the justice that will be dealt to you on the fearful
day of Judgment ... just as the knots of this wire are tied" ... To undo this binding ... undo the knots. You will say these words ... "Christ conquers, Christ
reigns, Christ rules.")[82]

In light of this contemporaneous text, the woodcut in the *Lozana andaluza* on the one hand seems to represent an efficacious object that can
be tied like a wire, while on the other, inserting a textual amulet into
the literary narrative itself. Its material presence is created by printing
the sigil of a Solomonic *ligatura*, complete with divine names, onto the
paper of the first and only 1527 edition.[83] Within the logic of the text, the
"ñudo" is instilled with a narrative power to bind and unbind, conjure
and release lovers from the seductive deceit and apocalyptic violence
of demons that will precede the Second Advent of Christ. In keeping
with the knot in the *Clavicula*, the fate of Rome and its condemned lovers is tied and sealed by the verbal conjuration and material fetishizing
engaged in by Lozana and her eponymous book, "desátela quien la quisiere." This also echoes a proclamation in the Apocalypse that the Seven
Seals will be broken only with the return of the Messiah (5:1–3). Revelation can be unveiled from the four corners of the "ñudo," in accordance
with the fourfold layout of Solomon's temple and quadripartite direc-
tionality of John the Divine's vision. In this way, Lozana's knot works
in conjunction with the inverted Tau woodcut, to mark performatively
the prophesized division between the damned and the saved and signal
pestilence and healing. These dual seals placed at the beginning and the
end of the book are efficacious in stigmatizing conversion as well as
the unconverted, exposing the corruption of the church, and heralding
the sacrilegious approach of its enemies.

In end, the irony of Lozana's escape from the hellish fate that awaits
Rome cannot be fully appreciated without considering Lipari's fame
as an infernal entryway, as opposed to the open "puerta" to "paraiso"

that she imagines. This idea stems from a pseudo-patristic work that was widely read throughout the Middle Ages and Renaissance, the *Pseudo-Gregorian Dialogues*. It is highly likely that Delicado would have been exposed to its well-known accounts of the punishments that awaited departed souls. The *Dialogi* was "the medieval equivalent of a bestseller," to the extent that no other eschatological work attributed to the Fathers of the Church "was more eagerly transcribed and read" (Clark 1987: 2.3).[84] According to this text, an opening to Hell was located among the volcanic peaks of Lipari: "To those craters were ferried the doomed souls of the young and dissolute ... because the Arian king Theodoric the Ostrogoth had persecuted unto death Pope John I, ... he was justly condemned to torments there ... We read how a hermit of great holiness saw the impious king being thrust down into hell in one of the craters of Lipari, watched by two of his illustrious victims" (Clark 1987: 2.645–6). The sixth-century pope was held prisoner by heretical Barbarian invaders of Italy, as was Clement VII in 1527 after fleeing to the Castel Sant'Angelo. For early audiences who were familiar with this "bestseller," Delicado's reference to Lipari could be understood as implicitly cursing the persecutors of the Pope and plunderers of Rome. Lozana calls the invaders Teutonic barbarians ("teutónicos bárbaros") and at the same time consigns the city's doomed and dissolute inhabitants to the flames (1985: 503). Lozana's final destination links her knot with an open entrance to Hell, contributing to its literary power to summon a demonic army and conjure the sacking of Rome.

Delicado's own escape to Venice, however, seems to correlate with the supposed effectiveness of the Tau against plagues and the apotropaic protection of Solomon's seal against every kind of demons. These two seals and the synecdochic disclosures at the start and finish of the narrative can be viewed as safeguarding the author from his own creation, since he claims to have found solace after escaping the cursed, diseased city of the *Lozana andaluza*. For the syphilitic profligates that inhabit Delicado's book, however, any doorway that might bring peace has been closed off. Their fate is forever captured by the woodcut picturing them being ushered one-by-one towards into a Plutonian underworld. This demise recalls the blind lovers of Rojas's tragicomedy, who meet their destruction not at the hands of a devil invoked by Celestina as "Plutón" but by seeking refuge and revelling in the mortal pleasures of what they imagine to be amorous wounds, open and festering. We have observed how salvific amuletic powers attributed to Christ's *vulnus* and its measure to safeguard life and enable rebirth are obscenely manipulated by the earlier bawd. Her verbal needle and thread are efficacious to the extent that she can pierce and bind willing victims for material profit. Like Lozana's sexual healing and treatment of syphilitic sores, Celestina deals in the infliction, treatment, and reopening of wounds that inevitably lead to death, turning sinners away from the transcendent aperture made in the body of Christ. Both works create a sense of fatalistic dread by inserting amuletic texts and images into the modernizing world of the printed book. Here, the efficacy of inscriptions to open and close, bind and loose could be fictively contained and corrupted in new ways, and also in new ways fetishized and ultimately turned against itself.

Chapter Five

Outlaw Prayers

In 1992, construction workers in the Spanish town of Barcarrota, south of Badajoz, Extremadura, discovered a round paper amulet or *nómina* (Figure 20) that was evidently intended to be carried or worn on the body. The object, measuring approximately eleven centimentres in diameter, had been concealed in a wall for more than four and half centuries. Concentric circles on the paper are inscribed with a blessing from Christ's heavenly letter, two *nómina sacra*, and further invocations from a prayer known as the Trisagion or *sanctus*. As I outlined at the beginning of this study, the apocryphal letter was first recorded in Eusebius of Caesarea's fourth-century *Historia ecclesiastica* and already being described as a protective amulet in the *Itinerarium Egeriae* (c. 400). During the Middle Ages, travellers and others sought to shield themselves from unexpected dangers and sudden death by carrying parts of the wondrous text reproduced on parchment. In the epistolary inscription on the Barcarrota amulet, Christ promises to heal Abgarus of an unspecified ailment after praising him for believing without seeing.[1] According to tradition, their correspondence began when news reached Edessa of a Nazarene miracle worker whose words could cure spiritual as well as bodily ailments: "I have heard ... of your healing ... by your word ... you heal sick spirits and those who are tormented with lunatic demons" (Leclerq 1907–22: 43).[2]

In keeping with this form of healing, the interlocking circles of the *nómina* could be expected to bind or repel demonic forces, not unlike the Solomonic woodcut in the *Lozana andaluza*. Its power to trap or drive away evil seems even more likely, considering that a five-pointed star had been traced at the centre of the circle, together with an anchor cross and the ineffable name of God discussed earlier. In other words, the

Figure 20. Paper amulet (11 cm. diameter) found at Barcarrota (Badajoz). Courtesy Biblioteca de Extremadura, from the "Biblioteca de Barcarrota" Collection, *nómina*.

amulet roughly simulates and redeploys the kind of seals, pentagrams, and naming formulae found in medieval and early modern grimoires. One of the *nómina sacra* inscribed around the centre of the paper, the cabbalistic "AGLA" is an abbreviation of the Hebrew acronym, "Atah Gibor Leolam Adonai" (אגלא), addressing "You, O Lord" as "forever mighty" (Kieckhefer 1989: 159). The same acronym can also be found on French, English, and Italian examples dating from the twelfth to the seventeenth centuries.[3] The other sacred name "Paracletus" Latinizes a Greek term (παράκλητος) from the Gospel of John used to call the Holy Spirit as comforter and advocate (Hastings 1911: 665). AGLA and Paracletus are grouped together with the Trisagion (thrice holy) prayer of "eleison imas," for "have mercy on us," along with "agios o theos," "athanatos" and "ischyros," signifying "holy God," "immortal" and "mighty" (Henry 1907–14: 211–12). These phoneticized Greek words were commonly used to protect against the plague, as well as other illnesses or accidents, but also would have been familiar from the Roman liturgy.[4] During the sixteenth century, the Trisagion was chanted twelve times every year on Good Friday as part of the *Improperia*.[5] Forming part of the Adoration of the Cross, the *Improperia* consisted of a repetitive series of "reproaches" in which God is made to accuse his ungrateful people ("popule meus") of subjecting Christ to the agonies of the crucifixion, after He had delivered and led them triumphantly to the Promised Land. As Keith Thomas has pointed out, the perceived efficacy of Latin formulas inscribed on textual amulets can be related to memorized prayers that, in some cases, "confessors required penitents to repeat a stated number of times" (1991: 41).

These elements suggest that the *nómina* was intended as a devotional apotropaic text for travellers and as a healing shield against evil forces, illness, and unexpected death. Further support can be derived from an Italian message that appears on the back of the paper, written in Rome and dated 1551: "a qui ben si vogliono non è cosa lontana e dificile. E ancora che la tua patria sia lontano dela mia, non chè tu ti ricordi di me, perchè io sempre me ricordero di te. E Dio te dia tanta bona ventura come io te desidero, e altro no ti prego" (May that which is wished for not be remote and difficult. And although your homeland is far from mine, you need not remember me, for I will always remember you. And may God grant such fortune as I desire for you, and not another fate, I pray thee) (Torrico 2010: 128).[6] In the outermost circle on the front of the amulet, the likely recipient of this note is identified as Fernão Brandão of Évora (a Portuguese city located some seventy kilometres west of Barcarrota). Thus it would seem that the *nómina* was given as a parting gift to a close friend who was preparing to embark on a return journey from the Italian to the Iberian Peninsula.

Additional clues can be gathered from the stack of twelve multilingual books that were hidden with the *nómina* in the same wall. These include a popular manual for exorcism and a collection of parallel prayers in Hebrew, Latin, and Greek that can clearly be related to the purposes and content of the amulet.[7] More critical attention, however, has been more focused on other books in the Barcarrota cache, and in particular a fifteenth-century pamphlet known as the *Alborayque* (2005, The Buraq). This text was intended to expose the vices of converts to Christianity or *conversos* like Delicado and his fictional anti-heroine. In a highly publicized book, Fernando Serrano Mangas claimed that only a secretly practising Jew would have taken the trouble to conceal this anti-*converso* polemic (2004). His approach to the *Alborayque* seems to draw on the theory that Inquisitorial edicts, published with lists of Judaizing activities, provided a guide for *conversos* wishing to preserve or reconstruct their former religious identity.[8] While members of the press in Spain were quick to popularize Serrano's thesis, many scholars remained unconvinced. As Benajamín Torrico has recently observed, the *Alborayque* is not primarily concerned with cataloguing prohibited religious practices *per se* but rather with viciously mocking *conversos* by portraying them as monstrously deformed hybrids (2010: 129). Serrano goes on to identify the alleged crypto-Jewish owner of the Barcarrota books as a physician named Francisco de Peñaranda. To support this claim, he presents somewhat vague evidence from a parish archive, indicating that Peñaranda once resided in a building at or near the site of the find. Serrano hypothesizes that Fernão Brandão was a student who gave it to Peñaranda expressly for the purpose of healing the sick. His interpretation of the amulet, in my view, not only oversimplifies the Heavenly Letter's promise of "healing" but also minimizes the powers that could be attributed to Christian *nómina sacra* transliterated from Greek and Hebrew.

Francisco Rico has provided a more convincing explanation for the find at Barcarrota (1999). Rico suggests that the cache could have belonged to a bookseller hoping to save his merchandise from censors. Whether the owner was actually operating a store, amassing a private collection, or both, there can be no doubt that Inquisitorial authorities would have confiscated many of the items found in the wall. Foreign editions immediately roused suspicion at a time when bookstores and libraries were subject to increased scrutiny and visited by censors without warning, and when the circulation of outlawed material – following a decree issued in 1558 – was punishable by death. Among these are works of chiromancy by Patritio Tricasso (prohibited on the Roman index of 1559), an underground manuscript of Antonio Vignali's pornographic *Cazzaria* (Book of the Prick 1525), and the satirical poetry of an accused French heretic, Clément Marot.[9] Three titles in the collection were explicitly banned by the 1559 index of Fernando de Valdés: a 1554 edition of the picaresque masterpiece *Lazarillo de Tormes*, an undated Portuguese translation of the *Oración de la Emparedada* (Prayer of the Immured Nun) – both unknown to modern scholars prior to the discovery – and a copy of the well-known treatise by Erasmus *De lingua* (On the Tongue, 1525), printed in Lyon in 1538. Needless to say, concealing an amulet together with these dangerous books would only have invited more scrutiny. During the sixteenth century, as discussed previously in this study, Catholic reformers were seeking to restrict such objects and expose superstitious abuses. Both Ciruelo and Castañega, writing in the 1520s, had already condemned *nóminas* for using esoteric words and acronyms like Tetragrammaton and AGLA that were incomprehensible for speakers of Latin and Romance, and in any case not condoned by the church (1978: 87–8; 1997: 131).

Apart from the precariousness of the Barcarrota collection in the context of Inquisitorial Spain, critics have found that the hidden materials share a number of other characteristics. For instance, Torrico has highlighted the importance of satire, eroticism, and popular religiosity. While the cache may seem heterogeneous, he points out that "any *Lazarillo* reader knowns that there can be sex together with Erasmism and with the *Prayer of the Emparedada* ... the stash can be considered a library ... through the identification of internal trends, patterns, themes" (2010: 127, 136). In this chapter, I will consider the relationship between these two works, as well as the *De lingua* of Erasmus. As we shall see, the *Oración de la Emparedada* is the only book discovered at the site that can be directly linked to both the story of *Lazarillo* and the power of textual amulets.[10] Like the Barcarrota *nómina*, the *Oración* could be expected to exert a power over those who carried it. Representations of these kinds of banned amuletic prayers in the picaresque have most often been understood as little more than a means of exposing religious hypocrisy. In the pages that follow, I will demonstrate how their presence and supposed efficacy contributed to the creation of narrative structures that are characteristic of the picaresque novel. This can be seen not only in the anonymous precursor, *Lazarillo de Tormes* but also in Francisco de Quevedo's early seventeenth-century revision and reprisal of the genre, *El Buscón* (The Swindler). Like his predecessor, the latter novelist's vision of delinquency exploits attributes of a notorious prayer that was carried as a *nómina* and explicitly banned by the Inquisitors – but does so as a means of reinforcing, as opposed to circumventing, the judgment of censors.

The Prayer of the Immured Woman and the Matter of *Lazarillo de Tormes*

The *Oración* is a sixteenth-century printed amulet that begins with the legend of an immured or "walled-in" woman living in a mountain retreat outside Rome, who fervently prayed that the number of wounds

Figure 21. *Oración de la Emparedada*, courtesy Biblioteca de Extremadura, from the "Biblioteca de Barcarrota" Collection, no. 3.

Christ received during His Passion would be known to her (Figure 21).[11] This unnamed nun seems to be associated with St Bridget of Sweden, a widow who experienced visions of the five *stigmata* wounds suffered during the crucifixion (in the hands, feet, and side) and to whom the popular *Quindecim orationes* (The Fifteen Prayers or "O's") had been attributed for over a century (Birgitta 2008, 1665). The elaboration on St Bridget's formula in the *Oración* consists of fifteen petitions for mercy and reflections on the suffering of Christ meant to be read every day of the year in conjunction with the same number of Ave Marias and Pater Nosters, forming a kind of threefold or Trinitarian representation of the five wounds. Because this number was used to factor the measure of Christ's body (the *mensura* or *longitudo Christi*), and the drops of blood shed during His martyrdom, multiples of fifteen were believed to possess apotropaic power and were widely used in the production of textual amulets (Skemer 2006: 142–3, 178).[12] The Saviour promises the immured woman that this symbolic formula will liberate fifteen souls from Purgatory in the hereafter, and in this world protect and bring happiness ("prazer") and the good life ("boa vida") to any mortal sinner who freely confesses (*A muyto devota oração* 1997: fols. 2–3).[13] Like the Barcarrota *nómina* and other examples from the period, the amuletic powers of the *Oración* are derived not solely from the inscribed efficacy of prayer but from its material presence: "E o que a rezar ... ou a trouxer consigo ... onde quer que esta oração estever ... eu guardarei aquella casa e livrarei aquella companha ... por pouco trabalho haverás grande galardão" (He who prays or carries it with him ... wherever this prayer is ... I will protect that house and deliver these people ... and with little work you will obtain great gifts) (1997: fol. 4v). The conclusion of the *Oración* explains how a hermit transcribed the text of the *Oración*, shared it with the abbess of a convent, and finally witnessed a raucous company of demons being tortured by the incessant praying of the walled-in woman, who is now described as an "encantadeira e mui palavreira" (sorceress and chatterbox) (1997: fol. 15r).

Scholars have noticed a reference to this prayer in the 1554 Alcalá de Henares's edition of *Lazarillo de Tormes*. The rogue's first master is a blind man who partly makes his living by reciting prayers for women of ill repute, identified as "mesoneras y por bodegoneras y turroneras y rameras, y ansí por semejantes mujercillas, que por hombre casi nunca le vi decir oración" (wives of innkeepers, tavern keepers, confectioners, prostitutes, and other such lowly women, as I almost never saw him saying prayers for a man) (1987: 37).[14] In a crucial scene that foreshadows Lazarillo's final destiny as a wine-peddling town crier and a domesticated cuckold (who is provided for by his wife's lover, the archpriest of Sant Salvador), the blind man comes to Escalona, where horns are mounted on the wall of an inn:

> Iba tentando si era allí el mesón adonde él rezaba cada día por la mesonera la oración de la emparedada, asío de un cuerno y con un gran sospiro dixo ... "algún día te dará este que de la mano tengo alguna mala comida y cena." (1987: 37)

> (He was feeling if this was the inn where he recited the prayer of the immured woman every day for the innkeeper's wife, and took hold of one of the horns

[a symbol of duped husbands] and said with a great sigh ..."one day this thing
that I've got in my hand will give you an ill-deserved day's meals.")

While the scene is traditionally viewed as one of four interpolations,
Manuel Ferrer-Chivite has more recently suggested that these could
have been removed from the author's original text.[15] Whatever the
case, critics like Jack Weiner have found that the Alcalá version creates
a more tightly connected structure in which the blind man's Escalona
prophesies are comically fulfilled through the corruption of Lazarillo,
ultimately leading him to consent to a dishonourable marriage. My purpose here is to show how connotations of the amuletic prayer of the
walled-in woman in sixteenth-century Spain contribute to this narrative sequence.

Like *Lazarillo de Tormes*, the *Oración de la Emparedada* was placed on the
1559 *Index of Prohibited Books* compiled by Fernando de Valdés (Reusch
1961: 237). Not surprisingly, the pamphlet found in Barcarrota was not
just hidden in a wall but also rebound in a liturgical folio so that its
contents could not be readily identified.[16] Inquisitors continued to condemn the *Oración* for what the later 1581 Index of Gaspar de Quiroga
classifies as its "promesas y esperanças temerarias y vanas" (vain and
reckless promises and hopes), not to mention the inclusion at the end
of the prayer of an apocryphal indulgence attributed to "Nicolao papa
v" claiming to reveal how many drops of blood were shed during the
Passion (Reusch 1961: 383).[17] Even more problematic, as María Cruz
García de Enterría has pointed out, the prohibited text likens medita-
tions on the Passion to exorcizing "conjuros" or incantations. Scholars
have found that vernacular versions first appeared in fifteenth-century
books of hours of the kind that were also listed in the Index of Valdés: "Mandanse quitar las Horas siguientes porque contienen muchas
cosas curiosas y supersticiosas" (It is ordered that the following Hours
be removed as they contain many strange and superstitious things)
(Bujanda 1984: 5.671). From the 1520s on, printing houses continued to
disseminate the prayer throughout the peninsula as "cordel" literature,
or cheaply reproduced broadsides that could be sold by street vendors
and tied with string to be hung around the neck like *nóminas*.[18]

Lazarillo de Tormes provides evidence of how the *Oración* also circulated in sixteenth-century Spain as part of the oral repertoire of blind
men who supported themselves by reciting such popular prayers.
Additional evidence of this tradition can be found in other satirical

texts from the period, some of which García de Enterría lists in her introduction. For example, in Sánchez de Badajoz's *Farsa del molinero* (Farce of the Miller, c. 1554 a blind man calls out "¡Ayudá, fieles hermanos / al ciego lleno de males! … si mandáis rezar, christianos / ¡Dios os guarde pies y manos, / vuestra vista conservada! / la oración de la enparedada" (Help faithful brothers, the blind man full of maladies! … if you would have me pray, good Christians / May God bless your feet and hands, and your sight be preserved! The prayer of the immured woman) (1970: vv. 249–55). It would seem that the blasphemous street performer in this way associates the *stigmata* commemorated in the prayer with "maladies" representing his moral failings and bodily infirmities.[19]

Other literary citations are more concerned with the problem of superstition than the disrepute of blind men. For instance, in the *Crónica burlesca del emperador Carlos V* (Burlesque Chronicle of the Emperor Charles V, c. 1528), a fearful nobleman crossing a flooded river is said to carry seven *nóminas* and a copy of the *Oración* (Zuñiga 1981: 120–1). This exaggerated scene can be compared to an episode from *Segunda parte del Lazarillo* (Part Two of Lazarillo, 1555). In the anonymous sequel, the protagonist recites the immured woman's prayer after being cast into the sea – and, in doing so, brings to mind the superstitious appeals to saints famously exposed in Erasmus's *Colloquy* of the Shipwreck (1990).[20] Even more striking is Alejo de Venegas's earlier Erasmian satire in *Agonía del tránsito de la muerte* (Agony of the Passage to Death, 1537). This book condemns phony pardoners, who use the same prayer to deceive ignorant believers: "los llevan en el sermón … dicen que tienen bulas … la oración del la emparedada. Item, traen consigo una nómina" (they trick them during the sermon … they say they have pardons … the prayer of the immured woman. Also, they have with them a textual amulet) (qtd. in Bataillon 1966: 570).[21] Interestingly, the Alcalá *Lazarillo de Tormes* fictionalizes the same problem. At one point, the narrator describes how he helped a pardoner sell fake indulgences by offering efficacious prayers to their victims: "con cinco paternostres y cinco avemarías … aun también aprovechan para los padres y hermanos y deudos que tenéis en el purgatorio" (with five Pater Nosters and five Ave Marias … they will even help your parents and brothers and sisters and other relatives who are in Purgatory) (1987: 123).[22] As Weiner has noticed, this is the first time Lazarillo actively participates in such a deception, and it thus anticipates his complicity in a materially beneficial *ménage et trois* (1985: 16). The episode also recalls the *Oración* evoked in the scene of the blind man's prediction, with its sequence of Our Fathers and Hail Marys in amuletic multiples of fives and promise to release family members from their purgatorial sentence.

The comic efficacy of the *Oración* in the life of Lazarillo cannot be fully understood without also considering how female characters invoked the walled-in visionary.[23] For instance, in Feliciano de Silva's *Segunda Celestina* (Second Celestina, 1534), the go-between offers to teach a girl named Poncia the prayer of the "Emparedada" (1988: *cena* 20, 314). Poncia becomes alarmed at the suggestion that she wall herself off from the world: "madre, nunca tuve desseo de ser emparedada; por tu vida, que no me lo muestres" (mother, I never had the desire to be immured; on your life, swear you won't teach it to me) (1988: 314). The wordplay continues as Celestina responds with a peal of devious laughter, realizing that the girl has not yet learned how to disguise carnal desires in sacred language. The old bawd advises her: "Hija, pues demparedar has tu voluntad para yr al cielo, que la vía de salvación estrecha es" (Well, daughter, to get to heaven you must unwall your will, for the way of salvation is narrow) (1988: 314). Just as the old bawd's joke seems to be lost on Poncia, Lazarillo fails to see how his blind master's prophesy and recitation of the *Oración de la Emparedada* at the inn can be interpreted as a premonition of the "unwalled" sexuality of his future wife. She is, in this sense, comparable to what Patricia Parker has characterized as the "dilatory" woman overcoming the "partitions" of Renaissance society and narrative discourse – so that her eroticized verbal and corporal uncontainability "stands as figure" for the deferred closure of the text (1987: 11–13).[24]

This connection between the immured woman and uncontrollable wives can be most clearly seen in a surviving fragment of Juan Lorenzo Palmireno's *Comedia Octavia* (Comedy of Octavia, 1564). In the Latin play, a husband is beaten and publicly humiliated after his wife Marcelia insults him, "coniugalem thorum fugiat" (flees from the wedding bed), and arranges for cloistered virgins to celebrate a novena in which they pray for her freedom from the obligation of marital sex by intoning a novena prayer "quæ uulgo *de la emparedada* uocantur" (that is vulgarly called *de la emparedada*) (1566: 117). In this way, promises in the *Oración* of a happy life and the release of souls from purgatory are reinterpreted as a plea for deliverance from the unhappy confines of marriage. Instead of contemplating the Passion, Marcelia's novena celebrates the suffering of an unworthy husband. In addition to the *Oración* text, her revenge humorously counteracts the traditional threat of husbands consigning unruly brides to confinement. For instance, the medieval historian Gregoria Cavero Domínguez documents the case of a Valencian "casa de reclusión que un caballero mandó construir para encerrar a su esposa y que hiciera penitencia por la vida licenciosa que hasta entonces había llevado" (house of reclusion that a gentlemen had constructed to enclose his wife so that she would do penance for the licentious life that she had led until then) (2006: 110).[25] In *Lazarillo de Tormes*, the blind man's clientele of "wives of innkeepers, tavern keepers, confectioners" and "other such lowly women" might have requested this *Oración* for much the same reason as Marcelia (1987: 137).

More important, the inversion of prayer in the *Comedia Octavia* sheds light on the characterization of the rogue's unruly spouse in the preordained conclusion of the Alcalá edition. The rumour has spread that she abandons her wedding bed to spend the night with the archpriest of Sant Salvador, and Lazarillo remembers the horns of the innkeeper in Escalona whose wife paid the blind man to recite the *Oración de la Emparedada* (1987: 132). When the cuckold brings up the subject of her adultery, she responds with a barrage of oaths and curses that he fears will bring down the walls of their house, reminiscent of the duplicitous efficacy of the pardoner's oath-taking. Also reminded of the archpriest's generosity, Lazarillo then promises to be content with her coming and going as she pleases: "Entonces mi mujer echó juramentos sobre sí, que yo pensé la casa se hundiera con nosotros; y después tomóse a llorar y a echar maldiciones … y había por bien de que ella entrase y saliese, de noche y de día" (Then my wife swore such oaths that I thought the house would cave in on us; and after that she broke into tears and curses … and I was content that she could go in and out of the house, night or day) (1987: 134). In accordance with the power of the *Oración de la Emparedada*, to protect the "home," and bestow a happy life with "little work," and plenty to eat and drink, Lazarillo ironically claims to have arrived at "la cumbre de buena fortuna" (the height of good fortune) in the last *tratado* – in fulfilment of the blind man's prediction of an "ill-deserved day's meals" (1987: 135, 37). This parody at the same time implicates the earlier-mentioned inversion at the end of the *Oración*, as a demon portrays the petitions of the immured woman as the cursed incantations of a "sorceress and chatterbox" (1997: fol. 15r). When the blind man's prediction at the inn where he recited the prayer finally comes to pass, the blessings of the bride of Christ in the *Oración* are transformed into the oaths, curses, and extramural sexuality of Lazarillo's wife.

Such an association reflects medieval and early modern anxieties over controlling the speech and sexuality of walled-in women, leading to what Peter Stallybrass has identified as the "*topos* that presents woman as that treasure which, however locked up, always escapes. She is the gaping mouth, the open window, the body that transgresses its own limits" (1986: 128). These kind of preoccupations can already be seen in Gonzalo de Berceo's thirteenth-century *Poema de Santa Oria* (Poem of St Aurea), where an anchoress shuts herself off from the temptations of fallen language and the urges of the flesh, and her body becomes an enclosure worthy to receive the Bridegroom: "ovo con su carne baraja e contienda ... que non salliessen dende vierbos desconvenientes ... un rencón angosto entró emparedada ... esta reclusa vaso de caridat" (with her body she clashed and battled ... to hold back indiscreet words ... she entered a narrow corner to be walled-in ... this enclosed vessel of God's love) (1981: sts. 16c, 18d, 20b, 25a). Julian Weiss (1996) has shown how Berceo portrays St Aurea as at once physically confined and spiritually opened up. It is also worth noting that this contrast is reflected in the dual meaning of the term *reclusum* in medieval Latin as *clausum* (closed) and/or *apertum* (open). In the fourteenth-century *Revelations* that informed the *Oración de la emparedada*, St Bridget similarly identifies herself an enclosed *sponsa Christi* receiving the espousals of the Saviour prefigured in the Song of Songs: "I have chosen you and taken you as my bride ... you ought to be ready for the wedding to my divinity, in which there is no carnal lust but the sweetest spiritual delight" (2008: 1.2.3–4, 1.20.7). According to Alfonso of Jaén, the Spanish anchorite who recorded and defended her *Revelations* – and might have inspired the unnamed hermit in the *Oración* – Bridget's detractors were sometimes punished with horrible afflictions.[26]

Nonetheless, denunciations persisted into the fifteenth century. For example, Jean Gerson cast doubt on the visions of ascetic women who engage their confessors in "continual conversations" and "lengthy accounts," displaying what he views as an "unhealthy curiosity which leads to gazing about and talking, not to mention touching," indicative of a "harmful love toward God or toward holy persons, rather than being moved by true, holy, and sincere charity" (Sahlin 2001: 165). During the same period, Spanish penitential writers and church synods repeatedly warned against the scandal of *emparedadas* breaking their vows of silence, receiving frequent visitors, and brazenly entering and leaving their cells.[27] As Stallybrass puts it in his study of feminine enclosure, "the mouth, chastity, the threshold ... these three areas were frequently collapsed into each other" (1986: 126). It is in this context that demons at the conclusion of the *Oración* depict the immured woman as a scandalizer. The bawd in the *Segunda Celestina* describes an unwalling of female desire, and Lazarillo relates the unconfined libido and unleashed tongue of his wife. Her carnal relationship with the aptly named Archpriest of the "Holy Savior" can be understood as a travesty of the divine love that Christ visits upon His *sponsa* in the alleged visions of saints like Bridget of Sweden and her legendary heterodox offshoot, the *emparedada*.[28]

During her lifetime, Bridget was repeatedly accused of witchcraft and threatened with prosecution for heresy. Sixteenth-century Spanish women who followed her example could expect to face the same kind of suspicions and were in some cases punished with ecclesiastical confinement. For instance, the nun Magdalena de la Cruz claimed to have experienced visions after making an opening in her cell wall to contemplate the sacred host, later confessed to having carnal relations with a demon, and was sentenced by the Inquisition in 1544 to "emparedamiento ... mandamos que esté encerrada perpetuamente en un monasterio" (immurement ... we order that she be perpetually confined in a monastery) (Imirizaldu 1977: 61).[29] The same condition of enclosure or *reclusum* that had enabled her to open up to the Divine and helped give credence to her revelations was ultimately used to shut off and silence her. Later mystics were also subjected to this penance or *murus strictus*, as in the case of María de la Visitación, who was condemned in the 1580s for falsely claiming to have received the five *stigmata* from her Bridegroom for fifteen days – the same talismanic number used in the *Oración de la emparedada* and other amuletic texts. Such rulings once again bring to mind the demonic characterization of the walled-in woman as a scandalous conjurer, as well as the revelations of her prayer. A particularly revealing example can be found in proceedings brought against the early seventeenth-century prophetess known as Juana de la Cruz or the "Enbustera" or Trickster, denouncing her as a heretic:

Tocada de los herrores de los alumbradoss, engañadora, escandalossa ...
diçiendo que a tenido muchas pláticas con ... Jesús ... es mentira aver

dicho que es doncella y que avía hecho boto de castidad y tanbien su
marido y que la verdad es averse comunicado carnalmente y confiesa ...
mentirossa, enbelecadora. (Imirizaldu 1977: 97, 104, 111)

(Influenced by Illuminist errors, a scandalous deceiver ... saying that she
has often spoken with ... Jesus ... she lies by claiming to be a maiden and
having made a vow of chastity, as does her husband, for the truth is they
have had carnal relations and she confesses ... she is a liar, a fraud.)[30]

These kinds of investigations suggest that early audiences could have
interpreted connotations of the *emparedada* in *Lazarillo de Tormes* as
alluding to the adultery of Lazarillo's wife as a parodic vision of mystical marriage. The idea of immurement might have also brought to mind
the Inquisitorial penalization of women, whether for masquerading as
visionary brides of Christ or for other crimes.

The sentence passed against María de la Visitación orders the
walled-in penitent to fast on bread and water, receive further unspecified mortifications, and recite the Psalm "miserere mei" (Have mercy
on me) (Imirizaldu 1977: 196).[31] Consonant with the treatment of other
false visionaries, the Inquisition mandates that all writings and relics related to her cult should be gathered and burned in public. The
penance of this visionary is distinctly reminiscent of the penance of St
Thais, a popular reformed sinner in late medieval and early modern
hagiographic collections that present her *vita eremitica* as the mirror
image of her former life, when she was closed off from faith and open
to the world. Thais famously confessed to an abbot who entered the
innermost chamber of her brothel to convert her, an enclosure where
no man had ever been received and only God could see her sins. She
expresses her contrition in the public square, throwing all of the goods
earned from her sin into a bonfire. The abbot then mandates that Thais
immure herself in a "cella pequeñuela," the entrance of which is sealed
with molten iron, leaving only a small opening to receive "un poco de
pan e de agua" (a little bread and water) (Beresford 2007: 135). When
the repentant prostitute asks where she should relieve herself, the confessor harshly chastises her: "¡aquí en tu celda como tú lo meresciste! ...
tú no eres digna de rogar a Dios nin de tomarle en tu boca suzia ... di
muchas vezes esta palabra ... 'ave mercet de mí'" (here in your cell as
you have deserved! ... you are not worthy to pray to God or speak his
name in your filthy mouth ... say these words repeatedly... have mercy

on me) (Beresford 2007: 134–5). Following a vision of three virgins on a celestial bed representing the immured woman's fear of God, shame for her past life, and newly found love of virtue, the abbot releases her. The freed Thais only lives for a period of fifteen days, a number that associates her triumph over evil and purified body with the apotropaic *mensura Christi*.

By the time *Lazarillo de Tormes* was published, this longstanding connection between visionary reclusion and the punishing and absolving of prostitutes and other promiscuous women had become something of running joke. In the *Lozana andaluza* (1528), a prostitute known as the "emparedada" seems to be making a burlesque allusion to the filthy cell of St Thais when she asks her madam "¿por qué no entró? … ¿pensó que estaba al potro?" (why didn't you come in? … Did you think I was on the pot?) (Delicado 1985: 312). An earlier commentary in the *Carajicomedia* (Prick Comedy 1519) portrays a walled-in prostitute known as Cáceres who remains in her chamber for thirty years: "es su costumbre estar a su puerta muy devota enclavijadas sus manos cantando lamentaciones muchas vezes, recibiendo el precio de su persona" (she is customarily found at the door with her hands crossed and nailed, very devoutly singing lamentations over and over, receiving a price for her person) (1981: st. 73).[32] As I have shown elsewhere, the *Carajicomedia* parodies Ambrosio de Montesino's 1514 translation of the *Vita Christi* of Ludolph of Saxony, in addition to the fifteenth-century *Laberinto de Fortuna* (*The Laughter* 2009: 25–32). In the gloss on Cáceres, the poet appears to be subverting Montesino's depiction of "una venerable matrona emparedada … que desseava saber el cuento de todas las llagas de Jesú Cristo e que por este desseo avia gastado muchos tiempos y lagrimas" (a venerable walled-in matron … who wished to know the number of all the wounds of Jesus Christ and for this desire spent long periods in tears) (1551: fol. 40r). While this *Vita Christi*, known as the *Cartuxano*, goes on to describe a numerological revelation and the prayer found in the *Oración de la emparedada*, the *Carajicomedia* features an unrepentant sex worker. Instead of praying for the visitation of her mystical husband, she continues to receive customers and moan mournfully within the walls of her enclosure. Instead of imitating the wounds of Christ, she graphically exhibits the stigma of a fallen woman. In keeping with these precedents, *Lazarillo de Tormes* links the immured woman with prostitutes and female clientele of the blind man, along with a wife whose adulterous affair with the archpriest of Sant Salvador marks the high point in a life of wounding humiliation.

Significantly, her affair occurs at a time when the Spanish church redoubled its efforts to enforce discipline among the clergy. This was partly in reaction to dangerous reform movements that, as Thomas Hanrahan notes, proposed "the abolition of clerical celibacy" (1983: 335). Lazarillo's precarious situation is first mentioned in the prologue as the "caso" or matter that he has been asked to relate "muy por extenso ... por que se tenga entera noticia de mi persona" (very extensively ... to have a full report of who I am) by request of an authority figure identified only as "Vuestra Merced" (Your Honour) (1987: 89, 130). Lazarillo responds by simultaneously justifying and incriminating himself with a tongue-and-cheek account that conceals and exposes. The narrator alternates between reflections on his formerly naive point of view and his cynical perspective in the final *tratado*. David Gitlitz has compared the narrator's strategies to Inquisitorial confessions in which *conversos* or new Christians were compelled to give reports of their own experiences as well as the lives of others. He finds that they appear to have engaged in comparable "rhetorical techniques of disclosure and evasion" (2000: 54).[33] Other scholars have emphasized the narrator's use of euphemism and preterition in anticipation of the sexual corruption of his "caso," as when Lazarillo takes refuge with spinner "mujercillas" (little women), "wears out his shoes" and other "cosillas" (little things) with a lecherous and apparently bisexual Mercedarian, and "grinds colors" for a painter of tambourines (1987: 93, 110–11, 125).[34] I have found that the *Oración de la Emparedada* invoked in the Alcalá edition plays into this sort of pseudo-confessional rhetoric. In sixteenth-century Spain, the prayer was linked with transgressions of the flesh and the Inquisitorial menace that Gitlitz and others have shown to be moulding and casting a shadow over the narrative. The banned *Oración* raised suspicions by offering the kind of "happiness in this world" that Lazarillo seeks together with extravagant promises of perfect contrition, confession, redemption through the Eucharist, and deliverance from evil forces and the pains of purgatory:

Ho que a rezar ou a fezer rezar ou ha trouxer consigo ... darlhej ... a comer o meu sanctisimo corpo, o qual o liurara da fome pa sempre. E darlhej a beber ho meu precioso sangue con o qual nunca auera sede ... darlhey a beber hũ singular beber da fonte da minha diuindad. Outrosi, qualquer pessoa que esteuer em pecado mortal ainda que aja trinta annos que se nan aja confessado, e se confessar con amarga contriçam e esta oraçam conprir, lhe perdoarey todos seus pecados, e o liurarey do poderio de justiça e do diabo. (1997: fol. 3)

(He who prays it or has it recited or carries it with him … I will feed him with my holiest body, which will free him from hunger forever; and I will quench his thirst with my precious blood, so that he is never again thirsty … I will give him an incomparable drink from the fountain of my Divinity … whosoever finds himself in mortal sin, though he has not confessed for thirty years, if he confesses with bitter contrition, and fulfills this prayer, I will pardon all sins, and I will free him from the forces of judgment and the devil.)

These benefits can be meaningfully contrasted with the decidedly uncontrite disclosures and quasi-Eucharistic redemption that characterize *Lazarillo de Tormes*. In fact, the narrator first recounts his early experiences of thirst and starvation as a kind of parodic excommunication in which the blind man bashes his head with a wine jug, deprives him of its "fuentecilla" (little fountain) – and, while cleaning his wounds with the fruit of the vine, entertains the innkeeper's wife and her friends by predicting that the same substance that now heals his wounds will someday bless him (1987: 31, 42–3). In the next *tratado*, a miserly priest refuses to share a store of bread that the starving rogue worships like the Corpus Christi: "por consolarme, abro el arca, como vi el pan, comencé de adorar, no osando rescebillo … contemplar en aquella cara de Dios" (to console myself, I open the trunk; as I looked upon the bread, I began to adore it, not daring to receive it … contemplating in it the face of God) (1987: 58). As we have seen, Lazarillo finally arrives at the "height of all good fortune" promised in the *Oración* and foretold by the blind man. He will earn an "ill deserved day's meals" as a town crier selling wines and profiting from his wife's extramarital affair with a salvific archpriest, though he swears to her honesty "sobre la hostia sagrada" (on the Sacred Host) (1987: 135, 37, 134).[35] In this way, the mock happy ending to the Alcalá narrative subverts the alleged efficacy of the prayer to grant even the most obstinate sinners absolution and admittance to the Lord's Supper.

The promise of forgiveness and penance made in the blind man's heterodox *Oración* can be fruitfully compared to Inquisitorial proceedings against walled-in women. These sinners could be readmitted to the *Coena Domini* only after confessing and receiving their sentence at an *auto de fé* where they were often expected to wear nooses around their necks and face a range of other public humiliations. For instance, when Magdalena de la Cruz was sentenced to immurement for a series of alleged crimes – including the earlier-mentioned use of sorcery to view the blessed sacrament through a hole in her cell – the tribunal specified that she appear with "una bela encendida en las manos y una mordaza a la lengua y una soga" (with a lit candle in her hand, a gag in her mouth, and a rope around her neck) (Imirizaldu 1977: 61). Juana the Illuminist "Trickster" was similarly paraded with "una bela de çera en la mano y una soga a la garganta y una coroça en la caveça … sea sacada en una bestia … con voz de pregonero que manifeste su delito" (a wax candle in her hand, a rope around her neck, and a conical hat on her head … may she appear on the back of a beast … with a town crier's voice declaring her crime) (Imirizaldu 1977: 118). The practice of condemning prisoners to *murus strictus* escorted by town criers and wearing esparto collars and gags corresponds to another prophecy that the blind man makes just before arriving at the Escalona inn. Touching the "sogas" that hang at a shoemaker's shop, he predicts: "mochacho, salgamos de entre tan mal manjar, que ahoga sin comerlo … según las mañas que llevas, lo sabrás y verás cómo digo verdad" (boy, let us flee from such bad fare, for it suffocates without even being eaten … with all of your tricks, you will come to know and see how I speak the truth) (1987: 37). In the Alcalá text, Lazarillo reflects on this divination after finding work as a town crier who, apart from peddling wines, accompanies criminals through the streets of Toledo:

> Tengo cargo de … acompañar los que padecen persecuciones por justicia y declarar a voices sus delictos, pregonero … En el cual oficio, un día que ahorcábamos a un apañador … llevaba una buena soga de esparto, conoscí y caí en la cuenta de la sentencia que aquel mi ciego amo había dicho … Teniendo noticia de mi persona el señor arcipreste de Sant Salvador … procuró casarme con un criada suya … y hasta ahora no estoy arrepentido … tengo de mi señor arcipreste todo favor y ayuda … mas malas lenguas … no nos dejan vivir diciendo no sé qué y sí sé qué de que ven mi mujer irle a hacer la cama y guisalle de comer … y habido algunas malas cenas por esperalla algunas noches hasta las laudes, y aún más, y se me ha venido a la memoria lo que mi amo el ciego me dijo en Escalona, estando asido del cuerno … Mi señor … me habló un día … delante de ella … "quien ha de mirar a dichos de malas lenguas nunca medrará." (1987: 129–32)[36]

(I am charged with ... following those who suffer persecution for the sake of justice and calling out their crimes, a town crier ... one day we hung a thief ... he wore a coarse noose, and I recognized and fell under the sentence that that blind master of mine had pronounced ... The reverend Archpriest of the Holy Savior having heard reports of me... arranged a marriage for me with a servant of his ... and I have repented to this day ... I have all the favours and help from my lord the Archpriest ... yet malicious tongues ... will not leave us be, saying I don't know what, and I do know what about having seen my wife go and make his bed and cook his food ... I have had some bad meals waiting up for her some nights until morning prayers, or even later, and I recalled what my master the blind man said to me in Escalona, when he was holding the horn ... My reverend Lord ... spoke to me one day ... in her presence ... "you'll never get on in life if you take notice of malicious tongues.")

In keeping with the oracular horns and prayer of a walled-in "chatterbox" at the Escalona inn, the meaning of the shoemaker's ropes becomes increasingly clear in subsequent episodes. First, when Lazarillo wears down the soles of his shoes – presumably made of esparto – in the company of the errant Mercedarian. This link between sexual corruption and worn-out ropes anticipates the rogue's role in promoting the wines of his wife's lover, while at the same time proclaiming the misdeeds of criminals bound with *sogas*. The rogue at once speaks as a town crier announcing his own crimes along with those of his associates, and as a haltered criminal, gagged and suffocated by what the blind man calls "bad fare." The narrator's discourse is stifled, euphemistic, marked by preterition and passing allusion. Yet it has the effect of loudly disclosing unsavoury truths in spite of the threat of censorship and the spectre of Inquisitorial punishment. He claims to have put a lid on the scandal of his wife by blasphemously swearing to her honesty, but instead succeeds in amplifying the clamour of "malicious tongues": "desta manera no me dicen nada, y you tengo paz en mi casa" (this way they tell me nothing, and I have peace in my house) (1987: 135). His pronouncement brings to mind last words of benediction, "in pace," from the *Ordo inclusorum* or ritual of immurement, which were also used by the Holy Office to designate the walled-in chambers of penitents.[37] While Lazarillo's unfaithful, cursing wife cannot be contained, he remains trapped. The "peaceable" confines of his house are ironically foreshadowed by the *Oración de la emparedada*'s power to protect the home of "he who prays or carries it with him" (1997: fol. 4v). They also recall the tomblike quarters that Lazarillo shares with the squire: "tener cerrada la puerta con llave ni sentir arriba ni abajo pasos de viva persona ... Todo lo que yo había visto eran paredes" (having the door closed and locked without a sign of any living person above or below ... All I had seen were walls) (1987: 73). Later in the same episode, Lazarillo hears a widow in a funeral procession crying out that her husband must now live in a dark and mournful dwelling and becomes convinced that the dead man will be brought to his house to rest *in pace*.[38] Like recurrent noose imagery, the squire's sepulchral dwelling takes on an especially ironic significance in the Alcalá narrative.

As I hope to have demonstrated, this version of *Lazarillo de Tormes* invokes the *Oración de la emparedada* to reveal key elements of the prophesized "matter" of the rogue's marriage and ultimate occupation. The amuletic prayer correlates with the pardoner's appeal to say five Hail Marys and Our Fathers for relatives in purgatory, and how the "unwalling" of the immured woman in other literary texts coincides with the revelation of the archpriest of Sant Salvador's "dilatory" lover. She too parodies visions of mystical espousal, wounds of the Passion, and vows of silence taken by walled-in female saints, subjecting her husband to a cuckold's martyrdom in the tradition of unruly women punished with immurement. Accordingly, the benefits of the prayer are comically fulfilled through Lazarillo's adulterous arrangement: material contentment is granted, the palate quenched, the belly filled, and an incorrigible sinner's confession leads to a mock Eucharistic supper. Denied the bread and cup of life by a string of abusive earlier masters, the town crier's meals and the wine he sells are now provided by the concubinary archpriest. Finally, we have seen how the apotropaic potency to safeguard the houses of those who say, hear, or wear the *Oración* is inverted by the "peace" of Lazarillo's house, and the connections between worn ropes, lost innocence, and the noosing and muzzling of prisoners condemned to *murus strictus*.

These findings suggest that the Lazarillo character is bound by the amuletic text that the blind man recites, as it seems to exert an ironic force over the course of his fictional life, equivalent to the binding physical presence of a *nómina* or *cordel* prayer hung around the neck or otherwise carried on the body. The stakes of the proleptic intertextual relationship between *Lazarillo* and the *Oración* that has concerned me can be further illuminated by turning to one last work from the Barcarrota cache, *De lingua* (On Language, 1525). A Spanish translation of the text went through several editions during the first half of the sixteenth century, until "Lengua de Erasmo, en Romance y en Latin" was placed on the 1559 index, along with the two books from Barcarrota that I have been discussing. In this treatise, Erasmus takes on his detractors by contrasting an uncontrolled torrent of printed books, many of them full of "indiscreet chattering, headlong lying" and the product of a "beguiling, impious and blaspheming tongue," with the restrained "new tongue" of true Christianity curing "men's souls with holy incantations" and offering "instead of accusation against our neighbor, confession of our own evils" (1989: 403–10). As Carla Mazzio points out, this torrent of escaping words can be related to "genital and lingual dilation" as an "analogue to the activity of narration itself ... to spread abroad or make large, to amplify, to tell" (1998: 101). Lazarillo demonstrates that he cannot control his tongue and speak the *lingua nova*, any more than demons can understand the prayers of the immured woman as anything other than incantatory chatter. His story both denies and verifies the allegations of "malas lenguas." In other words, it illustrates what Erasmus sees as a linguistic duplicity that breaks through the bounds of propriety represented by the tongue's natural, censoring enclosure behind its barrier of teeth. In spite of the rogue narrator's gestures of discretion and dissimulation, he remains incapable of controlling or walling-in his own tongue.[39]

The Prayer and Vision of the Just Judge in *El Buscón*

In an earlier-cited scene from the sequel to *Lazarillo de Tormes*, the shipwrecked rogue not only invokes the walled-in woman but also intones what is called the "Oración del Justo Juez" (Prayer to the Just Judge) (1988: 55). Unlike the *Oración de la Emparedada*, versions of this plea for justice had been circulating in written and oral form for centuries. The prayer can ultimately be traced back to a Latin text commonly attributed to Berenger of Tours. This eleventh-century theologian best known for infamously denying the doctrine of transubstantiation – that is, that the substance of Eucharistic bread is changed into the body of Christ. Berenger instead advanced a heretical theory known as *impanatio* in which God was said to transform Himself into bread during the consecration of the host, or in the words of his follower John of Paris, "The Body of Christ is impanated, i.e., has become bread" (Corpus Christi impanatum, i.e., panis factum) (Pohle 1914: 7.694). Berenger was excommunicated by Pope Leo XI and imprisoned by King Henry I of France, but refused to recant definitively and died in reclusion. Medieval adherents of his heresy were known as Berengarians, and the accusation of teaching "impanation" would be later levelled at Lutherans, as well as other Protestant reformers during the sixteenth century. By this time, a prayer known as the *Oratio Berengerii* and addressed to the *Juste Judex* was being widely disseminated with a plea for Christ to punish unspecified enemies, freeing and shielding supplicants like the souls ransomed from eternal imprisonment in the biblical Harrowing of Hell. While this Latin text does not allude to impanation, we will see how a later adaption of the prayer confuses the meaning of the Incarnation in a way that sheds light on early modern representations of superstition and heterodoxy.

A vernacular version of Berenger's plea for deliverance can be found in the early fifteenth-century *Leal Conselheiro* (Loyal Counselor) of Duarte I of Portugal (1842: 477–80).[40] The king uses the "Oraçom de Justo Juiz" as an example of accurate translation since it was based on a "Latin prayer sufficiently well known to his potential readers to allow them, without the text itself being present, to judge his methods" (Askins 2007: 252). While Duarte's rendering is faithful to the original, an erroneous Castilian translation later made its way into numerous sixteenth-century books of hours. It also passed into a popular meditation on the Passion of Christ entitled the *Fasciculus myrrhe* (The Little Bundle of Myrrhe), which went through at least fourteen editions between 1511 and 1553.[41] The corrupted prayer appears near the end of this book, when the anonymous author imagines Pontius Pilate as a righteous convert instead of an unjust judge:

Muchas maravillas ... [Poncio] avía oydo ... si una sola viera ... crexera en Él ... quitándole ... de los judíos ... embiándole a Roma al Emperador ... con propria fe y justicia no matando al ynocente. Siguesse la oración de nuestro señor jhesu christo muy devotíssima que dize ... Justo Juez ... "Tú en el vientre de la Virgen de los cielos descendiendo tomaste verdadera carne visitando este siglo: por la tu propia sangre después del mundo redemido ... Sea sienpre conmigo ... la tu defensión porque la malicia de los mis enemigos no perturbe el mi coraçón, ni el mi cuerpo sea engañado por el lazo dañoso y engañoso de trayción ... quebrantaste las puertas infernales: quebrántalos los mis enemigos ... que llamo en peccados captivo ... porque no se levanten los mis enemigos en denuesto mío. Sean destruydos y enfaqueacan los ... El lazo de la enbidia sea a ellos ... Tú seas mi escudo guardador ... Arriedres de mi a los que me aborrezcen y el su odio y error ... me haga vencedor porque vencido el enemigo fallezcan las sus fuerças con dolor ..." (1524: fol. 103)

(Many miracles ... [Pontius] had heard of ... had he seen only one ... he would have believed in Him ... freeing Him from the Jews ... sending Him to the Emperor in Rome ... by his own faith and justice not slaughtering the innocent. What follows is the very devout prayer to our Lord Jesus Christ that is called ... Just Judge ... "You in the womb of the Virgin, from the heavens descending, took on true flesh, visiting this age with your own blood after the world was redeemed ... May I always be ... defended by You, so that the malice of my enemies will not perturb my heart, nor my body be deceived by the damaging and deceptive snare of treachery ... you broke the doors of Hell: may you break my enemies ... I call out from the captivity of sin ... so that my enemies may not rise up against me ... May You destroy and weaken them ... may they be ensnared by their own envy ... May you be my protective shield ...")[42]

The error introduced into the prayer hinges on a misinterpretation of the Latin, "Tuum plasma redimendo sanguinem per proprium" (Redeeming creation with your own blood). The *Leal Conselheiro* accurately conveys the same line with the words "livraste ... per tuo sangue ... de perdiçom" (you freed ... by your blood ... from perdition) (Mone 1853–5: 1.359; Duarte 1842: 478). Unlike this earlier Portuguese version, the sixteenth-century Spanish translation of Berenger's prayer seems to be suggesting that the sinful world was redeemed prior to the Incarnation, "por la tu propia carne ... después del mundo redemido." The heterodox text was for this reason added to the *Index of Prohibited Books* in 1559. Undoubtedly, the notoriety of its original Latin author and his doctrine of impanation could have led to increased scrutiny and cast further suspicions on the "Oración del Justo Juez," as Counter-Reformation authorities sought to defend against a wave of perceived threats to orthodoxy.[43]

Not long after the publication of this *Index*, a prayer by the same name is identified as part of the repertoire of itinerant performers in fictional works like Lope de Vega's *Los peligros de la ausencia* (The Dangers of Absence, 1562). Reminiscent of *Lazarillo de Tormes* and its sequel, a character named Martín disguises himself as a disreputable blind man. Acquiring a "Lazarillo" or seeing-eye dog, he calls out: "¿hay quién me mande rezar la Oración del Justo Juez?" (is there someone who will have me intone the Prayer of the Just Judge?) (1902: 409). Another example can be found in a *villancico* or carol performed during the latter part of the seventeenth century, when a blind men wanders into the cathedral of Jaén offering to sing the same prayer. After worshipers threaten to eject him for so rudely interrupting feast-day celebrations with his heterodox chanting, the itinerant singer promises to take on the role of a just judge himself and make a ruling as to which is the greatest church in all of Spain. Ironically, his "just sentence" (in favour of Jaén, of course) is based on the experience of "seeing" them, "in the light" but with "eyes closed" (Medina 2008: 125–6).[44] Significantly, the blind judge is allowed to begin this song only after assuring listeners that the prohibited "oración" will be replaced with a new "obra y cosa de gusto" (work and thing of good taste) (2008: 125).

To my knowledge, the only literary reference from the period that claims to reproduce any part of the banned text is Francisco de Quevedo's classic *El Buscón* (composed c. 1604). What is more, characters repeatedly evoke this *Oración* in the novel: An initial allusion occurs when a female servant named Cypriana begins her nightly prayers with the Just Judge and ends with a mispronunciation of the *Quicumque vult* and *Salve regina* (pronounced as *Conquibules* and *Salva rehina*). Later, the titular rogue and first-person narrator, Pablos, meets a sacristan who has composed a prolific corpus of bad poetry, impossible-to-produce plays, and a song for the feast of Corpus Christi. Its verses blasphemously describe the Eucharistic wafer as an "immaculate lamb" humbling itself in the bellies and intestines of celebrants (1980: 178–9). When this ridiculous author later arrives in Madrid, a swarm of blind men ask him to recite the "Oración del Justo Juez" in what is described as "verso grave y sonoro, tal que provocase" (grave and sonorous verses, so that it would provoke) (1980: 181).[45] Near the end of the narrative, Pablos tries his hand at writing for theatre and composing poetry. He also claims to have written a famous rendition of the same prayer that the Sacristan sold to blind men. Pablos's version begins with the words "Madre del Verbo humanal, / Hija del Padre divino, / dame gracia virginal, etc." (Mother of the human Word, daughter of the Father Divine, give me virginal grace) (1980: 287).

It is clear that his petition, like the *Oración de la emparedada*, refers to a text that was not only performed, but also sold as portable *cordel* text to be carried or hung around the neck and more specifically employed as an amulet. Julio Caro Baroja has studied numerous seventeenth-century examples of the oral and material circulation of broadside prayers and other early modern materials that were trafficked by blind men and other street merchants (1969). Their business is described in two other works by Lope de Vega, *La octava maravilla* (The Eighth Wonder, c. 1609) and *Servir a señor discreto* (To Serve a Discrete Lord, 1618). In the first play, a servant carries "un papel … impreso" (printed paper) that he purchased after hearing a blind man recite all or part of its versified contents (1618: 159v). Similarly, *La octava maravilla* depicts two gentlemen discussing the problem of such verses: "un necio le escribe / y otro ciego le pregona … no sé cómo se consiente que mil inventadas cosas por ignorantes, se vendan por los ciegos que las toman. Allí se cuentan milagros, martirios … se venden y compran" (a fool writes it, and another blind man announces it … I do not know how it is allowed that thousands of inventions for the ignorant are sold by blind men to deceive. These tell of miracles, martyrdoms … they are sold and purchased) (1930: 255). In the later *Servir a señor discreto*, another servant disguises himself as a blind man, like Martín in the earlier-cited *Peligros de la ausencia*. The imposter then attempts to sell a *cordel* text that he supposedly authored: "Quién compra la obra nueva / recién impresa y famosa, della verso y della prosa? ¿quién la compra, / Quién la lleva?" (Who will buy this new work, recently printed and famous, in verse and in prose? Who will buy it?) (1901: 73).[46] These plays show how early seventeenth-century audience members would have understood the value and supposed efficacy of the *Prayer of the Just Judge* on the basis of its material possession, in addition to the performativity of spoken language. They also testify to the difficulty in controlling the proliferation of such texts in early modern Spain. It is no wonder that by 1684, Carlos II found it necessary to issue a royal decree restricting their spread: "se ha aumentado este abuso con demasía, por lo que toca a relaciones sueltas y otros papeles o coplas que suelen vender los ciegos" (this abuse as increased excessively, regarding broadside stories and other papers and verses that tend to be sold by blind men) (Zavala 1975: 398). While *cordel* literature from the seventeenth century has survived, a printed example corresponding to Pablos's prayer has yet to be found.

Editors have, however, noticed that his rhyme scheme corresponds to an orally preserved version, beginning with the invocation, "Justo Juez divinal." A number of Portuguese examples have been studied by Robert Ricard ("Du roi" and "Pour l'étude"), and more recently Manual de Costa Fontes in his compilation and analysis of *romanceiros* or popular songs that have been passed on for centuries.[47] Reminiscent of Pablos's version, some of these songs begin with the invocation, "Justo juiz divinal, filho da Virgen Maria," followed by variations like: "Entre toda a Judiaria crucificado ... se vierem nossos inimigos para nos prenderem / ou algum mal nos fazerem ... olhos tenham, nao nos vejam ... guardeis o meu corpo ... nao seja preso ... nem de justiça envolto" (Just Judge divine, son of the Virgin Mary ... He among all of the Jews crucified ... if our enemies come to arrest us / or do us any ill ... may they have eyes that cannot see us ... protect my body ... may it not be imprisoned ... nor caught in the arm of justice) (1987: 4–5).[48] While Costa Fontes does not take into consideration the precedent in the *Fasciculus myrrhe*, his oral texts exhibit an analogous fear of "captivity" and the desire to evade a "deceptive snare." Similar to the sixteenth-century devotional book, the Portuguese songs associate these threats with the injustice of Pontius Pilate and Jews being accused of wrongly condemning Christ to death in the gospels. The garbled prayer in the *Buscón*, in my view, provides additional evidence for such a connection.[49] It echoes the "Justo Juez divinal" rhythmic formula by parodically invoking Mary as daughter of the Father "divino," and Jesus as the Word "humanal," the son of God and the Blessed Mother "virginal." Quevedo's satirical invocation could also recall the prohibited translation of the *Oratio Berengerii*, with its notorious corruption of the meaning of the Incarnation and the redemption.

Costa Fontes goes on to suggest that the Portuguese tradition of the Just Judge hearkens back to the plight of *conversos* who, intent on secretly preserving their identity as practising Jews, sought to evade Inquisitorial authorities. In particular, he compares pleas for liberation from criminal "inquisições" (investigations) and the punishment of "fogo" (fire) that have been preserved as oral prayers with the documented petition of a seventeenth-century new Christian from Lisbon: "de Inquisição me livrares com brevidade pela tua Divina Piedade" (from the Inquisition quickly free me for your Divine Piety) (1997: 6–7).[50] Such a connection with the perceived injustice of the Holy Office seems at least plausible, considering Quevedo's vicious parody of *conversos* and their supposed sacrilege in the *Buscón*. In any case, it is clear that early modern authorities more broadly accused religious transgressors of employing the prayer that Pablos performs and sells as an incantation and textual amulet, irrespective of any perceived *converso* identity. For example, María Francisca, a suspect living in the Canary Islands in 1663, was said to carry around a bag full of talismanic papers, including the "Oración del Justo Juez"; and a similar Inquisitorial allegation was recorded in 1676, describing another alleged witch named María de los Ángeles who communed with demons after intoning "muchos versos en romance ... dezía que no podía ser preso por el Santo Officio de la Ynquisición porque sabía y traya consigo la Orasión del Justo Juez" (many verses in Romance ... saying that she could not be held prisoner by the Holy Office of the Inquisition because she knew and carried with her the Prayer of the Just Judge) (Gray Birth 1903: 654, 853). While neither of these women was accused of Judaizing or labelled as a New Christian, such an identification is certainly possible. Acquiring the names of Christian saints and feasts had long been associated with *converso* heritage, as can be seen in Quevedo's genealogy of Pablos's mother, "descendiente de la letanía" (descendent of the litany) (1980: 97).[51] Whether or not María de Francisca and María de los Ángeles were New Christians, their alleged crimes clearly illustrate that the physical presence of the prayer that I have been discussing, in addition to its oral pronouncement, was expected to confer an apotropaic power to evade capture and confinement. Such an amuletic efficacy would have appealed to a variety of superstitious criminals who – like Pablos and other characters in Quevedo's novel – had reason to fear prosecution for crimes against the church and state. Alonso de Villegas, for this reason, wrote that

Las nóminas ... usan con este intento por la mayor parte, gente ... mala, como ladrones, rufianes, y homicidas que ... con tales oraciones no morirán semejantes muertes, y a las vezes seles cumplen porque si dizen que trayeendo aquella oración no morirán sin confessión, suele ser assi: porque los prende la justicia, y a tormentos les hazen confessar sus delitos, y la confessión que hazen es ocassión de su muerte. (1603: 88r)

(Textual amulets ... are used with this intent primarily by bad people ... like thieves, rogues, and murderers that ... with such prayers they will not die certain deaths, and sometimes this comes to pass because if they say that wearing that prayer prevents dying without confession, it tends to happen like this: since they are caught by the justice system, and through torture made to confess their crimes; and the confession they make is the occasion of their death.)

In fact, a threat of prosecution by the Holy Office haunts the *Buscón* from start to finish. The rogue's mother is denounced for communing with the Devil, tarred and feathered, and arrested by the Inquisition for exhuming "piernas, brazos y cabezas" (arms, legs and heads) for her witchcraft (1980: 164). Recalling the ignominious punishment of his mother, the young rogue dons a hat festooned with feathers and rides through town in a festival, only to be pelted with vegetables. Thrown from his nag into a pile of manure, he pleads, "aunque llevo plumas, no soy ... mi madre" (although I wear feathers ... I am not my mother) (1980: 112). A number of other characters either implicitly or explicitly express anxiety over the prospect of being investigated by the Inquisition – a shared sense of dread that Pablos at times exploits to his advantage. During his early days as a student, a clerical schoolmaster named Cabra (Goat) whom the narrator characterizes as a grotesque personification of hunger "añadió a la comida tocino ... por no sé qué que le dijeron, un día, de hidalguía" (added to the meal bacon ... due to something that was said, one day, about his lineage) (1980: 125).[52] At the university town of Alcalá, the servant Cypriana – a name that brings to mind the magician Cyprian invoked in grimoires – is heard by Pablos calling out a Spanish homonym for the papal name Pius and the onomatopoeic chirping of chicks: "Yo no puedo dejar de dar parte a la Inquisición ... no os burléis con los inquisidores ... no neguéis la blasfemia ... que dijisteis a los pollos, 'pío, pío,' y es Pío nombre de los papas" (I have no choice but to inform the Inquisition ... do not make light of the inquisitors ... do not deny the blasphemy ... that you said to the chicks, "pío, pío," and Pío is the name of the popes) (1980: 154–5). Considering this overarching threat, it is fitting that Cypriana, Pablos, and the sacristan all recite a prayer that was specifically employed as an antidote to Inquisitorial prosecution.

Over the course of his criminal maturation, the *pícaro* manages to evade or manipulate authorities more than once. The young Pablos first learns to fear the law when he is beaten for calling a magistrate named Poncio de Aguirre by the infamous title "Poncio Pilato" (1980: 108). In later episodes, his partners in crime free him from a lawyer by impersonating inquisitors, and he manages to escape from the police just as his matronly lover is threatened with an *auto de fé* and taken prisoner for sorcery.[53] At another point in the story, as a means of facilitating his early release from jail, Pablos bribes numerous legal officials and then claims to possess the family tree of a prison guard's *converso* in-laws. On such occasions, the power of the prohibited prayer of the "Justo Juez" as a "defensión" against unjust judges like Pilate, and an "escudo" against capture and incarceration, seems all too efficacious in the life of the rogue. As promised in the *Fasciculus myrrhe* as well as Inquisitorial testimony, Pablos escapes imprisonment and other legal snares, eluding a number of enemies or persecutors – before being recognized by his upstart *converso* schoolmate and exposed as a fraud. Ironically, the prayer is also effective in demonstrating his guilt. By invoking the Blessed Mother, along with the Father and Son, as "madre del verbo humanal, hija del padre divino, dame gracia virginal," the rogue makes a mockery of the Trinity, the Holy Family, and divine justice brought about through the Incarnation (1980: 287). His prayer confuses the meaning of God putting on human flesh and thereby making possible the expiation of human guilt and the reconciliation of sinners. In other words, it distorts the essential Christian notion of God as the Just Judge found in moral treatises from the period, including Quevedo's later *La cuna y la sepultura* (1634): "Si me castigas, Señor, santificado sea tu nombre de Justo Juez en mis tormentos, si me perdona" (If you punish me, Lord, blessed be your name of Just Judge in my suffering, if you forgive me) (1963: 100).[54] Although Pablos repeatedly manages to escape justice, the presence of his amuletic "Oración del Justo Juez" in the novel also serves to condemn him further, in keeping with Inquisitorial cases brought against María Francisca and María de los Ángeles.

As such, the prayer inscribed into the narrative fits into a larger pattern of religious transgressors superstitiously misusing devotional objects in similar ways. For example, a companion of Pablos named Cosme makes his living as a vender of charms, and the narrator compares the bits of cloth that protect his band of rogues to the paper prayers that old women were known to collect and sell as *ensalmo* remedies for the most incurable maladies (1980: 236–7, 221).[55] Apart from her nightly prayer to the Just Judge, the aged Cypriana relies on the apotropaic power of a gigantic string of rosary beads, together with a clutter of superstitious images and talismans hung around her neck (1980: 152–3). Later, prayer beads in the novel are said to be fashioned from dead men's molars, to fall into soup and break unsuspecting teeth, and to resemble cords of firewood. Grotesque rosaries are similarly carried by gamblers disguised as hermits, monks, or by phony maidens and begging swindlers like Cosme and Pablos. Just as the language of the "Oración del Justo Juez" is corrupted and distorted, so is the physical presence of these prayer objects in the novel.

Of course, the prayer's ironic efficacy to deliver and convict criminals like Pablos is made possible by the broken state of the judicial system in seventeenth-century Spain. Rampant "corruption and greed of court officials" during this period has been well documented by historians and literary critics alike, who catalogue an increasing "acceptance of 'donations,' bribes, gifts and other kinds of payments under the table … to levels perceived to be those of state-sanctioned robbery" (Kagan 1981: 38–42; Carrión 2010: 30). We have seen how the "Oración del Justo Juez" in the *Buscón* forms part of a bitter satire in which guilty criminals are repeatedly shown lying and bribing their way out of legal jams. Undoubtedly, this preoccupation with corrupt officials can be related to Quevedo's decades-long struggle with the courts after inheriting a villa in 1598. The author's experience would have also influenced his condemnations of the Spanish legal system in other works: *Virtud militante* (Militant Virtue, 1633), for instance, evokes Christ's parable of the unjust judge who initially refused to come to the assistance of a widow; and *Política de Dios* (Politics of God, 1634) exposes the problem of "jueces delincuentes" (delinquent judges) giving rise to scandal like "Poncio Pilato" and his "sentencia sacrílega" (sacrilegious sentence) (1985: 154; 1966: 21, 75).[56] At the same time, in keeping with the *Buscón*, judicial authorities are depicted accepting bribes in Quevedo's other works. Most strikingly in his satirical masterpiece, *Sueños y discursos* (Dreams and Discourses, 1627), an unfair judge is condemned to forever wash his hands in the afterlife. In this way, he endlessly repeats Pilate's iconic ablution: "vi a un juez, que lo había sido, que estaba … lavándose las manos, y esto hacía muchas veces … Díjome que en vida, sobre ciertos negocios, se las hacía untado" (I saw one who was a judge, or had been, who was … washing his hands, and this he did many times … He said that in life, through certain dealings, he had them greased) (1993: 42–3). At another place in *Sueños*, a devil feasts on judges as the main course of an infernal feast that includes several other notorious members of the legal system (1993: 80).[57] God, as *Juste Judex*, has found the law courts of Quevedo's day guilty of defrauding the innocent, in spite of their pleas for justice, while at the same time routinely accepting bribes from criminals like Pablos who dare to blaspheme the "Justo Juez" with their petitions.

Significantly, the author compares both the hellish vision of *Sueños* and the criminal spectacle of the *Buscón* with the paintings of Hieronymus Bosch (1993: 76). *Sueños* refers to the Flemish painter's characteristic depiction of devils with talons, tails, and horns, while Quevedo's novel describes Pablos and his lowlife companions rivalling the contorted figures of Bosch, as they attempt to cover themselves with tattered fabric: "estirándole, hazía L. Uno hincado de rodillas, remedava un cinco … otro … metiendo la cabeza entre ellas, se hacía un ovillo. No pintó tan extrañas posturas el Bosco como yo vi" (stretching, he made an L shape. One of them, kneeling to do his mending, made a five …

another, with his head between his legs, became a ball of yarn. Bosch did not paint postures so strange as what I saw) (1980: 224). Such references come as no surprise, considering that Quevedo was known by his contemporaries as something of an art connoisseur. During his time at the royal courts of Philip III and his successor, the writer probably became familiar with works by this artist that belonged to the Habsburg kings and were on display at the Escorial royal palace and monastery.[58] For this reason, a number of critics have linked ekphrastic comparisons in *Sueños* and the *Buscón* to imagery from the *Garden of Earthly Delights*. The painting's centre panel (Figure 22) displays naked sinners twisting their bodies into shapes not unlike those described by Pablos, while in the right panel of the triptych (Figure 23), hybrid devils are shown torturing the bodies of Hell's occupants with objects associated with their sins, including brass, wind, and stringed instruments.

These musical punishments bring to mind another scene in the *Buscón* when Pablos's uncle, the hangman, "plays" the bodies of condemned prisoners: "Venía una procesión de desnudos ... y él ... tocando un pasacalles públicas en las costillas de cinco laúdes" (a naked procession approached ... with him ... playing a march on the ribs of five human lutes) (1980: 197). Although Quevedo invites such comparisons by frequently referencing Bosch in his works, scholars have also shown how the author's *conceptista* stylistic approach to the folly and judgment of humankind differs with the late medieval painter's theologized dreamscapes.[59] What has yet to be considered in such discussions is how satirical evocations of the "Justo Juez" in the *Buscón* can be related to and contrasted with the artist's moralizing treatment of this same divine figure.

Painted on the outer wings of the *Garden of Earthly Delights* is a transparent world globe that Peter Blum has linked to Bosch's *Table of the Seven Deadly Sins*. The top right corner of this table shows Christ as Just Judge seated above a similar globe, representing the fourth and final of the Last Things. Surrounded by His celestial court, the Redeemer displays the wounds of the Passion, as the bodies of the saved rise from their graves (Figure 24).[60] Variations on this theme of *Majestas Domini* can be seen in numerous Renaissance paintings of the Last Judgment, or the Divine Judge could be associated with the resurrected Man of Sorrows in woodcuts like the ones that sometimes accompanied the "Oración del Justo Juez" in books of hours. On Bosch's table, the *Juste Judex* image works in conjunction with God's omniscient vision, depicted in the circular form of an eye at the centre of the table – or

Figure 22. Body positioning. *Garden of Earthly Delights,* Hieronymus Bosch, Prado, Madrid. Center panel, detail (photo: Gianni Dagli Orti/ Art Resource, NY).

Figure 23. Musical instruments. *Garden of Earthly Delights*, Hieronymus Bosch. Prado, Madrid. Right panel, detail (photo: Gianni Dagli Orti/ Art Resource, NY).

what Erasmus calls the "Justitia oculus ... est oculus aequitatis omina intuens" (eye of Justice ... it is the eye of righteousness that notices all things) (Stolleis 2009: 16). The iris of this eye portrays the seven deadly sins, with avarice exemplified by a corrupt judge accepting a bribe (Figure 25). While the sinner accepts payment as if unseen, his crime is on full view within the *oculus* (Figure 26). Inside the pupil, the resurrected

Figure 24. Last Judgment, *Table of the Seven Deadly Sins*, Hieronymus Bosch,
Prado, Madrid. Upper right corner detail (photo: Erich Lessing/
Art Resource, NY).
Upper right corner, detail. (Photo: Erich Lessing/Art Resource, NY).

Figure 25. Avaricious judging accepting a bribe, *Table of the Seven Deadly Sins*, Hieronymus Bosch, Prado, Madrid. Segmented circle, upper left, detail (photo: Gianni Dagli Orti/Art Resource, NY).

Figure 26. *Table of the Seven Deadly Sins*, Hieronymus Bosch, Prado, Madrid
(photo: Erich Lessing/Art Resource, NY).

Saviour appears above a Latin inscription reading, "Cave, cave Deus
videt" (Beware, beware, God watches).[61]

Like Bosch's famous triptych, Quevedo could have seen this table at
the Escorial, where it formed part of the royal collection since the time
of Philip II.[62] Its striking contraposition of divine and earthly judges
demonstrates how visual as well as textual traditions can be used to
unpack further the ironic connotations of the "Justo Juez" invoked
throughout the *Buscón*.

In this early modern novel, prayers to the Just Judge subvert the
notion of God's all-seeing judgment that Bosch famously allegorized
in his ocular painting. Quevedo's characters recite the prayer as a
means of obscuring the light of justice in the world to avoid right-
ful punishment. It has been demonstrated how this supposed efficacy
is implicated in the apotropaic significance that accused witches like
María de los Ángeles attached to her amulet, and also specified in the

earlier-mentioned Portuguese supplication: "olhos tenham, nao nos vejam" (may they have eyes that cannot see us). As evidenced by the *villancico* from Jaén, and examples in Lope's dramatic works, interpretations of the Just Judge in the Golden Age consistently revolved around notions of vision and blindness. The petitionary appeals of real or fictional outlaws like Pablos were understood as attempts to obfuscate the sight of the *Justitiae oculus* with bias, as opposed to applying the impartial blindfold of justice.[63] They attribute the offering of an "Oración del Justo Juez" with the power to cloud the unrestricted vision of God, as if the *Juste Judex* were a short-sighted bribe taker comparable to the one exposed on Bosch's table – or like the many paid-off judges and other crooked representatives of the law satirized in Quevedo's works. In this sense, the prayer that Pablos claims to have authored is ultimately ineffective, in spite of his success at evading capture and freeing himself from legal binds. As opposed to temporarily blinding the eye of the law, the *Buscón* brings into full view and grotesquely exposes injustice as what Iffland has aptly called a "pure visual spectacle" (1978: 1.136). The novel's continual scenes of flagrant religious transgression and abject criminality are emphatically meant to be watched and judged.

Whereas Christ as *oculus Dei* and *Juste Judex* watches the entirety of sin through the doctrinal lens of Bosch's table, the spectacle of inequity in the *Buscón* is primarily viewed from the perspective of Quevedo's controlling, judgmental authorship – what Edward Friedman has identified as the "establishment position" and "conservative ideology" of the book's "implied author" (1987: 58–61).[64] Over the course of his narrative, Quevedo takes the position of a hostile onlooker, exposing a delinquent underworld in which the transcendent authority and orthodoxy of the "Justo Juez" that he so devoutly invokes in the *Cuna y sepultura* has been completely subverted. As Anne Cruz has pointed out, Pablos is exploited by his author as a "scapegoat," the target of "social anxieties of contamination" (1999: 131). Quevedo's embittered reaction to earlier picaresque narratives is consonant with that of the Augustinian, Luis de León, whose devotional writing he admired and promoted. In *De los nombres de Cristo* (The Names of Christ c. 1583), the friar writes: "si queremos mirar en ello con atención a ser justos juezes, no podemos dexar de juzgar sino destos libros perdidos y desconcertados" (if we are to look into this matter with attention and be just judges, we can reach no other judgment except that these are disorderly books of perdition) (1997: 143).[65] The disfigured, incongruous view from Quevedo's narrative lens puts this judgment on display, similar to the optics that

Rodrigo Fernández explicitly employs in the *Los anteojos de mejor vista* (Spectacles for a Better Vision 1625). In a recent study, Enrique García Santo-Tomás has explained how "Spanish lenses" in this satirical novel enable the viewer to look through deceptive appearances (*engaño*) and see the underlying truth (*desengaño*) as "a tableau of grotesque imagery" and "monstrous figures that resemble those of the Flemish painter Hieronymus Bosch" (2009: 64–5).[66] These visual effects, viewed from the top of the Giralda tower in Seville, allow the audience to perceive fully all that is rotten in society: "todo ... hoy se juzga a ciegas ... de ponerse estos anteojos, verá las cosas en el mismo ser que son, sin que el engaño común le turbe la luz de la vista más importante" (everything ... these days is judged blindly ... putting on these spectacles you will see things in the same way that they are, without common illusion blurring the light of the most important vision) (Fernández 1979: 64, 67).

Quevedo's satire elucidates in much the same manner, counteracting attempts by his picaresque subjects to cover and bias the eye of justice in keeping with the efficacy of the heterodox "Oración del Justo Juez." As has been demonstrated, the novelist's vision not only displays Boschian contortions of the body; but also exposes distortions of sacred language and prayer like the sacristan's blasphemous song, the petitions of Cypriana and Pablos, and the grotesque rosaries and other amuletic objects that characters apotropaically bind to their bodies, in relation to accusations of amuletic Judaizing.[67] Apart from casting light on the monstrosity of *pícaros* and the kind of writing they inspire, the implied author's all-seeing, surveilling eye seeks to capture and confine them within its vision. In doing so, he confirms the fears of guilty, heterodox criminals who appeal to the Just Judge not to be seen and ensnared. As Peter Dunn has explained, the *Buscón* forms part of a more widespread tendency among picaresque writers, living in an atmosphere of rampant corruption and worsening crime waves, to "create alternative worlds in which ... this irrational *vulgo*, this lawless mob ... may be symbolically brought under control" (1993: 313). In this sense, Quevedo's novel seems to anticipate an approach to disciplinary power that Michel Foucault finds taking shape at the end of the seventeenth century. This meaning of *surveiller* would culminate with Jeremy Bentham's later "panopticon" prison, in which an unseen yet all-seeing central tower casts a controlling light that is internalized by prisoners – named after the mythic giant, Panoptes, whose body was covered with eyes. Foucault, in his treatment of the early modern transition from a "culture of spectacle" to a "carceral culture," cites a plan for the town of Vincennes that was meant to be implemented in the event of plague: "the inspection functions ceaselessly. The gaze is alert everywhere ... the most absolute authority of the magistrates ... 'to observe all disorder, theft and extortion'; at each of the town gates there will be an observation post ... This enclosed, segmented space, observed at every point ... in which power is exercised ... according to a continuous hierarchical figure" (1977: 195–7).[68]

It would seem that Quevedo's surveillance comes closer to this kind of precursor to panopticonism than to the omniscient gaze of the *Justitiae oculus* painted centuries before by Bosch. As a reader of earlier novels, the author of the *Buscón*'s judgmental disciplinary gaze appears to have transformed the oversight of "Vuestra Merced" in *Lazarillo de Tormes* and the vantage point on humanity seen from the "atalaya" or watchtower in Mateo Alemán's 1604 sequel to *Guzmán de Alfarache* (Micó 2003: 74:). In the end, however, Quevedo's revision of the picaresque concerns that which cannot be seen and outbreaks of criminality that inevitably emerge and escape from the bounds of his novel.[69] As Dunn aptly puts it, although his "satirical overkill" is "intolerant of any behavior or belief that deviates from his own fiercely asserted norms" and characterized by "an obsession with status and boundaries, a rage for containment," ultimately the "failure of containment is what *El buscón* is about" (1993: 159, 297). Not unlike earlier-discussed anxieties exhibited by Erasmus, Luis de León, Habsburg kings, and Inquisitors, Quevedo's obsession with the impossibility of containment extends to the proliferation of what are seen as insidious books, as well as the corrupting influence of rogues. Similarly, Ariadna García-Bryce has recently found that, in his more overtly political work, Quevedo's "rhetorical ideals involve an alarmist view of emergent modes of circulation" (2011: 3). While his reactionary oversight over the picaresque in the *Buscón* can be productively likened to a tendency towards discursive "panopticonism," the author in fact novelizes a failure to contain the lawlessness of these criminals and their censored texts within the boundaries of his narrative.

Fittingly, Pablos makes his way to the Americas not long after selling his prayer. The text of this amulet recited in and inscribed onto the pages of the novel is effective insofar as law and order are successfully undermined inside the narrative and the rogue finds a place to hide and go unseen. In the final analysis, his prayer can be interpreted as an ironic shield that blocks the last word of his story from the judging purview of its implied author as well as the disapproving surveillance of early readers of the *Buscón*. Like Pablos, the forbidden *Oración del Justo Juez* slips away from this censorial, punishing gaze, along with other uncontrollable printed materials. As I hope to have demonstrated in this chapter, the intertextual relationship between the *Buscón* and earlier prototypes for the picaresque cannot be fully understood without taking into consideration the evasive powers assigned to outlaw prayers. In the edition of *Lazarillo de Tormes* published in Alcalá, we have seen how the proleptic insight of a printed amuletic prayer exerts an analogous force over the "caso" of this narrative, foretelling the uncontainability of a would-be *emparedada*. Foreseen by the blind man, her verbal and sexual outbursts cannot be held within the walls of Lazarillo's house – any more than Pablos and his ilk can be held within the reactionist pages of Quevedo's novel, or the sale of unapproved broadsides and other texts pouring out of early modern presses could be adequately suppressed by Spanish authorities. In different ways, both of these apotropaic prayers have been inscribed into modernizing novels as a means of exploring the limits of censorship, control, and containment.

Amuletic Afterlives

The spread of outlawed texts from Spain to the New World was not only implicated in the final pages of Quevedo's masterpiece but also documented by Inquisitors first brought to the Americas during the reign of Philip II. Notably, in 1619 a tailor named Miguel Pérez was investigated in New Spain and found to be in possession of a parchment inscribed with the "Oración de San León" that I examined in the introduction to this book. According to records published by Araceli Campos Moreno, the suspect claimed to have met an unidentified soldier and a local weaver at a public fountain in Mexico City, where they furnished him with the textual amulet.[1] Its contents were remarkably similar to those found in books of hours dating from late medieval and early sixteenth centuries, when an "Oración" by the same name, prior to its official prohibition, was owned by members of the Spanish royal family. Similar to peninsular versions, the Mexican tailor's text is identified as the amuletic prayer that Pope Leo III legendarily sent to Charlemagne and offers protection against all manner of ill fortune and threats of sudden death, ranging from journeys by land and sea to lightning strikes, work-related accidents, and the dangers of childbirth: "qualquiera que la rezace y trugueçe conçigo, nunca le sucedería mal … si alguna preñada estubiere de parto, diciéndosela o ponérsela encima de la barriga" (whoever prays and carries it on them, never will any evil befall them … if any pregnant woman is in labour, saying it for herself or placing it on her stomach) (Campos Moreno 1999: 63). Later Inquisitorial archives indicate that in addition to the "Oracion de San León," a rendition of the amulet that begins "Justo Juez divinal" – like the prayer Pablos sells on the streets of Madrid – had an afterlife in colonial Mexico, where criminals were still being accused of using its power to evade prosecution as late as the second half of the eighteenth century: "quebranta Señor la yra de la Justicia que a mi me persigue ... ojos tenga no me vean" (break, Lord, the wrath of Justice that pursues me ... may it have eyes that cannot see me) (González Gómez 2013: 87–8). Of course, New World belief in amulets had also been influenced by indigenous traditions. Notably, Hernando Ruiz de Alarcón wrote a treatise concerning what he saw as superstitions practised among native inhabitants of Mexico.[2] His *Tratado de las supersticiones de los naturales de esta Nueva España* (Treatise on the Superstitions of the Natives of New Spain, 1629) was possibly modelled on the frequently reprinted work of Ciruelo. It includes a section on "nóminas," although this writer's use of the term seems to be employed as an analogy for carrying apotropaic objects whether or not they included inscriptions (1984: chap. 8).

While petitions like the "Oración del Justo Juez" continued being reproduced and re-elaborated on the peninsula as well as its American colonies long after the publication of Quevedo's novel, the kind of intersections between literature and amulets that have concerned me in this book were coming to an end. Amuletic texts mentioned in subsequent works are increasingly demystified and disempowered. Their efficacious presence is dematerialized, deprived of a sacred and even subversive potency in the hands of authors and readers. For example, scholars have recently brought to a light a previously unpublished picaresque work dating from the 1650s that appears to have been written in Amsterdam.[3] This anonymous Spanish novel, entitled *Vida y costumbres de la Madre Andrea* (The Life and Times of Mother Andrea), tells the story of a Celestinesque prostitute and brothel keeper working in Madrid, and in the process engages in a complex pastiche that repeatedly alludes to scenes from *Lazarillo de Tormes* and *El Buscón*. In keeping with the latter novel, a blind man at one point purchases a prayer that starts with the words "Justo Juez divinal" (Zafra 2011: 90–5). The text is revealed to contain humorous pleas for the lame and crippled to become fast runners and adept jugglers and the mute to squawk like intoxicated parrots, among other punch lines. While the inserted prayer contributes to an ongoing satire of religious and societal corruption – demonstrating that "hasta en las cosas de la devoción está entremetido el contagio de los usos" (even devotional matters are contaminated by what's fashionable) – its presence in the novel remains devoid of any implied materiality or intertextual *historiola* that would affect the outcome of Andrea's life within the overall logic of the narrative. Nor is there any indication that the Just Judge is meant to be invoked in the context of escaping the Holy Office.[4] If anything, the novel shows how the prayer has been defanged and emptied of its former resonance, coming to function merely as a hypocritical performance intended to entertain and solicit money.

In this sense, it looks forward to later texts like the *Periquillo Sarniento* (Mangy Parrot, 1817–30), a Mexican picaresque novel written in the early nineteenth century by a proponent of Enlightenment values, José Joaquín Fernández de Lizardi. Here the first-person narrator is advised to learn the "Oración del Justo Juez," together with other empty "relaciones" (speeches), when he impersonates a blind beggar in Mexico City (1997: 121). On both sides of the Atlantic, the kinds of texts inscribed on amulets were being used to epitomize antiquated, though still persistent, superstitions and signs of cultural decadence. Not long before this, the Spanish writer Leandro Fernández de Moratín had annotated and republished (under a pseudonym) an account of a 1610 *auto de fé* celebrated in Logroño, in which he mocks the final Habsburg king. The deformed and demented Carlos II had suffered an untimely death in 1700, in spite of being treated with potions "de por dentro, y lleno de … nóminas y escapularios de por fuera … lo llevaron en ceremonia al Escorial" (on the inside, and covered with … *nóminas* and scapulars on the outside … they carried him ceremoniously to the Escorial) (1810: 105).[5]

In this study, I considered precisely the kind of amuletic powers and meanings that – put simply – no longer work in the *Vida y costumbres de la Madre Andrea*, the *Periquillo Sarniento*, or later novels. The first phase dealt with thirteenth-century amulets that worked in the world and in fiction, supernaturally and performatively. Healing, conversional attributes were attributed to Alfonso X's *Cantigas de Santa Maria* materially coming into contact with the king's body – attributes that apparently failed Carlos II. Similarly, the inclusion of an exorcistic prayer in the *Razón de amor* manuscript could be expected to purify real and imagined spaces under threat from evil forces and sinful contamination. Narrative accounts of Alexander the Great and Apollonius of Tyre from the same period also contained epicentres of amuletic power that worked materially and creatively. In one case, the representation of a parchment *nómina* served as an apocalyptic symbol for the organization of the emperor's legend; and in another an imbedded prayer for deliverance showed how the production and uses of amulets and poetry could provide a speaking voice for textual objects to identify their potency and deeper significance. These poems shed light on the relationship between what I have called "inscribed power" and the experience of copying, reading, touching, and being in possession of medieval literary manuscripts.

The second phase of my itinerary centred on amulets that made things happen in narratives by, as it were, backfiring. The intertextuality of fourteenth-century *Libro de buen amor* gave witness to an apotropaic inscription turned against its purveyors and users, challenging instead of safeguarding the moralizing authority of premodern narratives and the expectations and participation of their readers. An even more subversive fictionalization of the power of spoken and inscribed words took place in the pages of the *Celestina*, with its emphasis on materiality being stripped of Christian transcendence. This Renaissance masterpiece employed amuletic texts and objects to be fetishized by lovers who were denied healing and protection and were instead blinded and fatally wounded. A final juncture came when written amulets began to circulate in an early modern setting – the work they did was fuelled by their heterodox nature. The effects of the printing press were seen in the early sixteenth-century *La Lozana andaluza*, which reproduced a *nómina* also found in a manuscript grimoire that was seized by the Inquisition, turning this object into a woodcut that fatalistically signalled the unleashing of a demonic army. Two picaresque works of the Spanish Golden Age, *Lazarillo de Tormes* and *El Buscón* evoked printed amulets that functioned in comparable ways. The anonymous book used forbidden prayer to condemn the dissimulating narrator, just as the novel itself was prohibited when the Holy Office attempted to restrict a flood of unauthorized *nóminas* as well as other dangerous texts flowing from presses. Quevedo's novel exhibited a greater preoccupation with the inability to reign in and control a proliferation of superstitious and heretical writing or to stop criminals from buying, selling, and carrying amuletic prayers.

Although *nóminas* in later texts could not be expected to do the same kinds of fictional work, it was not because they had lost all of their powers. In spite of the gradual spread of Enlightenment ideas through the Iberian Peninsula and its colonies, ushering in a new emphasis on scientific reason, this and other forms of popular religiosity endured. In recent years, a number of scholars have shown how the idea of a modern "disenchantment," a phrase made famous by Max Weber, was and is more of a theoretical construct than a reality on the ground. They demonstrate how magical ways of thinking are always being reconfigured to persist alongside and even be interwoven with rational ideas of progress.[6] Such findings could certainly be applied to examples of inscribed words being re-enchanted in a post-Enlightenment context. One of the first modern histories of amulets, penned in the early eighteenth century by the German Martin Frederick Blumler (1887) – and reprinted in the Victorian era – studied what were perceived to be widespread, evolving practices. Prayers in Spanish manuscripts and printed books from the same period were said to be cleansed of the old superstitions but were still prefaced by warnings against attempts to use these new-and-improved texts as amulets.[7] Such warnings evidently had less than the desired effect. By the end of the nineteenth century, versions of the Prayer of the Just Judge were being reproduced on typewriters, and objects inscribed with variations on the invocation, such as votive candles and bottles of blessed oil, are now being advertised on Internet sites.[8] While amulets may have lost their former potency as literary devices, texts not unlike those uttered by Pablos are to this day being repackaged and resold in cyberspace.

Notes

Introduction: Literary Amulets

1 "Superveniunt Persi et girant civitatem istam. Sed statim Aggarus epistolam Domini ferens ad portam cum omni exercitu suo publice oravit … tenens manibus levatis epistolam ipsam … quotienscumque voluerunt venire et expugnare hanc civitatem hostes, haec epistola prolata est et lecta est in porta … expulsi sunt omnes hostes" (1960: 8–9, 13). The prayer that Abgar was said to have recited is as follows: "Domine Iesu, tu promiseras nobis, ne aliquis hostium ingrederetur civitatem istam, et ecce nunc Persae inpugnant nos" (O Lord Jesus, Thou hadst promised us that none of our enemies should enter this city, and lo! the Persians now attack.

2 On the societal and ritual significance of holy *presentia* of relics and their power or *potentia* in the early Christian Europe, see the classic study of Peter Brown (1981).

3 It is possible that more attention was given to the copied letter in Egeria's narrative than we can now appreciate, since – as editors have noted – the surviving account of her travels is fragmentary.

4 On Roman and early Christian attitudes towards and writings on the subject of amulets and related superstitious and magic practices, see the discussions of Daniel Ogden (1999: 51–4) and Richard Gordon (1999: 179–86), respectively. Evidence of the work of Eusebius circulating in medieval Spain can be found not only in the Alfonsine retelling that I discuss here, but also on the basis of surviving copies such as the late fourteenth-century one preserved at the Biblioteca Nacional (no. 8962). The letter can be compared to a later miraculous epistle that was supposedly written by the Saviour, descended from heaven during the 580s, falling into the unlikely hands of Vicentius of Ibiza, a bishop from

the Balearic islands off the coast of Spain (Menéndez y Pelayo 1992: 1.333–4, Ringwald 2007: 94–5). It urges Christians to observe strictly the Sabbath, refrain from pagan superstitions and rituals, and thus avoid temporal and eternal punishments. To a greater extent than this *Carta Dominica* (Lord's Day Epistle) – which was never widely accepted as authentic and was condemned not long after its appearance – the epistolary relic from Edessa continued to be copied and disseminated throughout the Middle Ages. See also Don Skemer (2006: 104).

5 In the version recorded by Egeria, Jesus promises to send St Thomas. Like Eusebius, she identifies the courier who delivered the letter as Ananias. According to Eusebius, it was Thaddeus – one of the Seventy – who came to Edessa on behalf of the apostle Thomas in keeping with Christ's promise. In Alfonso's chronicle, the city is also protected by the prayers and relics of Thomas deposited there (sent from India following his death, according to hagiographic tradition). Egeria also mentions that the apostle's body was in Edessa. Though not mentioned by Eusebius or Egeria, a tradition developed in which, along with the letter, the portrait of Christ protected the city from Persian enemies. The bishop tells Egeria that the Persians sought to deprive the city of water, but a miraculous fountain sprang forth to satisfy the thirst of its inhabitants and a darkness appeared to drive away their enemies.

6 For an example of this typology, see David Fuller (2010: 276). It is also apparent in Gonzalo de Berceo's thirteenth-century *Milagros de Nuestra Señora*: "Ella es dicha fonda de David" (2003: 34c). The Tree of Jesse was also often understood as a Marian symbol and used to depict the lineage of Christ during the Middle Ages. It is interesting to consider how this implicitly Davidic interpretation of the letter might relate to the biblical story of the Philistines being punished by the presence of the Ark of the Covenant (1 Sam. 5–12).

7 See Skemer (2006: 96–9). Editions of Leo's spurious *Enchiridion* (Handbook) of prayers began to appear in the sixteenth century. See also Alfred Edward Waite (1911: 39–45).

8 My approach to distinguishing between terms that are sometimes used interchangeably (such as talisman and amulet) follows that of Skemer. He also points out that Latin references to a *carmen* or recited spell (like the Spanish tradition of the healing "ensalmo" charm) may or may not have involved using the text as a physical apotropaic (2006: 9). Though popular devotional scapulars (unlike liturgical or monastic scapulars) are sometimes used like textual amulets, their development coincided with the spread of large lay confraternities during the latter part of the seventeenth century and thereafter.

9 As in other cases, Latin prayers known in French as the *Prière de Charlemagne* were at the same time disseminated through late medieval prayer books produced north and south of the Pyrenees (see Askins 2007: note 60).

10 Portuguese versions of the prayer also circulated at the same time, as Arthur Askins has shown (2007: 249). A Spanish version of the prayer published as a chapbook has been recently studied by Víctor Infantes (1995).

11 "Qualquier día que esta oración leyeres y sobre ti la truxieres con grand devoción en casa o en mar, o en batalla, o en todo lugar adonde ésto vieres, ninguno de tus enemigos avrá señorío en ti y vencedor permanecerás siempre de toda mala adversidad y enfermedad y peligro; serás librado … y acabasse santamente sus días … En aquel día no morirá a fierro ni en agua nin en fuego ni en muerte mala súbita ninguna sin confessión, ni sus enemigos nin el dyablo avrá poderío sobre él, dormiendo ni velando ni en camino ni fuera del camino ni en otro qualquier lugar … la tempestad de los relámpagos … E si fuere sobre la mar, digan la tres vezes en aquel día esta oración y no la avrá fortuna ninguna en el mar ni tempestad … espíritu maligno digan la sobre él con candela bendicta encendida tres vezes y luego será librado. E si alguna muger preñada no pudiere parir, digan la sobre ella tres vezes con candela bendicta encendida y luego será libre y parirá" (*Horas* 1502: fol. 502r–503v).

12 For instance, the "Oración" mixes Latin names for Christ with the Greek and Hebrew transliterated invocations "Agios" (Holy) and "Adonay" (Lord) that may not have been understood by Romance speakers as they recited the prayer (*Horas* 1502: 104v, 105r). The wounds of Christ are called on as a spiritual remedy, "las cinco llagas de Dios sean sienpre a mi melezina" (may the five wounds of God always be my medicine) – and there is also an implication that the prayer could be used to evade capture: "guardar me agora … librado de las manos dellos escape" (protect me now … free from their hands may I escape) (1502: 107r, 108v).

13 Alfonso's text draws both on Latin histories and the French epic cycle, as Christine Stresau has shown (1977: 231).

14 See John K. Walsh (1971); E. Michael Gerli (1980). Both Gerli and John R. Burt (1982) suggest an association between the Cid and Susanna being falsely accused. Another possibility is that the biblical figure's two lustful accusers foreshadow the perils faced by the Cid's daughters when they are attacked by their husbands.

15 It has been shown that these kinds of prayers were also inserted into French epics (Russell 1978) as well as hagiographical narratives (Baños

Vallejo 1994). For a bibliography on the tile, see Isabel Velázquez (2006) and Joseph Gwara's study (2005), where he suggests that it might also have been used as a votive offering.

16 On evidence for pilgrim badges made of clay, see for example the volume of Simon Coleman and John Elsner (1995). Skemer provides information on the amuletic qualities assigned to these badges (2006: 68–9). On Muslim amulets made of clay, see Sebastián Gaspariño García (2012).

17 The text allegedly authored by Christ was first listed as apocryphal in a fifth-century decree attributed to Pope Gelasius I, "Das Decretum Gelasianum de libris non recipiendis" (Books Not to Be Received) (Leclerq 1907–22: 43). Under the reign of Charlemagne, the epistle was again declared to be spurious by ecclesiastical authorities in the *Admonitio generalis* (c. 789) (Skemer 2006: 101).

18 The influence of Augustine's theory can be seen, for instance, in a sermon by Martin of Braga, called *De correctione rusticorum* (On the Correction of the Rustics) (c. 575). Intended to expose and root out residual paganism among peasants living in Galicia, this text warns that the invocation of non-Christian, demonic beings, even in combination with orthodox prayer, constitutes a renunciation of and rupture with the linguistic *pactum* through which supplicants can hope to communicate with God (1950: 16.3–7).

19 As a university student, William had undertaken an extensive study and experimentation with natural magic and occult knowledge. See the biographic study of Thomas B. de Mayo (2007).

20 Claire Fanger (1999) has compared this representation of the power of words with that of Roger Bacon (1900) and more fully considered William of Auvergne's scholastic argument in the context of magic. The mortal danger of the word is reminiscent of the power sometimes attached to hearing the ineffable four-letter name of God or Tetragrammaton, as I will discuss in the second chapter of this study.

21 As Richard Kieckhefer (1989: 15) and Skemer (2006: 30) note, the longstanding belief in the gospel's power stems in part from Christ's promise: "if you shall ask me any thing in my name, that I will do" (si quid petieritis me in nomine meo hoc faciam) (John 14:14).

22 These practices were also common among ancient physicians, who drew power from pagan texts as well as written formulas circulating among Jews and Christians such as *abracadabra*, often appearing as an inverted triangle. As Skemer points out, during the third century, Roman Quintus Serenus Sammonicus advocated treating malarial fevers with textual amulets, including papyrus inscribed with poetry from Homer's *Iliad* (2006: 25).

23 They were often used as means of Christianizing, as it were, the astrological power to discern the meaning of signs pointing to future events and its connection to ancient magic. See especially Michael L. Ryan's study (2011), as well as the work of Jennifer M. Corry (2005).

24 Access to classical sources, such as Galen, was mediated by Arabic commentaries. Just as distinctions between healing, amuletic, and literary texts were fluid during this period, physicians sometimes drew on fictional works such as the poetry of Ovid as a source for medical knowledge (Giles 2010).

25 The Arabic title of the work was *Ġāyat al-Ḥakīm* (غاية الحكيم). See the edition of David Pingree (1986).

26 As Skemer notes (2006: 132), the physician was at the same time required to recite from the psalmic verse "Iudica me, Deus, et discerne causam meam" (Judge me, O God, and distinguish my cause) (42:1). In this manner, the pope supposedly received a remedy for his kidney stones.

27 The Latin has been translated in the "Oración" as "catad la cruz del Señor, fuyd todas las partes contrarias" (*Horas* 1502, fol. 105r).

28 Apart from esoteric works like the *Picatrix*, this knowledge could also be derived from medieval lapidaries in which astrological as well as sacred influences are associated with gem stones that can be employed as healing amulets. The most well known of these was the *De lapidibus* (On Gemstones, c. 1100) of Marbode of Rennes (1977), who also wrote other works on the subject.

29 In addition to the explanation given by Virgilio Martínez Enamorado (2006), a concise overview of the uses of these names in Islamic culture can be found in Juan Eduardo Campo (see "Amulets and Talismans" and "Shahada" 2009).

30 For example, such texts can be found in Madrid at the Biblioteca de la Real Academia de la Historia in Madrid (ej. MS 11/9416), and the Biblioteca Nacional (ej. MS 5.223). See descriptions in the compilation of manuscripts recently made by Vincent Barletta (2011).

31 In some cases these spirits are associated with astrological bodies. In addition to Skemer (2006: 116–24), these texts are discussed by Owen Davies (2009) and in Claire Fanger's volume (2012).

32 Yet, at the same time, he sought to consolidate newly conquered territories by advocating a policy of conversion to Christianity and through policies that isolated minority religious groups, sometimes resulting in persecution and displacement. The clerical author of the prologue to the *Liber Razielis* (Book of Raziel) promises that a Castilian version is forthcoming, but this text was either never completed or has been lost.

33 His *Dialogi contra Iudaeos* (Dialogue against the Jews), alleges that some version of this book supplied proof for the trinitarian nature of God's name. While this assertion cannot be correlated with the Judaic angelology that made its way into Alfonso's *Liber Razielis*, a more familiar description is quoted in the Peter of Cornwall's early twelfth-century *Liber disputationum contra Symonem Iudeum* (Book of Disputation against Symon the Jew). He cites from a (now lost) dialogue by the Andalusian convert in which a text called the *Secreta secretorum* is said to give instructions on how to invoke the divinely inscribed names of angels, first revealed by "Rufielem" and passed on from Adam's third son, Seth, to wise Jews during the Christian era (Tolan 1993: 206).

34 "Et hoc fecit per os angeli Razielis, qui Raziel portavit Çeffer, et hoc significat quod portavit librum secretorum. Adam, qui erat tristis et dolens, quia videbat quod erat sepa[ra]tus et elongatus a sapiencia. Et erat iste liber scriptus in lapide saphirii. Et misit ei deus istum librum ad hoc quod propter vigorem et virtutem verborum istius sancti et preciosi libri sciret qualiter poterat recuperare maximum bonum quod amiserat ipse et alii qui post ipsum sequerentur precepta et vestigia Dei et obtinerent istum librum ... Sed quando placuit Deo quod iste liber ita sanctus presentaretur regi Salomoni filio regis David qui fuit ita nobilis et perfectus rex in sapiencia quod vocatur Sapiens in Sancta Scriptura ... in nostro tempore dominum iusticie que est cognitor boni et sobrietatis et est pius et requisitor et amator philosophie et omnium aliarum scientiarum. Et iste est dominus Alfonsus ... noster Rex cum ad manus eius pervenit ita nobilis et preciosus liber, sicut est Çeffer Raziel, quod vult dicere in ebrayco volumen secretorum Dei" (García Áviles 1997: 29–30). Translations are mine unless otherwise indicated.

35 According to the esoteric text, it is also possible for human bodies to be preserved from corruption and achieve a measure of celestial glory, like Enoch was.

36 The Castilian king Juan II authorized Lope Barrientos to investigate the library not long after Enrique de Villena had died. See the studies of E. Gascón Viera (1979) and Alejandro García Áviles (1997: 38). The Inquisitor, bishop, and royal confessor was immortalized as a book burner in Juan de Mena's *Laberinto de Fortuna* (1997: vv. 1014–17). According to Lope de Barrientos, the *Liber Razielis* was "más multiplicado en España que en otras partes del mundo" (reproduced more in Spain than in other parts of the world) (Girón Negrón 2000: 153).

37 Luis Girón Negrón notes that medicinal amulet knowledge was attributed by Villena to renown Jewish scholars of the day, such as the Toledan Rabbi

Jacob ben Asher or the philosopher from Barcelona, Hasdai ben Judah Crescas (2000: 153–4).

38 Ciruelo repeatedly condemns a reliance on words and "nombres bárbaros" (barbarous names) (1978: 77). He also disapproved of Christian Platonizing adaptations of the Jewish Kabbalah in a section from another book, *Paradoxae quaestiones numero decem* (Ten Paradoxical Questions). This text was published in Salamanca in 1538 and has been studied by François Secret (1959).

39 According to contemporaries of Ciruelo, it was believed that amuletic power could be derived not only from the use of virgin parchment but also from having an actual virgin stitch or tie the textual object (Azpilcueta 1557: 87).

40 Ciruelo provides instructions for licit prayer invocations to be inscribed and carry as a mnemonic act of devotion: "'Jesus Christus, María Virgo Mater Dei, kirie eleison, Criste eleison, Pater Noster, Ave Maria, Credo in Deum,' que se escriben todos enteros hasta el cabo. La razón desta regla es porque el evangelio dice que en nobre de Jesús hay mucha virtud y gracia maravillosa, y como leemos en las historias de los santos antiguos que unos con la oración del 'Pater Noster,' otros con el 'Credo in Deum,' otros con el 'Ave Maria,' sanaban a muchos enfermos de muy graves enfermedades, que es la principal intención de los ensalmos y nóminas. Y pues que esta mi nómina es muy breve y las palabras de ella son muy santas sacadas del Sancto Evangelio y muy probadas y usadas en toda la universal Iglesia" (1978: 82–3). These are presented as an alternative to popular *nóminas* containing long texts, mixed with languages and unknown words, foreign to the gospels. The sixteenth-century hagiographer Alonso de Villegas makes the same distinction, condemning amulets that promise to protect criminals from danger (1603: 88r).

41 An early example of this can be found in St Isidore's *De ecclesiasticis officiis* (On Church Offices, c. 610–15), where the bishop of Seville exposes a band of wandering monks who were known for selling the relics of supposed martyrs and hypocritically wearing their phylacteries like the Pharisees (2008: 2.16.6). Some eighty years later, on the eve of the Muslim invasion, a Visigothic canon was passed forbidding clergy from practising magic, performing incantations, and producing amulets that are again specifically identified as "phylateria" (supp. 21) (Menéndez y Pelayo 1992: 1.426).

42 Ironically, the positioning of the text "in petore" also reflects language in Vulgate for God's instructions to the Jews on wearing the tefillin (Deut. 11:18).

43 Of course, as Skemer has pointed out, it was a commonplace over the course of the Middle Ages for different religious groups to accuse each

other of introducing or attempting to profit from amuletic superstitions (2006: 26, 184). In this study, I do not consider fictional stories that are concerned with exposing this abuse and fraud of selling amulets as merchandise but only works that appear to re-convey fictionally powers believed to be inherent in the words and materiality of these objects. For late medieval stories about cases of fraudulence in the *Decameron* and elsewhere see Skemer (2006: 182–4).

44 The theories that Bynum considers (2011) are representative of different ways of approaching the question of an object's agency or its active blurring of a perceived or assumed distinction between object and subject. She cites the classic studies of the social scientists Bruno Latour (1993) and Alfred Gell (1998), as well as the literary critic Barbara Johnson (2008). These can be distinguished from non-material verbal performativity in the work of J.L. Austin (1962) and later literary theorists.

45 Specifically, my approach to the study of manuscripts has been influenced by the insights of scholars like Stephen Nichols, Andrew Taylor (2002), in addition to John Dagenais (1994). The kinds of questions I ask in the analyses performed in these chapters are broadly shaped by notions of reader response, speech acts, intertextuality, gender construction, representations of the other, and New Historicist ways of understanding how objects and texts can "resonate" through time (Greenblatt 1990).

1. Amuletic Manuscripts

1 Amuletic Manuscripts[1] He threatens the demons in a way that is later imitated in Celestina's hex and also corresponds with Solomonic magic, both of which will be more fully discussed in chapter 4 of this study.

2 The Latin verses from the *Officium Beatae Mariae* draw on Psalms 125–7: "Memento salutis auctor / quod nostri quondam corporis, / ex illibata virgine / nascendo, formam sumpseris ... Beatus vir ... non confundetur cum loquetur inimicis ... Pulchra es et decora filia Hierusalem" (1599).

3 See especially *De doctrina Christiana* (1841: 2.21–4).

4 The same kind of *sigillum* can be found in versions of the following medieval Solomonic grimoires: the *Liber iuratus or Sacer* (The Sworn Book of Honorius), the *Ars Notoria* (Notary Art), and in particular the *Clavicula Salomonis* (Key of Solomon).

5 For example, in the early thirteenth century, Caesarius of Heisterbach recommended using the Ave Maria to protect against the devil's deceptions (1851: 1.36). Skemer also cites Johannes Herolt, who tells of an

inscribed Ave Maria text serving as a "demon repellent" in his fifteenth-century collection of Marian miracles (2006: 92).

6 The sermons occupy in fact a total 161 folios in the codex, versus the five folios that concern me in this chapter. Their possible relationship to the Spanish *cuaderno* has been only explored partially (Dagenais 1994: 43–7).

7 All citations from the edition of Enzo Franchini (1993). The titles of the two parts follow headings in the manuscript: "Razón acabada feyta damor y bien rymada" (The Complete Reason Made of Love and Well Rhymed) and "Aquí copiença adenostar el vino y el agua" (Here Begins the Debating of Wine and Water) (1993: 3, 87). The Latin name of the scribe appears in the manuscript, "Lupus me fecit de Moros" (Lope of Moros made me) (1993: 29).

8 According to medieval tradition, the Christ's cross was made from the wood of an olive tree. The pomegranate was linked to the fruits of the church as the bride of Christ. The image of the apple tree in the Song of Songs was understood as typological prefiguration of the wood on which the Saviour's body hung like fruit (Norris 2003: 108, 284). The exorcistic prayer invokes the cross as an apotropaic ("ecce crucem domini") and also seems to allude to the invention or discovery of this relic by St Helen ("de umbra en Sancta Elena in petra marmorea sede") (Franchini 1991: fol. 123). On legends and amorous representations of St Helen and the cross during the Middle Ages, see my earlier study (*The Laughter* 2009: 15–24).

9 It is first described as being perched in the apple tree and later appears in the pomegranate (Franchini 1993: vv. 82–6).

10 Scholars have compared the poem's imagery of "fin amor" to Old French and Provençal traditions of the *pastourelle*, the related Iberian *cantar de amigo*, and allegories of the redeeming Marian garden and Incarnation as seen in the "Introducción" to Gonzalo de Berceo's miracle collection (Franchini 1993).

11 In the Gospel of Luke, John the Baptist prophesizes that a Saviour will come and baptize not with water but with the Holy Spirit (3:16). Another comparison is made when, unlike the Baptist, Christ drinks wine instead of water (Luke 7:34). Medieval commentators spoke of the church being born from Christ's side wound (Bynum, 2010, 113). Images of this wound were also commonly depicted on amulets from the period, as I will discuss in chapter 4 of this study.

12 The synoptic gospels all describe how the Holy Spirit descended on Christ like a dove at his baptism in the river Jordan (Matt. 3:13–17; Mark 1:9–11; Luke 3:21–3; John 1:30–5).

13 Medieval scribes often recorded a request for wine at the end of a copied text. Apart from the earlier *Poema de mío Cid* (1980: vv. 3732, 3734), this occurs in a number of French manuscripts from the period. See, for

example, the *Roman de Fauvel* (Dillon 2002: 171). In the case of the *Razón de amor*, however, the pun suggests the influence of drinking masses and related practices associated with end-of-the-year festivities (Bayless 1996: 353–62; and Giles "The Liberties" 2009).

14 More highly developed exorcistic rituals began to appear in manuals during the fifteenth century. Hilaire Kallendorf (2003) has studied the influence of these later rituals on early modern Spanish literary texts. During the Middle Ages, exorcism could refer to the initiation for baptism that I briefly discuss here or, more broadly, to the tradition of Christ and the saints (imitated by priests or lay people) commanding and exorcizing demons believed to have taken possession of individuals or groups. These are described in miracle collections and hagiographic works.

15 Following the verbal binding of Satan, the Trinitarian invocation of the Holy Spirit appears in the Latin prayer: "Recordare Sathanas ... in nomine Patris, filii, spiritus sancti" (1991: 82). I have consulted the English translation of the Mozarabic rite by T.C. Akeley (1967). For a transcription of the Latin text, see the *Liber Ordinum* edited by Dom G. Férotin (1904: 26).

16 Bells were themselves viewed as apotropaic objects on the basis of sacred inscriptions made on them as well as the potent sound of their ringing. The poem mentions that a small bell had been attached to the dove's foot ("un cascabiello dorado" 1993: v. 150). This was a common practice for domestic birds during the Middle Ages but in the context of the poem is also suggestive of a liturgical bell-ringing.

17 I discuss this feast in my earlier study (*The Laughter* 2009: 88–9). For a medieval Spanish account of the dragons' aerial contamination of water sources, see Fernando Baños Vallejo and Isabel Uría Maqua (2000: 182).

18 The Trisagion can also be found in later medieval texts studied by Skemer (2006: 181, 187), as well as the sixteenth-century paper I will discuss in the last chapter of this study, providing an example of how the same elements were copied, recopied, and recontextualized in the production of textual amulets through the centuries.

19 Priests were sometimes blamed for storms if they refused to perform an abjuration (Zilka 2003:166). Mermeut, together with the giant Fasolt, were demigods in Norse mythology who held power over storms on land and at sea (Grimm 1883: 2.636). The church had, in fact, instituted a yearly rogation ceremony that would come to coincide with the feast of St Mark (25 April), in which parish priests led a procession to bless the fields and prayer for their protection against damaging storms (Martín Cebrián 2012). "Las rogativas" was also a popular time to arrange and conduct marriages, as can be seen in the archpriest of Hita's subversive evocation

these festivities in the *Libro de buen amor* (Ruiz 1988: sts. 1321–8). Other ceremonies, later condemned by reformers like Ciruelo (1978: chap. 10), sometimes involved counteracting locust infestations by putting the pests on trial or excommunicating them (Christian 1981b: 31, 55, 61–3).

20 In late antiquity and throughout the Middle Ages, variants of this word could also be repeatedly written to form squares or triangles (sometimes inverted) of diminishing and increasing letter combinations. Apart from the incantatory repetition of these sounds, the numerology of the lines was believed to impart additional power to such magic words. Skemer has studied a thirteenth-century example of an illustrated "O" from the Canterbury Cathedral Library (2006: 49, 116, and 204).

21 "Super flumina et super fontes aquarum ... factus est sanguis ... facta sunt fulgora et voces et tonitrua ... calicem vini indignationis irae eius ... grando magna ... descendit de caelo in homines et blasphemaverunt homines Deum propter plagam grandinis quoniam magna facta est vehementer." The word "milia" is repeated in Latin prayer (Franchini 1991: 83), and appears in Revelation more than a dozen times, most notably in the context of the famous Millennium prophecy of the Devil being bound for a thousand years (1991: 20).

22 The Latin text renders the first of these "Sabbadon" – apparently confusing "Abaddon" (אֲבַדּוֹן) with the word for Sabbath, "Sabbaton" (Greek σάββατον, Hebrew שַׁבָּת). According to Revelation, Abaddon and Apollyon (Ἀπολλύων) are respectively the Hebrew and Greek names for the same personified star called "Abaddon" that falls from the heavens in Revelation, opening a pit from which a swarm of locusts arises. In the Hebrew Bible the name signified a place of destruction (Job 26:6, 28:22, 31:12; Psalm 88:11; Proverbs 15:11, 27:20). This spirit is called on in a late medieval *Clavícula de Salamón*, preserved during the 1520s by the Spanish Inquisition that I will discuss later in this book (Caro Baroja 1967).

23 These were thought to have been prefigured by the meteorological punishment of Pharaoh in Exodus (9:13–35). In addition to fires in the sky, Berceo evokes the image of blood erupting from plants at the end of time ("Los signos" 2003, vv. 1–24).

24 At the end of the prayer, Christ is also invoked as "Pantocrator" or the Almighty Lord (Franchini 1991: 83). Skemer records a number of textual amulets in which the Trisagion and Alpha Omega appear. Both invocations will be discussed at greater length in another part of this study.

25 In the Old Testament, the metaphor is employed, for example, in Hosea (10:1). Cf. the parable from the Gospel of John on the vine, branches, and fruit was traditionally interpreted as an illustration of

the mediating role of Christ through the institution of the Eucharist (15:1–11, Thune 2002: 95).

26 The pattern of images that correlates so closely and consistently with the *Razón de amor* can be found in *Cantar de Cantares* 2:1, 4:12; 4:13, 2:12, 5:14, among other places.

27 The commentaries of Robert of Tombelaine have sometimes been wrongly attributed to Gregory the Great. Such commentators could have drawn on the influential gloss of the Venerable Bede, who also likened the bride to the church (Matter 1990: 101, 130). Ann Astell has considered some other medieval examples of literary writers linking the Song and Songs and the Apocalypse (1990: 132, 155).

28 For commentators like Honorius, the image of "drinking from the mouth" could also allude to Mary being, as it were, kissed by the divine Word made incarnate in her (Norris 2003: 24–5). The verse from the Vulgate reads, "Osculetur me osculo oris sui quia meliora sunt ubera tua vino." Specifically, Matter cites a prayer book in which Christ and the church are "locked in a kiss" within the capital "O" of "Osculetur" (1990: 101).

29 "Columbam autem ecclesiam ... eo quod nullo sit malitiae felle perfusa, sed et quod columba apud Graecos peristera dicitur, cuius nominis litterae per computum Graecum in summam redactae unum et octigentos faciunt; unum autem et alpha et omega graece signantur; unde et ipse dominus, cuius est caro ecclesia, 'ego sum' inquit 'alpha et omega', quo numero nomen columbae signatur; unde et spiritus sicut columba descendens super Christum in Iordanen indicat trinitatem ... spiritus sanctus in columba" (Gregory of Elvira 1994: 3.10–11).

30 In addition to the descent of the Holy Spirit like a dove, Jesus also asks his followers to remain innocent as doves in the gospels (Matt. 10:16).

31 Bestiary writers followed exegetes in linking the gospel image of the dove not only to the Song of Songs but also the bird that appeared to Noah with an olive branch in its mouth (Gen. 8:11), symbolizing the soul that loves God and fears damnation pleading for mercy (for example, *Aberdeen* 2002: fol. 26v).

32 Alfonso's first son, Fernando de la Cerda, had died while trying to put down a spreading Muslim revolt. Fernando had married the sister of the French king, Blanche, who bore him two sons – both of them under the age of six at the time of his death. This turn of events led to Alfonso's second-born son, Sancho, declaring himself heir to the throne in opposition to the rights of Fernando's eldest. Philip III of France then sent his forces across the Pyrenees to capture Pamplona, ostensibly in support of his other sister, Isabella, the widowed queen of Navarra. As Alfonso lay in agony,

his younger brother was supposed to be leading an army north in support of the Castilian cause, but these troops never reached the city to offer any resistance. For an overview, see the biography of Salvador Martínez (2010).

33 All citations from the edition of Walter Mettman (1986–9). Translations based on the English version of Kathleen Kulp-Hill (Alfonso X 2000).

34 See, for example, the biographical works of Joseph O'Callaghan (1998) and Salvador Martínez (2010), as well as the co-authored study of John Keller and Richard Kinkade (1983). On the condition of the king, resulting in severe pain, tumours, and visible ulcers, see the study of Marcel E. Presilla (1987). The casket was moved several times before being permanently relocated to the Cathedral of Seville (except for the king's heart, which was sent to Murcia). In 1948, a forensic examination was conducted on the remains of Alfonso and his mother (see J. Delgado Roig 1948).

35 As Prado-Vilar (2011) points out, according to the legal text known as the *Siete partidas* (Seven Parts), Christians were prohibited from receiving medicines prepared directly by Jewish physicians (2004: 7.24.8). He cites Dwayne Carpenter's helpful edition of materials from the Alfonsine code (1986).

36 This theory is noted, for instance, by Salvador Martínez (2010: 262). However, the visual representation of other books in the *Cantigas* is similar, and the use of such binding quite common. The manuscript in question is currently housed at the Biblioteca Nacional in Madrid (BNE, Ms. 10069).

37 Prado-Vilar mentions two historical Jewish physicians, Abraham Ibn Waqar (who personally served the king for many years) and Yehuda Mosca (who is mentioned in the prologue to Alfonso X's *Lapidario*) (2011: 116). On the conventional vilification of Jews in the *Cantigas*, see the studies of Albert Bagby (1971) and Angus Mackay (1983). Prado-Vilar also compares the visual presentation of Jews in biographical versus non-biographical Latin sources (2011: 121–2).

38 Specifically, they call her a "heretic" and "renegade": "'ereja' a chamavan / muit' e 'renegada' e 'crischãa tornada'" (1986–9: vol. 1, vv. 58–60) Cf. *cantiga* 306, in which an image of the pregnant Virgin provokes the mockery of a heretic. As he looks at the painting, Mary's swollen belly miraculously shrinks.

39 This illustrates how Merlin used the boy to correct or cause the Jews to be "released from their error" and so "convert them" (e polos judeus tirar de seu erro, pois creceu, con el os convertia) (1986–9: vol. 2, vv. 82–4) The verses do not describe how the position of the boy's head was restored or "turned" through conversion. As Prado-Vilar rightly points out, the faces or facial expressions of Jewish men are in several cases (though

not in *cantiga* 209) caricatured, whereas Jewish women are visually indistinguishable from their Christian counterparts in the collection's illuminations.

40 The same tale is found in the Gonzalo de Berceo's *Milagros de Nuestra Señora* (see the study of Patricia Timmons 2012), and was widely disseminated during the Middle Ages, as Miri Rubin as shown (2004). Interestingly, this "oven miracle" topic can be compared to a Muslim legend, recorded in the eleventh-century by Al-Tha'labi, in which the mother of Moses (Mūsā) hides him from Pharaoh in an oven. When the fire is lit, he emerges unscathed (see John Renard 2008).

41 Prado-Vilar refers to this status as *iudeus sacer*: "From the point of view of the father/Jewish law, he is *sacer* (accursed) ... while from the point of view of the mother/Mary/Christianity, he is *sacer* (sacred) in the positive sense as a sacredly begotten figure ... a pure figure of potentiality ... undergoing processes of becoming" (2011: 133).

42 The gospel verse in question condemns religious pride and ostentation: "For they make their phylacteries broad and enlarge their fringes" (enim phylacteria sua et magnificant fimbrias). Don Skemer has considered the influence of this passage of Jerome's commentary (*Commentaria in Matthaeum*) as it relates to medieval discussions of textual amulets (2006: 36–7).

43 Of equal interest, these texts could be attributed with amuletic powers in Jewish communities (see Skemer 2006: 33–5). Recently, Yehudah Cohn (2008) has studied the early history of tefillin, including possible connections with phylacteries in ancient Greek culture.

44 Translation by Thomas Scheck. "Dominus cum dedisset mandata Legis per Moysen, ad extremum intulit: 'Ligabis ea ... sint ante oculos tuos' ... Hoc Pharisaei male interpretantes, scribebant in membranulis Decalogum Moysi, id est decem verba Legis, complicantes ea, et ligantes in fronte ... ut quomodo in corporibus circumcisio signum Judaicae gentis daret, ita et vestis haberet aliquam differentiam ... Pictatiola illa Decalogi, phylacteria vocabant: quod quicumque habuisset ea, quasi ob custodiam et monimentum sui haberet ... Pharisaeis quod haec in corde portanda sint, non in corpore ... Hoc apud nos superstitiosae ... in parvulis Evangeliis usque hodie factitant" (1845: 0168A–C).

45 Pauline notions of the letter and the flesh versus the spirit were also influentially applied by the church fathers and later medieval writers to ways of reading and employing poetic language, carnally or inwardly and figuratively. See David Nirenberg's (2006) groundbreaking study of how this legacy manifests itself in fourteenth and fifteenth-century Castilian

poetry. On the monstrous representation of religious others in earlier
centuries, see the study of Michael Uebel (1996).

46 "Puto quod illorum tunc scribarum et Pharisaeorum exemplo et nunc
multi aliqua nomina Haebraica angelorum configunt, et scribunt, et
alligant sibi ... vani sunt, sicut illi fuerunt ... De hominibus itaque nostri
temporis exponentes, de illis videmur exponere. Ergo sacerdotes ex eo
quod ab hominibus volunt videri justi, phylacteria alligant ... partem
aliquam Evangelii scriptam ... Deinde ubi est virtus Evangelii, in figuris
literarum, an in intellectu sensuum? Si in figuris, bene circa collum
suspendis; si in intellectu, ergo melius in corde posita prosunt" (1862:
0877–9). While such commentators only evoke images of inscription, Paul's
letter to the Romans also contrasts hearing the law with acting on it.

47 "In principio erat Verbum et Verbum erat apud Deum et Deus erat Verbum ... et
Verbum caro factum est et habitavit in nobis ... plenum gratiae et veritatis."
Skemer has edited French, Italian, and English textual amulets that date
from the latter part of the Middle Ages and also prominently feature the
Incarnational opening to the Gospel of John.

48 This seventh-century miniature codex (5.4 × 3.6 inches), known as the
Anglo-Saxon Cuthbert gospel, was supposedly removed from the saint's
casket during the early twelfth century and has been preserved at the
British Library (Additional MS 89000).

49 "Quale remedium posuit Dominus contra aegritudines animae ... et
non ad ligaturam cucurreris ... ita plangendi sunt homines qui currunt
ad ligaturas, ut gaudeamus quando videmus hominem in lecto suo
constitutum, jactari febribus et doloribus, nec alicubi spem posuisse, nisi
ut sibi Evangelium ... non quia ad hoc factum est, sed quia praelatum
est Evangelium ligaturis ... ut quiescat dolor ... ad cor non ponitur ut
sanetur a peccatis? ... Ponatur ad cor, sanetur cor. Bonum est, bonum, ut
de salute corporis non satagas, nisi ut a Deo illam petas ... Rogavit eum
Paulus apostolus, ut auferret stimulum carnis ... 'Sufficit tibi gratia mea;
nam virtus in infirmitate perficitur'" (1888: 1443, 1841). On the profound
influence of Augustine's *Tractates* on medieval interpretations of John's
gospel, see William M. Wright (2009).

50 Christians interpreted Daniel's vision as the Heavenly court and a
prefigurement of the opening of books at the Last Judgment in Revelation:
"I beheld till thrones were placed, and the ancient of days sat ... the
judgment sat, and the books were opened" (aspiciebam donec throni positi
sunt et antiquus dierum sedit ... iudicium sedit et libri aperti sunt).

51 "Et qui libri aperti, nisi conscientiae nostrae, velut libri peccatorum
nostrorum seriem continentes? ... aperietur liber cordis tui ... recitabitur ...

Si bene egeris, manebit Scriptura. Vide ne tollas Spiritus sancti gratiam ... deleas, et scribas atramento flagitia tua" (1845: 0949C–0950B).

52 On Alfonso's will and the postmortem fate of his *Cantigas*, see Kirstin Kennedy (2004: 202). In particular, artists visualized the following passage from Revelation: "And I saw the dead, great and small, standing in the presence of the throne. And the books were opened: and another book was opened, which was the book of life. And the dead were judged by those things which were written in the books, according to their works" (et vidi mortuos magnos et pusillos stantes in conspectu throni et libri aperti sunt et alius liber apertus est qui est vitae et iudicati sunt mortui ex his quae scripta erant in libris secundum opera ipsorum) (20:12). A *cantiga* near the end of the collection cites a related passage from the Apocalypse in anticipation of the deeds of sinners being textually revealed on their foreheads (1986–9: vol. 3, no. 422, v. 37; cf. Rev. 13:16–17).

53 "Non clauditur codex eorum, nec plicatur liber eorum; quia tu ipse illis hoc es" (1841: bk. 13, chap. 5. 18).

54 This can be compared to male and female saints who sometimes composed texts to be used as amulets, in addition to employing sacred books (Skemer 2006: 58).

55 It is significant, as Jager suggests, that earlier texts read by Augustine are identifiable as scrolls, as opposed to the codices that came to be associated closely with his ultimate conversion experience. Before the scene in the garden of Milan, he is reminded of a similar story after he sees open codex of Paul's epistles lying on a table. In it, a man is converted after coming across and reading an open book containing the life of St Anthony. Anthony himself was said to have been transformed after he happened to hear a reading from the gospel.

56 On the influence of Petrus Comestor on Alfonsine historiography, see Charles F. Fraker (1996). Jager also cites a thirteenth-century contemporary of Alfonso, Hugh of Saint-Cher, who viewed the "liber cordis sive conscientie" (Book of the Heart or Conscience) as the individual's own self-authored work to "read within" (intus legere) (2000: 58). In this way, his *De doctrina cordis* (On the Teaching of the Heart) figures the text that each "reader/scribe will present to Christ at the Last Judgment as a manuscript codex that has been visually examined and corrected" (2000: 59).

57 I have added an ellipsis in the last line of Jager's translation to indicate the omission of a phrase that Petrus Comestor adapted from the Gospel of Matthew (5:26), "solvamus novissimum quadrantem" (we pay off the last farthing). "Ecce in hoc folio primo scribuntur ea quae pertinent ad dilectionem Dei proprie, et exprimitur hic Trinitas. In secundo folio scribes

ea quae pertinent ad dilectionem proximi (1855: 0816D–17A) ... Loquitur homo ad cor suum, in libro cordis sui opera sua diligenter legendo. Liber iste duo folia habet. In uno legunt peccatores; in alio poenitentes ne forte ... quae de terra protraximus" (1855: 0675C–D). J.P. Migne follows the mistaken attribution of this sermonic material to Hildebert of Lavardin and Hugh of Saint-Victor, respectively, but Petrus Comestor has since been identified as the author. See the corrected reattributions of Palémon Glorieux (1952).

58 Augustine was also concerned with the danger of music to delight and arouse the senses. On the influence of the spiritual and worldly powers attributed to music in medieval culture, see chapter 3 of this study.

2. Naming God

1 Diacritic marks for the name Elohim could also be applied (see Singer et al. 1901–6: 9.160–1). Prior to the publication of the King James Bible (1611), an early instance in English of this derivation appears as "Iehouah" in William Tyndale's translation of the Pentateuch (1530). Latin examples of this confused pronunciation go back much further, however, at least to the thirteenth-century (Mass 1907–22).

2 These citations are from the thirteenth-century translation in the Biblioteca Universitaria de Salamanca M. 1997, known as *Fazienda de Ultramar* (Overseas Deeds), and fourteenth-century translations housed at the Escorial: I.i.3, I.i.4, I.i.5, I.i.7, and I.ii.19.

3 Fourteenth-century peninsular witnesses also include *Victoria adversus impios Ebreos* (Victory over the impious Hebrews) by the Portuguese Carthusian, Victor Porchet de Salvaticis, and from the Jewish perspective, the polemical *Eben Bohan* (Touchstone) of Shem Tob Ibn Shaprut. See Williams (1935) and Sainz de la Maza (1992).

4 For a recent discussion of Jewish influences, see Skemer (2006: 26, 112–14). Examples of Syriac and Gnostic amulets (collected in the British Museum) can be found in the work of E.A. Wallis Budge (1930).

5 R.P.H. Green makes a note of this possible connection in his work on sources for the *Ecloga Theoduli* (1982: 103).

6 Harry Vredeveld makes reference to this allusion (1987: 104, 110). Medieval readers interpreted such imagery through a process of allegoresis, in the tradition of Augustine drawing on language from the *Aeneid* to describe his conversion in *Confessiones*. On the mythologizing of Proserpina and Troy during the Middle Ages, see Marcia A. Dalbey (1974), Mark Amsler (2001: 72–6), and Jane Chance (1995: 31, 246).

7 "E terra verum corpus Salvator Iesus assumpsit quae nunc." Another example of this meaning can be found in Cyprian's *De resurrectione mortuorum* (On the Resurrection of the Dead) (see Vredeveld 1987: 110).

8 In this way, the image of Christian resurrection simultaneously recalls the fall of Satan and the raising of Adam from the dust, as well as the ascension of Christ.

9 This stanza appears to contrast the power of the four-lettered name of the One God with Pythagoras's legendary veneration of the sun in medieval biographies (Joost-Gaugier 2006: 67–71).

10 On the medieval tradition of riddling, see also Archer Taylor's classic study (1948). For contemporary readers, this problem of named namelessness may bring to mind Derrida's discussion of *dénégation*: "does something like the secret itself, properly speaking, ever exist? The name of God (I do not say God, but how to avoid saying God here, from the moment when I say the name of God?) can only be *said* in the modality of this secret denial [*dénégation*]" (1992: 95).

11 The hero marries an Amazonian queen, defeats Porus of India, journeys into the heavens on a gondola pulled by griffins, and sinks to the bottom of the ocean in a metal capsule – before his life is cut short by a Satanic conspiracy to poison him in Babylon.

12 Like a Christian pilgrim, Alexander also makes offerings at the city's holy sites or "estaçiones" (1988: 1095b).

13 On the sources for these scenes, see Raymond S. Willis (1933: 44). The relationship between the *Alexandreis* and the Spanish poem has also been studied by Matthew Agnew (2001). The *Historia de Preliis* has been attributed to the tenth-century writer, Leo Archipresbyter. Its relationship to the *Libro de Alexandre* has been studied by Ian Michael (1982). The biblical phrase describing the mitre with the inscribed plate can be found in Exodus (28.36–8, 29.6) and Leviticus (8.9). Skemer points out that the Latin phrase *laminae* could, in any case, be used in reference to metal sheets used as textual amulets (2006: 13, 81). The *Historia de preliis*, in turn, draws on the late first-century *Antiquitates Judaicae* (Jewish Antiquities) of Josephus (2006: 11.317–45). For more information on the treatment of the scene in medieval romance Alexander legends, see Lida de Malkiel (1957: 191).

14 This was a popular sequel to one of the *Libro de Alexandre*'s primary sources, the *Roman d'Alexandre*. References to other uses of textual amulets in French Romance from the period can be found in Skemer (2006: 109–10). This *Prière de Charlemagne* not only served as a literary device but continued to be copied throughout the Middle Ages as well as in later

grimoires in spite of specific denunciations by the church (Skemer 2006: 98). In a later version of the story, it was sent by Pope Leo III (Askins 2007: 249–51). The idea could be related to the tradition of the "heavenly letter" sent by Christ to Abgar.

15 For example, in the later catalogue of precious stones (1988: sts. 1468–92).

16 "Tetagrammaton, id est quatuor litterarum, *iod-he-vau-he*. Sed his litteris non repraesentantur elementa illa" (Tetragrammaton, that is four letters, *yod-he-vau-he*. But these letters do not represent its elements).

17 "Dicitur 'Tetragrammaton' non est nota alicujus conceptus mentis, non est proprium nomen Dei vel alterius ... ineffabile est, non nominans sed nominatum." As this book was going into production, a new study by Robert Wilkinson (2015) was published that traces the history of Christian expropriations of the Tetragrammaton, from late antiquity into the early modern period.

18 "Non extrinsecus verba exciperet" (did not receive words from the outside) (*De Genesi contra Manichaeos* 2.4). Translation by Roland J. Teske (1991: 99). The poem also features an allegorized treatment of the mythic Apple of Discord from the Trojan legend, marked by the "mala escriptura" (evil inscription) of Sin, and a later account of linguistic disunity in the biblical city "de nombre de confusión ... Babilón" (with the name of confusion ... Babylon) (1988: sts. 341c, 1522d).

19 Instead, this neoplatonic writer finds that "we know him from the arrangement of everything, because ... this order possesses certain images and semblances of his divine paradigms" (1987: 108; 7.3).

20 He specifically cites his source as the *Secretis secretorum*, but this could refer to a number of different works (Alfonsi 2006: 172).

21 This Cistercian bishop associates the letters *yod-he-vau* with the "principle of life itself" (Maurer "The Sacred" 1979, 978).

22 "Nomen eius in frontibus eorum" (Rev. 22.4). "Dominus in carne… vexillum crucis, quo suorum frontes signaret … Nam et ipsa crucis figura dilatatum ubique Domini significat regnum, sicut vetus dictum comprobat: 'Respice distinctis quadratum partibus orbem, ut regnum fidei cuncta tenere probes.' Neque enim frustra in fronte pontificis nomen Domini tetragrammaton scribebatur, nisi quia hoc est signum in fronte fidelium." The marked forehead image also occurs earlier in Revelation 9.4, 13.16, 14.1, and 20.4.

23 "Vidi quattuor angelos stantes super quattuor angulos terrae tenentes quattuor ventos terrae (1850)." See Jonathan T. Lanman's study of these maps (1981). On mapping in medieval Spain, see Simone Pinet.

24 In search of the other side of the world, Alexander ventures beneath its surface into the realm of the Devil and the deadly sins. On the question

of geography and the antipodes in the poem, see Alan Deyermond (1996: 2002). The third and fourth panels of Alexander's tent depict the *mappa mundi* and his deeds. The first two show the months of year and the legends of Hercules and the Trojan War (1988: sts. 2554–775). The ceiling portrays the sacred history of the Fall of Lucifer and humanity, including the biblical episode of the Tower of Babylon (1988: sts. 2551–3).

25 On the influence of Joachim of Fiore, see Marjorie Reeves (1969: 40–132).

26 He inscribes both A and Ω with the characters of the Tetragrammaton and the three persons of the godhead. Joachim's triangular Alpha was probably influenced by the earlier-mentioned illustration of Petrus Alfonsi's dialogue, as was Garnerius of Rochefort's arrangement (c. 1208–10) of the holy letters at the angles of an equilateral triangle (Reeves 1969: 44).

27 In a second allegory, Daniel alludes to the Macedonian as one of four beasts, a leopard with four wings and heads that represent his conquests and successors (Dan. 7.6).

28 "No firié más aprissa Judas el Macabeo; / diz' el rey Alexandre ... 'de bevir estos omes non han mucho deseo'" (not even Judas the Maccabean was wounded so hurriedly; King Alexander remarked ... "these men do not much desire to live"). The biblical texts reads, "Alexander ... fought many battles ... even to the ends of the earth ... And his servants made themselves kings ... after his death, and their sons after them ... evils were multiplied in the earth ... And there came out of them a wicked root, Antiochus" (constituit proelia multa... usque ad fines terrae... obtinuerunt pueri eius regnum... multiplicata sunt mala in terra... et exiit ex eis radix peccatrix Antiochus) (Macc. 1.1–11).

29 The Antichrist was expected to simulate God by enthroning himself in the Temple (Adso 1979: 91). As a precursor to his reign of terror, Alexander's twelve-year rule was also connected to the Last World Emperor reigning for the same duration and ushering in the Messianic Age (Cary 1956: 134).

30 "Solvetur Satanas de carcere suo ... super quattuor angulos terrae Gog et Magog ... in proelium quorum numerus est sicut harena maris." The names Gog and Magog come from Genesis (10.1–5) and Ezekiel (38–9). The meaning of the verse in the Spanish poem is clear in a version of the *Historia de preliis*: "inclusit Alexander duas gentes immundas, scilicet Gogh et Machgogh, quos tamen Antichristus inde reducet" (Alexander enclosed two foul peoples, surely God and Magog, those who are to be retrieved by the Antichrist) (Hilka 1976: 140–4).

31 By describing them celebrating a continuous Passover, the Castilian poet equates the enclosure and release from captivity of the lost tribes to the

ordained release of the Antichrist, as opposed to the deliverance God's chosen people.

32 He supposedly tried – with no success – to convert a Jewish friend with the diagram. See Anna Sapir Abulafia, who also discusses Peter of Blois's earlier adoption of Petrus Alfonsi's version of the Tetragrammaton in his late twelfth-century polemic, *Contra perfidiam Judaeorum* (Against the Perfidious Jews) (2002: 75–9; 1855).

33 In the *Liber figurarum*, Joachim (1940: no. 14) saw the Islamic conqueror of Jerusalem, Saladin, as the sixth head that immediately precedes the coming of the Antichrist, or the seventh head of the dragon from Revelation (chapter 12).

34 Corominas also speculates that the word "encordado" could describe a process of embroidering letters onto the wooden surface: "las letras podían ponerse como bordadas con un tranzado de cuerdecitas" (Ruiz 1967, 590). While Corominas is no doubt correct in his gloss of "tabletas," I have found little evidence testifying to a practice of physically embroidering shields in fourteenth-century Iberia. The appearance of heraldic embroidered shield designs on vestments was not uncommon, however (see, for example, Hayward 1971). In his edition, Alberto Blecua noted "no se sabe bien a qué alude" (Ruiz 2001: 265).

35 The influence of Perault has been considered by Félix Lecoy (1938), Gerli (1982), Louise Vasvari (1985), and Jacques Joset (2004). On the ordering of the sins, see in addition to Lecoy's book the studies of Lida de Malkiel (1940) and Robert Ricard (1973). For comparison between their organizations in different parts of the text, see Julián Bueno (1983). In this poet's allegory, the sins are depicted in Hell with Satan, a tradition that supports Gerli's reading (1982) of Amor's identity as the Satanic father of sin in the *Libro de buen amor*.

36 The names are abbreviated with suspension marks. In the *Libro* manuscript, the abbreviation is used "Spūt buen consejo" (1988: st. 1598d; 1965: 542, 646). In keeping with the anonymous illustrator (and Alan of Lille's *Tractatus de virtutibus et de vitiis et de donis Spiritus Sancti*), each of the remaining attributes of the Holy Spirit precedes the shield in the archpriest's allegory: "Spíritu Santo de buena sabidoría ... temer a Dios ... de piedat ... fortaleza ... entendimiento ... çiencia" (Holy Spirit of good knowledge [sapientiae] ... fear of God [timoris Domini] ... piety [pietatis] ... strength [fortitudinis] ... understanding [intellectus] ... wisdom [scientiae]) (Evans 1982: 16; 1988: sts. 1588–96).

37 As in other illuminations from the period, including Matthew of Paris's well-known *Chronica majora*, the spoke connecting the central roundel

(*Deus*) to the bottom (*Filius*) appears as a Cross (see Evans 1982: 73; Lewis 1987: 194–6).

38 This heraldic element can also be related to emblazoned patterns described by the Marqués de Santillana as "cón nudos ligada" (tied with knots) in his description of the Navarrese coat of arms (1976: v. 60).

39 In the words of Peter Lombard (2007: 45–6): "tenses … are used of God, such as 'was', 'will be', 'is,' 'used to be' … yet they do not distinguish temporal movements … but indicate simply the essence or the existence of the Divinity. And so God alone is properly called essence or being (temporum de Deo dicantur, ut fuit, erit, est, erat, non tamen temporales motus tunc distinguunt … sed essentiam sive existentiam divinitatis simpliciter insinuant. Deus ergo solus proprie dicitur essentia vel esse) (1855: *liber* 1, *distinctio* 8, *cap.* 1). As a protective amulet, the shield can be related to endless knot images of Solomon's pentacle that I discuss in a later chapter (see Skemer 2006: 204, 302; Arthur 1987: 26–39).

40 These statements can also be clearly seen in an earlier thirteenth-century illumination from a manuscript containing Peter of Poitiers's *Compendium historiae in genealogia Christi* (Historical Compendium on the Genealogy of Christ) (Evans 1982: 73).

41 Translation by John Patrick Crichton-Stuart (1879: 1.834). "Minus enim jacula feriunt, quae praevidentur: et nos tolerabilius mundi mala suscipimus, si contra haec per praescientiae clypeum munimur" (Gregory 1849: 1259c). St Gregory's sermon explicates a passage from the Gospel of Luke: "For I will give you a mouth and wisdom, which all your adversaries shall not be able to resist and gainsay" (ego enim dabo vobis os et sapientiam cui non poterunt resistere et contradicere omnes adversarii vestri) (21.15).

42 Of particular interest is Accursius's gloss of the *Corpus Juris Civilis* (Body of Civil Law) and *Placides et Timéo ou li secrés as philosophes* (Placidius and Timaeus or The Secrets of the Philosophers). In his discussion of these sources, Lecoy finds that the tale satirizes the scholastic disputes and sign language used in monasteries (1938: 164).

43 In the example discussed by Gerli (2002), Augustine describes how the letter "Y" means different things for the Greeks and Romans (*Doctrina Christiana* 1841: *liber* 2, *cap.* 24).

44 Building on Augustine's portrayal of *caritas*, and later Trinitarian theology, Aquinas writes of the love that is "proper to the Holy Spirit – the love by which God loves us. So also does the love by which we love God, for he makes us lovers of God" (quod ad spiritum sanctum pertinet amor quo Deus nos amat. Similiter etiam et amor quo nos Deum amamus: cum

nos Dei faciat amatores) (1957: bk. 4.23.11). Translation from the study of Dennis Ngien (2005: 106).

45 On Abulafia's version, see Moshe Idel (1988, 30). The three-finger Christian blessing is attested to by Jean Beleth and Guillaume Durand (Didron 1851–91: 1.408).

46 "'Llamat me Buen Amor' ... 'Buen Amor' dixe al libro, e a ella" ("Call me Good Love" ... I said my book was "Good Love," as was she) (1988: 932b, 933b).

47 The first citation is from Psalm 53: "Deus in nomino tuo salvum me fac; et in virtute tuo judica me" (Save me, O God, by thy name, and judge me in thy strength) (v. 3). The reference to Eve comes from the hymn, "O Gloriosa Domina" (O Glorious Lady), sung at laudes: "Quod Eva tristis abstulit, tu reddis almo germine" (What man had lost in hapless Eve, thy sacred womb to man restores) (v. 5–6, see Green 1963).

48 "The soul plays your unfaithful lover ... men mount a grotesque imitation of you ... was I imitating you – in, admittedly, some grotesque and twisted way? (1955)" (Ita fornicatur anima… perverse te imitantur omnes… in quo dominum meum vel vitiose atque perverse imitatus sum?) (*Confessiones* 1841: 2.14, 2.6).

49 In accordance with the recycling of imagery from the *Libro de Alexandre* (1988: sts. 2182–233) in the archpriest's initial treatment of seven deadly sins (1988: sts. 217–320). See Nicolás Emilio Álvarez (1976), and John K. Walsh's study of influences (1979).

50 The archpriest's parodic interpretation is also suggested in a stanza near the end of the *Libro de Alexandre* that recalls the triumphant procession in Jerusalem, after the hero prays to God on the eve of his death: "fue bien ora de nona, medio día passada; / emperador del mundo a proçessión honrada / con *Te Deum laudamus* tornó a su posada" (it was well into the hour of nones, midday having passed; the world emperor returned to his quarters with an honorary procession singing "Lord we worship you") (1988: st. 2601). The archpriest takes the phrase *venite exultemus* from the *invitatorium* of the Divine Office, the *Te Deum laudamus* (or Ambrosian Hymn) was sung at the close of matins, the words *exultemus et laetemur* come from the antiphon of lauds for Easter, and *benedictus qui venit* is from the paschal offertory (see Bueno 1983).

3. Amuletic Voices

1 Ángel Ruiz Sainz found the object in a covered hole when renovating his house. It is still owned by the same family, kept in a safety deposit box near Burgos and only occasionally displayed. In his book, José Hernando

Pérez (1995) has studied the discovery of the tile as part of his speculative theory that the *Poema de Fernán González* was composed by the chancellor of Castile, Diego García, author of the scholastic Latin text known as the *Planeta* (1218). In recent years, Isabel Velázquez has published a useful descriptive study of the ostracon, also showing how its verses vary from the other manuscript containing the poem. The bottom of the shingle includes a notarial mark together with a typical abbreviation for "en testimonio de la verdat," and on the broken right-hand corner an incomplete, unexplained inscription, "philosopho sure [...]" (2006: 29).

2 On this prayer in particular, see Ruth House Webber (1995) and E. Michael Gerli ("*Ordo*" 1980). For a history of hagiographic motifs in Spanish literature, see the study of Ángel Gómez Moreno (2008).

3 In *Loores de Nuestra Señora* (In Praise of Our Lady), Gonzalo de Berceo includes two stanzas of a similar litany after his poetic recitation of the seven days of creation and ten commandments (2003: sts. 91–2). In Berceo's *Milagros de Nuestra Señora*, a longer version is recited in a liturgical context when a pregnant nun miraculously recovers her virginity: "ficieron un buen cántico toda la confradía, / podriélo en la glesia contar la clerecía" (all of the brothers sang a goodly song, as the clergy would sing in church) (2003: st. 452cd). These passages suggest that the prayer also functioned as a thanksgiving for the saving grace of God.

4 This corner of the shingle is partly missing, and the verse has itself been scratched. It is immediately followed by a stanza from another section of the *Poema de Fernán González*: "fues la tu mesurra / que tornaste la rrueda que [anda a la ventura]" (it was at your discretion, that you turned the wheel that [moves fortune]) (Gwara 2005: 117, cf. st. 180abc). This quatrain can be understood as linking Fortune's wheel, "la rueda que anda a la ventura," to the rotary torture of St Catherine implied in subsequent verses of the inscribed prayer, "valiste a Catalina y de muerte libreste" (*Libro de Apolonio* 1987: 180b, cf. 106a). The following invocation of the virgin Marina indicates that the object was connected to the cult of this saint at a Villamartín hermitage. Heather Bamford has recently considered whether it might have been used to protect the building itself, comparable to uses of Koranic texts or the Jewish mezuzah and so intended to work through "knowledge of the text's physical presence in the area" (2012).

5 This work contained riddles from the *Aenigmata* of Symphosius (1928: no. 59), as was also included in the *Gesta Romanorum* (1959: no. 158) by the end of the thirteenth century.

6 "El precio que daría para con vos pecar, quiérovoslo en donado, ofrecer y donar ... el Criador vos quiera ayudar y valer" (the price that I would

have paid to sin with you, I want to give it to you as a donation, to offer
and donate ... may the Creator wish to protect and cherish you) (1987:
416ab, 417c).

7 Grieve has noted that with the exception of the virgin's status as a priestess
and her homicidal act, the case of Seneca's *sacerdos prostituta* (prostitute
priestess) closely corresponds with the story of Tarsiana found in the *Libro
de Apolonio,* as well as its Latin models.

8 Ronald Surtz has also studied hagiographic discourse in the poem ("The
Libro de Apolonio" 1980). These interpretations seem even more plausible
considering that the earliest surviving versions of the *Historia Apollonii,*
dating from the late fifth and early sixth century, already contained a
number of Latin images that only occur in hagiographic texts written
during the same period. On Christian meanings in the poem, see also the
recent work of Matthew Desing (2012).

9 Translations of the *Gesta* (or *Vita*) *Sanctae Agnes* are taken from William
Granger Ryan's translated edition of the *Golden Legend* (Voragine 1993).
This text draws on Ambrose's *De viginibus* (1845), a Greek passion, as well
as the Prudentius hymn (*Peristephanon* 1950: 14).

10 Also, doctrinal works use versions of this phrase. See G.A.A. Kortekaas
(2004: 21) and (2007).

11 The book was based on sermons, one of which was given for the feast of St
Agnes to convince his sister, Marcellina, to become a nun (1997: 71).

12 For a comparison between the question of *incestum* with Vestals and later
meaning among Christians, see for example Thomas Worsfold (1997:
63). On incest as the breaking of a religious woman's vows in medieval
Christianity, see Graciela Daichman (1986: 11).

13 As T.E. Pickford points out, during the Middle Ages the name would have
been associated with the scriptural Antiochus Epiphanes "who wrought
terrible persecution on Jerusalem ... as a type of Satan" and linked with
concupiscentia (1975: 601; James 1.15). Cf. the incestuous poetics of Gower's
Confessio amantis in its later retelling of the legend of Apollonius (discussed
by Nowlin 2005).

14 On this poetic school, see especially the work of Francisco Rico (1985) and
Julian Weiss (2006).

15 These riddles were adapted from the late fourth or early fifth-century
Aenigmata of Symphosius. Another enigma, the "wheel," seems to refer to
Fortune.

16 She is consigned to the temple of Diane in the *Historia Apollonii.* In the
Latin text, Tarsiana is asked to worship Priapus in the Mytilene brothel.

17 The question is asked by the angel when followers look for Christ in his tomb.

18 On the other hand, transcendence remains incomplete in the lives of
   saintly characters, as the fullness of *anagnorismo* can be reached only when
   the soul no longer sees, in the earlier-mentioned words of Paul, "through a
   glass darkly" but finally encounters God "face to face" (Cor. 1:13).

19 The poem contains a number of hymns that reverently invoke both Christ
   and the Virgin, interspersed with prayers for students and blind men as
   well as parodic prayers in the tradition of the Goliards. See, in particular,
   the study of Otis Green (1958).

20 "Intus enim crines mihi sunt, quos non videt ullus; / Meque manus
   mittunt manibusque remittor in auras" (I have hair that no one sees.
   Hands send me and by hands am I sent back into the air) (Symphosius
   1928: no. 59, 90–1). I follow the Latin text and translation from the edition
   of Raymond Theodore Ohl.

21 The *Aenigmata* of Symphosius cited in the *Historia Apollonii* were widely
   circulated during the Middle Ages, as were other collections. During this
   period, syllogistic language was used to reveal the "paradox and mystery
   inherent in humble things," as well as central theological truths like "Quis
   est mortuus et non est natus? Adam ... Quis habet de virgine carnem?
   Christus" (Who is dead and not born? Adam ... Who has flesh of a virgin?
   Christ) (Law 2006: 24; Alvar 1984: 58). These questions, which Alvar cites
   in his discussion of the scholarly function of riddles in the *Libro de Apolonio*,
   are taken from Eberhard the German's thirteenth-century *Laborintus*, a
   didactic allegory for instruction in grammar and poetry (see Purcell 1993).
   Such exercises often employed personification and the first-person voice.

22 Gwara notes that this amuletic pronouncement can be compared to
   the personification of the *Libro de buen amor*, but does not consider the
   implications of this in his brief description of the tile (2005: 132–3).

23 Anglo-Saxon crosses were, for example, inscribed in the first-person with
   verses from the *Dream of the Rood* (Gwara 2005: 133; Swanton 1970: 9).

24 Another possible link between the *Libro de Apolonio* and *Libro de buen
   amor*, which was first commented upon by Felix Lecoy, occurs not long
   before the archpriest's assumption of his predatory alter ego Don Melón.
   Advising the narrator how to be a successful worldly lover, Amor warns
   against drinking too much wine and cites the example of Lot sleeping with
   his daughters, followed by an exemplum told by medieval preachers of
   a prayerful hermit who was convinced by the Devil to commit rape and
   murder (1988: 530d). This same tale is used to illustrate Antíoco's sin with
   his daughter and attempted murder of Apolonio (1987: 55a). Amor, who is
   himself closely associated with the Devil, tells the story not as a negative
   exemplar intended to warn readers how one sin can lead to another, but
   rather as an illustration of how to become a more effective carnal lover.

4. The Bawd's Amulet

1 The object was listed by the Les Enluminures gallery in Paris, but now belongs to the Princeton University Library (Ms. 138.44). According to descriptions of its provenance, the parchment and other items in the purse formerly belonged to a certain Mademoiselle Lacroix de Nogaro "for the use of her friends" (à l'usage de ses amis") (Skemer 2006: 247).

2 Famously, a girdle or pregnancy belt of the kind worn above the belly is mentioned in the *Legenda aurea* as having been dropped by the Virgin Mary during the Assumption, just as she disappeared into the heavens (vol. 1, p. 468). Thomas the Apostle, who had arrived late for the occasion, was chosen to retrieve it. For centuries a belt known as the *cintola* of Thomas was preserved in Tuscany and used as an amulet to ensure safe childbirth – a tradition that probably also drew on the doubting Apostle's special connection to the side wound.

3 Although the Virgin is the most common patron saint of labouring mothers in Spain, female saints such as Margaret and Felicitas were also popular (see Herradón Figueroa 2001, 39). As Skemer points out (2006: 240), the former holy woman was conferred these powers due to a story of her cutting or otherwise breaking her way out of a dragon's stomach, as recorded in the *Golden Legend*: "the dragon burst open and the virgin emerged unscathed" (Voragine 1993: 1.369).

4 On the valence of the horizontally represented side wound as a speaking mouth, see the analysis and visual examples commented on by Caroline Walker Bynum (2010: 109; 2011, 197–8). These objects could have been positioned over different parts of the birthing mother's body, including her mouth and genitals (Gwara and Morse 2012: 45).

5 As Bynum observes in a recent essay (2010), some theologians followed Augustine's interpretation (*Tractate* 120 on the Gospel of John) of the salvific aperture as being made not so much from the outside in (egress), but rather – as it were – from the inside out so that the body of Christ itself opened up (ingress) to receive sinners and give birth to the church.

6 Numerous badges from the period also include similar vulvic and phallic representations. Sherry Lindquist has considered visual and linguistic associations (French *coquille*) between the symbol of Compostela, the scallop shell, and the "vulva-as-pilgrim" (2012: 20). James F. Burke has pointed out that in a Romanesque portrayal of St Thomas the Apostle inserting his figure in the side wound, Christ raising an overly stiff and elongated arm in blessing is suggestive of and spirtualizes what could have been interpreted as a sign of carnal arousal (1998: 135).

7 His persecutors are conventionally identified in the *Tragicomedia* verses
  as false Jews ("falsos judíos") and associated with the Bad Thief. The
  rhymed epilogue by Alonso de Proaza that appears in later editions
  positions the text as a warning for lovers. On the critical tradition of
  questioning the sincerity of these verses (and the *converso* author's
  commitment to Christianity), see especially the work of Stephen Gilman
  (1972). Alan Deyermond, on the other hand, suggests that this expression
  of Christian faith in the *Tragicomedia* version could be a sign of genuine
  recommitment to the faith (2001). On the question of a secular materialism
  that either implicitly denies or fundamentally calls into question Christian
  transcendence in the *Celestina* – and in some strands of fifteenth-century
  humanist culture – see E. Michael Gerli's recent book (2011: especially
  chapter 9).
8 Evocations of the arrows of love and the lancing of Christ in the *Libro de
  buen amor* can be found in stanzas 597, 653, and 1066. Burke has studied
  these passages and also the portrayal of Longinus and his spear in the final
  miracle of Berceo's *Milagros de Nuestra Señora* (1998: 166–9, 117–42).
9 The name first appears in the seventh-century Gospel of Nicodemus
  ("Longinus miles lanceam aperuit latus eius"), a popular apocryphal work
  that was widely circulated throughout the Middle Ages (Kim 1973: 25).
10 Cf. the motif known as "Ecclesia et Synagoga" in medieval art, in which
  a blindfolded woman personifying the synagogue appears to the left of
  a sighted female representation of the church. In crucifixion scenes, the
  former is pictured on the sinister side of Christ like the Bad Thief, while
  the latter faces the side wound and sometimes collects its Eucharistic
  outpouring in a chalice (see the study of Nina Rowe 2011).
11 Bynum cites examples from the end of the thirteenth century tracing the
  increasing popularity of devotion to the bleeding heart during the late
  Middle Ages (2010: 102–6). It also examines the exegetical figuring of the
  side wound as a cleft or cavern for the dove from the Song of Songs to
  take refuge (2.14) – or as a dovecot – that was popularized by Bernard of
  Clairvaux (2010: 106).
12 On the medieval commentary tradition of Mary's maternal participation in
  the Passion, see the study of Luigi Gambero (2000).
13 This sort of contemplation of the side wound can be seen not only in
  Montesino's translation, but also in the devotional work of another
  Carthusian, Juan de Padilla (1516). At the time of his death in 1541, Rojas
  owned a copy of the *Retablo de la vida de Cristo* (Valle Lersundi 1925), first
  published three years after the *Tragicomedia* (1505) and reprinted several
  times thereafter (see fols. 450v–452r in the 1545 edition).

14 "Transfige, dulcissime domine Jesu, medullas animae meae suavissimo ac saluberrimo vulnere amoris tui ... aninam Mariae passionis gladius pertransivit ... curre, curre, Domine Jesu, curre et me vulnera" (qtd. in Stewart 2003: 151).

15 Rojas owned another work by Boccaccio during his lifetime, a translation of *De mulieribus claris* (Valle Lersundi 1925: 382). The malady of *amor eros* in the tragicomedy has been studied by Ricardo Castells, Marcelino Amasuno Sárraga, and Bienvenido Morros Mestres, among others (2000; 2000; 2004). For a bibliography on the many studies that deal with the influence of Ovid's amatory works and lovesickness in the *Celestina*, see my study (2010). During the Middle Ages, Christ was sometimes depicted as a paramour suffering the same symptoms as those ascribed to *amor eros* (see Wack 1990: 24–7). On the importance of Eros in later neoplatonic approaches to magic see Culianu (1987).

16 The image of a sacred birth was sometimes connected to martyrdom in 2 Maccabees (7:20–3) and also appears as a metaphor for sacrifice and salvation in the letters of Paul and the Book of Revelation (Rom. 8:20–241, Thess. 5:3; 12:2).

17 This can be compared to Ovid's warning against letting Love's *vulnus* fester: "I have known wounds which might easily have been cured if taken in hand at once, but which, through being neglected, grew past all healing" (Vidi ego, quod fuerat primo sanabile, vulnus / Dilatum longae damna tulisse morae) (*Remedia amoris* 2003: vv. 101–2).

18 Petrarch's poetry evokes the image of an amorous side wound inflicted on the lover and implanted in his heart: "Amor co la man destra il lato manco m'aperse, et piantòvvi entro il mezzo 'l core" (Love, with its right hand opened my left side and planted within, in the center of my heart) (1976: no. 228, v. 1–2).

19 A number of scholars have asserted that audiences would have attributed magic powers to the skein – as opposed to powers of suggestion and verbal fascination (see Gifford 1981) or the kind of linguistic and material fetishism that concern me. See, for example, Peter E. Russell (1963), Deyermond (1977), and Javier Herrero (1984).

20 The scene is somewhat reminiscent of a story found in Boccaccio's *Decameron* (2009: 9.5) in which a love amulet is prepared using a live bat (Celestina uses bat's blood) and other allegedly magical objects (see Skemer 2006, 182–3). In this case, however, the power of the amulet is completely exposed as a hoax. The eroticism of the thread has long been recognized by critics. See, for example, Rosario Ferré (1983). The demonization of female healers as alleged corrupters of young women

and wives coincided with an increased control and professionalization
of medicine during the fifteenth century that has been discussed by Jean
Dangler (2001: 34–43). See also the study of David Harley (1990).

21 Skemer indicates that medieval instructions sometimes called for ritualistic
applications of animal blood and observes that many textual amulets were
thought to have the power to staunch bleeding in case of injury (2006: 76,
130–1, 55, 80, 207–12). He also describes an early sixteenth-century English
birthing amulet that is stained with "a dozen irregular brownish spots,
which may well be congealed blood" from a birth (2006: 260–1). As Bynum
observes, for medieval Christians, "the blood Christ shed ... is analogous to
the blood of birthing" (2011: 197).

22 As Gerli has pointed out, the old bawd obviously takes erotic delight in
applying this remedy before voyeuristically urging her new co-conspirator,
Pármeno, to enter Areusa's bed (2011: 113–15). Burke has observed that
the disease called "mal de la madre" in fact functions as an epithet for
Celestina's presence and influence (1993: 92–4). The medical context of
the wandering womb that informs the tragicomedy has been studied by
Dangler (2001).

23 Midwives typically brought thread to births, and in addition were
sometimes called on to perform emergency baptisms after carrying out
caesarians on mothers who died before the infant could be removed
(Wigelsworth 2006: 110; Blumenfeld-Kosinski 1990; and Taglia 2001).

24 The *ensalmo* invokes St Apollonia, a martyr who had her teeth removed by
tormentors (see Beresford 2001). It is also possible that the *cordón* recalls the
girdle of Venus in the *Iliad*, used to enchant Zeus (v. 254–429). On classical
meanings that could have been attached to the item, see Ángel Gómez
Moreno ("A vueltas" 1995). References to the fall of Troy abound in the
tragicomedy, and Rojas owned a translation of Homer's epic at the time of
his death (Valle Lersundi 1925).

25 In addition to Peter Brown's study (1981), the materiality of relics has been
productively studied in more recent years by scholars like Charles Freeman
(2011). On Celestina's "linguistic sorcery," see also Olga Valbuena (1994).

26 The first appearance of this word can be found in a Portuguese legal
documents that were compiled by the order of King João I from 1385 to
1403, condemning "obrar fetiços ou ligamentos ou chamar diabos" (work
artifices or cast binding spells or call on Devils) (Sansi 2011: 21).

27 On Celestina as a parody of the Virgin Mary in a more general sense, see
Costa Fontes (2005, 101–42).

28 In Berceo's *Milagros de Nuestra Señora*, the Virgin is in one tale praised as
a miraculous midwife (2003: no. 19, vv. 431–60). She is the new, sinless

Eve, and in this sense her demonic counterpart is the sexually aggressive Lilith (legendarily created before Eve) who was said to cause the death of labouring mothers and newborns – and, in Jewish tradition, could be protected against through the use of birthing amulets (see Hurwitz 1992; Hamilton 1998).

29 The wound is also figured as the window in Noah's Ark (Bynum 2010: 99).

30 Mercedes Turón (1988) was among the first to emphasize the importance of this allusion. In his influential sixth-century reading of this myth, Fulgentius developed this etymology from the Greek, also interpreting the first sister "Clitos" as drawing out the "summons" of birth and "Lachesis" as spinning the present into one's "destiny": "Clitos enim Grece euocatio dicitur, Lacesis uero sors nuncupatur, Atropos quoque sine ordine dicitur." (Whitbread 1971: 1.8). Isidore's detailed explanation, with its emphasis on time (2007: 8.11.92–3), provides a model for how the figures are moralized by later Christian scholars, such as Bersuire (1979: 312, 314). For more on this mythography and how it might relate to the *Celestina*, see my essay (2012). The medieval figure of Atropos has been studied by Siegfried Guthke (1999). See the visual examples analysed by Millard Meiss (1971).

31 On the iconography of the *Parcae*, see Thomas Blisniewski (1992). In keeping with medieval visualizations of the Furies invoked in Celestina's hex (that is, the mythological sisters sent by the Fates), Atropos flies with bat wings. Scholarship has shown that the hex also draws on imagery from Juan de Mena's *Laberinto de Fortuna* (1997).

32 "Pansez de vos monteplier, / si porrioz ainsinc conchier / la felonesse, la ruvesche / Atropos, qui tout anpeesche." Translations by Charles Dahlberg.

33 "Atropos mourir ne me doigne / fors en fesant vostre besoigne, / ainz me praigne en meïsmes l'euvre / don Venus plus volentiers euvre ... puissent dire: ... 'bien ierte ceste mort convenable / a la vie que tu menoies.'" Translation by Frances Horgan.

34 "Un' insegna oscura e trista ... di gioventute e di bellezze ... troiana ... con la mia spada la qual punge e seca ... vostro dolce qualche amaro metta" (Petrarca 1984). In Petrarch's poem, Death triumphs over the World, Love, and Chastity, but is outlived by Fame as well as Time and Eternity. Similarly, after Melibea announces that "the Fates have cut their threads" and lies before her father lifeless and broken, audiences familiar with this popular death motif could visualize Atropos hovering triumphantly with her sisters over a fallen figure of Chastity. This can be seen, for example, in a Flemish tapestry, c. 1510–20, called the "Triumph of Death" that is housed in the Victoria and Albert Museum in London. On other Petrarchan reworkings in the *Celestina*, see Deyermond (1961).

35 "Vanitatibus quas mulieres exercent in suis lanificiis, in suis telis; quae ...
   cum incantationibus illarum ... fila staminis et subtegminis in invicem ita
   commisceantur ut ... totum pereat." Translation by A.L. Meaney and John
   Ward (1981). On medieval associations of women with spinning, see also
   Laura F. Hodges (1990).

36 The binding power of amuletic textiles could also be used as a deadly
   curse. This could be implied in the earlier-mentioned first miracle of
   Berceo, recounting how a pretender to the archbishopric of Toledo was
   suffocated by a chasuble that Mary made to only be worn by St Ildefonsus.

37 The three sisters were also believed to visit when a table with food and
   drink was prepared for them, and the *sylvaticae* or "women of the forest"
   were said to come and take pleasure with their hosts (1853: 538–1066; Harf-
   Lancner 2000: 526). These mythic creatures can also be related to the wild
   women described by Richard Bernheimer (1952).

38 Translation by Robert M. Durling.

39 The Grimm version draws on a text from the seventeenth century by
   Johannes Prätorius (the pen name of Hans Schultze) based on earlier
   folk tales involving the night visit of Three Spinners, classified by Stith
   Thompson as "Type 501" (1977: 48). On their connection with medieval
   fairies, see Harf-Lancner (2000).

40 A good example can be found in a text that exerted a significant influence
   on the *Celestina*, the *Arcipreste de Talavera* or *Corbacho*, whose palinode shows
   the narrator being attacked with "ruecas" (Martínez de Toledo 1970: 305).

41 As Pedrosa points out, such incantations were mocked in Cristóbal de
   Villalón's *Crotalón* (2000: 184–5). Similar prayers can be found in sixteenth-
   and seventeenth-century Inquisition records studied by Julio Caro Baroja
   (*Vidas mágicas* 1967). On how the Three Fates reemerge as characters in the
   Celestinesque work *Comedia de Polidoro y Casandrina* (c. 1565), see Stefano
   Arata (1988) and Ana Herrero (1997). For variations passed on in later
   centuries as part of a Sephardic oral tradition, see Susana Weich-Shahak
   (2002).

42 See also José Manuel Blanco Prado (2008) and Isabel Botas San Martín
   (1992).

43 This is also reminiscent of Penelope's weaving. The contest of Arachne
   is famously portrayed in a painting by Diego Velázquez, *The Spinners*.
   Interestingly, three female helpers appear in foreground assisting Arachne
   and Athena.

44 This can be compared to the tripartite danger of Celestina's visits: "Tres
   veces que entra en una casa engendra sospecha" (1994: 248). Fittingly, the
   bawd's penetrating "intellectuales ojos" will also fail in the end (1994: 117).

45 It is possible that Rojas read the *Libro de buen amor* in the library at the
   University of Salamanca, which had possessed a copy of the poem since
   1440 (Gerli 1995: 30).
46 See Jean Dangler (2001) and Patricia Botta (2002).
47 The papal court of Alexander VI was accepting of the thousands of Jewish
   refugees that arrived from Spain and Portugal. In the prologue to the
   Lozana andaluza (1985: 169–70), Delicado cites Hernando del Pulgar, who
   lamented the treatment of *conversos* in Andalucía (see MacKay 1998).
48 This hospital was known as Santiago de Carreteras. The Imperial forces
   had defeated the French army and then mutinied after never receiving
   their pay. They were able to compel their commander, the Duke of
   Bourbon, to continue the march to Rome. On Delicado's later editorial
   work in Venice, see especially Lucia Binotti (2012). He also wrote a
   third, now lost work, which was entitled *De consolatione infirmorum* (On
   Consoling the Infirm).
49 The symptoms would have consisted of open sores on the face, genitals,
   and elsewhere, the appearance of which could be influenced by hormonal
   changes during menstruation.
50 The first part of this poem, as Allaigre points out in his edition, is derived
   from the "Descomunión de amores fecha a su amiga" by Hernando de
   Ludueña, which was included in the fifteenth-century *Cancionero general.*
51 Delicado would later publish an edition of the *Cárcel de Amor* in Venice. See
   Bruno Damiani (1974) and Binotti (2010).
52 In the introduction to his edition, Allaigre (Delicado 1985: 118) relates
   Lozana's scar to marks made on the foreheads of Roman slaves as recorded
   in Martial's *Ad Refum* and the lexicography of Covarrubias (1611: 537, 178).
53 Notable examples would include the monsters of Ravenna and Bologna
   (see Niccoli 1990: 30–59). The former is described at the beginning of
   Guzmán de Alfarache (1599) as having portentous features, letters, and a
   cruciform marking. This disfigured creature was said to foreshadow the
   defeat of the papal army by the French in 1512. Another was supposed
   to have washed up in the river Tiber in 1496 and had the features of an
   ass, scales, a pig hoof, a bird claw, female breasts, and an old man's face.
   It purportedly reflected the state and fate of the papacy (Edwards 2004:
   294–5).
54 In the Roman Rite, the words of the sacrament for anointing the forehead
   are "signo te signo crucis, et confirmo te chrismate salutis" (I sign you
   with the sign of the cross, and confirm you with the chrism of salvation)
   (Jackson 1877: 104). Receiving the confirmation was also an imitation of the
   Saviour, as *Christos* means "the anointed one."

55 The custom was not to remove the oil for seven days. During the medieval and early modern period in Spain, confirmation generally occurred as soon as a bishop could be present to conduct the ceremony – in any case, within a year of the baptism.

56 Syphilis was commonly associated with *amor eros* or lovesickness, as can be seen in the preliminaries of the book, when Delicado implies that his dialogue can either relieve or exacerbate the erotic passions (1985: 167, 170, 173). In an epilogue, the syphilitic author similarly characterizes his work as "malencónica," combining the humoral diagnosis of melancholy with the Spanish word for disease ("mal") and an obscene reference to the vagina ("coño" or Italian *conno*): "como mi pasion antes de sanarse ... siendo atormentado de una grande y prolija enfermedad" (like my passion before being healed ... having been tormented by a great and prolonged illness) (1985: 485). In contrast to Lozana's Galenic coital therapy, moralizing preachers and medical authorities insisted that syphilitics be made to suffer and purify themselves, undergoing "the just rewards of unbridled lust" (Allen 2000: 41–60). Accordingly, Delicado's *De modo de adoperare* calls for a forty-day fast and sudorific infusions made from the sawdust of guaiacum wood that were meant to cure "ogni piaga" (all sores) (2011: 485).

57 The wearing of badges by Roman Jews is pointed out to Lozana shorty after she arrives, although not described in detail (Delicado 1985: 240).

58 Later, circular badges were introduced that presumably symbolized coin. See Damiani and Raphael Patai (1974: 59; 1977: 156). Jeremy Cohen (1999) has studied the eschatological belief in the final conversion of the Jews, which was supported by the writings of Augustine and St Paul's Epistle to the Romans (11:25–6).

59 Witnesses also report how the Tiber flooded the same year, leading to a famine and further epidemics (see Partner 1980: 80–1). Delicado recalls these further disasters in his "epístola" epilogue (1985: 490).

60 The Spanish word for wound, "llaga," was itself derived from the Latin *plaga*.

61 This treatise combines Castilian, Latin, and Italian. A modern Spanish translation has been recently completed by Ignacio Ahumada (Delicado 2011).

62 Rome is first portrayed as full of brothels and personified as a "putana" when Rampín gives the recently arrived Lozana a tour of the city (Delicado 1985: 216).

63 The same anonymous letter in the anthology of Rodríguez Villa describes this situation: "hizo una neblina al entrar, que apenas se conocían los unos

a los otros" (a fog developed as we entered [the city], so that we could barely tell one from another) (1875: 141).

64 Delicado makes a millennial allusion by evoking the legend of the Wandering Jew. This figure, known as in Spanish as "Juan espera en Dios," was legendarily cursed to walk the earth until the return of Christ (Delicado 1985: *Mamotreto* 42). On allusions to the "judío errante" in other early modern Spanish texts, see Caro Baroja (1967: 355–65).

65 See the studies by Brakhage and Edwards on the Jewish messianism of figures like Solomón Molcho, David Reubeni, and Asher Lemmlein (1986; 2004). They also consider how the eschatology of spiritual Franciscans influenced works like the *Libro de las profecías* of Columbus and the *Apocalypsis nova* attributed to João Mendes de Silva (known as "Amadeo").

66 Jerome's *Vita Pauli primi eremitae* (Life of Paul the First Hermit, 1893) and other *Vitae* of the church fathers were frequently reprinted during the sixteenth century.

67 Corsi's apocalyptic, mythographic allusions have been unpacked by Kenneth Gouwens (1998: 86–7). In the words of Sanuto: "tutta questa città è in tanta tribulatione" (this whole city is in so much tribulation) that the urban landscape resembles "l'inferno" (Hell) (qtd. in Gouwens 1998: xviii). As Carla Perugini has pointed out (2000), this woodcut together with another one showing characters from Delicado's dialogue on a Venetian gondola share visual parallels with the pictorial scheme of the late fifteenth-century *Stultifera navis* (Ship of Fools).

68 Lozana describes these mountains in the dream as the Andalusian Sierra Morena. As in other instances, such as the digression concerning the appearance of the Magdalene in province of Córdoba (Delicado 1985: 396–8), events in Rome are conflated with the author's homeland.

69 This well-known account of Pompey's conquest first appears in Josephus (2006: bk. 14, chap. 4, line 72).

70 Castiglione was a papal ambassador in Madrid, engaged in an open dispute with Alfonso de Valdés, who was a member of the Imperial court and twin brother of the humanist more famous Spanish humanist, Juan de Valdés.

71 This can be compared to Paul's first letter to the Corinthians: "Or know you not, that your members are the temple of the Holy Ghost, who is in you, whom you have from God" (6.19).

72 Characteristically, Delicado engages in a pun that associates the name of the island with the Spanish word for pairs and peers, "pares" (1985: 487).

73 Allaigre and Macpherson also discuss related adaptations of the myth of Gordian's knot, including its use in the royal heraldry of the Catholic

monarchs who were responsible for the 1492 expulsion of the Jews from Spain. The fourfold layout of the First Temple was thought to reflect the creation of the universe and was also interpreted on the basis of Pythagorean ideas. It is possible that Delicado saw the common endless-knot motif on an ancient Roman mosaic during his time in Italy. The same critics cite the note made in Luis de Usoz y Rio's nineteenth-century edition of earlier mentioned "pregunta" from the *Cancionero de obras de burlas* (Songbook of Works of Jest): "Áludese aquí al llamado sello, sigilo o signo de Salomón cuy figura es ... el famoso pentalfa que significa salud, y que antiguamente tenía en España el vulgo por amuleto, y preservativo contra las brujas" (1841: 115–17).

74 Such a connection can be seen, for example, in Fray Íñigo de Mendoza's "invención" addressed to "un signo de Salomón" (Rodríguez-Puértolas 1968: 347). The sign is used in different ways in another *Cancionero* work by the same author, punning the word "signo," as well as by the poet known as Serrano, and in an anonymous "Pregunta" (associated it with a dishonourable facial scar) (see Macpherson 1998: 205–9; and Allaigre's edition of Delicado 1985: 142).

75 According to Josephus: "He obtained also by inspiration the art of magic ... and left the method of conjuration in writing whereby the devils are enchanted and expelled" (qtd. in Hattaway 1968: 504). The most detailed scriptural portrayal of Solomon's submission to women can be found in 1 Kings: "Solomon loved many strange women ... And to these was Solomon joined with a most ardent love ... and the women turned away his heart ... to follow strange gods ... for all his wives that were strangers ... the Lord was angry with Solomon" (11:1–9). This is mentioned elsewhere in the Hebrew Bible: "Did not Solomon king of Israel sin in this kind of thing ... women of other countries brought even him to sin" (Neh. 13:26). Written during the first centuries of the Christian era, the *Testament* gives an account of Solomon's sealing of demons and portrays the Queen of Sheba as a witch. In medieval Latin dialogues, Solomon engages in a dispute with a carnivalesque fool named Marcolf who subverts his famed wisdom (see the edition of Ziolkowsi 2008). Solomonic magic also informs the earlier-mentioned Alfonsine *Liber Razielis*. In Renaissance Spain, these traditions were recorded as vernacular legends, such as the "Vida de Salomón y duda si se salvó" by Alonso de Villegas.

76 This version of the text was apparently attributed to Ramon Llull. The Aragonese Inquisitor, Nicolau Eymerich was best known for writing the *Directorium Inquisitorum*, which provides instruction in uncovering witchcraft and sorcery.

77 "A quien atribuyen ... otro gran volumen ... lleno de sacrificios y encantamientos de demonios. Los judíos y alárabes de España dejaban por derecho hereditario a sus sucesores este libro, y por él obraban algunas maravillas y cosas increíbles. La Inquisición entregó a las llamas cuantos ejemplares pudo haber de estas obras" (To whom is attributed ... another great text ... full of sacrifices and demonic enchantments. The Jews and Arabs of Spain passed this book on to their heirs by right of inheritance, and with it worked great marvels and incredible things. The Inquisition consigned to the flames as many copies of these works as could be had) (qtd. in Fernández Guerra y Orbe 1852: 320).

78 It is clear that the Canterbury parchment was meant to be folded in a particular way and carried. As in the case of other amulets, the folds correspond to sacred numbers that were believed to contribute to the object's power.

79 AGLA (also found on the exorcistic prayer in the *Razón de amor* manuscript) was a common acronym on textual amulets that had been derived from the Hebrew blessing, אתה גבור לעולם אדני or "Atta gibbor leolam adonai" (Thou, Lord, are forever might) (Skemer 2006: 112).

80 Other details in these instructions correspond with aspects of Celestina's hex, such as the use of bat's blood. They also coincide with Ciruelo's description of nóminas, as when the *Clavicula* claims that virgin parchment must be used (Lamb 1963: 137, 139, 140).

81 These promises include avoiding sudden death and becoming invisible. In several instances, specifics are given on how the inscribed material object is to be worn or carried: "sy quisyeres dormir con la muger quantas vezes quisyeres, escryve en plegamyno vírgen estas letras y métalas devajo de las espaldas" (to sleep with a woman as many times as you like, write on virgin parchment these letters and place them under the back) (Lamb 1963: 137, 139, 140).

82 These words were also invoked by crusaders during the Middle Ages. Later in the sixteenth century, Pope Sixtus V had this acclamation of *Laudes regiae* inscribed on an Egyptian obelisk that was placed at the center of St Peter's square in Rome.

83 During the late Middle Ages, different kinds of wire were used for making for wool cards, pins, and for a number of other purposes (including jewellery). A metal thread and fine, pliant wires like the one described in the *Clavicula* were produced either by cutting strips of foil or drawing "short rods of cast metal ... through successively diminishing holes in a draw plate" (Campbell 1991: 134).

84 This *Dialogi*, as Francis Clark points out in his study, had a marked influence on everything from medieval folklore, to sermons, religious

literature and art for centuries to come (1987: 8). Disputes of the authenticity of its authorship began with the work of sixteenth-century humanists and continued for centuries.

5. Outlaw Prayers

1 The letter states that an apostle will be sent (Eusebius 1960: 1.13.5–13).
2 Abgar specifies that according to what he has heard, this healing requires no medicine: "Dicitur mihi te curare homines sine medico ac sine herbis. Dicitur mihi homines cæcos curari ... te ejacere diabolos" (1960: 1.13.14–32).
3 Don Skemer cites "all-purpose" apotropaic texts, to protect mothers as they gave birth, or even as "portable" grimoires (2006: 71, 112, 167, 203, 216, 244, 256, 300–2). Esoteric models from grimoires that were meant to be precisely followed by master magicians during their rituals became popularized through the spread of such amulets.
4 For examples, see Skemer (2006: 181, 187, 224, 263).
5 In the Latin Adoration of the Cross, the Trisagion is sung both in phoneticized Greek and also Latin translation: "sanctus deus, sanctus fortis, sanctus immortalis, miserere nobis" (Henry 1907–14: 211–12).
6 A specific date is also given: "fu fata a di xxiii d'aprili l'anno [1]551." As Benjamin Torrico points out, the possibility of intimate same-sex relationship cannot be ruled out and is supported by the relative prevalence of homosexual themes in the library – from the open advocation of sodomy in the *Cazzaria* to the pederastic innuendos in *Lazarillo de Tormes* (see Shipley 1982, and Thompson and Walsh 1988), as well as references in other books discussed by Torrico (2010: 134–6).
7 These volumes are the entitled *Exorcismo mirabile da disfare ogni sorte di maleficii* (Exorcism, Wonderful for Counteracting All Kinds of Evil, Venice 1540), and *Precationes aliquot celebriores, e sacris Bibliis desumptae, ac in studiosorum gratiam lingua Hebraica, Graeca, & Latina* (Some Well-Known Prayers, Selected from the Bible, Lyon 1538) (Torrico 2010: 124–5). Also included is the polemical *Confusione della Setta Machumetana* (Confusion of the Muhammadan Sect, Venice 1543), translated from the 1537 Spanish work of an Iberian convert from Islam to Christianity who took the name Juan Andrés (Torrico 2010: 125).
8 This theory has been advanced by scholars like David Gitlitz (2002: 233), but remains somewhat controversial, since it – of necessity – relies heavily on Inquisitorial testimony that, of course, could have been coerced or otherwise misrepresented (see, for example, Salomon 1998).
9 Policies of censorship during this period have been studied in depth by Virgilio Pinto Crespo (1983) and Henry Kamen (1985: 62–100). The books

on palmistry are *Super chyromantiam* (Concerning Chiromancy, 1525) and *Chyromantia del Tricasso* (Chiromancy of Tricasso, 1543) (see Reusch 1961, 203). The Counter-Reformation church was increasingly denouncing such works as heretical by the end of the century. Marot's poetry is collected in an anthology published in Paris in 1539 and discovered at the site: *Plusiers traitez* (Various Works, Paris 1539). His work resonates with the subject matter of *Lazarillo de Tormes* as its tone is often anticlerical and contains a well-known poem concerning a wily servant or "valet." Antonio Vignali wrote the *Cazzaria* in Siena during the 1520s and went on to serve in the court of Philip II, living in Spain during the 1540s (see the study of Elisa Ruiz García 1999).

10 It is clear that the prayer was translated from Castilian (Carrasco González 2005: 51–2) to create the 1500 Portuguese version that appears in a book of hours. This version has been studied by Arthur Askins (2007) and closely relates to the later Barcarrota text.

11 In the *Oración*, Jesus appears and reveals that His wounds totaled 6,676, a number that could have been linked to exorcism (the belief that 6,666 demons comprised the legion in Luke 8:36), the Apocalypse (three sixes as the number of the Beast), together with prayers in memory of the seven wounds (the scourging and crown of thorns combined with the five *stigmata*) or possibly the even last words or utterances of Christ (Mark 15.34 and Matt. 27:46; Luke 23:34, 43, 46; John 19:26–30). Other sources give the number as 6,666, as in the case of Ambrosio de Montesino's sixteenth-century translation of the *Vita Christi* of Ludolph of Saxony (the 1514 *Cartuxano* cited in the last chapter), and the examples discussed by Robin Flowers (1927). Graphic representations of the wounds and drops of blood also appear in amulets and were believed to increase their power (see Skemer 2006: 143, 248, 265).

12 Uses of the number fifteen to calculate the length of Christ's body were based on the measurements of the Golden Cross relic in the Hagia Sophia and specifically believed to protect "against evil, misfortune, and sudden death," in keeping with the promises of the *Oración* (Skemer 2006: 143). Fifteen Mysteries were sometimes used in rosary prayers (consisting of Joyful, Sorrowful, and Glorious sets of five), though this was not yet standardized during the period (see Winston-Allen 1997). Fifteen can also refer to the number of steps of the Temple, or the cubits needed to build the ark – the latter was interpreted by Ambrose as a threefold (Trinitarian) product of the five senses (Hopper 1938: 1115–16). See also Arthur Askins, who notes fifteen is "the talisman number in a variety of legends," and thus frequently used in these kinds of prayers (2007: 243). Fittingly, the

number is twice associated with healing in *Lazarillo de Tormes* after the
rogue is beaten by the priest (1987: 70, 71).

13 "Sejam livradas das penas do purgatório quinze almas ... Outrossi,
qualquer pessoa que estever em pecado mortal ainda que haja trinta anos
que se não haja confessado: e se confessar ... será outorgada ... boa vida ...
darei em este mundo prazer" (2010: fols. 2–3).

14 In my translations from *Lazarillo*, I have consulted the English text of
Michael Alpert, *"Lazarillo De Tormes" and "The Swindler": Two Spanish
Picaresque Novels*, rev. ed. (New York: Penguin, 2003: 13). Spanish citations
of *Lazarillo* are from the edition of Francisco Rico (1987).

15 The *Oración* is to be said every day, presumably to arrive at a
numerological formula for the counting of Christ's wounds. As opposed
to scholars and editors like Alberto Blecua (*Lazarillo* 1974: 58), Ferrer-
Chivite wonders whether the interpolations were not expurgated parts of
the original text (2000). The Alcalá printer, Salcedo, specifically presents
the book as follows: "nuevamente impresa, corregida y de nuevo añadido
en esta segunda impresión ... a veinte y seis de Febrero" (newly printed,
corrected and again amended in this second edition ... on 26 February)
(*Lazarillo* 1987: 13). In addition to this reissue, and the newly discovered
Medina del Campo, 1554 versions were published in Burgos and Amberes.
While Rico and others have proposed a plausible stemma, the sequence
remains impossible to determine definitively, as Jesús Cañas Murillo
has pointed out (1996: 92–3). The authorship of *Lazarillo* also remains a
mystery, although candidates continue to be proposed. Mercedes Agulló
(2010) has most recently found suggestive though not totally conclusive
evidence supporting the theory that Diego Hurtado de Mendoza at the
very least contributed in some way to the 1573 expurgated edition of
Lazarillo.

16 María Cruz García de Enterría notes that such prayers first appeared
in books of hours, and Askins discusses versions dating prior to the
association with St Bridget (1997; 2007). García de Enterría documents a
manuscript possessed by María de Aragón in the mid fifteenth century,
mentioned in an inventory as *"De la dona emparedada"* (1997: xi).

17 The prayer had already been banned in the 1551 index (García de Enterría
1997: xv). While the indulgence of Pope Nicholas V is particular to the
Barcarrota prayer, the amuletic count of blood drops spilled during
the Passion can be found in versions outside the peninsula. Unlike the
Trinitarian number given in the *Oración*, Skemer notes that the count
was sometimes calculated using multiples of 365, similar to the totals of
Christ's wounds (2006: 143).

18 García de Enterría notes early printed copies of the *Oración de la Emparedada* listed by book dealers in Barcelona in 1524, and Askins documents a number of other sixteenth-century editions in Catalan and Castilian (1997; 2007: 238).

19 The sightless performer could also be equating his condition to the blindfolding of Christ during the Passion, as an image that was sometimes evoked in popular prayers.

20 The prayer – showing how the anonymous sequel likely drew on the Alcalá version of *Lazarillo* – is listed in a litany of others supposedly taught to him by the blind man, "tienen virtud contra los peligros del agua" (because they had power against the dangers of water) (1988: 55). This claim correlates with the alleged promise made to the immured woman to protect against sudden death, "como livrey a são pedro das ondas do mar" (like I saved Peter from the waves of the sea) ("A muyto devota" 1997: fol. 3v).

21 Marcel Bataillon (1950) has related this text to Erasmian thinking, in particular the *Modus orandi* (Manner of Prayer). The *nómina* has an inscription reading "si ergo me quaeritis" (if therefore you seek me). This phrase is from the Gospel of John, a favourite source for textual amulets, as we have seen (Skemer 2006: 87–9). When Jesus is about to be arrested he says, "I have told you that I am he. If therefore you seek me, let these go their way that the word might be fulfilled" (dixi vobis quia ego sum si ergo me quaeritis sinite hos abire ut impleretur sermo) (18:8–9).

22 Lazarillo also helps stage a fake exorcism in this episode, and, as Jack Weiner points out, the Alcalá interpolation stresses his complicity when the pardoner asks him not to reveal the deception of the burning cross (1987: 828; 1985, 123–4).

23 Anne Cruz (2014) has very recently published an essay on the meanings of female enclosure in relation to the prayer that provides further historical contexts and theoretical reflections on the practice as it continued later in the Golden Age.

24 Her subversion can also be compared with that of later female rogue characters or *pícaras*. In Cruz's discussion of Francisco López de Ubeda's 1605 *La pícara Justina* (2011), she points out that early modern manuals such as Fray Luis de León's *La perfecta casada* (1987) explicitly compared the virtue of a wife's "closed mouth" with the "enclosed state in which she should ideally remain" (1999: 154).

25 In the fifteenth-century *Arcipreste de Talavera o Corbacho*, a wife complains that her controlling husband would have her immured (1970: 128). Centuries later, the idea of immuring unfortunate brides provides the ghastly subject matter for "La inocencia castigada" in María de Zayas's 1647 *Desengaños amorosos* (1989).

26 For example, a warden is described by Alfonso of Jaén as suffering from a painful swelling of the groin after making false accusations against Bridget (Sahlin 2001: 155).

27 Three of Gerson's works deal with the discernment of divine versus malevolent spirits, including *De distinctione verarum revelationum a falsis* (On Distinguishing True and False Revelations, 1401), *De probatione spirituum* (On Testing the Spirits 1415), *De examinatione doctrinarum* (On Investigating Teachings 1423). On the question of *discretio spirituum*, see the study of Rosalynn Voaden (1999). For example, in the *Libro de confesiones* Martín Pérez urges "enparedadas" to maintain their enclosure at all times so as to avoid the grave scandal that arises from "las entradas a ellas o de las sus salidas" (entering to visit them or their leaving) (2002: 416).

28 As Rico notes in his edition, the Sant Salvador parish in Toledo had no archpriest (1987: 130). This suggests that the title was meant to allude to the unsavoury reputation of archpriests, legendary by this time, in contrast to the meaning of "Holy Savior."

29 Henry Kamen points out that in such cases perpetual sentences could be shortened considerably (1985: 88, 201).

30 Prior to her condemnation in 1588, the cult of María de la Visitación had spread far and wide, to the extent that Luis de Granada penned an account of her life (see Imirizaldu 1977: 122–75). Another visionary sentenced to reclusion, Lucrecia de León, was linked with the court of Philip II and brought before the Inquisition for prophesizing the defeat of the Armada and collapse of the Empire (Imirizaldu 1977: 63–9). On the story of Lucrecia, see Richard Kagan's *Lucrecia's Dreams* (1990).

31 The sentence specifies "cárcel perpetua … en una celda o apossento … cada semana saldrá para recibir una disciplina que durará en quanto dixere un miserere mei" (perpetual imprisonment … in a cell or chamber … once a week she will emerge to receive a discipline that will last until she says a *misere*) (Imirizaldu 1977: 196).

32 This poem appeared at the end of an expanded reprint of the *Cancionero de obras de burlas provocantes a risa* and published in Valencia. It recently inspired the title of a novel by Juan Goytisolo.

33 This view is also supported by sixteenth-century proceedings against heretical women, like the earlier-discussed case of Juana the "Trickster," that investigate husbands and other men found to be complicit in the concealment of illicit activities (Imirizaldu 1977: 104).

34 See, in particular, the studies of Bussell Thompson and John Walsh, and also George Shipley (1988; 1982).

35 Elsewhere I have linked this imagery to Lazarillo's simultaneous parodic imitation of the life of John the Baptist and festive aspects of his cult (*Laughter* 2009: 83–91). See also Javier Herrero's study (1979) of this water and wine pattern. Not surprisingly, the rogue's final oath was censored from expurgated editions printed after the appearance of the 1554 *Lazarillo* in the Index.

36 The image from the Beatitudes, "los que padecen persecuciones por la justicia" (those who suffer persecutions for the sake of justice), recalls the arrest of Lazarillo's father, "confesó y no negó, y padesció persecución por la justicia" (he confessed and did not deny, and suffered persecution for the sake of justice), evoking the biblical phrase applied to Juan the Baptist, "confessus est et non negavit" (1987: 14, 129; Matt 5:6, John 1:20). This can be compared to Celestina's portrayal of Claudina being accused of witchcraft.

37 The phrase forms part of the Office of the Dead. The association of the quarters of walled-in visionaries with tombs can be seen in an account of the fifteenth-century mystic María de Toledo: "tomó un aposentillo tan estrecho y oscuro que 'más parecía sepultura de muertos que aposento de vivos'" (she took a small room so narrow and dark that "it more closely resembled a tomb for the dead than a room for the living") (Cavero Domínguez 2006: 117).

38 The rogue complains, "'¡Oh desdichado de mí, Para mi casa llevan este muerto!'" ("Oh woe is me, they are taking this dead man to my house!") (1987: 73).

39 Eliciting the question: "tongue, where have you gone?" (1989: 22). This aspect of Erasmus's *De lingua* has been studied by Shane Gasbarra (1991). The final Alcalá interpolation hints at Lazarillo's continued chattiness (inviting a sequelization of "casos"), "de lo que de aquí adelante me suscediere, avisaré a Vuestra Merced" (concerning what has happened from here on, I will give Your Honor notice) (1987: 136).

40 Earlier vernacular invocations of *Juste Judex* in medieval Iberia, can be found in Alfonso X's late thirteenth-century *Cantigas de Santa Maria* (1986–9: vol. 1, *cantiga* 70, "Eno nome de Maria"), and the *Rimado de Palacio* (Palace Rhymes) that Pero López de Ayala completed at the close of the fourteenth century (1987: sts. 144–5).

41 The introduction to the prayer in this book draws on a popular legend to exonerate Pilate, hearkening back to a fourth-century text called *Acta Pilati* or *Gospel of Nicodemus* (see Hourihane 2009). Like other devotional manuals from the period, it emphasizes the experience of Mary (see Rubin 2009: 360). Its title alludes to images from the Old and New Testaments (Cant. 1:13; Matt. 2:11). The anonymous Franciscan author of the text

briefly explains the etymology and symbolic virtue of this name, "la myrra es amarga e tiene virtud de conservar" (1524: fol. 5v). On editions of the *Fasciculus myrrhe*, see Alexander Wilkinson (2010: 341–2).

42 The error was later transmitted into Portuguese translations and found in a number of Spanish books of hours published during the sixteenth century, including the 1510 version that I cited earlier (see Askins 2007: 253–4).

43 The initial proscription, of 1559, affected the text only "en quanto dize, después del mundo redimido" (Reusch 1961: 237).

44 "La Oración del Justo Juez / me manden cantar / que no siempre los ciegos han de rezar … La sentencia vengo a dar … siendo en ella juez justo … es nueva obra y cosa de gusto … que de vista … un ciego ser testigo … mas este a ojos cerrados … es de ver / por la luz … y en la sentencia que ha dado, / ha procedido tan ajustado, / pues aunque ciego … bien puede un ciego ser justo juez" (the Prayer of the Just Judge, have me sing it, for blind men need not always pray … I come to give the ruling … being in this matter just judge … it is a new work and something of good taste … that being seen … a blind men being witness … and this with eyes closed … it is to be seen in the light … In the sentence that has been given, he has proceeded so justly, that although blind … a blind man can well be a just judge) (Medina 2008: 125–6).

45 On religious parody in the *Buscón* and its carnivalesque elements, see the studies of R.M. Price, Edmond Cros, and Anne Cruz (1971; 1975; 1999). For a list of Golden Age allusions to the prayer, see Arthur Askins's summary of the work of Ricard and others (2007: 252n74). These include Pedro Espinosa's satirical dialogue *El perro y la calentura* (The Dog and the Fever, 1625), in which a prostitute is said to ensure the salvation of her soul partly by having a blind man pray the "Justo Juez" (1736: 304); Jerónimo de Alcalá Yáñez's picaresque novel *El donado hablador* (The Gifted Lay Talker, 1624), in which a phony blind man with a boy makes his living by praying the "Justo Juez" along with other popular prayers (1847: 39); Lope de Vega's anti-Semitic play *El niño inocente de la Guardia* (The Innocent Child of La Guardia, c. 1594–7), in which a blind woman offers to recite the prayer for a disconsolate mother (1985: 96); and the Protestant sympathizer Cipriano de Valera's *Tratado para confirmar en la fe cristiana a los cautivos de Berbería* (Treatise for the Confirmation to the Christian Faith of Prisoners in Barbary, 1594), in which the "Justo Juez" is listed as one of the superstitious prayers of *beatas* whom God allows to be deceived by demons as His "justo juzio" (just judgment) (1854: 9).

46 See also a scene in *Vida y hechos de Estebanillo González* (Life and Deeds of Little Esteban González, 1646), in which the autobiographical protagonist

plays the role of a blind man chanting and selling printed religious texts (González 1978: 546).

47 As Ricard notes, both Julio Cejador y Frauca and Américo Castro also refer to related popular prayers invoking the formula "Justo Juez divinal" in their earlier critical editions of *Lazarillo* and the *Buscón,* respectively (1954: 415). Ricard has authored a number of other studies of more modern versions of the prayer recorded in Latin America (see Askins 2007: 252n72).

48 These variations are excerpted from *romances* nos. 1512 and 1508 (1987: vv. 1–2, 4–5, 9–10, 12–14; vv. 7, 10).

49 Both Ricard and Costa Fontes have noticed that verses of the prayer in the *Buscón* corresponds with Portuguese versions (Ricard 1966: 33–5; 1987: 4).

50 Costa Fontes compares oral prayers passed on to twentieth-century Portuguese speakers in Iberia and North America with texts recorded by Amílcar Paulo (1985) in his study of communities thought to maintain vestiges of Jewish identification or "crypto-Judaism" in Portugal.

51 It is also possible that these women came from families that converted from Islam. According to the file, María de Francisca lived on the "calle de los Moriscos" (street of the Moorish converts) (Gray Birth 1903: 645). The name María de los Ángeles resembles the kind of religious epithets acquired by *beatas* like the ones discussed earlier in this chapter. The mother of the novel's rogue, "Aldonza de San Pedro," is said to be the daughter of "Diego de San Juan," and the granddaughter of "Andrés de San Cristóbal ... Sospechábase ... que no era cristiana vieja ... por los nombres y sobrenombres de sus pasados" (it was suspected ... that she was not an old Christian ... due to the names and nicknames of her ancestors) (Quevedo 1980: 96–7). Pablos also refers to the Moriscos, who are reluctant to welcome the "Santísimo Sacramento" when he arrives at an inn (1980: 141). Possession of textual amulets by women was, by this time, associated both with witchcraft and Judaizing (Valderrama 1608: 77).

52 A grotesque personification of hunger and death, Cabra is also implicitly compared to Judas (1980: 116). After a student dies of starvation and receives his final communion (bringing the presence of Christ into the school), Pablos and his schoolmate finally receive justice and are ransomed in a comic allusion to the Harrowing of Hell (1980: 128–9). The rogue later compares himself to Judas (1980: 151). Another possible reference to the Inquisition's pursuit of so-called *converso* "marranos" comes when Pablos has to avoid "justicia" after sentencing to death the neighbour's pigs (1980: 149–50).

53 He compares his trial at the hands of the lawyer to that of Christ, "lo que pasó con ellos vivo" (what he went through because of them while alive)

(1980: 255). In another parodic reference to the gospels, Pablos identifies himself as not "Ecce Homo" after a group of supposed Moriscos and *conversos* cover him with mucus from "las mayores narices que se han visto jamás en paso" (noses greater than have ever been seen in a Passion parade) (1980: 144).

54 Pious references to the "Justo Juez" in sixteenth- and seventeenth-century Spain are frequent. See also the Franciscan Ambrosio Montesino's meditation on the Last Judgment (1608: 313–14), or the prayers and invocations in the devotional works of Jesuits Juan Eusebio Nieremberg and Pedro de Ribadeneyra (1665: 272; 1616: 1.872).

55 "La vieja recogía trapos … como las que tratan en papel para acomodar incurables cosas de los caballeros" (The old women picked up rags … like those that traffic in papers for the healing of incurable things suffered by gentlemen) (1980: 221). The narrator here likely refers to syphilis or another venereal disease. Cosme is pictured with a group of sick boys: "se había hecho ensalmador con unas santiguaduras y oraciones que había aprendido de una vieja" (he had made himself a magic healer with some blessings and prayers that he had learned from an old woman) (1980: 221).

56 In the parable, the "iudex iniquitatis" (unrighteous judge) finally gives in to the widow's pleading, leading to Christ's prophecy that God as a Just Judge will avenge those who ceaselessly cry out to Him in prayer (Luke 18:1–8).

57 See also, the reflection on injustice in *Sueños*: "si no hubiera cárcel, no hubiera jueces; si hubiera jueces, no huberia pasión, no hubiera cohecho" (if there were no jail, there would be no judges; if there were no judges, there would be no biased feelings, there would be no bribery) (1993: 270–1). Quevedo also singles out the corruption of jurists, attorneys, and constables (*letrados, procuradores, alguaciles*), and in the *Buscón* bribes are similarly offered to an "alguacil" (police official), "relator" (court clerk), and "alcalde" (municipal official), in addition to the jailer (1980: 244–5). In *Política de Dios* (Politics of God, 1626), Quevedo writes: "El juez delincuente merece todos los castigos … menos mal hacen los delincuentes, que un mal juez …el juez que, en lugar de darles castigo, les da escándulo" (the delinquent judge deserves every punishment … criminals do less harm than a bad judge … the judge that, instead of giving them punishment, gives rise to scandal) (1966: 21). He also discusses the topic of judges in *Hora de todos* (The Hour of All Men [1634] 1975).

58 There are also other references to Bosch in Quevedo's work. See also "Pintura de la mujer de un abogado, abogada ella del demonio" (Painting of a lawyer's daughter, she being an advocate of the Devil) (1963: 980).

This and other images by the painter also circulated as engravings that have been reproduced in Walter Bosing's book (2004). Paintings from the Escorial by Bosch are now housed at the Prado Museum in Madrid.

59 As a number of art historians have pointed out, Quevedo draws parallels between Bosch and his own work. See especially the work of Margarita Morreale, Margarita Levisi, and Helmut Heidenreich (1956; 1963; 1970). Critics who deemphasize connections between the painter and writer include Xavier de Salas and James Iffland (1943; 1978). According to the latter critic, while the genius of Quevedo lies in his witty and grotesque satire of "types," the fantastical, allegorical imagination of Bosch is inhabited by a "generic Man, an abstraction" (1978: 2.45–6). In a polemic against Quevedo known as the *Tribunal de la justa venganza* (Trial of Just Revenge) (1635), the author is denigrated as an atheist, due to Boschian influences on the *Sueño.* "El Bosco" was also sometimes thought to be a non-believer and represented as a farcical figure (see Salas 1943: 34–5). Quevedo, ironically, also accused his literary enemy Luis de Góngora of being the "Bosch of poets" (1963: 151).

60 The globe also appears under the feet of Christ, seated as *Juste Judex*, in a Last Judgment in Madrid painted by a sixteenth-century imitator of Bosch's *Garden of Earthly Delights* (Bosing 2004: 45, 48). Descriptions of the Last Judgment and Christ as Judge can be found in the gospels, Acts, and epistles of the New Testament (see, especially, Matt 25:31–41, Acts 17:31, Rom. 2:16, 2 Cor. 5:10, Heb. 9:27–8 and 20:12).

61 For a discussion of the table's ocular significance, see the study of Marc Bensimon (1972).

62 Indeed, in the words of Carmen Pereira-Muro: "it does not seem coincidental that Philip placed in his personal chamber this reminder … since geopolitically, he was trying to reproduce the same centripetal effect; El Escorial was the precise geographical center from which he overlooked his empire (2010: 140). Philip II compared festive devils to those found in the paintings of Bosch (see Salas 1943: 11).

63 An early, negative literary image of this kind can be found in Sebastian Brant's *Das Narrenschiff* (Ship of Fools 1494), in which a fool is shown blindfolding Lady Justice to represent the corruption of courts (1944: 236–7). For a discussion of visual representations of Justice's vision and blindfolding, see the study of Martin Jay (1999).

64 Even in *the Garden of Earthly Delights*, with its less overt moralization, in the words of Pereira-Muro, "God and Salvation still occupy a reduced space of the representation" (2010: 138). In Quevedo's satire, however, the transcendent viewpoint of the "Justo Juez" can only be perceived from a

distant, contextual space. The watchful eye of God, in the words of Pereira-Muro, seems to be "hidden behind a thick rhetorical cloud of metaphors and ellipses … acting somewhere," but "more divorced from Man's reckoning" (2010: 138).

65 On Quevedo's promotion of Luis de León, see Donald W. Bleznick's literary biography (1972: 113, 131, 137). Becoming a "just judge," in this context, entails imitating Christ through one of his names. The friar wrote this while imprisoned on false charges of potential heresy, yet instinctively trusted that the Holy Office would sooner or later correctly judge his case (Kamen 1985: 91–2).

66 The metaphorical spectacles of "Maestro Desengaño" (Master Undeceiver) influenced a lesser-known picaresque novel from the same period, Luis Vélez de Guevara's *Diablo Cojuelo* (1641). Also, legal officials like notaries and bailiffs are shown through these lenses (2009: 48–56). Concerning optics in Golden Age Spain, see the full-length study of García Santo-Tomás (2015).

67 See the studies of José Carlos Vela Bueno, who compares these scenes to Ramón del Valle-Inclan's *esperpento* (critical, reifying distortion), and William Clamurro who observes a similar pattern of "cosificación" (reification) in which objects take precedence over persons, who are presented as "fragmented, grotesque ensembles" (1996: 307–8; 1980: 297).

68 As Anne Cruz points out, the *Buscón* was written not long after the plague that hit Valladolid in 1599 (1999: 131).

69 The longstanding question as to whether Quevedo's parody of genre in the *Buscón* should be considered formally a picaresque novel or anti-picaresque reaction to such novels has been recently taken up by Francisco Garrote Pérez (2003).

Postcript: Amuletic Afterlives

1 He is said to have come into possession of the amulet at the "Salto del agua," a site that was then supplied by an Aztec aqueduct, and now provides the name of an important metro stop (Campos Moreno 1999: 142).

2 Hernando was the brother of the well-known Golden Age dramatist, Juan Ruiz de Alarcón.

3 J.A. Van Praag discovered the novella in 1950 at an auction house for antique books in Utrecht and published it in *Revista de literatura* (1958). This manuscript, identified as a copy made during the eighteenth century, has since disappeared. In addition to the language of the text, allusions to earlier picaresque works and other Golden Age authors led to the dating

of the work. Scholars have suggested, on the basis of Portuguese spellings and word choices, that the anonymous author was from Portugal and they have also speculated that his citations of the Old Testament and criticisms of the church may point to a *converso* background (Zafra 2011: 15–18).

4 Critics have speculated, partly on the basis of allusions to the Inquisition, that the author of Andrea's life might have been a *converso*.

5 In other words, he was brought to the monastery and palace where Philip II had buried his father, Carlos I, and died in excruciating pain just over one hundred years earlier, after attempting to heal himself with relics preserved in Escorial, a collection that included a number of manuscripts that were believed to have been written or used by saints, and thus attributed with amuletic qualities (see Lazure 2007).

6 See, most recently, the concluding chapter of Michael D. Bailey's study (2013). Enlightened thinkers were not only interested in writing and studying superstitions, but also in some cases seem to have engaged in aspects of these practices. A striking instance of this is a mystical text and seeming amulet that Blaise Pascal carried on his person, hidden beneath his clothes. It is being studied by Hall Bjørnstad.

7 One example can be found at Indiana University's Lilly Library, Spanish History Box, MSS. 18th cent. This miscellaneous collection of documents contains copies of a "Remedia contra toda peste," supposedly translated from a sixteenth-century Latin text that was approved by members of the Council of Trent: "se mandó no se traxesen, nin usassen sin su declaración" (it was ordered these not be carried, nor used without their declaration) (18th cent: fols. 21–2).

8 A numbered copy of the typed prayer can be found in the *Colección de Pliegos Sueltos* of the Fundación Joaquín Díaz in Valladolid. Another such copy is conserved at the Biblioteca de Castilla y León (control no. CYL20090073531).

Works Cited

"A muyto devota oração da Empardeada em linguagem português." 1997. *La muy devota oración de la emparedada.* Edited and translated by Juan M. Carrasco González. Extremadura: Junta de Extremadura; Consejería de Cultura y Patrimonio.

Aberdeen Bestiary. 2002. Edited by Morton Gauld and Colin McLarens. Aberdeen Bestiary Project. Aberdeen University.

Abulafia, Anna Sapir. 2002. "The Intellectual and Spiritual Quest for Christ and Central Medieval Persecution of Jews." In *Religious Violence between Christians and Jews: Medieval Roots, Modern Perspectives,* edited by Anna Sapir Abulafia, 61–85. New York: Palgrave.

Adso of Montier-en-Der. 1979. "Letter on the Origin and Time of the Antichrist." In *Apocalyptic Spirituality: Treatises and Letters of Lactantius, Adso of Montier-en-Der, Joachim of Fiore, the Spiritual Franciscans, Savonarola,* translated by Bernard McGinn, 89–96. New York: Paulist Press.

Agnew, Matthew. 2001. "'Como en libro abierto': La construcción de un model exegético en el Libro de Alexandre." *La corónica* 29 (2): 159–83.

Agulló, Mercedes. 2010. *A vueltas con el autor del "Lazarillo."* Madrid: Calambur.

Akeley, T.C. 1967. *Christian Initiation in Spain, c. 300–1100.* London: Darton, Longman, and Todd.

Alborayque. 2005. Edited by Dwayne Eugène Carpenter. Mérida: Editora Regional de Extremadura.

Alcalá Yáñez y Rivera, Jerónimo de. 1847. *El donado hablador: vida y aventuras de Alonso, mozo de mucho amos.* Paris: Fain y Thunot.

Alfonsi, Petrus. 2006. *Dialogue against the Jews.* [Dialogus contra Iudaeos]. Translated by Irven M. Resnick. Washington, DC: Catholic University of America Press.

Alfonso X. 1858. *Gran conquista de ultramar*. Edited by Pascual de Gayangos. Madrid: Rivadeneyra.

Alfonso X. 1906. *Primera crónica general. Estoria de España*. Vol. 1. 2 vols. Edited by Ramón Menéndez Pidal. Madrid: Bailly-Bailliere.

Alfonso X. 1957. *General estoria. Primera parte*. Edited by Antonio García Solalinde. Madrid: CSIC.

Alfonso X. 1986–9. *Cantigas de Santa Maria*. 3 vols. Edited by Walter Mettmann. Madrid: Castalia.

Alfonso X. 1986. *Picatrix*. Edited by David Pingree. London: Warburg Institute, University of London Press.

Alfonso X. 1991. *Facsímil del códice B.R.20 de la Biblioteca Nazionale Centrale de Florencia*. Edited by Ana Domínguez Rodríguez, Agustín Santiago Luque, and Victoria Chico Picaza María. Madrid: Edilan.

Alfonso X. 2000. *Songs of Holy Mary of Alfonso X, the Wise*. Translated by Kathleen Kulp-Hill. Tempe: Arizona Center for Medieval and Renaissance Studies.

Alfonso X. 2004. *Las siete partidas*. Edited by José Sánchez-Arcilla Bernal. Madrid: Reus.

Alfonso X. 2011. *Códice rico facsimile, Ms. T-I-1 de la Real biblioteca del Monasterio de San Lorenzo de El Escorial*. Edited by Laura Fernández Fernández and Juan Carlos Ruiz Souza. Madrid: Patrimonio Nacional; Testimonio Compañía Editorial.

Allen, Peter Lewis. 2000. *The Wages of Sin: Sex and Disease, Past and Present*. Chicago: University of Chicago Press.

Alvar, Manuel. 1984. "Apolonio, clerigo entendido." In *Symposium in honorem prof. M de Riquer*, 51–73. Barcelona: U de Barcelona, Quaderns Crema.

Álvarez, Nicolás Emilio. 1976. "El recibimiento y la tienda de Don Amor en el *Libro de buen amor* a la luz del *Libro de Alexandre*." *Bulletin of Hispanic Studies* 53: 1–14.

Amasuno Sárraga, Marcelino. 2000. "Entre el *amor heroes* y una terapia falaz." *DICENDA: Cuadernos de filología hispánica* 18: 11–49.

Ambrose of Milan. 1845. *De virginibus. Patrologia latina 16*. Edited by J.P. Migne. Paris: Migne.

Ambrose of Milan. 1879. *Sermones. Opera Omnia*. Patrologia Latina 17. Paris: J.P. Migne.

Ambrose of Milan. 1997. *On Virgins. Ambrose*. Edited and translated by Boniface Ramsey. London, New York: Routledge. 71–116.

Amsler, Mark. 2001. "Rape and Silence: Ovid's Mythography and Medieval Readers." In *Representing Rape in Medieval and Early Modern Literature*, edited by Elizabeth Robertson and Christine M. Rose, 61–96. New York: Palgrave.

Aquinas, Thomas. 1957. *Summa contra Gentiles*.Book 4. Translated by Charles J. O'Neil. New York: Hanover House.

Arata, Stefano. 1988. "Una nueva tragicomedia celestinesca del siglo XVI." *Celestinesca* 12 (1): 45–50.

Arinze, Francis. 2008. "Letter to the Bishops Conferences on the Name of God." *Congregatio de Cultu Divino et Disciplina Sacramentorum.* Prot. no. 213/08/L.

Arthur, Ross G. 1987. *Medieval Sign Theory and "Sir Gawain and the Green Knight."* Toronto: University of Toronto Press.

Askins, Arthur Lee-Francis. 2007. "Notes on Three Prayers in Late 15th. Century Portuguese (the *Oração da Empardeada,* the *Oração de S. Leão, Papa,* and the *Justo Juiz*): Text History and Inquisitorial Interdictions." *Península: Revista de Estudos Ibéricos* 4: 235–66.

Astell, Ann W. 1990. *The Song of Songs in the Middle Ages.* Cornell: Cornell University Press.

Auerbach, Erich. 1993. *Literary Language and Its Public in Late Latin Antiquity and in the Middle Ages.* Translated by Ralph Manheim. Princeton: Princeton University Press.

Augustine. 1841. *Confessiones. Patrologia Latina 32.* Edited by J.P. Migne. Paris: Migne.

Augustine. 1841. *De Doctrina Christiana. Patrologia Latina 34.* Edited by J.P. Migne. Paris: Migne.

Augustine. 1841. *De Trinitate. Patrologia Latina 42.* Edited by J.P. Migne. Paris: Migne.

Augustine. 1841. *Joannis Evangelium Tractatus. Patrologia latina 35.* Edited by J.P. Migne. Paris: Migne.

Augustine. 1888. *Tractates on the Gospel of John.* Translated by John Gibb. *Nicene and Post-Nicene Fathers.* First Series. Vol. 7. Edited by Philip Schaff. 14 vols. Buffalo, NY: Christian Literature Publishing. 452.

Augustine. 1955. *"Confessions" and "Enchiridion."* Edited and translated by Albert Cook Outler. Louisville, KY: Westminster John Knox Press.

Augustine. 1984. *The City of God.* Translated by Henry Bettenson. New York: Penguin Books.

Augustine. 2002. *On the Trinity.* Edited by Gareth B. Matthews. Cambridge: Cambridge University Press.

Austin, J.L. 1962. *How to Do Things with Words. The William James Lectures.* Cambridge, MA: Cambridge University Press.

Auvergne, William of. 1963. *De Legibus.* Vol. 1. *Opera Omnia.* 2 vols. Frankfurt: Minerva.

Avitus, Alcimus Ecdicius. 1997. *The Poems of Alcimus Ecdicius Avitus.* Translated by George W. Shea. Medieval and Renaissance Texts and Studies 172. Temple: Arizona State University Press.

Azpilcueta, Martín de. 1557. *Manual de confessores y penitentes.* Anvers: Juan Steelsio.

Bacon, Roger. 1900. *"Opus majus": Supplementary Volume*. Edited by John Henry Bridges. Oxford: Clarendon.

Bagby, Albert I. 1971. "The Jew in the *Cántigas* of Alfonso X, *el Sabio*." *Speculum* 46: 670–88.

Bailey, Michael D. 2013. *Fearful Spirits, Reasoned Follies: The Boundaries of Superstition in Late Medieval Europe*. Ithaca: Cornell University Press.

Bamford, Heather. 2012. "Faith in Fragments." Unpublished lecture. 129th Convention of the Modern Language Association. Chicago, IL.

Baños Vallejo, Fernando. 1994. "Plegarias de héroes y de santos. Más datos sobre la oración narrativa." *Hispanic Review* 62: 205–15.

Baños Vallejo, Fernando, and Isabel Uría Maqua, eds. 2000. *La leyenda de los santos: "Flos Sanctorum" del ms. 8 de la Biblioteca de Menéndez Pelayo*. Santander: Ayuntamiento de Santander, Sociedad Menéndez Pelayo.

Barletta, Vincent. May 2011. *Relación de manuscritos aljamiados conocidos*. http://www.academia.edu/13761907/Relación_de_manuscritos_aljamiados_conocidos.

Bataillon, Marcel. 1950. *Erasmo y España: Estudios sobre la historia espiritual del siglo XVI*. 2 vols. Translated by Antonio Alatorre. México, DF: Fondo de Cultura Económica.

Bataillon, Marcel. 1966. *Erasmo y España. Estudios sobre la historia espiritual del siglo XVI*. Madrid: Fondo de cultura económica.

Bayless, Martha. 1996. *Parody in the Middle Ages: The Latin Tradition*. Ann Arbor: University of Michigan Press.

Bensimon, Marc. 1972. "The Significance of Eye Imagery in the Renaissance from Bosch to Montaign." *Yale French Studies* 47: 266–90.

Berceo, Gonzalo de. 1981. *Poema de Santa Oria*. Edited by Isabel Uría Maqua. Madrid: Castalia.

Berceo, Gonzalo de. 2003. *Obras completas*. Edited by Carlos Clavería and Jorge García López. Madrid: Fundación José Antonio de Castro.

Beresford, Andrew. 2001. "'Una oración, señora, que le dixeron que sabías, de Sancta Polonia para el dolor de las muelas': *Celestina* and the Legend of St. Apollonia." *Bulletin of Hispanic Studies* 78 (1): 39–58.

Beresford, Andrew. 2007. *The Legends of the Holy Harlots: Thais and Pelagia in Medieval Spanish Literature*. Woodbridge, Suffolk, UK; Rochester, NY: Tamesis.

Bernheimer, Richard. 1952. *Wild Men in the Middle Ages: A Study in Art, Sentiment, and Demonology*. Cambridge: Harvard University Press.

Bersuire, Pierre. 1979. *Metamorphosis Ovidiana moraliter [Ovidius moralizatus]*. Edited by Stephen Orgel. The Philosophy of Images 1. New York: Garland.

Bible. 1941. Douay-Rheims Version. New York: Benziger Brothers.

Biblia Sacra. 1994. Iuxta Vulgatam Versionem [Vulgate]. 4th ed. Edited by Robert Weber. Stuttgart: Bibelgesellschaft.

Binet, Alfred. 1887. "Le fétichisme dans l'amour." *Revue Philosophique* 24: 143–67, 252–74.

Binotti, Lucia. 2010. "Humanistic Audiences: *Novela sentimental* and *Libros de caballerías in Cinquecento* Italy." *La corónica* 39 (1): 67–113.

Binotti, Lucia. 2012. *Cultural Capital, Language and National Identity in Imperial Spain*. Woodbridge, UK: Tamesis.

Birgitta of Sweden. 1665. *Las quinze devotíssimas oraciones de Santa Brígida*. Barcelona: Sebestián de Cormellas.

Birgitta of Sweden. 2008. *Revelations*. Translated by Denis Searby. Edited by Bridget Morris. 2 vols. Oxford: Oxford University Press.

Blanco Prado, José Manuel. 2008. "Las enfermedades de la vista y de las lombrices en la provincia de Lugo. Ensalmos y rituales etnomédicos." *Culturas Populares. Revista Electrónica* 6: n.p.

Bleznick, Donald W. 1972. *Quevedo*. New York: Twayne.

Blisniewski, Thomas Maria. 1992. *"Kinder der dunkelen Nacht": die Ikonographie der Parzen vom späten Mittelalter bis zum späten XVIII*. Berlin: Kommissionsvertrieb, Wasmuth.

Blois, Peter of. 1855. *Contra perfidiam Judaeorum. Patrologia Latina 207*. Edited by J.P. Migne. Paris: Migne.

Blumenfeld-Kosinski, Renate. 1990. *Not of Woman Born: Representations of Caesarean Birth in Medieval and Renaissance Culture*. Ithaca: Cornell University Press.

Blumler, Martin Frederick. 1887. *A History of Amulets*. Translated by S.H. Gent. Rpt. Edinburgh: E.G. Goldsmid.

Boccaccio. 1951. *De genealogia deorum gentilium*. 2 vols. Bari: Scrittoria d'Italia.

Boccaccio. 2009. *Decameron*. Translated by J.G. Nichols. New York: Knopf.

Bonaventure. 1864–71. *Sententiarium. Opera Omnia*. 3 vols. Paris: Ludovicus Vivès. 1:58 (*Liber* 1, *Distinctio* 2, *Quaestio* 4).

Bosing, Walter. 2004. *Hieronymus Bosch, c. 1450–1516: Between Heaven and Hell*. London: Taschen.

Botas San Martín, Isabel. 1992. "Oraciones, ensalmos y conjuros." *Revista de folklore* 141: 90–9.

Botta, Patricia. 2002. "La *Celestina* vibra en *La lozana*." *Cultura neolatina* 62 (4): 275–304.

Boulhol, Pascal. 1996. *Anagnōrismos: la scène de reconnaissance dans l'hagiographie antique et médiévale*. Provence: Université de Provence.

Bouza, Fernando. 2001. *Corre manuscrito: una historia cultural del Siglo de Oro*. Madrid: Marcial Pons.

Brakhage, Pamela S. 1986. *The Theology of "La lozana andaluza."* Potomac, MD: Scripta Humanistica.

Brant, Sebastian. 1944. *The Ship of Fools*. Edited and translated by Edwin H. Zeydel. New York: Dover.

Brown, Peter. 1967. *Augustine of Hippo: A Biography*. Berkeley: University of California Press.

Brown, Peter. 1981. *The Cult of the Saints: Its Rise and Function in Latin Christianity*. Chicago: University of Chicago Press.

Brownlee, Marina Scordilis. 1983. "Writing and Scripture in the *Libro de Apolonio*: The Conflation of Hagiography and Romance." *Hispanic Review* 51 (2): 159–74.

Budge, E.A. Wallis. 1930. *Amulets and Superstitions*. Oxford: Oxford University Press.

Bueno, Julián F. 1983. *La sotana de Juan Ruiz: elementos eclesiásticos en el "Libro de buen amor."* York, SC: Spanish Literature Publications.

Bujanda, J.M. de, ed. 1984. *Index de l'Inquisition espagnole, 1551, 1554, 1559*. Vol. 5 of *Index des livres interdits*. Centre d'études de la Renaissance, Editions de l'Université de Sherbrooke. 11 vols. Genève: Droz.

Burchard of Worms. 1853. *Decretum. Patrologia Latina 140*. Ed. J.P. Migne. Paris: Migne.

Burke, James F. 1993. "The *Mal de la Madre* and the Failure of Maternal Influence in *Celestina*." *Celestinesca* 17 (2): 111–12.

Burke, James F. 1998. *Desire against the Law: The Juxtaposition of Contraries in Early Medieval Spanish Literature*. Stanford: Stanford University Press.

Burke, James F. 2000. *Vision, the Gaze, and the Function of the Senses in "Celestina."* University Park, PA: Pennsylvania State University Press.

Burt, John R. 1982. "The Metaphorical Suggestions of Jimena's Prayer." *Crítica hispánica* 4: 21–8.

Bynum, Caroline Walker. 2010. "Violence Occluded: The Wound in Christ's Side in Late Medieval Devotion." In *Feud, Violence and Practice: Essays in Medieval Studies in Honor of Stephen D. White*, edited by Belle S. Tuten and Tracey L. Billado, 95–116. Burlington, VT: Ashgate.

Bynum, Caroline Walker. 2011. *Christian Materiality: An Essay on Religion in Late Medieval Europe*. Cambridge, MA: MIT Press.

Campbell, Marian. 1991. "Gold, Silver, and Precious Stones." In *English Medieval Industries: Craftsmen, Techniques, Products*, edited by John Blair and Nigel Ramsey, 108–66. London: Hambeldon Press.

Campo, Juan Eduardo et al. 2009. "Amulets and Talismans." *Encyclopedia of Islam*, 40–1. New York: Infobase.

Campo, Juan Eduardo et al. 2009. "Shahada." *Encyclopedia of Islam*, 618–19. New York: Infobase.

Campos Moreno, Araceli. 1999. *Oraciones, ensalmos y conjuros mágicos del archivo inquisitorial de la Nueva España*. México, DF: Colegio de México.

Capellanus, Andreas. 1982. *On Love (De amore)*. Edited and translated by P.G. Walsh. London: Duckworth.

Carajicomedia. 1981. Edited by Carlos Varo. Madrid: Playor.

Caro Baroja, Julio. 1967. "El libro mágico: La *Clavícula* de Solomón." In *Vidas mágicas e inquisición*. 2 vols. Madrid: Taurus. 1.159–76.

Caro Baroja, Julio. 1969. *Ensayo sobre la literatura de cordel*. Madrid: Revista de Occidente.

Carpenter, Dwayne E. *1986. Alfonso X and the Jews: An Edition of and Commentary on "Siete pártidas."* Berkeley: University of California Press.

Carrasco González, Juan M. 2005. "Portugal en la biblioteca de Barcarrota: la *Oración de la Emparedada*." *Anuario de estudios filológicos* 28: 21–34.

Carrión, María M. 2010. *Subject Stages: Marriage, Theatre and the Law in Early Modern Spain*. Toronto: University of Toronto Press.

Cary, George. 1956. *The Medieval Alexander*. Cambridge: Cambridge University Press.

Castañega, Martín de. 1997. *Tratado de las supersticiones y hechicerías. Libros raros, olvidados y curiosos*. Edited by Fabián Alejandro Campagne. Buenos Aires: Universidad de Buenos Aires.

Castells, Ricardo. 2000. *Fernando de Rojas and the Renaissance Vision: Phantasm, Melancholy, and Didacticism in "Celestina."* University Park, PA: Pennsylvania State University Press.

Cavero Domínguez, Gregoria. 2006. "Fuentes para el estudio del emparedamiento en la España medieval (siglos XII–XV)." *Revue Mabillon* 17: 105–26.

Chance, Jane. 1995. *The Mythographic Chaucer: The Fabulation of Sexual Politics*. Minneapolis: University of Minnesota Press.

Châtillon, Walter of. 1978. *Alexandreis*. Edited by Marvin Colker. Padua: Antenore.

Christian, William A. 1981a. *Apparitions in Late Medieval and Renaissance Spain*. Princeton: Princeton University Press.

Christian, William A. 1981b. *Local Religion in Sixteenth-Century Spain*. Princeton: Princeton University Press.

Ciruelo, Pedro. 1978. *Reprovación de las supersticiones y hechizerías*. Edited by Alva V. Ebersole. Valencia: Albatros Hispanófila.

Clamurro, William H. 1980. "The Destabilized Sign: Word and Form in Quevedo's *Buscón*." *Modern Language Notes* 95 (2): 295–311.

Clark, Francis, ed. 1987. *Pseudo-Gregorian Dialogues*. 2 vols. Leiden: Brill.

Coffey, Heather. 2010. "Between Amulet and Devotion: Islamic Miniature Books in the Lilly Library." In *The Islamic Manuscript Tradition: Ten Centuries of Book Arts in Indiana University Collections*, edited by Christiane Gruber, 78–115. Bloomington, IN: Indiana University Press.

Cohen, Jeremy. 1999. *Living Letters of the Law: Ideas of the Jew in Medieval Christianity*. Berkeley: University of California Press.

Cohen, Judith R. 2001. "'Ca no soe joglaresa': Women and Music in Medieval Spain's Three Cultures." In *Medieval Woman's Song: Cross-Cultural Approaches*, edited by Anne L. Klinck and Ann Marie Rasmussen, 66–80. Philadelphia: University of Pennsylvania Press.

Cohn, Yehudah. 2008. *Tangled up in Text: Tefillin and the Ancient World*. Providence: Brown Judaic Studies.

Coleman, Simon, and John Elsner. 1995. *Pilgrimage: Past and Present in the World Religions*. Cambridge, MA: Harvard University Press.

Cook, Eleanor. 2006. *Enigmas and Riddles in Literature*. Cambridge: Cambridge University Press.

Copeland, Rita. 1991. *Rhetoric, Hermeneutics, and Translation in the Middle Ages: Academic Traditions and Vernacular Texts. Cambridge Studies in Medieval Literature 11*. Cambridge: Cambridge University Press.

Corry, Jennifer M. 2005. *Perceptions of Magic in Medieval Spanish Literature*. Cranbury, NJ: Associated University Press.

Costa Fontes, Manuel da, ed. 1987. *Romanceiro da Província de Trás-os-Montes*. Coimbra: Universidade de Coimbra.

Costa Fontes, Manuel da. 1993. "Anti-Trinitarianism and the Virgin Birth in *La Lozana andaluza*." *Hispania* 76 (2): 197–203.

Costa Fontes, Manuel da. 1997. "O Justo Juiz Cristão e a Inquisição em Duas Orações Criptojudaicas de Rebordelo." *Hispania* 80 (1): 1–8.

Costa Fontes, Manuel da. 2005. *The Art of Subversion in Inquisitorial Spain: Rojas and Delicado*. Purdue Studies in Romance Literatures 30. West Lafayette, IN: Purdue University Press.

Covarrubias Orozco, Sebastián de. 1611. *Tesoro de la lengua castellana o española*. Madrid: L. Sanchez.

Crichton-Stuart, John Patrick. 1879. *The Roman Breviary*. 2 vols. London: William Blackwood.

Cros, Edmond. 1975. *L'aristocrate et le carnaval de gueux: Etude sure le "Buscón" de Quevedo*. Montpellier: CERS.

Cruz, Anne J. 1999. *Discourses of Poverty: Social Reform and the Picaresque Novel in Early Modern Spain*. Toronto: University of Toronto Press.

Cruz, Anne J. 2014. "The Walled-In Woman in Medieval and Early Modern Spain." In *Gender Matters: Discourses of Violence in Early Modern Literature and the Arts*, edited by Mara R. Wade, 345–65. Amsterdam: Repoli.

Culianu, Ioan P. 1987. *Eros and Magic in the Renaissance*. Translated by Margaret Cook. Chicago: University of Chicago Press.

Dagenais, John. 1994. *The Ethics of Reading in Manuscript Culture: Glossing the "Libro de buen amor."* Princeton: Princeton University Press.

Daichman, Graciela S. 1986. *Wayward Nuns in Medieval Literature.* Syracuse, NY: Syracuse University Press.

Dalbey, Marcia A. 1974. "The Devil in the Garden: Pluto and Prosperine in Chaucer's 'Merchantes Tale.'" *Neuphilologische Mitteilungen* 75 (3): 408–15.

Dallaway, James, ed. 1793. *The 1486 Boke of St. Albans. Heraldic Miscellanies.* London: T. Cadell.

Damiani, Bruno M, ed. 1971. "*El modo de adoperare el legno de India Occidantale*: A Critical Transcription." *Revista Hispánica Moderna* 36 (4): 251–71.

Damiani, Bruno M, ed. 1974. *Francisco Delicado. Twayne World Author Series 335.* New York: Twayne.

Dan, Joseph. 1996. "The Name of God, the Name of the Rose, and the Concept of Language in Jewish Mysticism." *Medieval Encounters* 2 (3): 228–48.

Dangler, Jean. 2001. *Mediating Fictions: Literature, Women Healers, and the Go-Between in Medieval and Early Modern Iberia.* Lewisburg, PA: Bucknell University Press.

Dante Alighieri. 1996. *The Divine Comedy [Divina commedia].* 3 vols. Edited and translated by Robert M. Durling. Oxford, New York: Oxford University Press.

Davies, Owen. 2009. *Grimoires: A History of Magic Books.* Oxford: Oxford University Press.

Delgado Roig, Juan. 1948. "Examen médico-legal de unos restos históricos: Los cadáveres de Alfonso X el sabio y Doña Beatriz de Suabia." *Archivo Hispalense* 9: 135–53.

Delicado, Francisco. 1985. *La Lózana andaluza.* Edited by Claude Allaigre. Madrid: Cátedra.

Delicado, Francisco. 2011. *El modo de usar el palo de la India Occidental, saludable remedio contra toda llaga y mal incurable.* Edited and translated by Ignacio Ahumada. Jaén: Universidad Jaén.

De Looze, Laurence. 1998. "To Understand Perfectly Is to Misunderstand Completely: 'The Debate in Signs' in France, Iceland, Italy and Spain." *Comparative Literature* 50: 136–54.

Derrida, Jacques. 1992. "How to Avoid Speaking: Denials." In *Derrida and Negative Theology,* 73–142. Albany: SUNY Press.

Desing, Matthew V. 2012. "De pan y de tresoro: Sacrament in the *Libro de Apolonio.*" *La corónica* 40 (2): 93–120.

Desmond, Marilynn, and Pamela Sheingorn. 2003. *Myth, Montage, and Visuality in Late Medieval Manuscript Culture: Christine de Pizan's Epistre Othea.* Ann Arbor: University of Michigan Press.

Deyermond, Alan. 1961. *The Petrarchan Sources of "La Celestina."* Oxford: Oxford University Press.

Deyermond, Alan. 1977. "*Hilado-cordón-cadena*: Symbolic Equivalence in *La Celestina*." *Celestinesca* 1 (1): 6–12.

Deyermond, Alan. 1996. "Building a World: Geography and Cosmology in Castilian Literature of the Early Thirteenth Century." *Canadian Review of Comparative Literature* 23: 141–59.

Deyermond, Alan. 2001. "Fernando de Rojas from 1499 to 1502: Born-Again Christian?" *Celestinesca* 25 (1–2): 3–20.

Deyermond, Alan. 2002. "El Alejandro medieval, el Ulises de Dante y la búsqueda de las Antípodas." In *Maravillas, peregrinaciones y utopías: Literatura de viajes en el mundo románico*, edited by Rafael Beltrán, 15–32. València: Universitat de València.

Didron, Adolphe Napoleon. 1851–91. *Christian Iconography: The History of Christian Art in the Middle Ages*. 2 vols. Translated by E.J. Millington. London: Henry G. Bohn.

Dillon, Emma. 2002. *Medieval Music-Making and the "Roman de Fauvel"*. Cambridge: Cambridge University Press.

Duarte, I. 1842. *Leal Conselheiro*. Edited by J.E. Roquete. Paris: J.P. Aillaud.

Dunn, Peter N. 1993. *Spanish Picaresque Fiction: A New Literary History*. Ithaca: Cornell University Press.

Edwards, John. 2004. "The Friars and the Jews: Messianism in Spain and Italy, circa 1500." In *Friars and Jews in the Middle Ages and Renaissance*, edited by Steven J. McMichael and Susan E. Myers, 273–98. Leiden: Boston: Brill.

Egeria of Galicia. 1960. *Itinerarium Egeriae*. Edited by Otto Prinz. Heidelberg: Carl Winter Universitätsverlag.

Erasmus. 1989. *De Lingua*. Edited and translated by Elaine Fantham. *Collected Works of Erasmus*. 86 vols. Toronto: University of Toronto Press. 29.247–412.

Erasmus. 1990. "Shipwreck (*Naufragium*)." *Erasmus Reader*. Edited by Erika Rummel and translated by Craig R. Thompson, 239–48. Toronto: University of Toronto Press.

Espinosa, Pedro. 1736. *El perro y la calentura: novela peregrina*. Madrid: Pedro Joseph Alonso y Padilla.

Eusebius of Caesarea. 1952–60. *Histoire ecclésiastique, Livres I–IV*. Edited and translated by Gustave Bardy. 4 vols. Paris: Cerf. 1.41–5.

Evans, Michael. 1982. "An Illustrated Fragment of Peraldus's *Summa* of Vice: Harleian MS 3244." *Journal of the Warburg and Courtauld Institutes* 45: 14–68.

Fairclough, Henry Rushton. 1916. "The Meaning of *Caelum* in the Sixth Book of the *Aeneid*." *Leland Stanford Junior University Publications* 2: 108–13.

Fanger, Claire. 1999. "Things Done Wisely by a Wise Enchanter: Negotiating the Power of Words in the Thirteenth Century." *Esoterica* 1: 97–131.

Fasciculus myrrhe. 1524. Sevilla: Juan de Varela.

Fernández Guerra y Orbe, Aureliano. 1852. *Obras de Don Francisco de Quevedo Villegas.* Vol. 1. 3 vols. Madrid: Rivadaneyra.

Fernández, Rodrigo. 1979. *Los anteojos de mejor vista. El mesón del mundo.* Edited by Víctor Infantes de Miguel. Madrid: Legasa.

Fernández de Lizardi, José J. 1997. *El periquillo sarniento.* Edited by Carmen Ruiz Barrionuevo. Madrid: Cátedra.

Fernández de Moratín, Leandro [pseud. Ginés de Posadilla]. 1810. *Auto de fe celebrado en la ciudad de Logroño.* Madrid: Collado.

Férotin, Dom G., ed. 1904. *Liber Ordinum.* Paris: Firmin-Didot.

Ferré, Rosario. 1983. "Celestina en el tejido de *cupiditas.*" *Celestinesca* 7 (1): 3–16.

Ferrer-Chivite, Manuel. 2000. "Sobre las así llamadas interpolaciones de Alcalá." *Actas del XIII Congreso de la Asociación Internacional de Hispanistas, Madrid 6–11 de julio de 1998.* 4 vols. Edited by Florencio Sevilla Arroyo and Carlos Alvar Ezquerra. Madrid: Castalia; Fundación Duques de Soria. 1.318–26.

Flint, Valerie I.J. 1994. *The Rise of Magic in Early Medieval Europe.* Princeton: Princeton University Press.

Flores, Juan de. 2003. *La historia de Grisel y Mirabella.* Edited by Maria Grazia Ciccarello di Blasi. Dipartimento di Studi Romanzi, Università di Roma "La Sapienza," testi, Studi e Manuali 18. Rome: Bagatto.

Flowers, Robin. 1927. "The Revelation of Christ's Wounds." *Béaloideas* 1 (1): 38–45.

Foucault, Michel. 1977. *Discipline and Punish: The Birth of the Prison.* Translated by Alan Sheridon. New York: Vintage.

Fraker, Charles F. 1996. *The Scope of History: Studies in the Historiography of Alfonso el Sabio.* Ann Arbor: University of Michigan Press.

Franchini, Enzo. 1991. "'Abracalabra' (Los exorcismos hispanolatinos en el Códice de la Razón de amor)." *Revista de literatura medieval* 3: 77–94.

Franchini, Enzo. 1993. *El manuscrito, la lengua y el ser literario de la "Razón de amor."* Madrid: CSIC.

Frankfurter, David. 2001. "Narrating Power: The Theory and Practice of the Magical *Historiola* in Magical Spells." In *Ancient Magic and Ritual Power,* edited by Marvin W. Meyer and Paul Allan Mirecki, 457–76. Leiden: Brill.

Freeman, Charles. 2011. *Holy Bones, Holy Dust: How Relics Shaped the History of Medieval Europe.* New Haven: Yale University Press.

Friedman, Edward. 1987. *The Antiheroine's Voice: Narrative Discourse and Transformations of the Picaresque.* Columbia: University of Missouri Press.

Frye, Northrop. 2008. *Words with Power: Being a Second Study of the Bible and Literature*. Edited by Michael Dolzani. University of Toronto Press: Harcourt.

Fuller, David. 2010. "Lyrics, Sacred and Secular." In *A Companion to Medieval Poetry*, edited by Corinne Saunders, 258–76. Malden, MA: Wiley-Blackwell.

Gambero, Luigi. 2000. *Mary in the Middle Ages: The Blessed Virgin Mary in the Thought of Medieval Latin Theologians*. San Antonio: Ignatius.

Ganim, John. 2007. *Place, Space, and Landscape in Medieval Narrative*. Edited by Laura L. Howes. Knoxville: University of Tennessee Press.

García Áviles, Alejandro. 1997. "Alfonso X y el *Liber Razielis*: imágenes de la magia astral judía en el *scriptorium* alfonsí." *Bulletin of Hispanic Studies* 74: 21–39.

García-Bryce, Ariadna. 2011. *Transcending Textuality: Quevedo and Political Authority in the Age of Print*. University Park, PA: Pennsylvania State University Press.

García de Enterría, María Cruz. 1997. "Una devoción prohibida: la *Oración de la Emparedada*." *La muy devota Oración de la Emparedada*. La Biblioteca de Barcarrota 2. Edited by Juan M. Carrasco González. Badajoz: Junta de Extremadura. ix–xlv.

García Santo-Tomás, Enrique. 2009. "Fortunes of the *Occhiali Politici* in Early Modern Spain: Optics, Vision, Points of View." *PMLA* 124 (1): 59–75.

García Santo Tomás, Enrique. 2015. *La musa refractada: Literatura y óptica en la España del Barroco*. Madrid: Iberoamericana Vervuert.

Garrote Pérez, Francisco. 2003. "Reflexiones en torno a la picaresca y el *Buscón* de Quevedo." *Lógos Hellenikós: Homenaje al Profesor Gaspar Morocho*. Edited by Jesús María Nieto Ibáñez. León: Universidad de León. 951–7.

Gasbarra, Shane. 1991. "'Lingua quo vadis?' Language and Community in Erasmus's *Lingua*." *Viator* 22: 343–55.

Gascón Viera, E. 1979. "La quema de los libros de don Enrique de Villena: una maniobra política y antisemítica." *Bulletin of Hispanic Studies* 56: 317–24.

Gaspariño García, Sebastián. 18 January 2012. "Amuletos de al-Andalus." http:www.amuletosdealandalus.com.

Gell, Alfred. 1998. *Art and Agency: An Anthropological Theory*. Oxford: Clarendon.

Gerbert de Montreuil. 1922, 1925, 1975. *La continuation de Perceval*. Edited by Mary Williams and Marguerite Oswald. 3 vols. Les Classiques Français du Moyen Age 20, 50, 101. Paris: Honoré Champion.

Gerli, E. Michael. 1980. "The *Ordo Commendationis Animae* and the Cid Poet." *Modern Language Notes* 95: 436–41.

Gerli, E. Michael. 1982. "Don Amor, the Devil, and the Devil's Brood: Love and the Seven Deadly Sins in the *Libro de buen amor*." *Revista de estudios hispánicos* 16 (1): 67–80.

Gerli, E. Michael. 1995. "Complicitous Laughter: Hilarity and Seduction in *Celestina*." *Hispanic Review* 63: 19–38.

Gerli, E. Michael. 2002. "The Greeks, the Romans, and the Ambiguity of Signs: *De doctrina christiana*, the Fall, and the Hermeneutics of the *Libro de buen amor*." *Bulletin of Spanish Studies* 79: 411–28.

Gerli, E. Michael. 2011. *Celestina and the Ends of Desire*. Toronto: University of Toronto Press.

Gerli, E. Michael. 2016. "Reading Error, Finding Fault: On the Uses of Heresy in the *Libro del Arcipreste*." *Reading, Performing, and Imagining the Libro del Arcipreste*. Chapel Hill: University of North Carolina Press.

Gesta Romanorum. 1959. Translated by Charles Swan and Wynnard Hooper. New York: Dover.

Gesta (Vita) Sanctæ Agnetis. *Acta Sanctorum*. 1863. Vol. 2. 68 vols. Edited by Joannes Bollandus. Paris: V. Palme. 715–18.

Gifford, D.J. 1981. "Magical Patter: The Place of Verbal Fascination in *La Celestina*." In *Mediaeval and Renaissance Studies on Spain and Portugal in Honour of P.E. Russell*, edited by F.W. Hodcroft et al., 30–7. Oxford: Society for the Study of Mediaeval Languages and Literatures.

Giles, Ryan D. 2009. *The Laughter of the Saints: Parodies of Holiness in Late Medieval and Renaissance Spain*. Toronto: University of Toronto Press.

Giles, Ryan D. 2009. "The Liberties of December and Gonzalo de Berceo's Miracle of St. Ildefonsus." *Hispanófila* 156: 1–12.

Giles, Ryan D. 2010. "A Galen for Lovers: Medical Readings of Ovid in Medieval and Early Renaissance Spain." In *Ovid in the Age of Cervantes*, edited by Frederick A. de Armas, 3–19. Toronto: University of Toronto Press.

Giles, Ryan D. 2012. "El Triunfo de Átropos en la *Celestina*." *Anales de Historia del Arte* 22: 285–94.

Gilman, Stephen. 1972. *The Spain of Fernando de Rojas: The Intellectual and Social Landscape of "La Celestina."* Princeton: Princeton University Press.

Gilo of Paris. 1997. *Historia vie hierosolimitane*. Edited by C.W. Grocock. Oxford: Clarendon.

Girón Negrón, Luis M. 2000. *Alfonso de la Torre's "Visión Deleytable": Philosophical Rationalism and the Religious Imagination in Fifteenth-Century Spain*. Leiden: Brill.

Gitlitz, David M. 2000. "Inquisition Confessions and *Lazarillo de Tormes*." *Hispanic Review* 68 (1): 53–74.

Gitlitz, David M. 2002. *Secrecy and Deceit: The Religion of the Crypto-Jews*. Albuquerque, NM: University of New Mexico Press.

Glorieux, Palémon. 1952. *Pour revaloriser Migne: tables rectificatives*. Mélanges de science religieuse 9. Cahier supplémentaire. Lille: Facultés catholiques.

Goldstein, Morris. 1950. "Toledoth Yeshu." In *Jesus in the Jewish Tradition*, 147–66. New York: Macmillan.

Gómez Moreno, Ángel. 1995. "A vueltas con Celestina-bruja y el cordón de Melibea." *Revista de Filología Española* 75: 85–104.

Gómez Moreno, Ángel. 2008. *Claves hagiográficas de la literatura española (del Cantar de mío Cid a Cervantes)*. Madrid: Iberoamericana.

González, Esteban. 1978. *Vida y hechos de Estebanillo González*. Edited by Nicholas Spadaccini and Anthony Zahareas. Clásicos Castalia 86. Madrid: Castalia.

González Gómez, José Antonio. 2013. "La Santa Muerte como el Justo Juez en el México colonial: contrucciones tridentinas y africanas." In *Magia, brujería, Idolatría y herejía en el México colonial*, 85–90. DF, México. https://www.scribd.com/doc/118161195/ Magia-Brujeria-Idolatria-y-Herejia-en-el-Mexico-Colonial.

Gordon, Richard. 1999. "Imagining Greek and Roman Magic." In *Witchcraft and Magic in Europe: Ancient Greece and Rome*, 159–266. Vol. 2. Edited by Bengt Ankarloo and Steward Clark. Philadelphia: University of Pennsylvania Press.

Gordonio, Bernardo de. 1993. *Lilio de medicina*. Edited by Brian Dutton, Jineen Krogstad, and María Nieves Sánchez. Madrid: Arcos.

Gouwens, Kenneth. 1998. *Remembering the Renaissance: Humanist Narratives of the Sack of Rome*. Leiden: Brill.

Gray Birth, Walter de, ed. 1903. *Catalogue of a Collection of Original Manuscripts Formerly Belonging to the Inquisition in the Canary Islands*. London: Blackwood.

Green, Otis H. 1958. "On Juan Ruiz's Parody of the Canonical Hours." *Hispanic Review* 26 (1): 12–34.

Green, Otis H. 1963. "Medieval Laughter." *Spain and the Western Tradition: The Castilian Mind in Literature from "El Cid" to Calderón*. 4 vols. Madison: University of Wisconsin Press. 1: 27–71.

Green, R.P.H. 1982. "The Genesis of a Medieval Textbook: The Models and Sources of the *Ecloga Theoduli*." *Viator* 13: 49–106.

Greenblatt, Stephen. 1990. "Resonance and Wonder." *Bulletin – American Academy of Arts and Sciences* 43 (4): 11–34.

Gregory. 1849. *Homiliae in Evangelia*. Patrologia Latina 76. Edited by J.P. Migne. Paris: Migne.

Gregory of Elvira. 1994. *Epithalamium sive explanatio in Canticis canticorum*. Edited by Eva Schulz-Flügel. Freiburg: Herder.

Grieve, Patricia E. 1998. "Building Christian Narrative: The Rhetoric of Knowledge, Revelation, and Interpretation in the *Libro de Apolonio*." In *The*

Book and the Magic of Reading in the Middle Ages, edited by Albrecht Classen, 149–69. New York: Taylor & Francis.

Grimm, Jacob. 1883. *Teutonic Mythology*. 3 vols. Translated by James Steven Stallybras. London: George Bell.

Grimm, Jacob. 1892. *Grimm's Fairy Tales*. Translated by Lucy Crane. New York: F.M. Lupton.

Guillaume de Lorris, and Jean de Meun. 1971. *Romance of the Rose [Roman de la rose]*. Translated by Charles Dahlberg. Princeton: Princeton University Press.

Guillaume de Lorris, and Jean de Meun. 2008. *Romance of the Rose*. Translated by Frances Horgan. Oxford: Oxford University Press.

Guthke, Siegfried Karl. 1999. *The Gender of Death: A Cultural History in Art and Literature*. Cambridge: Cambridge University Press.

Gwara, Joseph J. 2005. "The *Poema de Fernán González*, the Villamartín Tile and the Diffusion of *Cuaderna Vía* Verse." In *Historicist Essays on Hispano-Medieval Narrative in Memory of Roger M. Walker*, edited by Barry Taylor and Geoffrey West, 115–34. London: Maney.

Gwara, Joseph J. 2012. "A Possible Hebraism in *Grisel y Mirabella* and Its Implications: Old Spanish *Cultre* '(Textual) Amulet.'" *Journal of the Early Book Society* 15: 1–40.

Gwara, Joseph J., and Mary Morse. 2012. "A Birth Girdle Printed by Wynkyn de Worde." *Library* 13 (1): 33–62.

Hamilton, Michelle. 1998. "Celestina and the Daughters of Lilith." *Bulletin of Hispanic Studies* 75 (2): 153–72.

Hanrahan, Thomas. 1983. "*Lazarillo de Tormes*: Erasmian Satire or Protestant Reform?" *Hispania* 66: 333–9.

Hardison, O.B. 1965. *Christian Rite and Christian Drama in the Middle Ages: Essays in the Origin and Early History of Modern Drama*. Baltimore: Johns Hopkins University Press.

Harf-Lancner, Laurence. 2000. "Fairies." In *Encyclopedia of the Middle Ages*, edited by André Vauchez and Michael Lapidge, 526. New York: Routledge.

Haring, N.M. 1953. "A Latin Dialogue on the Doctrine of Gilbert of Poitiers." *Mediaeval Studies* 15: 243–89.

Harley, David. 1990. "Historians as Demonologists: Myth of Midwife-Witch." *Social History of Medicine* 3: 1–26.

Hastings, James, ed. 1911. "Paraclete." *Dictionary of the Bible*. 4 vols. New York: Scribners. 3: 665–8.

Hattaway, Michael. 1968. "Paradoxes of Solomon: Learning in the English Renaissance." *Journal of the History of Ideas* 29 (4): 499–530.

Hayward, Jane. 1971. "Sacred Vestments as They Developed in the Middle Ages." *Metropolitan Museum of Art Bulletin, New Series* 29 (7): 299–309.

Heffernan, Thomas. 1988. *Sacred Biography: Saints and Their Biographers in the Middle Ages*. Oxford, New York: Oxford University Press.

Heidenreich, Helmut. 1970. "Hieronymus Bosch in Some Literary Contexts." *Journal of the Warburg and Courtauld Institutes* 33: 171–99.

Heisterbach, Caesarius. 1851. *Dialogus miraculorum*. 2 vols. Edited by Joseph Strange. Cologne: Lempertz.

Henry, Hugh. 1907–14. "Agios O Theos." *The Catholic Encyclopedia*. 17 Vols. New York: Robert Appleton. 1: 211–12.

Herradón Figueroa, María Antonia. 2001. "Cintas, medidas y estadales de la Virgen (Colección del Museo Nacional de Antropología)." *Revista de Dialectologia y Tradiciones Populares* 56 (2): 33–66.

Herrero, Ana Vian. 1997. "Tranformaciones del pensamiento mágico: el conjuro amatorio en *La Celestina* y en su linaje literario." In *Cinco Siglos de Celestina: Aportaciones interpretativas*, edited by Rafael Beltrán and José Luis Canet, 209–38. Valencia: Servei de Publicacions de la Universitat de València.

Herrero, Javier. 1979. "The Ending of *Lazarillo*: The Wine against the Water." *Modern Language Notes* 93 (2): 313–19.

Herrero, Javier. 1984. "Celestina's Craft: The Devil in the Skein." *Bulletin of Hispanic Studies* 61: 343–51.

Hilka, Alfons von, ed. 1976. *Historia Alexandri Magni (Historia de preliis): Rezension J2*. Beiträge zur klassischen Philologie Heft 79. Meisenheim am Glan: Hain.

Historia Apollonii Regis Tyri. Apollonius of Tyre: Medieval and Renaissance Themes and Variations. 1991. Edited and translated by Elizabeth Archibald, 107–81. Cambridge: D.S. Brewer.

Hodges, Laura F. 1990. "Noe's Wife: Type of Eve and Wakefield Spinner." In *Equally in God's Image: Women in the Middle Ages*, edited by Julia Bolton Holloway, Constance S Wright, Joan Bechtold, 30–9. New York: Peter Lang Publishing.

Hopper, Vincent Foster. 1938. *Medieval Number Symbolism: Its Sources, Meaning and Influence on Thought and Expression*. New York: Columbia University Press.

Horas de Nuestra señora con muchos otros oficios y oraciones. 1502. Paris: Thielmam Keruer.

Hourihane, Colum. 2009. *Pontius Pilate, Anti-Semitism, and the Passion in Medieval Art*. Princeton: Princeton University Pres.

Howard, Donald R. 1966. *The Three Temptations: Medieval Man in Search of the World*. Princeton: Princeton University Press.

Howes, Laura L. 1997. *Chaucer's Gardens and the Language of Convention*. Gainesville, FL: University Press of Florida.

Hugh of St. Victor. 1854. *Eruditio didascalica. Opera omnia. Patrologia Latina 176.* Paris: Migne.

Hurwitz, Siegmund. 1992. *Lilith, the First Eve: Historical and Psychological Aspects of the Dark Feminine.* Daimon: Einsiedeln.

Idel, Moshe. 1988. *The Mystical Experience of Abraham Abulafia.* Albany: SUNY Press.

Iffland, James. 1978. *Quevedo and the Grotesque.* 2 vols. London: Tamesis.

Imirizaldu, Jesús, ed. 1977. *Monjas y beatas embaucadoras.* Madrid: Nacional.

Infantes, Víctor. 1995. "El gran hallazgo de un pequeño libro que una vez fue incunable. La *Oración de las ordenanzas de la Iglesia del Papa León III Magno.*" *Gutenberg Jahrbuch* 70: 93–101.

Isidore of Seville. 2007. *Etymologies.* Edited and translated by Stephen A. Barney et al. Cambridge: Cambridge University Press.

Isidore of Seville. 2008. *De Ecclesiasticis Officiis.* Edited and translated by Thomas L. Knoebel. Mahwah, NJ: Paulist Pres.

Jackson, William. 1877. *History of Confirmation.* London, Oxford: James Parker.

Jager, Eric. 2000. *The Book of the Heart.* Chicago: University of Chicago Press.

Jay, Martin. 1999. "Must Justice Be Blind? The Challenge of Images to the Law." In *Law and the Image: The Authority of Art and the Aesthetics of Law,* edited by Costas Douzinas and Lynda Nead, 19–35. Chicago: University of Chicago Press.

Jeffrey, David L, ed. 1992. *Dictionary of Biblical Tradition in English Literature.* Grand Rapids: Eerdmans.

Jerome. 1570. *Vita Pauli primi eremitae [Vitae Patrum]. De probatis sanctorum historiis.* Edited by Laurentius Surius. Cologne: Agrippinae.

Jerome. 1845. *Commentaria in Matthaeum.* Patrologia latina 26. Edited by J.P. Migne. Paris: Migne.

Jerome. 1845. *Epistolae.* Patrologia Latina 22. Edited by J.P. Migne. Paris: Migne.

Jerome. 1893. *Vita Pauli primi eremitae [Vitae Patrum].* Translated by W.H. Fremantle, G. Lewis, and W.G. Martley. *Nicene and Post-Nicene Fathers, Second Series.* Vol. 6. 14 vols. Edited by Philip Schaff and Henry Wace. Buffalo: Christian Literature Publishing.

Jerome. 2008. *Commentary on Matthew.* Translated by Thomas P. Scheck. Fathers of the Church 117. Washington DC: Catholic University of American Press.

Joachim of Fiore. 1940. *Il libro delle figure [Liber Figurarum].* Edited by Leone Tondell. Torino: Società Editrice Internazionale.

Johnson, Barbara. 2008. *Persons and Things.* Cambridge, MA: Harvard University Press.

Jolly, Karen. 2002. "Medieval Magic: Definitions, Beliefs, Practices." In *Witchcraft and Magic in Europe: The Middle Ages*, 1–66. Vol. 3. Edited by Bengt Ankarloo and Stuart Clark. Philadelphia: University of Pennsylvania Press.

Joost-Gaugier, Christiane L. 2006. *Measuring Heaven: Pythagoras and His Influence on Thought and Art in Antiquity and the Middle Ages*. Ithaca: Cornell University Press.

Josephus, Flavius. 2006. *Jewish Antiquities*. Translated by William Whiston. Hertfordshire: Wordsworth.

Joset, Jacques. 2004. "El pensamiento de Juan Ruiz." In *Actas del Primer Congreso Internacional del Centro para la Edición de los Clásicos Españoles*, edited by Francisco Toro Ceballos, Bienvenido Morros Mestres, 105–28. Alcalá: Ayuntamiento de Alcalá La Real.

Julien, Philippe. 1994. *Jacques Lacan's Return to Freud: The Real, the Symbolic, and the Imaginary*. Translated by Devra Beck Simiu. New York: New York University Press.

Kagan, Richard L. 1981. *Lawsuits and Litigants in Castile, 1500–1700*. Chapel Hill: University of North Carolina Press.

Kagan, Richard L. 1990. *Lucrecia's dreams: Politics and Prophecy in Sixteenth-Century Spain*. Berkeley: University of California Press.

Kallendorf, Hilaire. 2003. *Exorcism and Its Texts: Subjectivity in Early Modern Literature of England and Spain*. Toronto: University of Toronto Press.

Kamen, Henry. 1985. *Inquisition and Society in Spain in the Sixteenth and Seventeenth Centuries*. Bloomington: Indiana University Press.

Keller, John K., and Richard P. Kinkade. 1983. "*Iconography and Literature: Alfonso Himself in* Cantiga 209." *Hispania* 66 (3): 348–52.

Kelly, Kathleen Coyne. 2000. *Performing Virginity and Testing Chastity in the Middle Ages*. London, New York: Routledge.

Kennedy, Kirstin. 2004. "Alfonso's Miraculous Book: Patronage, Politics, and Performance in the *Cantigas de Santa Maria*." In *The Appearances of Medieval Rituals: The Play of Construction and Modification*, edited by Nils Holger Petersen et al., 199–212. Brepols: Turnhout.

Kermode, Frank. 2000. *A Sense of Ending: Studies in the Theory of Fiction*. Rpt. Oxford: Oxford University Press.

Kieckhefer, Richard. 1989. *Magic in the Middle Ages*. Cambridge: Cambridge University Press.

Kim, H.C., ed. 1973. *The Gospel of Nicodemus: Gesta Salvatoris*. Toronto: Pontifical Institute of Mediaeval Studies.

Kortekaas, G.A.A. 2004. *The Story of Apollonius, King of Tyre*. Leiden, Boston: Brill.

Kortekaas, G.A.A. 2007. *Commentary on the "Historia Apollonii Regis Tyri."* Leiden, Boston: Brill.

Labarta, Ana. 1983. "Supersticiones moriscas." *Awrāq* 6: 161–90.

Lamb, Úrsula, ed. 1963. "La Inquisición en Canarias y un libro de magia del siglo XVI." *El museo canario* 24: 113–44.

Lanman, Johnathan T. 1981. "The Religious Symbolism of the T in T-O Map." *Cartographica* 18 (4): 18–22.

Latini, Brunetto. 1982. *The Medieval Castilian Bestiary: From Brunetto Latini's "Tesoro."* Edited by Spurgeon Baldwin. Exeter: University of Exeter Press.

Latour, Bruno. 1993. *We Have Never Been Modern.* Cambridge, MA: Harvard University Press.

Law, Vivien. 2006. *Wisdom, Authority and Grammar in the Seventh Century.* Cambridge: Cambridge University Press.

Lazure, Guy. 2007. "Possessing the Sacred: Monarchy and Identity in Philip II's Relic Collection at the Escorial." *Renaissance Quarterly* 60 (1): 58–93.

Lazarillo de Tormes. 1974. Edited by Alberto Blecua. 2nd ed. Clásicos Castalia 58. Madrid: Castalia.

Lazarillo de Tormes. 1987. Edited by Francisco Rico. 2nd ed. Letras hispánicas 44. Madrid: Cátedra.

Leclerq, H. 1907–22. "Abgar, Legend of." *The Catholic Encyclopedia.* 17 vols. New York: Robert Appleton Company. 1:42–3.

Lecoy, Félix. 1938. *Recherches sur le "Libro de buen amor."* Paris: Librairie E. Droz.

Lee, Harold. 1974. "*Scrutamini Scripturas*: Joachimist Themes and *Figurae* in the Early Religious Writing of Arnald of Villanova." *Journal of the Warburg and Courtauld Institutes* 37: 33–56.

León, Luis de. 1987. *La perfecta casada.* Edited by Mercedes Etreros. Madrid: Taurus.

León, Luis de. 1997. *De los nombres de Cristo.* Edited by Cristóbal Cuevas. Letras hispánicas 59. 6th ed. Madrid: Cátedra.

Levisi, Margarita. 1963. "Hieronymus Bosch y los *Sueños* de Francisco de Quevedo." *Filología* 9: 163–200.

Lewis, Suzanne. 1987. *The Art of Matthew Paris in the "Chronica majora."* Berkeley: University of California Press.

Libro de Alexandre. 1988. Edited by Jesús Cañas. Letras hispánicas 280. Madrid: Cátedra.

Libro de Apolonio. 1987. Edited by Carmen Monedero. Madrid: Castalia.

Lida de Malkiel, María Rosa. 1940. "Notas para la interpretación, influencia, fuentes y texto del *Libro de buen amor.*" *Revista de Filología Hispánica* 2: 105–50.

Lida de Malkiel, María Rosa. 1957. "Alejandro en Jerúsalen." *Romance Studies* 10: 185–96.

Lindquist, Sherry C.M. 2012. "The Meanings of Nudity in Medieval Art: An Introduction." In *The Meanings of Nudity in Medieval Art*, edited by Sherry C.M. Lindquist, 1–46. Burlington, VT: Ashgate.

Llull, Ramon. 2006. *Cent noms de Déu*. Alicante: Biblioteca Virtual Joan Lluís Vives. http://www.cervantesvirtual.com/obra/cent-noms-de-deu-manuscrit--0/

Lochrie, Karma. 1997. "Mystical Acts, Queer Tendencies." In *Constructing Medieval Sexuality*, edited by Karma Lochrie, Peggy McCracken, and James A. Schultz, 180–200. Minneapolis: University of Minnesota Press.

Lombard, Peter. 2007. *The Sentences*. Translated by Giulio Silano. Toronto: Pontifical Institute of Mediaeval Studies.

Lope de Vega. 1618. *La octava maravilla. Decima parte de las comedias de Lope de Vega Carpio*. Madrid: Juan de la Cuesta. fols. 151v–176v.

Lope de Vega. 1901. *Servir a señor discreto. Obras escogidas*. 4 vols. Madrid: Hernando y compañía. 4: 69–91.

Lope de Vega. 1902. *Los peligros de la ausencia. Obras escogidas*. 4 vols. Madrid: Hernando y compañía. 2: 405–24.

Lope de Vega. 1985. *El niño inocente de la Guardia*. Edited by Anthony J. Farrell. London: Tamesis.

López Álvarez, Ana María, ed. 1986. *Catálogo del Museo Sefardí, Toledo*. Madrid: Ministerio de Cultura.

Lopez de Ayala, Pero. 1987. *Rimado de Palacio*. Edited by Germán Orduna. Clásicos Castalia 156. Madrid: Castalia.

López de Ubeda, Francisco. 2011. *La pícara Justina*. Edited by Luc Torres. Madrid: Castalia.

López-Ríos, Santiago. 2012. "'Señor, por holgar con el cordón no querrás gozar de Melibea': la parodia del culto a las reliquias en la *Celestina*." *Modern Language Notes* 127: 190–207.

Luber, Aaron Krista. 1999. *Text and Image in Ulrich Molitor's "De lamiis et phitonicis mulieribus."* Tempe: Arizona State University Press.

Ludolph of Saxony. 1551. *Vita Christi Cartuxano*. 4 vols. Translated by Ambrosio Montesino. Sevilla: Casa de Jacobo Cromberger.

Macdonald, Fiona. 2009. *The Plague and Medicine in the Middle Ages*. Charlotte, NC: Baker and Taylor.

Mackay, Angus. 1983. "Anti-Semitism in the *Cantigas de Santa Maria*." *Bulletin of Hispanic Studies* 61: 189–99.

Mackay, Angus. 1998. "The Whores of Babylon." In *Love, Religion, and Politics in Fifteenth Century Spain*, by Ian Macpherson and Angus MacKay, 179–87. Leiden: Brill.

Macpherson, Ian. 1998. "Solomon's Knot." In *Love, Religion, and Politics in Fifteenth Century Spain*, by Ian Macpherson and Angus MacKay, 205–22. Leiden: Brill.

Marbode of Rennes. 1977. *De lapidibus*. Translated by C.W. King and John M. Riddle. Wiesbaden: Steiner.

Martin of Braga. 1950. *De Correctione Rusticorum. Opera Omnia*. Edited by Claude W. Barlow. New Haven: Yale UP. 159–203.

Martín, Raimundo. 1651. *Pugio Fidei*. Paris: apud Ioannem Henault.

Martín Cebrián, Modesto. 2012. "Las rogativas." *Revista de folklore* 32 (361): 38–51.

Martínez Enamorado, Virgilio. 2006. "El amuleto de los 'Nombres más bellos de Allāh' hallado en Alberite (Villamartín, Cádiz)." *Almajar* 3: 27–36.

Martínez de Toledo, Alonso. 1970. *Arcipreste de Talavera o Corbacho*. Edited by J. González Muela. Clásicos Castalia 24. Madrid: Castalia.

Mass, Anthony. 1907–22. "Jehovah (Yahweh)." *The Catholic Encyclopedia*. 17 vols. New York: Robert Appleton Company. 8: 267–8.

Matter, Ann E. 1990. *The Voice of My Beloved: The Song of Songs in Western Medieval Christianity*. Philadelphia: University of Pennsylvania Press.

Maurer, Armand A. 1979. "The Sacred Tetragrammaton in Medieval Thought." *Actas del V Congreso Internacional de Filosofía Medieval*. Madrid: Editora nacional. 2: 975–83.

Maurer, Armand A. 1990. *Being and Knowing: Studies in Thomas Aquinas and Late Medieval Philosophy*. Toronto: Pontifical Institute of Mediaeval Studies.

Mayo, Thomas B. de. 2007. *The Demonology of William of Auvergne: By Fire and Sword*. New York: Edwin Mellen.

Mazzio, Carla. 1998. "Sins of the Tongue in Early Modern England." *Modern Language Studies* 28 (3): 95–124.

McAvoy, Liz Herbert. 2003. "Monstrous Masculinities in Julian of Norwich's *A Revelation of Love* and *The Book of Margery Kempe*." In *The Monstrous Middle Ages*, 55–74. Edited by Bettina Bildhauer and Robert Mills. Toronto: University of Toronto Press.

McInnis-Domínguez, Meghan. 2011. "The Diseasing Healer: Francisco Delicado's Infectious *La Lozana andaluza*."*eHumanista* 17: 311–33.

Meaney, Audrey L. 1981. *Anglo-Saxon Amulets and Curing Stones. BAR British*. Vol. 96. Oxford: British Archaeological Reports.

Medina, Alfonso. 2008. *Villancicos barrocos en la catedral de Jaén*. Jaén: Blanca.

Meiss, Millard. 1971. "Atropos-Mors: Observations on a Rare Early Humanist Image." In *Florilegium historiale: Essays Presented to Wallace K. Ferguson*, edited by J.G. Rowe and W.H. Stockdale, 152–9. Toronto: University of Toronto Press.

Mena, Juan de. 1997. *Laberinto de Fortuna*. Edited by Maxim P.A.M. Kerkhof. Clásicos Castalia 223. Madrid: Castalia.

Menaldi, Veronica. Oct. 2015. "Enchanting Go-Betweens: Mediated Love Magic Within and Without *El Libro de buen amor*." Unpublished conference paper. "The Cleric's Craft" Symposium, El Paso, TX.

Menéndez Pidal, Ramón. 1905. "Razón de amor con los denuestos del agua y el vino." *Revue hispanique* 13: 1–32.

Menéndez y Pelayo, Marcelino. 1992. *Historia de los heterodoxos españoles*. 3 vols. Madrid: CSIC.

Michael, Ian. 1970. *The Treatment of Classical Material in the "Libro de Alexandre."* *Publications of the Faculty of Arts of the University of Manchester 17*. Manchester: Manchester University Press.

Michael, Ian. 1982. "Typological Problems in Medieval Alexander Literature." In *The Medieval Alexander Legend and Romance Epic: Essays in Honour of David J.A. Ross*, edited by Peter Noble, Lucie Polak, and Claire Isoz, 131–47. Millwood, NY: Kraus International.

Micó, José María. 2003. "Introducción." In *Guzmán de Alfarache*, edited by José María Micó, Letras hispánicas, 86–7. Madrid: Cátedra.

Miller, Sarah Alison. 2010. *Medieval Monstrosity and the Female Body*. New York: Routledge.

Mone, Franz Joseph. 1853–5. *Hymni Latini medii aevi*. 3 vols. Friburgi Brisgoviae: Sumptibus Herder.

Montesino, Ambrosio de. 1608. *Epístolas y enangelios para todo el año*. Barcelona: Miguel Menescal.

Morel-Fatio, Alfred. 1987. "Textes castillans inédits due XIII." *Romania* 16: 364–82.

Morreale, Margarita. 1956. "Quevedo y el Bosco: Una apostilla a los *Sueños*." *Clavileño* 7: 40–4.

Morros Mestres, Bienvenido. 2004. "*La Celestina* como *remedium amoris*." *Hispanic Review* 72 (1): 77–99.

Murillo, Jesús Cañas. 1996. "Un Lazarillo de Medina del Campo: peculiaridades y variantes de una edición desconocida de 1554." *Anuario de estudios filológicos* 19: 91–134.

Musgrave, J.C. 1976. "Tarsiana and Juglaría in the *Libro de Apolonio*." In *Medieval Studies Presented to Rita Hamilton*, edited by A.D. Deyermond, 129–38. London: Tamesis.

Nepaulsingh, Colbert I. 1986. "The Song of Songs and the Unity of the *Razón de amor*." *Towards a History of Literary Composition in Medieval Spain*. Toronto: University of Toronto Press. 41–62.

Névelon, Jean Le. 1931. *La venjance Alixandre*. Edited by Edward Billings Ham. Princeton: Princeton University Press.

Newman, Barbara. 2003. *God and the Goddesses: Vision, Poetry, and Belief in the Middle Ages*. Philadelphia: University of Pennsylvania Press.

Ngien, Dennis. 2005. *Apologetic for Filioque in Medieval Theology*. Bletchley: Paternoster.

Niccoli, Ottavia. 1990. *Prophecy and People in Renaissance Italy*. Princeton: Princeton University Press.

Nieremberg, Juan Eusebio. 1665. *La imitación de Cristo y menosprecio del mundo de Tomás de Kempis.* León: Huguetan-Ravaud.

Nirenberg, David. 2006. "Figures of Thought and Figures of Flesh: 'Jews' and 'Judaism' in Late-Medieval Spanish Poetry and Politics." *Speculum* 81: 398–426.

Norris, Richard A. 2003. *The Song of Songs: Interpreted by Early Christian and Medieval Commentators*. Grand Rapids: Eerdmans.

Nowlin, Steele. 2005. "Narratives of Incest and Incestuous Narrative: Memory, Process, and the *Confessio Amantis*'s "Middel Weie.'" *Journal of Medieval and Early Modern Studies* 35 (2): 217–44.

O'Callaghan, Joseph F. 1998. *Alfonso X and the "Cantigas de Santa Maria": A Poetic Biography*. Leiden; Boston: Brill.

Office of the Blessed Virgin Marie [Officium Beatae Mariae], in Latin and English. 1599. Antwerp: Arnold Conings.

Ogden, Daniel. 1999. "Binding Spells: Curse Tablets and Voodoo Dolls in the Greek and Roman Worlds." In *Witchcraft and Magic in Europe: Ancient Greece and Rome*, Vol. 2, edited by Bengt Ankarloo and Stuart Clark, 1–96. Philadelphia: University of Pennsylvania Press.

Osternacher, Johannes, ed. 1902. *Theoduli Eclogam*. Urfahr-Linz: Kollegium Petrinum.

Ovid. 2003. *Carmina amatoria: Amores, Medicamina faciei femineae, Ars amatoria, Remedia amoris*. Edited by Antonio Ramírez de Verger. München: Saur.

Padilla, Juan de. 1516. *El Retablo de la vida de Cristo*. Sevilla: Cromberger.

Palmireno, Juan Lorenzo. 1566. *Fragmentum ex Comœdia Octavia. Rhetoricę Laurentii Palmyreni: Tertia et ultima pars*. Valencia: J. Mey. 117–37.

Parker, Patricia. 1987. *Literary Fate Ladies: Rhetoric, Gender, Property*. London: Methuen.

Parks, M.B. 1992. *Pause and Effect: Punctuation in the West*. Aldershot, UK: Scolar.

Partner, Peter. 1980. *Renaissance Rome 1500–1559: A Portrait of a Society*. Berkeley: University of California Pres.

Paulo, Amílcar. 1985. *Os judeus secretos em Portugal*. Lisboa: Labirinto.

Patai, Raphael. 1977. *The Jewish Mind*. Detroit: Wayne State University Press.

Peachy, Frederic, ed. 1957. *Clareti Engimata [The Latin Riddles of Claret]*. Folklore Studies 7. Berkeley: University of California Press.

Pedrosa, José Manuel. 2000. *Entre la magia y la religión: Oraciones, conjuros, ensalmos*. Biblioteca mítica 2. Oiartzun, Guipúzkoa: Sendoa.

Perault, William. 1519. *Summa virtutum ac vitiorum*. [Summa de vitiis et virtutibus] Paris: Venundantur Parisius.

Pereira-Muro, Carmen. 2010. "When an Image is Not Worth a Thousand Words: Divergent Codes of Representation of Death and the Afterlife in Francisco de Quevedo's Satirical Works and the Art of Hieronymus Bosch." *Hispanic Issues On Line* 7: 126–43.

Pérez, José Hernando. 1986. "Nuevos datos para el estudio de *Poema de Fernán González*." *Boletín de la Real Academia Española* 66: 135–52.

Pérez, José Hernando. 1995. *Hispano Diego García en la interpretacion del ostrakon de Villamartin sobre el "Poema de Fernán González."* Burgos: Facultad de Teologia del Norte de España.

Pérez, Martín. 2002. *Libro de confesiones. Libro de las confesiones: una radiografía de la sociedad medieval española.* Edited by Antonio García y García, Bernardo Alonso Rodríguez, and Francisco Cantelar Rodríguez. Madrid: Biblioteca de Autores Cristianos.

Perugini, Carla. 1999. "Contaminaciones ideológicas en *La lozana andaluza*." *Ínsula: revista de letras y ciencias humanas* 635: 10–11.

Perugini, Carla. 2000. "Las fuentes iconográficas de la *Editio princeps* de la *Lozana andaluza*." *Salina: Revista de la Facultat de Lletres de Tarragona* 14: 65–72.

Peters, Edward. 1978. "The Systematic Condemnation of Magic in the Thirteenth Century." In *The Magician, the Witch and the Law*, 85–109. Philadelphia: University of Pennsylvania Press.

Petrarca, Francesco. 1512. *Los seys triunfos: de toscano sacados en castellano.* Translated by Antonio de Obregon. Logrono: Arnao Guillen de Brocar.

Petrarca, Francesco. 1976. *Lyric Poems: The Rime Sparse and Other Lyrics.* Edited and translated by Robert M. Durling. Cambridge, MA: Harvard University Press.

Petrarca, Francesco. 1984. *Trionfi.* Milan: Rizzoli.

Petrus Comestor. 1855. *Historia Scholastica.* Patrologia Latina 198. Edited by J.P. Migne. Paris: Migne.

Pickford, T.E. 1975. "Apollonius of Tyre as Greek Myth and Christian Mystery." *Neophilologus* 59 (4): 599–609.

Pineda, Juan. 1963–4. *Diálogos familiares de la agricultura cristiana.* 5 vols. Edited by Juan Meseguer Fernández. Madrid: Atlas.

Piñero, Pedro M., ed. 1988. *Segunda parte del Lazarillo.* Edited by Pedro M. Piñero Ramírez. Madrid: Cátedra.

Pinet, Simone. 2016. *The Task of the Cleric: Cartography, Translation, and Economics in Thirteenth-Century Iberia.* Toronto: University of Toronto Press.

Pinto Crespo, Virgilio. 1983. *Inquisición y control ideológico en la España del siglo XVI.* Madrid: Taurus.

Pingree, David, ed. 1986. *Picatrix: The Latin Version of the Ghayat al-hakim.* London: Warburg Institute.

Pizan, Christine de. 1970. *The Episte of Othéa*. Translated by Stephen Scrope. Edited by Curt F. Bühler. Early English Text Society 264. London: Oxford University Press.

Poema de Fernán González. 1983. Edited by Juan Victorio. Madrid: Cátedra.

Poema de mío Cid. 1980. Edited by Ian Michael. 2nd ed. Madrid: Castalia.

Pohle, Joseph. 1907–14. "Impanation." *The Catholic Encyclopedia*. 17 vols. New York: Robert Appleton. 7.694–5.

Prado-Vilar, Francisco. 2011. "*Iudeus sacer*: Life, Law and Identity in the 'State of Exception' Called 'Marian Miracle'." In *Judaism and Christian Art: Aesthetic Anxieties from the Catacombs to Colonialism*, edited by Herbert L. Kessler and David Nirenberg, 115–42. University of Pennsylvania Press.

Presilla, Marcel. 1987. "The Image of Death in the 'Cantigas de Santa Maria.'" In *Studies on the "Cantigas de Santa Maria": Art, Music and Poetry*, edited by Israel J. Katz and John E. Keller, 432–40. Madison: Hispanic Seminary of Medieval Studies.

Price, Percival. 1983. *Bells and Man*. Oxford: Oxford University Press.

Price, R.M. 1971. "On Religious Parody in the *Buscón*." *Modern Language Notes* 86 (2): 273–9.

Prudentius, Aurelius. 1950. *Obras completas de Aurelio Prudencio*. Translated by D. José Guillén. Edited by Isidoro Rodríguez. Madrid: La Católica.

Pseudo-Chrysostom. 1862. *Opus imperfectum in Matthaeum*. Opera Omnia. Patrologia cursus completus, series Graeca 56. Edited by J.P. Migne. Paris.

Pseudo-Chrysostom. 2010. *Incomplete Commentary on Matthew*. 2 vols. Edited by Thomas C. Oden. Translated by James A. Kellerman. Downer's Grove, IL: InterVarsity Press.

Pseudo-Dionysius. 1987. *The Complete Works*. Translated by C.E. Rolt and J. Jones. New York: Paulist Press.

Purcell, William M. 1993. "Eberhard the German and the Labyrinth of Learning: Grammar, Poesy, Rhetoric, and Pedagogy in *Laborintus*." *Rhetorica* 11 (2): 95–118.

Quevedo, Francisco de. 1963. *Obras completas I*. Edited by J.M. Blecua. Barcelona: Planeta.

Quevedo, Francisco de. 1966. *Política de Dios, govierno de Christo*. Edited by James O. Crosby. Urbana: University Illinois Press.

Quevedo, Francisco de. 1975. *La hora de todos*. Edited by Luisa López-Grigera. Clásicos Castalia 67. Madrid: Castalia.

Quevedo, Francisco de. 1980. *Historia de la vida del Buscón*. Edited by Domingo Ynduráin. Letras hispánicas 124. Madrid: Cátedra.

Quevedo, Francisco de. 1985. *Virtud militante*. Edited by Alfonso Rey. Santiago de Compostela: Universidade de Santiago de Compostela.

Quevedo, Francisco de. 1993. *Sueños y discursos*. Edited by James O. Crosby. Clásicos Castalia 199. Madrid: Castalia.

Reeves, Marjorie. 1969. *The Influence of Prophecy in the Later Middle Ages: A Study in Joachimism*. Oxford: Clarcendon.

"Remedia contra toda peste." 18th cent. Spanish History Box, MSS. Lilly Library, Indiana University. Fols. 21–2.

Renard, John. 2008. *Friends of God: Islamic Images of Piety, Commitment and Servanthood*. Berkeley: University of California Press.

Reusch, F.H., ed. 1961. *Die Indices Librorum prohibitorum des sechzehnten Jahrhunderts*. Nieuwkoop, Graaf.

Reynolds, Suzanne. 1996. *Medieval Reading: Grammar, Rhetoric and the Classical Text*. Cambridge: Cambridge University Pres.

Ribadeneyra, Pedro de. 1616. *Flos sanctorum*. 3 vols. Madrid: Luis Sánchez.

Ricard, Robert. 1954. "Du roi D. Duarte de Portugal à Ciro Alegría: *La Oración del Justo Juez*." *Bulletin Hispanique* 56 (4): 415–23.

Ricard, Robert. 1966. "Pour l'étude de la priére magique du 'Justo Juge' dans le monde hispano-portugais." *Revista de Etnografía* 11: 33–46.

Ricard, Robert. 1973. "Las armas del cristiano en el *Libro de buen amor*." In *El Arcipreste de Hita. El libro, el autor, la tierra, la época*, edited by M. Criado de Val, 95–103. Actas del I Congreso Internacional sobre el Arcipreste de Hita. Barcelona: S.E.R.E.S.A.

Richard of Saint-Victor. 1855. *De Trinitate. Patrologia Latina 196.16*. Edited by J.P. Migne. Paris: Migne.

Rico, Francisco. 1985. "La clerecía del *mester*." *Hispanic Review* 53 (1–2): 1–23, 127–50.

Rico, Francisco. 1999. "Preliminar." In *La Cazzaria*, edited by G.M. Capelli, i–x. Mérida: Editorial Regional de Extematura.

Rigg, A.G. 2008. "The Eclogue of Theodulus: A Translation." University of Toronto Centre for Medieval Studies. http://medieval.utoronto.ca/ylias/web-content/theoduli.html.

Riehle, Wolfgang. 1981. *The Middle English Mystics*. Translated by Bernard Strandring. London: Routledge.

Ringwald, Chistopher D. 2007. *A Day Apart: How Jews, Christians, and Muslims Find Faith, Freedom, and Joy on the Sabbath*. Oxford: Oxford University Press.

Río, Martín del. 1991. *La magia demoníaca: libro II de las Disquisiciones mágicas*. Edited by Jesús Moya. Madrid: Hiperión.

Rodríguez-Puértolas, Julio, ed. 1968. *Cancionero*. Madrid: Espasa-Calpe.

Rodríguez Villa, Antonio. 1875. *Memorias para la historia del asalto y saqueo de Roma en 1527*. Madrid: La biblioteca de instrucción y recreo.

Rojas, Fernando. 1994. *La Celestina*. Edited by Dorothy Severin. Madrid: Cátedra.

Rowe, Nina. 2011. *The Jew, the Cathedral, and the Medieval City: Synagoga and Ecclesia in the Thirteenth-Century*. Cambridge: Cambridge University Press.

Rubin, Miri. 2004. *Gentile Tales: The Narrative Assault on Late Medieval Jews*. Philadelphia: University of Pennsylvania Press.

Rubin, Miri. 2009. *Mother of God: A History of the Virgin Mary*. New Haven: Yale University Press.

Ruiz García, Elisa. 1999. "Estudio material del manuscrito 1 de Barcarrota." In *La Cazzaria* by Antonio Vignali, xl–xli. Edited by Guido M. Cappellini. Translated by Elisa Ruiz García. Mérida: Editora Regional de Extremadura.

Ruiz, Juan. 1965. *Libro de buen amor*. Edited by Manuel Criado de Val and Eric W. Naylor. Madrid: Consejo Superior de Investigaciones Científicas.

Ruiz, Juan. 1967. *Libro de buen amor*. Edited by Joan Corominas. Biblioteca románica hispánica 4. Textos 4. Madrid: Gredos.

Ruiz, Juan. 1988. *Libro de buen amor*. Edited by G.B. Gybbon-Monypenny. Clásicos Castalia 161. Madrid: Castalia.

Ruiz, Juan. 2001. *Libro de buen amor*. Edited by Alberto Blecua. Clásicos y modernos 7. Barcelona: Crítica.

Ruiz de Alarcón, Hernando. 1984. *Treatise on the Heathen Superstitions and Customs That Today Live Among the Indians Native to New Spain [Tratado de las supersticiones de los naturales de esta Nueva España]*. Edited and translated by J. Richard Andrews and Ross Hassig. Norman, OK: University of Oklahoma Press.

Russell, Peter E. 1963. "La magia como tema integral de *La Celestina*." *Studia philologica: homenaje a Dámaso Alonso*.3 vols. Madrid: Gredos. 3: 337–54.

Russell, Peter E. 1978. "La oración de doña Jimena (*Poema de mío Cid*, vv. 325–367)." In *Temas de "La Celestina" y otros estudios, del "Cid" al "Quijote,"* 113–58. Barcelona: Ariel.

Ryan, Michael L. 2011. *A Kingdom of Stargazers: Astrology and Authority in the Late Medieval Crown of Aragon*. Cornell: Cornell University Press.

Sáenz-López Pérez, Sandra. 2014. *The Beatus Maps: The Revelation of the World in the Middle Ages*. Translated by Peter Krakenberger and Gerry Coldham. Burgos: Gil de Siloé

Sahlin, Claire L. 2001. *Birgitta of Sweden and the Voice of Prophecy*. Woodbridge, Suffolk; Rochester, NY: Boydell Press.

Sainz de la Maza, Carlos. 1992. "El *Toledot Yeshu* castellano en el maestre Alfonso de Valladolid." In *Actas del II Congreso Internacional de la Asociación Hispánica de Literatura Medieval,* edited by José Manuel Lucía Megías, Paloma Gracia Alonso, and Carmen Martín Daza, 2:797–805. Alcalá: U Alcalá.

Salas, Xavier de. 1943. *El Bosco en la literatura española*. Barcelona: J. Sabater.

Salomon, Herman Prins. 1998. "Crypto-Judaism or Inquisitorial Deception?" *Jewish Quarterly Review (Philadelphia, Pa.)* 89 (2): 131–54.

Salvador Martínez, H. 2010. *Alfonso X, the Learned: A Biography.* Translated by Odile Cisneros. Leiden: Brill.

Sánchez de Badajoz, Diego. 1970. *Farsa del molinero.* Diccionario bibliográfico de pliegos sueltos poéticos (siglo XVI). Edited by Antonio Rodríguez-Moñino. Madrid: Castalia. 85–6.

Sansi, Roger. 2011. "Sorcery and Fetishism in the Modern Atlantic." In *Sorcery in the Black Atlantic,* edited by Luis Nicolau Parés and Roger Sansi, 19–39. Chicago: University of Chicago Press.

Santa Cruz, Melchior de. 1997. *Floresta española.* Edited by María Pilar Cuarteto and Maxime Chevalier. Barcelona: Crítica.

Santillana, Iñigo López de Mendoza. 1976. *La comedieta de Ponza.* Edited by Maximiliaan Paul Adriaan Maria Kerkhof. Groningen: Rijksuniversiteit te Groningen.

Scannell, Thomas. 1908. "Confirmation." In *The Catholic Encyclopedia.* 17 vols. New York: Robert Appleton Company. 4.23–4.

Scarborough, Connie L. 2011. "Sexual Imagery as Unifying Factor in *Razón de amor y los denuestos del agua y el vino.*" *Hispanic Research Journal* 12 (3): 207–20.

Schaff, Philip. 1919. *The Creeds of Christendom.* 6th ed. rev. New York, London: Harper and Bros.

Secret, François. 1959. "Pedro Ciruelo: Critique de la kabbala et de son usage par les chrétiens." *Safarad* 19:49–50.

Serrano Mangas, Fernando. 2004. *El secreto de los Peñaranda: el universo judeoconverso de la biblioteca de Barcarrota, siglos XVI y XVII.* Huelva: Universidad Huelva.

Shakespeare, William. 1975. *Macbeth. The Complete Works.* New York: Gramercy.

Shipley, George. 1982. "A Case of Functional Obscurity: The Master Tambourine-Painter of *Lazarillo,* 'Tratado' VI." *Modern Language Notes* 97: 225–53.

Silva, Feliciano de. 1988. *Segunda comedia de Celestina.* Edited by Consolación Baranda. Madrid: Cátedra.

Singer, Isidore et al. 1901–6. "Amulet." *Jewish Encyclopedia.* 12 vols. New York: Funk and Wagnalls. 1.546–50.

Singer, Isidore et al. 1901–6. "Phylacteries." *Jewish Encyclopedia.* 12 vols. New York: Funk and Wagnalls. 10.21–8.

Singer, Isidore et al., eds. 1901–6. "Names of God." *Jewish Encyclopedia.* 12 vols. New York: Funk and Wagnalls. 9.160–5.

Skemer, Don. 2006. *Binding Words: Textual Amulets in the Middle Ages.* University Park: Pennsylvania State University Press.

Stallybrass, Peter. 1986. "Patriarchal Territories: The Body Enclosed." In *Rewriting the Renaissance: The Discourses of Sexual Difference in Early Modern Europe,* edited by Margaret W. Ferguson, Maureen Quilligan, and Nancy J. Vickers, 123–42. Chicago: University of Chicago Press.

Steffens, Karl von, ed. 1975. *Die "Historia de preliis Alexandri Magni": Rezension J3.* Meisenheim am Glan: A. Hain.

Stewart, Dana E. 2003. *Arrow of Love: Optics, Gender, and Subjectivity in Medieval Love Poetry.* Bucknell: Bucknell University Press.

Stock, Brian. 1996. *Augustine the Reader: Meditation, Self-Knowledge, and the Ethics of Interpretation.* Cambridge, MA: Harvard University Press.

Stolleis, Michael. 2009. *The Eye of the Law: Two Essays on Legal History.* New York: Birkbeck Law.

Stresau, Christine R. 1977. *"La gran conquista de ultramar:* Its Sources and Composition." PhD diss. University of North Carolina.

Surtz, Ronald E. 1980. "The *Libro de Apolonio* and Medieval Hagiography." *Medioevo Romanzo* 7: 328–41.

Swanton, Michael. 1970. *The Dream of the Rood.* Manchester: Manchester University Press.

Symphosius. 1928. *The Enigmas.* Edited and translated by Raymond Theodore Ohl. Philadelphia: Published Dissertation.

Taglia, Kathryn. 2001. "Delivering a Christian Identity: Midwives in Northern French Synodal Legislation, c. 1200–1500." In *Religion and Medicine in the Middle Ages,* edited by Peter Biller and Joseph Ziegler, 77–90. Woodbridge, UK: York Medieval Press.

Taylor, Andrew. 2002. *Textual Situations: Three Medieval Manuscripts and Their Readers.* Philadelphia: University of Pennsylvania Press.

Taylor, Archer. 1948. *The Literary Riddle before 1600.* Berkeley: University of California Press.

Tertullian. 1917. *Apologeticus.* Cambridge: Cambridge University Press.

Teske, Roland J. 1991. *On Genesis: Two Books on Genesis against the Manichees.* Washington, DC: Catholic University Press.

Thomas, Keith. 1991. *Religion and the Decline of Magic.* New York: Penguin.

Thompson, B. Bussell, and J.K. Walsh. 1988. "The Mercedarian's Shoes (Perambulations on the Fourth *Tratado* of *Lazarillo de Tormes*)." *Modern Language Notes* 103 (2): 440–8.

Thompson, Stith. 1977. *The Folktale.* Berkeley: University of California Press.

Thorp, Nigel, ed. 1992. *Chanson de Jérusalem.* Vol. 4. The Old French Crusade Cycle. 9 vols. Tuskaloosa: University of Alabama Press.

278 Works Cited

Thune, Erik. 2002. *Image and the Relic: Mediating the Sacred in Early Medieval Rome*. Rome: Analecta Romana Instituti Danici.

Thurston, Herbert. 1908. "Chalice." In *The Catholic Encyclopedia*. 17 vols. Edited by Charles G. Herbermann et al. New York: Robert Appleton. 3.563–4.

Timmons, Patricia. 2012. "Convivencia and Conversión in Gonzalo de Berceo's Judïezno." In *Marginal Voices: Studies in Converso Literature of Medieval and Golden Age Spain*, edited by Amy I. Aronson-Friedman and Gregory B. Kaplan, 91–116. Leiden: Brill.

Tolan, John. 1993. *Petrus Alfonsi and His Medieval Readers*. Gainesville: University of Florida Press.

Toner, Patrick. 1909. "Exorcism." In *The Catholic Encyclopedia*, 17 vols. New York: Robert Appleton. 5.709–11.

Torrico, Benjamín. 2010. "Hiding in the Wall: Lazarillo's Bedfellows: The Secret Library of Barcarrota." In *The Lazarillo Phenomenon: Essays on the Adventures of a Classic Text*, 120–38. Lewisburg, PA: Bucknell University Press.

Turón, Mercedes. 1988. "El hilado de Celestina: Símbolo del tema y eje de la obra." *Cuadernos Hispanoamericanos* 459: 140–9.

Uebel, Michael. 1996. "Unthinking the Monster: Twelfth-Century Responses to Saracen Alterity." In *Monster Theory: Reading Culture*, edited by Jeffrey J. Cohen, 264–91. Twin Cities: University of Minnesota Press.

Usoz y Rio, Luis, ed. 1841. *Cancionero de obras de burlas provocantes a risa*. London: Luis Sánchez.

Valbuena, Olga Lucia. 1994. "Love, Magic, and the Inquisition of Linguistic Sorcery in *Celestina*." *PMLA* 109 (2): 207–24.

Valderrama, Pedro de. 1608. *Exercicios espirituales*. Barcelona: Hieronymo Margarit.

Valdés, Alfonso de. 1952. *Alfonso de Valdés and the Sack of Rome: "Dialogue of Lactancio and an Archdeacon*. Trans. John Edward Longhurst. Albuquerque: University of New Mexico Press.

Valera, Cipriano de. 1854. *Tratado para confirmar en la fe cristiana a los cautivos de Berbería*. Rpt. San Sebastián: I.R. Baroja.

Valle Lersundi, Fernando del. 1925. "Testamento de Fernando de Rojas, autor de *La Celestina*." *Revista de Filología Española* 12: 385–96.

Van Praag, Jonas A., ed. 1958. "Vida y costumbres de la madre Andrea." *Revista de Literatura* 14: 111–69.

Vasvari, Louise O. 1985. "La digresión sobre los pecados mortales y la estructura del *Libro de buen amor*." *Nueva revista de filología hispánica* 34 (1): 156–80.

Vela Bueno, José Carlos. 1996. "Historia y distorción formal en El Buscón." *DICENDA* 14: 297–312.

Velázquez, Isabel. 2006. *La teja de Villamartín de Sotoscueva (Burgos): los versos más antiguos del "Poema de Fernán González."* Burgos: Instituto Castellano y Leonés de la Lengua.

Venerable Bede. 1878. *The Explanation of the Apocalypse.* Translated by Edward Marshall. London: James Parker.

Vilanova, Arnau de. 1504. *Hec Sunt Opera Arnaldi de Villanova.* Lyon: Gabiano.

Vilanova, Arnau de. 2005. *Discurso sobre el nombre de Dios.* [*Allocutio super Tetragrammaton*]. Edited and translated by Carmen de la Maza. Barcelona: Obelisco.

Villegas, Alonso de. 1603. *Flos sanctorum: Quarte parte.* Barcelona: Jayme Cendrar.

Voaden, Rosalynn. 1999. *God's Words, Women's Voices: The Discernment of Spirits in the Writing of Late-Medieval Women Visionaries.* York; Rochester, NY: York Medieval Press.

Voragine, Jacobus de. 1993. *Golden Legend.* 2 vols. Edited by William Granger Ryan. Princeton: Princeton University Press.

Vredeveld, Harry. 1987. "Pagan and Christian Echoes in the '*Ecloga Theoduli*': A Supplement." *Mittellateinisches Jahrbuch* 22: 101–13.

Wack, Mary. 1990. *Lovesickness in the Middle Ages.* Philadelphia: University of Pennsylvania Press.

Waite, Alfred Edward. 1911. *Book of Spells: A Magical Enquiry in the Rituals of Sorcery and Witchcraft.* London: Wordsworth.

Walsh, John K. 1971. "Religious Motifs in the Early Spanish Epic." *Revista hispánica moderna* 26 (4): 165–72.

Walsh, John K. 1979. "Juan Ruiz and the *mester de clerezía*: Lost Context and Lost Parody in the *Libro de buen amor.*" *Romance Studies* 33: 62–86.

Walsh, John K. 1983. "The Names of the Bawd in the *Libro de buen amor.*" In *Florilegium Hispanicum: Medieval and Golden Age Studies Presented to Dorothy Clotelle Clarke*, edited by John S. Geary, 151–64. Madison: Hispanic Seminary of Medieval Studies.

Webber, Ruth House. 1995. "Jimena's Prayer in the *Cantar de Mío Cid.*" In *Oral Tradition and Hispanic Literature: Essays in Honor of Samuel G. Armistead*, edited by Mishael M. Caspi, 619–47. New York: Garland.

Weich-Shahak, Susana. 2002. "Observaciones sobre el romancero sefardí de tradición oral—motivos y folo temático." *LEMIR* 6: n.p.

Weiner, Jack. 1985. "Las interpolaciones en *El Lazarillo de Tormes* (Alcalá de Henares, 1554) con énfasis especial sobre las del ciego." *Hispanófila* 29 (1): 15–21.

Weiss, Julian. 1996. "Writing, Sanctity, and Gender in Berceo's *Poema de Santa Oria*." *Hispanic Review* 64 (4): 447–65.

Weiss, Julian. 2006. *The Mester De Clerecía: Intellectuals and Ideologies in Thirteenth-Century Castile*. Woodbridge, UK; Rochester, NY: Tamesis.

Wellbery, David E., Judith Ryan, and Hans Ulrich Gumbrecht. 2004. *A New History of German Literature*. Harvard: Harvard University Press.

Whitbread, Georg Leslie. 1971. *Fulgentius the Mythographer*. Columbus: Ohio State University Press.

Wigelsworth, Jeffrey R. 2006. *Science and Technology in Medieval European Life*. Westport, CT: Greenwood Press.

Wilkinson, Alexander S., ed. 2010. *Iberian Books: Books Published in Spanish or Portuguese or on the Iberian Peninsula before 1601*. Leiden: Brill.

Wilkinson, Robert J. 2015. *Tetragrammaton. Western Christians and the Hebrew Name of God: from the Beginnings to the Seventeenth Century*. Leiden: Brill.

Williams, A. Lukyn. 1935. *Adversus Judaeos: A Bird's-Eye View of Christian Apologiae until the Renaissance*. Cambridge: Cambridge University Press.

Willis, Raymond S. 1933. *The Relationship of the Spanish "Libro de Alexandre" to the "Alexandreis" of Gautier de Châtillon*. Published Dissertation. Princeton University.

Winston-Allen, Anne. 1997. *Stories of the Rose: The Making of the Rosary in the Middle Ages*. University Park: Pennsylvania State University Press.

Wolfenzon, Carolyn. 2007. "La *Lozana andaluza*: Judaísmo, sífilis, exilio y creación." *Hispanic Research Journal* 8 (2): 107–22.

Worsfold, Thomas Cato. 1997. *History of Vestal Virgins of Rome*. Rpt. Kessinger Publishing.

Wright, William M. 2009. *Rhetoric and Theology: Figurative Reading of John 9*. Berlin: Gruyter.

Zafra, Enriqueta, ed. 2011. *Vida y costumbres de la Madre Andre: The Life and Times of Mother Andrea*. Translated by Anne J. Cruz. Woodbridge, UK: Tamesis.

Zavala, Iris M. 1975. "Clandestinidad y literatura en el setecientos." *Nueva revista de filología hispánica* 24 (2): 398–418.

Zayas y Sotomayor, María. 1989. "La inocencia castigada." In *Tres novelas amorosas y tres desengaños amorosos*, edited by Alicia Redondo Goicoechea, 272–312. Madrid: Castalia.

Zilka, Charles. 2003. *Exorcising Our Demons: Magic, Witchcraft, and Visual Culture in Early Modern Europe*. Leiden: Brill.

Ziolkowsi, Jan M., ed. 2008. *Solomon and Marcolf*. Cambridge, MA: Harvard University Press.

Zuñiga, Francesillo de. 1981. *Crónica burlesca del emperador Carlos V*. Edited by Diane Pamp de Avalle-Arce. Barcelona: Crítica.

Index

Frye, Northrop, 62
Fulgentius, 229n30
Fuller, David, 200n6
Furies, 119, 229n31

Galen, 52, 203n24, 232n56
Galicia, 3, 202n18
Galician-Portuguese, 20, 39
Gambero, Luigi, 226n12
Ganim, John, 31, 41
García, Diego, 221–2n1
García Áviles, Alejandro, 204nn34, 36
García-Bryce, Aradna, 191
García de Enterría, María Cruz,
    160–1, 238nn16, 17, 18
García Santo-Tomás, Enrique, 190,
    246n66
Garden of Earthly Delights (painting
    by Bosch), 183–5, 245n60,
    245–6n64
gardens, 30–1, 33, 38, 52; Eden, 60,
    82; Song of Songs, 39, 41–2, 56,
    207n8. See also *locus amoenus*
Garrote Pérez, Francisco, 246n69
Gascón Viera, E., 204n36
Gascony, 109–10, 116, 120–1, 126
Gaspariño García, Sebastián, 202n16
Gelasius I (pope), 202n17
General estoria (General History), 59
Gerli, E. Michael, 8, 79, 82–3, 121,
    132, 201n14, 219n35, 220n43,
    222n2, 226n7, 228n22, 231n45
Germanus (St), 130
Gerson, Jean, 164, 240n27
Gesta Romanorum (Deeds of the
    Romans), 4, 222n5
Gesta Sanctae Agnes (Deeds of St
    Agnes), 95–7, 223n9
Gifford, D.J., 227n19
Gifts of the Holy Spirit, 73–4

Gil (Archbishop of Toledo), 103
Gilman, Stephen, 226n7
Girón Negrón, Luis, 204nn36, 37
Gitlitz, David, 17, 138, 168, 236n8
Glorieux, Palémon, 214–15n57
Glossa ordinaria (Ordinary Gloss), 39,
    42, 46, 50
gnostics, 215n4
Gog and Magog, 70, 73, 218n30,
    226n10
Golden Legend, 4, 55, 95–6, 130, 223n9,
    225nn2, 3
goliards, 32, 224n19
Goliath, 5
Gómez Moreno, Ángel, 222n2,
    228n24
Góngora, Luise de, 245n59
González, Estéban, 242–3n46
González, Fernán, 91
González Gómez, José Antonio, 194
Good Friday, 155
Gospel of Nicodemus, 226n9,
    241–2n41
Gospels. *See* New Testament
Gouwens, Kenneth, 233n67
Gower, John, 223n13
Goytisolo, Juan, 240n32
grace, 11–12, 27, 31, 33, 38, 49, 50–1,
    131, 137, 176, 222n3
Gran conquista de ultramar (Great
    Conquest Overseas), 7–8, 13
Granada, 17, 240n30
Granada, Luis de, 240n30
Gray Birth, Walter de, 179, 243n51
Greek, 6, 16, 34, 37, 40, 47–8, 57, 59–60,
    63, 65, 68, 115, 117, 126, 138, 144,
    146, 154–6, 201n12, 209n22, 212n43,
    220n43, 223n9, 229n30, 236n5
Greeks and Romans (characters in the
    Libro de buen amor), 78–81, 83, 86

TORONTO IBERIC